Norman Dott

WITH SHARP COMPASSION

AUP Titles of Related Interest

PILGRIM SOULS
Mary and Hamish MacIver

NORMAN COLLIE, A Life in Two Worlds
Christine Mill

KATHARINE ATHOLL 1874–1960
Against the Tide
S J Hetherington

HALDANE
the life and work of J B S Haldane
with special reference to India
Krishna R Dronamraju

SIR JAMES MACKINTOSH 1765–1832
The Whig Cicero
Patrick O'Leary

REGENCY EDITOR
life of John Scott 1784–1821
Patrick O'Leary

WITH SHARP COMPASSION

NORMAN DOTT
FREEMAN SURGEON OF EDINBURGH

by CHRISTOPHER RUSH and
JOHN F SHAW, FRCS

The wounded surgeon plies the steel
That questions the distempered part;
Beneath the bleeding hands we feel
The sharp compassion of the healer's art.
T S Eliot

ABERDEEN UNIVERSITY PRESS
Member of Maxwell Macmillan Pergamon Publishing Corporation

First published 1990
Aberdeen University Press
Member of Maxwell Macmillan Pergamon Publishing Corporation

© Christopher Rush and John F Shaw, FRCS 1990

British Library Cataloguing in Publication Data

Rush, Christopher
    With sharp compassion.
    1. Edinburgh. Medicine. Surgery. Dott, Norman
    I. Title II. Shaw, John F.
    617'.092'4

    ISBN 0 08 037975 3

Printed in Great Britain by BPCC AUP Ltd, Aberdeen
Member of BPCC Ltd.

Contents

List of Illustrations

Jacket Illustrations
Portrait of Professor Norman Dott by Sir William Oliphant Hutchison. The original hangs in the Royal College of Surgeons, Edinburgh.

Edinburgh Royal Infirmary from George Heriot's.

Acknowledgements

Many hands and heads have been active in helping us in our research and in preparing the ground for this biography.

We should particularly like to thank Dr Eric Dott, Professor Norman Dott's brother, for his help and enthusiastic cooperation. He readily agreed to and encouraged the idea of this life and tribute. The passing years seem to have taken little toll and his memory to have been least affected. Without his carefully preserved family papers and photographs, much of this book might never have seen the light of day. What a pleasure it was to sit with him in his Edinburgh home and listen to his tales of the close-knit family and of childhood in Colinton.

Miss Cathy Morrison, still a doughty inhabitant of Colinton village, was also able to give us some marvellous descriptions of the village and its inhabitants at the turn of the century and during the First World War, as was Mr George Smith, also of Colinton.

It was Dr Calvin Hider, Norman Dott's son-in-law, who first suggested that 'Uncle Eric' should be approached and we thank him for this excellent advice and for all his subsequent help. His wife Jean, Dr Jean Hider, the adored only child of Professor and Mrs Dott, was so encouraging and provided many family photographs before her tragically early death.

Jaqueline, Katherine and Susan (née Hider) collaborated to tell us what life was like with 'Granda' as opposed to the eminent brain surgeon. The unexpected contrast of relaxed family life was amply borne out by Miss Jacqueline Robertson, Mrs Dott's sister, who sadly, has now also died; Barbara, the faithful housekeeper at Chalmers Crescent; and Mrs Joan Henderson, a close friend of Jean Dott from schooldays. These ladies opened a window for us into the life of Dott the Man.

A pleasant surprise too it was to visit Brig o' Turk at the invitation of Mrs Mary Macfarlane, to find more than one lively survivor from those days during and just after the First World War when the Dott family used to holiday there; to hear from them of their affection for young Norman and all the family, and also to see that much was still unchanged in this unspoiled Highland village. We are grateful to all these people who have contributed so willingly to our picture.

For precious help of a practical and time-saving nature, we should also like to thank the Headmaster, Mr Keith Pearson, and librarian, Ruth Reid, of George Heriot's School; and Katy Chapman, Matron, who is in charge of the F.P. section of *The Herioter*. Further research inquiries were courteously, promptly and fruitfully answered by: the Headmistress and the librarian of St George's School for Girls; William C M Jackson, Managing Director of The Scottish Gallery; Dr Lindsay M Errington, Assistant Keeper of British Art in The National Gallery of Scotland; Joanne Soder, Library Assistant in The Royal Scottish Academy; Mr Jack Firth, RSW; John Nice, Secretary of the Edinburgh College of Art; the Very Reverend William B Johnston, DD, Minister of Colinton Parish Church; and David and Liz Nicolson, the present owners and inhabitants of Hailes Brae, who not only facilitated access to important domestic and legal papers, but also invited us hospitably into their home, to photograph and peruse at will.

The photographs in this book were initially prepared for publication by Mr Ian McHaffie of George Watson's College, sometimes working, of necessity, from old and inferior pictures. He not only advised and developed but willingly went wherever the Dott story led us, to take pictures of his own.

Much of the labour of typing and correction was taken out of our hands by the patient, skilful and astoundingly swift care of Mrs Florence Millar, to whom we owe a debt of gratitude.

To none are we more indebted however than to our wives, who have shown the proverbial patience of Job in what has been a demanding year.

Fortunately Professor Dott was meticulous in retaining his personal papers, which ranged widely from carefully pencilled reports on his early pituitary experiments, through various scientific papers and extensive correspondence, to dinner invitations and comments on fishing. It was a great privilege to study these at leisure and learn so much about the man and his struggles to establish Surgical Neurology as a viable speciality in Scotland. For this we are greatly indebted to Drs Jeanine Alton and Harriet Weiskettel of The Contemporary Scientific Archives Centre, who had so carefully and skillfully arranged and catalogued the papers. Our thanks also go to Mr J V Howard and his staff, particularly Mrs J O Currie of the Special Collections Department in the Edinburgh University Library where these papers are deposited, for facilitating their study and directing us to other records of Professor Dott and the University of Edinburgh. Dr Mike Barfoot, Archivist to the Lothian Health Board, was also most helpful, as was Mr Wilson, Archivist to Edinburgh City Council, who provided us with some details of The City of Edinburgh Freedom Ceremony.

At the Royal College of Surgeons in Edinburgh, Miss Margaret Bean, the Clerk to the College, and Miss Alison Stevenson in the library, have helped with details of the Professor's work and offices held within the College.

Among the many publications which we have studied, three deserve special mention and the authors have given us permission to quote freely, for which we thank them. Mr J Ross's *The Edinburgh School of Surgery after Lister* and Mr E F Catford's *The Royal Infirmary of Edinburgh 1929-1979* add much to our picture of Edinburgh surgery during the time with which we are concerned. Mr Charles McKean's *Edinburgh: An Illustrated Architectural Guide* gave valuable information and illustration of the well known Edinburgh buildings which feature in Dott's career.

The Dott Memorial Trust and particularly the Secretary of the Trust, the late Dr W Sneddon Watson, are to be thanked for their backing of the project and a generous donation towards the initial expenses. Several past patients of Professor Dott responded similarly, in token of their gratitude, and we thank them for this invaluable help.

Despite the passage of years, innumerable people from all parts of the world wrote in response to our appeals, with personal knowledge of Norman Dott. Senior doctors and surgeons who had worked with him long years, junior doctors who had worked long hours, theatre sisters, ward sisters, more junior nurses, occupational therapists, physio- and speech-therapists—all contributed. Above all, patients wrote. There were stories of triumphant success, of sad failure, mitigated by kindness and concern. Some wrote detailed accounts, others amusing fragments. Some will recognise their contribution: others, failing to find their piece of the mosaic, should rest assured that each and every one has helped to build up our portrait of this exceptional man.

Lastly, it would be wrong not to acknowledge Mr David Gerrard, a very long-term patient and great admirer of Professor Dott. He, stemming from an East Neuk of Fife fishing community, and knowing, because of similar roots, of one of the co-authors and the success of his descriptive pen, stimulated this unusual collaboration in a tale that really unfolds itself.

C R and J F S

PART ONE

The Man in the Making

Thou art not thyself
For thou exists on many a thousand grains
That issue out of dust.

(Shakespeare *Measure for Measure*)

CHAPTER ONE

The Convergence of the Twain

Alien they seemed to be:
No mortal eye could see
The intimate wedding of their later history.
(*Thomas Hardy*)

Thy foot He'll not let slide, nor will
He slumber that thee keeps.
(*Psalm121*)

On the twenty-ninth day of August 1913 a young man called Norman Dott was riding to work on his newly acquired motor bike. He had come into Edinburgh earlier that morning from his home in Colinton Village and was now making for Loanhead, where he was apprenticed to McTaggart Scott & Co the engineering firm.[1] The young man had reached his sixteenth birthday only three days previously and in fact had lied about his age when purchasing his machine a little before then. The then fifteen year old had told Willie McLeod in Juniper Green that he was seventeen.

Willie was a benign old bachelor who hired out pushbikes to youngsters at the rate of sixpence per two hours and never batted an eyelid if the bikes were brought back to the shop four hours later by children wearing the wind in their hair and euphoria in their faces. But perhaps Mr McLeod wondered and worried a little for the machine-mad boy to whom he had hired bicycles in the past and who had now bought a motor bike from him.

'Don't go on the thoroughfares yet,' he told hm. 'Keep to the quiet streets.'

Norman Dott arrived at the West End of Princes Street and turned into Lothian Road, making for Tollcross.

By today's standards it might not have been thought busy, even by the quiet-headed Willie McLeod. Yet it carried a stranger mix of traffic then than it does towards the end of the twentieth century. Henry Ford had made the first motor car just twenty years ago and the motor cycle was an invention not as old as the boy who was riding it. Cable-cars, the cumbersome ships of the street, trundled noisily up and down, ferrying their passengers from stop to stop. A new power house to convert the horse tramways and drive the underground cables had recently been completed at Tollcross when Norman Dott was a toddler of two. Motor taxis, among them the green-breeked drivers of Croall's taxi company, sped on their faster courses like the stars against Sisera. The Edinburgh District Motor Omnibus Company had first sent their buses up Lothian Road in 1906 but the firm had failed and now it was the taxis, all glittering glass and chrome, terrible as an army with banners, that passed the lumbering horse lorries and carts. The old and new eras were yoked together in a brief partnership in the same street.

Norman Dott roared past the Caledonian Station yard, now straddled by the huge colossus of the Sheraton Hotel. In front of him he saw a horse lorry which he decided to overtake.

It was a momentous decision.

The horse lorry, without warning, made a sudden swerve to the right. Looming up fast in front of the motor cyclist were the great brown flanks of a Clydesdale, a soft enough point of collision perhaps, but one which would have done the animal little good. Norman Dott's own iron horse stood the likelier chance of surviving the charge. In the second or less he had in which to consider the matter he also swerved sharply to the right. Bearing down on him was one of the stars of the street, a shining new motor taxi, travelling at the same speed . . .

On the same day another young man, six years Norman Dott's senior, was travelling down Lothian Road towards the West End. John Baillie Watson, since coming of age, had not wasted the first year of what was then formally considered his manhood. In 1912 the twenty-one year old, carried on the adventurous wings of the travelling Scot, had joined the Ottawa Fire Service, where he drove to the sound of brigade bells. The following year found him again at the wheel, this time of a military-style jeep, property of the Ottawa Police, into which he had drafted himself.

After the events of August 1914 another draft awaited him and millions like him, and the restless adventurer was to find himself detained for some time at his Majesty's pleasure in the front line trenches of Western Europe, clutching the King's shilling and dreaming of Auld Reekie. But chance or an inscrutable law had dictated that between his two Canadian love liaisons and his prolonged spell of soldiering he would be, like Norman Dott, driving his own newly obtained machine—a motor taxi—down Lothian Road.

John Watson's mother was at that moment in hospital with a brain tumour, a condition which in those days, once diagnosed, was roughly

1 John Baillie Watson in 1913 at the wheel of his taxi: possibly the same vehicle which altered the course of neurosurgery in Edinburgh. The elegant young lady about to step into the cab is his wife.

ROYAL INFIRMARY

GEORGE HERIOT'S HOSPITAL

2 and 3 Sketches from G G Thornby's *Sketchbook of Edinburgh* show the Royal Infirmary in 1912 and George Heriot's School. The two buildings face one another across Lauriston Place.

equivalent to a death sentence. Mr Watson was on his way to visit his stricken mother. Doubtless his thoughts were fastened on sickness and surgery and grief, the depressing sadness of a mother in extremis, when, shooting across the street in front of him, he saw a youth on a motor bike.

There was no time to think.

The young man who had commanded a fire engine and a police jeep in Ottawa by the power of his hands could make no possible manoeuvre to avoid what was certain. It must have seemed to him inevitable that he had come back to Edinburgh to be on Lothian Road at that particular place and time merely to collide with the boy on the bike.

Nothing in their lives could have brought the two together in any meaningful way, their backgrounds and class were so different, and it would be a fruitless prospect to calculate the odds against its happening. It was to be, this strangely Hardyesque meeting in Lothian Road. Several months later Thomas Hardy published a poem called 'The Convergence of the Twain' concerning a more famous collision which had occurred in the frost-bitten North Atlantic on the night of 14 and 15 April 1912, when the White Star liner, the *Titanic*, pronounced unsinkable, collided with an iceberg on her maiden voyage and sank into the dark, drowning 1,517 people.

In Hardy's mind the iceberg and the ship, seemingly unconnected, were wedded by fate. They had courted since the beginning of time and evolution was their long love's day, destiny the mad priest who married them. Had Hardy known what was to happen to Norman Dott as the result of his meeting with John Baillie Watson, in the year following the loss of the *Titanic*, his pessimism might have taken a dent.

> Alien they seemed to be:
> No mortal eye could see
> The intimate wedding of their later history,
>
> Or sign that they were bent
> By paths coincident
> On being anon twin halves of one august event.
>
> Till the Spinner of the Years
> Said 'Now!' And each one hears,
> And consummation comes, and jars two hemispheres.[2]

The consummation that drowned fifteen hundred souls was not one devoutly to be wished: the one which sent Norman Dott to hospital that day was destined, if not designed, to save many more lives, and indirectly speaking more than could subsequently make up the passenger lists of many *Titanics*.

Sixty years later, on the tenth day of December 1973, the *Edinburgh Evening News* seller, standing outside the Royal Infirmary of Edinburgh at the top of the Middle Meadow Walk, wrote on his newsboard the three words: DOTT IS DEAD. Hundreds of home-returning workers were slowed in their tracks that day as they passed along under the winter vaults of interlocking boughs that lined the meadow walk, a straight crow-flown line between the Infirmary and No. 3 Chalmers Crescent, both for many years Dott's place of work and his unpretentious home. There was something appropriate about those bare, ruined choirs, where birdsong was silenced for December, and those bowed heads buried in the front page story.

Dott is dead.

Yet even as the newsvendor penned this piece of stark alliteration, ship-loads of Edinburgh citizens, and indeed people who had travelled to Edinburgh across the world, were alive and well, not merely because of what Professor Norman Dott might have personally achieved with them, but due to his considerable contributions to the field of neurosurgery during those sixty intervening years.

Neither the motor cyclist nor the taxi driver could have had any such thought in his head as each ground his teeth for the inevitable.

It was a head-on collision.

The impact was sufficient to damage both vehicles severely. In the comparative safety of his cab the taxi driver was uninjured, but the motor cyclist was catapulted through busy space and onto the side of the road. It was his first experience of extreme pain and must have been agonising. He sustained multiple fractures of the left leg and had to be rushed to hospital. There, in the Infirmary, he was admitted under the care of Mr Wade.

When the resident saw the condition of Norman Dott's leg he at once telephoned Mr Wade and suggested that an amputation would be necessary. Mr Wade went to the Infirmary to examine the injured youth for himself.

'No,' he said, after close examination, 'I think we can save the leg.'

Given his condition and the best that medical science could offer at that time, the boy Norman was fortunate not to lose the shattered limb at once; fortunate too that the slow healing processes took place so successfully, once the decision had been made to preserve rather than to destroy. For both gifts of fortune and skill the Dott family remained forever grateful. The letter is not extant but the boy's father also wrote to John Watson, excusing him from all blame for the accident. The taxi driver came to visit the victim in hospital and to view his injuries.

These were compound fractures with spicules of bone which subsequently went on to suppuration and detained him in the Infirmary for eight weeks. By the time he was discharged the last October winds had stripped the trees and he hirpled out onto a Middle Meadow Walk that was a long gusty carpet of leaves. The new academic session for schools, colleges and the university was already well under way.

The first thing Norman Dott did was to enrol at Skerry's College for tuition in Latin. He had limped out into what was for him an altered world and Latin was now an absolutely vital key to his plans for the future. During his painful sojourn in the Royal Infirmary the pivot of life had changed dramatically for him. So fascinated had he become by surgery, so obsessed by the dream of practising medicine himself, that the young apprentice engineer now wished to become a doctor. When his family visited him in hospital they found him already discussing aspects of his own case and expatiating learnedly upon the details of other cases in the ward, commenting with great interest and understanding upon his fellow patients' progress. There were even moments in his own case where he took it upon himself to advise his doctors and made no secret about the fact that he felt he could handle some of the practicalities of his treatment, such as bandaging, rather better himself!

His behaviour was not precocious. Rather the twin fascinations of surgery now held him in thrall: to cure sick people and to do so by the skill of his own hands. From now on those talents which had encouraged him to be an engineer would be directed to the tending of human beings, not machines That close harmony of fingers and brain was to become popularly known, in Norman Dott's case, as the ballet of hands. There's a divinity that shapes our ends, rough-hew them how we may. The metaphor is from joinery, a trade to which this engineer-not-to-be had also been at one time more informally apprenticed. And if the God of Psalm 121 had failed to live up to his reputation as a protector, in letting Norman Dott's foot slide on 29 August 1913, Dott senior would have argued that there's a special providence in the fall of a sparrow. The very hairs of his son's head were numbered.

He encouraged him in his new choice of profession and in less than a year Norman had taken his Latin. He entered Edinburgh University for the medical course in the autumn of 1914. By that time the first red wave of war had broken over the globe and the seventeen year old student was now eager to join the forces as soon as he was of age. In particular he yearned to enter the Royal Flying Corps.

As things turned out he was rejected. His accident had left him with a permanent limp. The military authorities who later in the war sent wounded men back to the Front could in that first year of carnage afford to be more selective than to choose lame young medics for the slaughter. The flower of the country was ready for the fall.

Had the leg been amputated, on the other hand, it is most unlikely in those days that he could have pursued a career in surgery. The meeting of John Baillie Watson and Norman Dott in Lothian Road in 1913 and the subsequent happenings ensured, quite simply, that the young man would not become an engineer; that he would enter the medical profession instead; and that he would be prevented from enlisting in the Flying Corps, in which he would have stood a glorious chance of losing more than his leg. The resultant benefit for society, in the light of Professor Norman Dott's achievements in neurosurgery, might have made Thomas Hardy pause in his conviction, hardened by the Great War, of a blindly mechanistic universe governing (or misgoverning) human affairs. The poem on the *Titanic* appeared in a collection called *Satires Of Circumstance*, published in 1914. Fourteen years later its gloomy author was dead and Norman Dott had embarked on his career as a surgeon with remarkable success. The doctor with the limp and the somewhat crab-like gait was to become a famous sight. If the events which made this possible were purely circumstantial, they are a cause not for satire but for triumph. Dott is now regarded the world over as one of the surgical giants of all time.

His story is of a great surgeon, a surgeon set upon his course by a strange twist of fate. He was a surgeon in that unforgiving field of brain and spinal cord, whose name is literally found in the same roll of honour as Lister and Simpson; a teacher who expounded to world-wide audiences, yet found friendly plane with both ghillie and child. What follows is a biography, a tribute of joint authorship, but factual scientific reports, former colleagues, buildings and services instituted, and above all, the hearts of patients all tell the tale.

It is the tale of a strangely human being whom fate decreed to be a pioneer of neurosurgery in Scotland and a world leader of his time. It tells of a man who laid the foundation of his reputation by acting courageously upon cool deductive reasoning, to pioneer in the dangerous field of intracranial aneurysm surgery, and who built upon it by dogged determination and unflinching discipline. His achievements in the surgery of the vital pituitary gland are well known and acclaimed, but there are few neurosurgical pathologies which did not interest him and receive his meticulous attention, with benefit to all concerned.

Ironically he was afflicted by constant pain stemming from the original injuries suffered in his accident. A surgeon to the end however, the lessons of this and of each disability which assailed him with the passing years, were turned to the benefit of mankind.

Above all he taught and his work continues in the advances made and in the surgeons and world-wide healing services which he has set forth on the right lines.

Before the text of this book was begun, a far-flung multitude of patients movingly confirmed that, though the years have taken their toll, yet many hearts still hold an unyielding place of honour and affection for Dott, their surgeon and friend.

CHAPTER TWO

Under the Spreading Huguenot Tree

Our conscious years are but a moment in the history
of the elements that build us.
(*Robert Louis Stevenson*)

I am a native of Edinburgh only by adoption.
(*Norman Dott*)

A bloody cocktail of politics and religion brought the Dotts to Scotland
more than two centuries before Norman Dott was born. In his laurelled
years the grand old man of neurosurgery loved to inform assembled
companies that he was really a latter day Huguenot of French–Belgian
extraction. And a Huguenot he was, genetically, if not by denominational
persuasion. So how did history contrive to being him to Scotland's capital
city?

It is by indirections that we find directions out. Having shown Christian
men and women their own image for more than fifteen hundred years, the
clear glass of Christ's church suffered a massive fracture in the sixteenth
century. Historians call it The Reformation and the anti-Catholic reaction
to it the Counter-reformation. The ecclesiastical breakage occasioned
quarrels, martyrdoms and wars well into the seventeenth century. On one
side of the fracture the Catholics saw clearly that Luther and Calvin were
hacking at the unbroken umbilical cord of St Peter's original Church, the
Rock of Ages against which heresy dashed itself in vain. On the other side
the Protestants saw through the glass darkly that the Church itself had been
a heretic for years. It was blocking the very door to salvation where the dear
Christ entered in.

In France the Catholic rulers struck the first blow. Thousands of
Huguenots were massacred on 24 August 1572, St Bartholomew's day, and
in the days following. Many who escaped the massacre fled the country.
Those who remained did so under the watchful Catholic eye and they
longed for a statement that would free them to worship God in their own
image without looking over their shoulder. The statement came twenty-six

years later when Henri IV issued the Edict of Nantes. It was full of flaws but was a measure of tolerance and brought an uneasy tranquillity which lasted almost a hundred years.

Then came the deluge.

Louis XIV was only five years old when he succeeded his father as King of France in 1643. In his twenties, pursuing his ideal of splendid uniformity for French citizens, he was already issuing edicts which made life difficult for the Huguenots. To begin with there was little in the way of direct persecution, but privileges were withdrawn and rewards were put in the way of those who decided to embrace Catholicism. A Treasury of Conversions was instituted in 1677 to administer the work of theological bribery. Be a Huguenot and stay poor or unprivileged: become a Catholic and enjoy posts and pensions. As the Sun King shone longer on the Pope and turned his cloudier countenance oftener on the Protestants, the measures against them grew steadily more draconian. The doors to various careers in the state were slammed shut in their faces; the doors of many of their schools and churches were nailed up for good. With Orwellian insidiousness the children of 1684 could divorce themselves from their Huguenot parents and kiss the papal toe, and the Treasury of Conversions held out the francs and candy to help them calculate the attractions of a royal-backed gospel. Even by 1680 the velvet glove was slipping off the mailed fist.

It is impossible to pin a proof to the precise year in which Norman Dott's ancestors eluded its iron blows, but the decision was not taken before 1676. A Flemish dresser bearing that date still remains in the family, an heirloom which assuredly pre-dates their departure. By the year 1680 thousands of their brethren were already fleeing to England and Scotland and other parts of Europe. Earlier settlements had been established in Canterbury, London, Norwich and Southampton. The later emigrants established centres as far west as Bristol and Plymouth and in Ireland.

Those who fled after 1682 did so in defiance of an edict which made emigration an offence for the galleys. Of those who were caught some might have reflected that a great Scottish reformer had also sweated at the end of a French oar, following the murder of Cardinal Beaton and the capture of St Andrews Castle. But that was a century and a half ago and in Scotland, where the Great Whore of Babylon kindled a fanaticism quite remarkable even in the annals of church history. The Huguenots were not led by a John Knox; where possible they trod the path of easiest resistance by making good their escape. When they demonstrated pacifically in the Cevennes in 1683 they were visited by the ferocious Dragonnades, whose licensed debauchery and cruelty to women and children proved an added incitement to fearful waverers to undergo a good Catholic conversion.

Reports of rapes and infanticides frizzle up as they approach the house of the sun and *Le Roi Soleil* was not well informed. By October 1685 he must have felt pretty satisfied. Henri Quatre's Edict of Nantes now seemed to him, cynically assessed, an antiquated irrelevance, its toleration of Protestants largely unnecessary in a country where so many Protestants had already seen the Catholic point of view, whether by force of purse or privilege or by whatever forms of persuasion. In October 1685 the Edict of Nantes was revoked. Protestantism was now forbidden by law. Its ministers were banished from the land, its churches closed, its adherents compelled to stay and worship graven images to the sound of the Mass.

About a quarter of a million decided not to stay.

In itself the figure is a conservative one. Many a one made the decision to flee the country only to fall into the hands of the military and eke out a galley slave's miserable existence, fruitlessly ploughing the waves. Whether through emigration, slavery or death, the result was the same: France lost the economic benefit of a golden thread in the fabric of her people. Douce, dedicated and highly skilled, the Huguenots were the masters of industry and commerce. No philosophers or artists rose from their ranks; they were not, generally viewed, the stuff of which Pascals and Voltaires were made. Instead their solid commonsense and energy swelled the treasury. And now came the brain drain. Wherever they went they fattened the public purses of other nations. Those with a military background leagued themselves with the countries of their adoption, fighting against their tyrant mother like the soldiers of God, with puritanical zeal, so that France was weakened both militarily and economically.

Such was the stock from which Norman Dott sprang. Sturdy, sensible, practical rather than heroic, hardworking realists, many of them nonetheless had the courage of their convictions when it mattered most. To a family called De Ott or D'Ott (an alternative spelling d'Aoust meaning August or harvest) the risk of slavery or death mattered less than living a life of shoddy compromise. Honour was at the stake.

So: on an unknown day after the year 1676, and by family tradition before the Revocation of 1685, Norman Dott's ancestors, seeking freedom of conscience, boarded a vessel bound for Scotland. The Reformation had not killed the Auld Alliance's best by-products: the trade of wine and mind, together with other commodities cultural and mercantile, and droves of Huguenots had already brought their weaving skills from Lyons and Flanders to parts of Scotland. An invisible lifeline floated up the North Sea for the D'Otts to follow—a twining of Celtic blood and the pull of politics.

In all probability they embarked on a merchant ship trading with the Scottish kingdom of Fife, where the influence of the Low Countries still glints in the white-washed crow-stepped gables and red-pantiled roofs of the East Neuk. The huge dresser they brought along with them is a substantial piece of furniture, undoubtedly outweighing the combined members of the family, for whom it could easily have served as a common sea-coffin, such are its dimensions. They were a solid, well-heeled crop of bourgeoisie and did not simply jump into the nearest tub and make off. Nor did they ship a dresser alone. A canny skipper was paid well to risk flitting an entire household of furnishings and folk to the mercy of the sea. The North Sea is a web of storms and many a seaman's drowning mouth has closed on the rocky bottom of the Firth of Forth. But these people were willing to put even the most notorious waves between themselves and the wrath of the French Catholic police.

The ship discharged its cargo, and along with it a quiet, sober family of refugees, who stood for the first time among the tar and tangle of the Fife fishing townships: Anstruther, St Andrews, St Monans, Cellardyke, Crail. The head of the family was a shoemaker to trade. Not academically inclined, he had no reason to have heard that St Andrews University was the work not merely of a Pope but of the Anti-Pope, Pedro da Luna, nearly three centuries earlier. Where were they to go? No archives give off the least whisper of sea-winds. Maybe they blew briskly that day on the coasts of Fife. At any rate the D'Otts made their way to the sheltered inland farms and the father found for himself and his family both hospitality and a niche in the ancient burgh of Cupar, where he quickly plied his trade. Eventually he became Dean of the Guild of Shoemakers there, that fact grandly emblazoned on his gravestone in the parish churchyard, where the family tombs tell their story, the rich proud cost of outworn buried age. Nowadays they are leprous with lichens and their inscriptions illegible as the wind, but the fact that they are there at all is monumental evidence of the D'Otts' success. The seekers of freedom had flourished.

They were not the only D'Otts so to do. In the next two centuries scions and saplings from the D'Ott tree scattered themselves about the world. One emerges as the owner of The Garrick Theatre in London; another as the Goods Manager for the Caledonian Railway Company at Dundee; the Docks and Railway Manager at Bo'ness; a shipper in Liverpool; a Bank Agent in Lochmaddy; a merchant in the East Indies; a tailor, a compositor; and Head of the Public Dams and Waterworks of Holland, this one having found honour close to his own country after 250 years of mouldering royal bones. And before the red blind of 1917 came down on Moscow, one was gynaecologist to the last Tsarina of Russia.

Quite a tradition. Written into the D'Ott genes, it seems, are the works and ways of hands, a mind to plan and the determination to succeed. Small wonder then that a seed scattered in Edinburgh by an art-dealing and picture-framing member of the family was to pioneer brain surgery in Scotland and become first Professor of Surgical Neurology in Edinburgh's University. The genius of craftsmanship, initiative and adventure shouted along the arteries, filled the heart and ignited the brain.

Norman Dott's family remained proud of its place on the Huguenot tree

4   An early photograph of Aitken Dott, Norman's paternal grandfather, who was born in the year of Napoleon's defeat at Waterloo.

5   Rebecca Morton's father. Norman's maternal grandfather, Mr Morton was a Scottish Ulsterman who moved to Birkenhead where Rebecca was brought up.

6   Peter McOmish Dott, Norman's father as a young man.

7   Rebecca Morton as a young woman. This picture was taken in Odessa, Russia, around 1885, where she was looking after her adventuring brother.

and Norman Dott himself was always interested in its various falls and driftings. Leaves upon leaves of letters were carried between Edinburgh and all parts of the world.

When Norman was already keeping up the family tradition by making wheelbarrows at eight years old, one of his Cupar ancestors was alive and well in Alexandria, South Dakota. Judge Robert Dott was born in The Chance Inn at Cupar on 9 September 1824. As a journeyman tailor he left Cupar for Toronto where he set up as a clothier. Later he moved to Illinois and was a merchant in Anamosa, Iowa. He fought in the Civil War in the 14th Iowa Volunteer Infantry, was captured, exchanged and discharged, and at the age of fifty-eight travelled to the unbroken prairies of Dakota territory and started farming in Sanborn County. In 1886 at the age of sixty-two he moved to Alexandria, South Dakota, and set up in law. Later he became County Judge for Hanson County.

Able adventurers all.

Norman Dott relished and revelled in his feeling of kinship with this heritage and related it gleefully to the specifically Scots heritage, renowned for its ready absorption of stravaigers and for a similar predilection to wanderlust. Speaking to the Congress of Neurological Surgeons at Toronto in 1968 at which he and Mrs Dott were Honoured Guests, he carved his name with pride on the Scottish stone of destiny:

> The Scots are what they are because their land was at the outermost north-western fringe of Europe. There, arrived from the hinterland of Europe and beyond, and there settled for a while wave upon wave of the non-conformists, the searchers of freedom, the adventurers, the curious, the malcontents, the unwanted and the criminous. This heritage gave them their character . . . For my own part my roots are deep in Scotland.[1]

Quite clearly he was including in this catalogue the adventuring D'Otts who chose Scotland as their home from home.

Of the original family that came to Cupar around the year 1680, a grandchild who was a stonemason to trade heard tell of the glittering opportunities for builders in the construction and development of the New Town of Edinburgh. This grandchild was Henry Dott, Norman Dott's great-grandfather, who took himself and his tools to the capital city and played his part in the great Georgian plan. As the century turned he was still a comparatively young man and was content as a bachelor to concentrate on his building. Only after he was well established did his thoughts turn to his other responsibilities as a builder and breeder of men: a responsibility bleakly acknowledged from scripture by the theological inheritors of Knox and Calvin. To aid him in his obedience to the call to be fruitful and multiply, he chose Margaret Farquharson from Invercauld near Braemar. She was housemaid in a genteel Edinburgh family and was herself out of a family of Deeside farmers and crofters, but in marrying the successful Henry Dott she at once acquired a gentility of her own. Their third son was Aitken Dott, born in 1815, the year the Iron Duke found Napoleon and Waterloo to be such a damned close-run thing.

Of Aitken Megget Dott, Norman's grandfather, little enough is known, unless one were uselessly to speculate on his character from his portrait. He seems, however, to have witnessed the execution of William Burke, the infamous bodysnatcher, on 28 January 1829. Norman Dott's great-aunt, Elizabeth Brown wrote to her son, David Brown, that Wednesday morning. Later to become an Edinburgh chemist, David Brown was apprenticed at the time in Berwick-Upon-Tweed. At the end of the letter there is a postscript signed A. Dott, describing the execution.

David Brown's great-grandson, David Rainy Brown, wrote to Norman Dott in 1962, enclosing a copy of this letter. In his reply Norman Dott expresses some doubt that the postscript was written by Aitken Dott, who, he says, was born only eleven years before Burke's execution. He gives it as his opinion that the piece was penned by William Alexander Dott, Aitken's eldest sibling, commonly known by his middle name rather than his first. The facts of the matter, however, are that the handwriting is similar to Aitken Dott's as it appears in later family papers (Norman Dott's own calligraphy as a teenager is strikingly different from that of his maturity) and that Norman Dott makes a simple error when giving Aitken Dott's age in 1829 as eleven. He was in fact fourteen years of age and is perfectly likely to have been the Dott who wrote that part of the letter. It was moreover quite natural that a fourteen year old Edinburgh boy should want to write to his newly apprenticed cousin in Berwick-Upon-Tweed, telling him about the grisly event he had missed that morning. Mortar and pestle were nothing to this.

Whether it was Norman's grandfather or great-uncle who saw the famous drop, this is what he says he saw.

> Burke, the murderer was executed this morning, but such a scene I never saw. The windows about the Lawnmarket were let for 10 shillings apiece and upwards, but they were disappointed, as they expected him to make a speech, but he never spoke a word. When he ascended the scaffold the multitude gave three cheers, and another three when he was thrown off. When he heard them cheering when he ascended the scaffold he burst into tears, but you may expect a paper in the course of the week, with a full account of how he spent the night previous to his execution, and behaviour on the scaffold. Yours A D—I forgot to tell you that the multitude gave three cheers for Hare and three for Dr Knox.[2]
>
> A Dott

The passage, with its matter-of-fact details and tone, does not appear to have been composed by a person on flame with imagination. After he had drunk his glass of early morning wine, Burke faced a crowd of twenty thousand and upwards, all screaming for his blood. Among the gentlefolk at the Lawnmarket windows, observed by Aitken Dott, was Sir Walter Scott, who more graphically recorded the event in his diary with the inner eye of the novelist. Scott had already pictured in his mind the spectacle of the Edinburgh mob in hanging mood during the Porteous Riots. The ugly dregs of humanity that surged along the High Street in *The Heart of Midlothian* were outnumbered by the gross and genteel rabble that saw Burke turned off, his Catholic's creed strangled in his mouth by rope and drop and the yells of execration. 'Multitude' is the closest Aitken Dott's politely turned pen can come to a description of that bloodthirsty congregation.

Aitken Dott it was, his head more attuned to business than to letters, who in 1842 founded the family picture-framing service, later to become Aitken Dott & Son. It was the son who developed it from a small affair of peddling materials and framing pictures into the renowned shop and gallery of 36 North Castle Street. That son, who joined his father in the business in 1876, was Peter McOmish Dott.

The middle name is his mother's surname. Aitken Dott married twice, his first wife being Jane McOmish. After she died he wed Graham (yes, a female!) Gilston, Jane's half cousin. The McOmishes, Norman Dott's paternal grandmother's relations, said to be a sept of the outlawed McGregors, were from Comrie, Perth and Crieff. Jane McOmish's father, Peter, was a lawyer, practising his bewigged and gowned trade in Lauriston Place, Edinburgh, and married to Elizabeth Arrott, one of the Arrotts of Dumbarrow, Forfarshire, the owners of this estate since the days of King Robert the Bruce. Her brother Peter, named after his father, became Headmaster of John Watson's School, also in Edinburgh. The family surname falls away among the various relatives as the tree spreads its branches down the years. Most of those who had no issue were women who changed their names on marriage and it looked as though Aitken and Jane had no intention of keeping the surname alive. The leaves issue forth meticulously labelled like shop stock, but no tag reading McOmish. Their first child was Elizabeth Arrott Dott (after the maternal grandmother) who died at twenty-one years old. Margaret Farquharson Dott (after her paternal grandmother) died unmarried. Then came David Brown Dott and John Lumgair Dott, their middle names reaching out even further to the tributaries of the tree. Finally they called an end to their breeding and perhaps ran out of middle names. Their last genetic act was to produce Peter McOmish Dott.

He was born in Edinburgh on 29 June 1856 when the first cigarette factory was established at Walworth, smoking having been popularlised by soldiers returning from the Crimean War. The new born pink little thing called Peter McOmish was destined to smoke a great many cigarettes before he died, as was his son, Norman McOmish Dott, the inheritor of the middle name not quite vanished from the telephone directories of Scotland.

And neither was to die of lung cancer.

It was now Peter McOmish Dott's turn to seek a spouse. He chose Rebecca Morton, the seventh child of Fraser Morton, a general produce dealer near Belfast. Fraser Morton had married a Miss Liddell, like himself of Scottish Ulster breed, and they moved early in life to Birkenhead near Liverpool, where Rebecca was born on 2 January 1864, following in the wake of three brothers and three sisters. One of her brothers, Liddell, was a wanderer. He married twice, left a daughter on the continent from his first marriage, wedded again without issue, then ventured to Russia, where he was burned out in the Peasant Riots of 1905. As a young woman Rebecca Morton went out to Russia and looked after this brother in Odessa. After that her own thoughts turned less lightly to marriage and she came home to join herself to Cosmo Innes Burton, the son of a Scottish historian. She was at once whisked off again on the wings of travel when Cosmo was appointed Professor of Chemistry in Shanghai. Only six months after going out there he died.

Rebecca wore widow's weeds for a long time to come.

It was Peter McOmish Dott who took her out of mourning and dressed her in bridal whiteness to the wrists. They were married on 2 April 1894. He was thirty-eight, she was thirty—not too old to think about raising up seed to the Dott tree, but certainly by the standards of the day a late starter. Nevertheless they were to have five children before the end of the century.

Norman Dott came into leaf from the old Huguenot tree twenty-eight months before the new century put out its first shoot.

TABLE I. Dotts
(Original Huguenots)

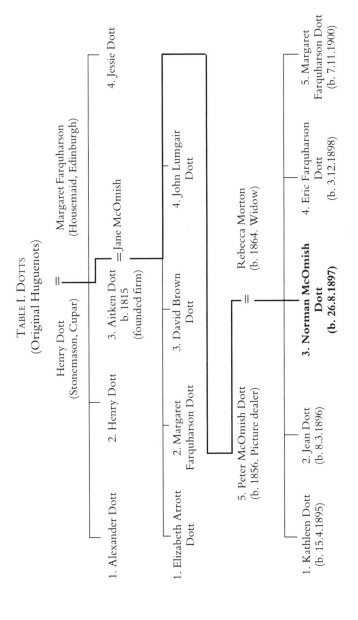

Henry Dott
(Stonemason, Cupar)

=

Margaret Farquharson
(Housemaid, Edinburgh)

1. Alexander Dott

2. Henry Dott

3. Aitken Dott
b. 1815
(founded firm)

= Jane McOmish

4. Jessie Dott

1. Elizabeth Arrott
Dott

2. Margaret
Farquharson Dott

3. David Brown
Dott

4. John Lumgair
Dott

5. Peter McOmish Dott
(b. 1856. Picture dealer)

=

Rebecca Morton
(b. 1864. Widow)

1. Kathleen Dott
(b. 15.4.1895)

2. Jean Dott
(b. 8.3.1896)

**3. Norman McOmish
Dott
(b. 26.8.1897)**

4. Eric Farquharson
Dott
(b. 3.12.1898)

5. Margaret
Farquharson Dott
(b. 7.11.1900)

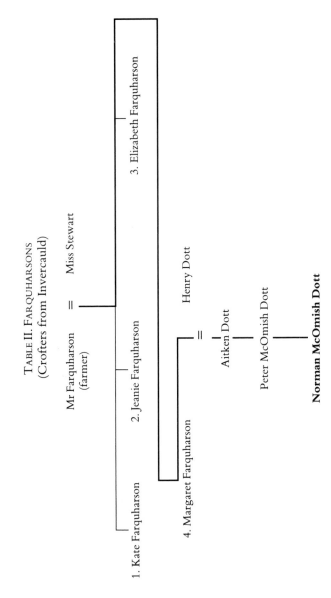

TABLE II. FARQUHARSONS
(Crofters from Invercauld)

Mr Farquharson
(farmer)
=
Miss Stewart

1. Kate Farquharson
2. Jeanie Farquharson
3. Elizabeth Farquharson
4. Margaret Farquharson
=
Henry Dott

Aitken Dott
Peter McOmish Dott

Norman McOmish Dott

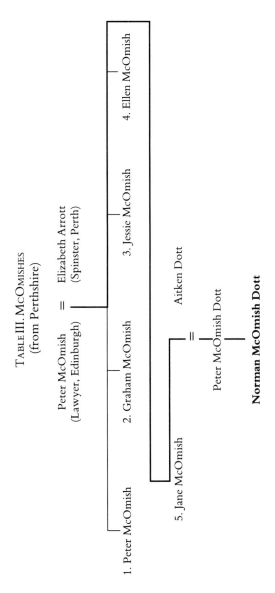

TABLE III. MCOMISHES
(from Perthshire)

Peter McOmish = Elizabeth Arrott
(Lawyer, Edinburgh)   (Spinster, Perth)

1. Peter McOmish

2. Graham McOmish

3. Jessie McOmish

4. Ellen McOmish

5. Jane McOmish = Aitken Dott

Peter McOmish Dott

Norman McOmish Dott

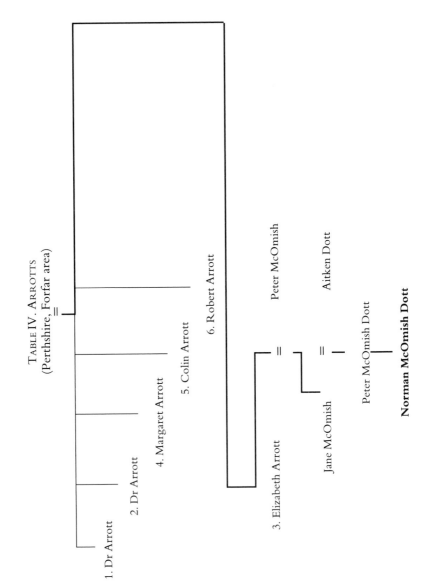

TABLE IV. ARROTTS
(Perthshire, Forfar area)

1. Dr Arrott

2. Dr Arrott

4. Margaret Arrott

5. Colin Arrott

6. Robert Arrott

3. Elizabeth Arrott

Peter McOmish

Jane McOmish

Aitken Dott

Peter McOmish Dott

Norman McOmish Dott

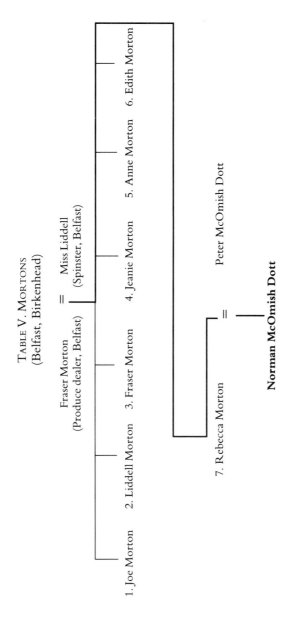

Table V. Mortons
(Belfast, Birkenhead)

Fraser Morton
(Produce dealer, Belfast)
=
Miss Liddell
(Spinster, Belfast)

1. Joe Morton
2. Liddell Morton
3. Fraser Morton
4. Jeanie Morton
5. Anne Morton
6. Edith Morton
7. Rebecca Morton

Peter McOmish Dott
=
Norman McOmish Dott

CHAPTER THREE

The Squirrel and the Bear

Bears and squirrels *are* marvellous.
(*John Osborne*)

We are what our parents make us.
(*Norman Dott*)

Our roots lie in places and people.

Places are their own memorial but people perish as though they had never been. And yet, if our offspring are our immortality and we live again in theirs, then no-one who begets children ever quite dies. The begetting that went on in the Bible should convince us of that, if not the argument of Shakespeare's sonnets, that bachelors and spinsters make worms their heirs. Look at the case of Norman Dott. A single leaf sprouts suddenly against the sky, green and bright, and a great surgeon comes into being. In truth, the roots of his tree have been spreading unseen, tapping darkly for generations; for centuries. Norman Dott, Huguenot though he liked to present himself, took his birth and breeding from a hardy mixture of races: Scots, Celtic, Continental.

In the end two people have to get down to it and must bear the brunt of the responsibility or accept posterity's praise. If Norman Dott's direct progenitors lived to be proud of him, he in turn could not have hoped for better parents and he lived to make that pronouncement many times over. He was the outcome of a truly perfect match: that of the squirrel and the bear.

Right through their lives together Peter Dott used to draw a squirrel and a bear to represent Rebecca and himself and she reciprocated. They did not speak these terms as everyday endearments but used them emblematically in letters and gifts. One of Rebecca's bibles has a squirrel and a bear drawn on the fly-leaf, clearly indicating that the book is a present from the bear to the squirrel. From their photographs it is not hard to interpret the underlying symbolism. She was the busy but dainty little woman with her finesse and charm, he the strong man, protective, hard-headed and energetic, perhaps feeling a trifle clumsy beside her. In John Osborne's play

Look Back In Anger, first performed in 1956, the principal characters, Jimmy and Alison Porter, play at being squirrels and bears in those affectionate oases that sweeten the wilderness of their stormy relationship. It is a curiously ironic chance to find this Victorian couple predating Osborne by half a century and more. In fact Mrs Dott was very much a woman of her own time.

Rebecca Morton was born to be a Martha rather than a Mary, in spite of certain inclinations in the latter direction. A deeply religious soul, gentle and loving, she trod the active path to salvation in looking after first her brother, then her home and family, with Victorian scrupulosity and a wry Edwardian smile. Brought up in Birkenhead as an Ulster Protestant and living latterly among the clang of good Scots tongues, her own voice bore not a trace of any accent whatsoever but remained peculiarly her own. In that neutral chiming of hers she sang her children to sleep from her hoard of old Irish songs, sometimes giving herself and the family impromptu recitals and tinkling out her own rough accompaniment on the grand piano.

She also read a lot to her children: from the Arthurian literature for youngsters, Andrew Lang's Fairy Books of all colours, poetry, the classics— and above all else the Bible, her rod and staff, with which she meted out comfort in the true sense of the word, strength as well as solace. As happens with intelligent children who are read to and given books, the young Dotts quickly began reading for themselves. Norman read less than the others, preferring his more practical bents, but he enjoyed being read to out loud, and right up to the time she died Rebecca continued the habit of reading to him alone.

By that time he was a medical student, well into his course. Exhausted by a day spent in study and in hospital work in Edinburgh, he would roar home to Colinton on his motor bike and sit down to tea, to be read to while he ate. From R M Ballantyne, W H Hudson, Victor Hugo, and, most frequently, the Waverley Novels of Sir Walter Scott or the works of Robert Louis Stevenson, his favourite author. He found his mother's reading relaxing, and she, realising the importance of the work on which he had embarked and proud of her boy, loved to soothe him in this way. There were times he came home from the Deaconess Hospital in the dark small hours, tired beyond eating or talking. On one of these occasions he dozed off on his Sunbeam Combination motor cycle, and bike, sidecar and driver almost had a second accident. No matter how late he came home, Rebecca was always ready to cook for him, to read to him, to talk, to sing, to give him her complete mother's devotion.

She did this in spite of the fact that she was often herself unwell. A small, slight woman, hard wrought and hungry for work, she suffered terribly from very bad migraines, for which there was little in the way of real treatment. As thoughtful and concerned for his mother as she was for him,

the young boy Norman used to run down to the local chemist's in Colinton
to buy her powders of phenacetin and caffeine: ten grains and two grains
respectively made up. Usually she was so sick she simply could not keep the
mixture down and dragged herself through three days of abject misery.
Even without the ironic benefit of a leg-shattering injury, a young child
seeing his mother suffer in this way might well have had his thoughts turned
to medical advance and advantage.

This particular boy was to cure many a headache in his time.

Victorian or Edwardian headaches had to run their course and the work
of a large house had to be carried on through sickness, dizziness and pain.
Rebecca saw to most of the household chores on her own, dealing shrewdly
with the butcher and with Mr Hislop the grocer, who came to the front
door with pencil and notebook in hand, poised for the orders from a substantial home.

She ordered nothing special. Cathy Morrison, the sexton's child, who
delivered the half gallon pitchers of morning milk to the house at the turn
of the century, remembered two sensory details: Mrs Dott's white,
scrubbed kitchen table and the heart-entrancing smell of her porridge.
Breakfasts contained no fripperies and all other meals were ample but basic:
the kind on which work could be done. Porridge was in fact their daily
bread and the Dott youngsters slipped easily into that frame of mind
enjoined by Christ's gospel, to take no thought what they should eat. There
was no need; they knew what their mother would be serving up. Dr Samuel
Johnson defines oats as 'a grain which in England is generally fed to horses
but in Scotland supports the people'. Less often quoted is the reply: 'but
what horses—and what people'! The Dotts were little workhorses, trained
to busy themselves to good purpose by their sedulous mother.

Accordingly she never gave them pocket money *gratis* but they were
encouraged to earn just a little from housework. A penny an hour was the
going rate under the character-forming Rebecca Dott's work ethic: *Radix
malorum est cupiditas* and who steals my purse steals trash. For this remuneration each one of the five chilren looked after an allotted part of a room or
hallway and always kept it polished and tidy. Norman's preference was for
part of the garden which he kept in good trim. Other helping hands that
appeared on the domestic deck from time to time belonged to a variety of
charwomen, signing on casually for two or three hours a week; rum
customers sometimes, who smoked clay pipes and were not always helpful.
One of them had to be dismissed one day for some unforgivable
transgression, collected her pay and barged out in a temper, the inevitable
insult preparing itself on the barb of her tongue, to be grumphed out in her
wake. As she passed the scullery she passed Rebecca Dott standing in a wild
sea of foam, her cuffs pulled back to the elbows, bubbles rainbowing her
hair, and her bare red arms beating the dirt out of the household blankets.

'Well, I must say this for you, Mrs Dott, you're a hard-working woman!'

This made Rebecca laugh, but it speaks volumes in folio on her behalf that even a disgruntled dismissee could not find a point of slander against her employer, turning an intended aspersion into a compliment in spite of herself, when there was nothing left to lose. The best she could come up with was that this middle-class woman was behaving like one of the working class. At any rate there is no doubt that the lovely character of this little lady, strong, tireless and kind, had a bigger bearing on Norman Dott than can be easily estimated: that sense of steadiness, purposefulness, earnest-mindedness, industry and compassion he carried with him to his own grave.

The one part of his mother's spirit he did not inherit was her formal piety, absorbing instead his father's later free-thinking socialism, which replaced the conventional religious beliefs of his younger days. Rebecca Dott was a complete Christian. Keir Hardie, who founded the Independent Labour Party in 1894, the year Peter Dott proposed to her, used to jibe that you could not be a Christian on a pound a week. As it happens Mrs Dott never had to put that to the test and so was not led unto temptation, but had she done so, or had she been so led, the evidence suggests that her Christianity would not have been compromised by one jot or tittle. And this at a time when 80 per cent of the populace never darkened the kirk door. The blood and the fire were running and burning low.

As things stood Rebecca had married a man who, though he entertained a great reverence and admiration for the Bible as God's Word, felt no compulsion or desire to go to church. Indeed the self-contained Dotts were covertly viewed as atheists by the inhabitants of Colinton village, and the closest picture of Mrs Dott taken in the heads of the local folk was of 'a small person who never went to the kirk'. Secretly it was rumoured that Peter McOmish Dott, an imposingly caped silhouette on the rustic horizon, dominated his wife and family, refusing them access to local worship. The truth was that when Peter Dott stepped out under the Colinton sky he believed himself to be standing in the biggest church of all, and the real marvel was that Rebecca and Peter, while taking their religion in different ways and to different ends, remained in total harmony on the subject all the days of their life.

In time Mrs Dott and the children did go to church. It happened by accident, as recalled by Dr Eric Dott, Norman's younger brother.

> One of my father's many artist friends lived in Edzell, in a house called Blithewood. We were holidaying there in the summer of 1909 and we were walking one Saturday past the church near this house, when we heard the organist inside practising his hymns and voluntary for the Sunday service. A lost chord was struck in me, I suppose. Though aged only eleven, I had already grown into something of an earnest youth and begged to be allowed into church next morning to hear the service. My mother was delighted. We all went, including Norman, who'd have been twelve at the time, and as soon as we returned to Colinton I was eager to continue the experiment.[1]

8   The Ferguson's thatched cottage at Wester Brig o' Turk where Peter McOmish Dott and Rebecca Morton were married in 1894. The watercolour is by John Blair, one of many artists who set up their easels amid the idyllic scenery of the Trossachs.

9   On moving to Hailes Brae, the new house in Colinton Village, Peter McOmish Dott designed and laid out the huge garden entirely on his own

10   Rebecca Dott in the garden of Hailes Brae with one of the cats, possibly Spunkie, which Norman trained to ring a bell as a means of achieving entry to the house.

11   Mr and Mrs Dott outside the main front room of Hailes Brae.

12   Peter Dott in the famous Inverness cape. The local Colintoners thought him a somewhat forbidding eccentric.

And so the Dotts shed their aloofness and atheism (apparently) and became church goers. The Colinton Parish Church had undergone major alterations in the previous year, including a tasteful redesigning of the interior. God's white radiance flooded into the apse unbroken and onto Rebecca Dott's bowed head through the nine windows embodying the Fruits of the Spirit: Love, Joy, Peace, Patience, Kindness, Goodness, Fidelity, Gentleness and Self-Control. An eloquent summation of the spiritual character of the little woman who sat there. Norman himself sat there as little as possible, finding other more practical affairs to attend to whenever he could on Sundays, and his father never attended once, but entirely approved of the new family custom. Only the formalities were new, however. The children were already steeped in the hymns, paraphrases and psalms as well as in basic Christianity, as learned through scripture from both parents.

At that time the pulpit of the Parish Church was occupied by the Reverend Thomas Marjoribanks, a man of fine mind and character. He welcomed the Dotts and was gratified by the mother's increasing interest in church work. He could see that Rebecca's interpretation of her rôle as a servant of God through His Church differed from that of some of her grander and wealthier neighbours in Colinton. The great good ladies of the Women's circle enjoyed the tea parties and the genteel visiting, where they sipped prettily enough, sometimes passing the scandal potion from cup to cup to sweeten the hour. What they heartily disliked was the difficult part of church business: visiting those who really did need basic human help as opposed to cold chapter and verse. The result was that Mr Marjoribanks had failed to find anyone in his flock who would visit the most distant part of the Colinton Parish, a district called Drumbrydon, adjacent to Kingsknowe. Mrs Dott took it upon herself gladly to visit the poorer folk in this farthest-flung outpost of her church's pastoral empire. She went there regularly, summer and winter, in all weathers, on foot and alone, the staff of life in her heart, soul and mind; she went bearing bread, a sturdy little pilgrim, and was particularly kind and caring to many of these forgotten folk through the hardships of the First World War.

Her reward was in heaven. Before the worst effects of the war were felt at home, Mr Marjoribanks had committed Mrs Dott to the earth and consigned her to the care of her first Lord and Master.

Her other lord and master, her earthly soul's mate, Peter, was the rock on which all her worldly hopes were founded.

Worldly, yes. Peter Dott built up a successful business by purchasing and selling pictures: he knew how to count. Addressing a gathering after his own retirement, Norman Dott talked about his father:

He was educated at the Royal High School. A few years since I had occasion to visit Persia or Iran in a medical capacity. I thought I should refresh my memory on *The Arabian Nights*. I knew there was a copy in the house and found it. Here it is, a beautifully calf-bound volume, an 1869 edition with the crest stamped in gold. It is First Prize in Arithmetic,won by my father in July 1870 (aged 14), vouched by his Maths Master, David Munn, FRSE. It contains copious footnotes.[2]

A cultured business man in embryo. But the man who fooled the Colintoners by never going to church had done more than his share of theological thinking by the time he married Rebecca Morton. Several of his personal notebooks, still extant, chart his spiritual journeyings from the time of his late teens in 1873 right up to the year before his marriage in 1893: twenty years both of self-scrutiny and rigorous examination of the scriptures. He was a lone mariner on the perilous seas of Victorian religious consciousness. Perilous seas because the old certainties of the soul were under attack from the new philosophies that called all in doubt. The philosophy of the next century, the twentieth, was to be that our doubts unite as our convictions divide us, and so there is a value in not being sure. This was not so new, of course. Francis Bacon had long since expressed the need for scepticisim and the dangers of an undiscriminating faith.

> Now if a man will begin with certainties he will end in doubts; but if he will be content to begin with doubts, he will end in certainties.[3]

The Victorian age began with doubts. Sir Charles Lyell, the Scottish geologist, published his *Principles of Geology* several years before Victoria grew to the throne and Darwin's *Origin of Species* appeared in 1859. Peter Dott gobbled up both books and inwardly digested. The dogmas of Genesis were crumbling under the theories of biological and geological evolution. A six-day week on the part of a God who had performed the modern miracle of not working on a Sunday now no longer seemed to satisfy intelligent men's insatiable thirst for knowledge.

Nineteenth-century scepticism was epitomised by another piece of Peter Dott's set reading: Tennyson's *In Memoriam,* the black rose of the Victorian garden, in bloom almost a decade before Darwin's theories appeared in print. Geology rather than biology is the true villain of this key poem. Not that the wicked character's actual costume matters much. If science can prove we are creatures without souls, then what does science really matter to us? What does anything matter any more? So shrieks Tennyson as he contemplates his 'Nature red in tooth and claw' and observes the meaningless dispersal of life.

McOmish Dott imbibed the Tennysonian uncertainties. He also drank down the poem's desperate faith, quoting it in a letter to his son Eric in 1917:

We have but faith: we cannot know;
For Knowledge is of things we see,
And yet we trust it comes from Thee.
A beam in darkness: let it grow.[4]

The bereaved Victoria read this poem up to the day of her death, when Norman Dott was four years old. She kept it next to her bible. Peter Dott's own bible is a well-thumbed copy, heavily marked in particular in the Book of Psalms, which seems to have inspired him above all else. A simple system of symbols indicates his annotated preferences (three pencilled dots in a row signifying his specially favoured numbers) and plainly the faith and the despair of the Psalmist affected his thinking deeply and found a mirror in his mind. Interestingly Norman Dott adopted the same mannerism when appending his signature to letters, often concluding them with his father's triple stab of the pen after his name.

As a young man Peter McOmish Dott read his way through the entire Bible, analysing what he read and systematically commenting upon it in a spirit of shrewd critical inquiry in which there is not a trace either of sentimentality or of prejudice. He approaches the Bible variously in his exegesis: as a work of literature; as an historical document; above all as a verbalised experience of religion, the writings of men in search of God and the product of God-inspired authors rather than the Word itself from the ultimate Author. His notes also reveal that current biblical scholarship formed a major part of his youthful reading. He did his homework. The various remarks he makes are not in themselves interesting or unusual except in so far as they lay bare a ruthlessly honest intelligence and an inquiring mind at work on what it considers to be a deeply important area of human experience. These might pass for the notebooks of an aspiring divinity student but for the open rigour of the process. He is completely in touch with the intellectual movement which subjected the scriptures to historical and literary analysis, and, like the scientific movement, made a fundamentalist interpretation literally impossible for an educated mind to take. It is the unique blend of reverence and hard-nosed logic that gives the Dott mind its stamp. Like Peter Abelard seven centuries earlier, he has to understand in order that he may believe. Revolutionary enough for some Victorian divines who shut their minds to the new free thinking. There is also an organised energy that is Miltonic in its tone. McOmish Dott's notebooks suggest that he might well have been preparing the background for a mighty religious epic. Of course he was not: he was simply responding with his own ferocious intelligence to what his forefathers were content to swallow whole.

The process continued to the end of his life. Into his sixties he was still quoting a prayer which he had composed in his twenties. It ran:

Heavenly Father, I would worship you this day with my body. Make it sufficiently strong for thy service. Keep my senses clean and pure.

Heavenly Father, I would worship you this day with my intellect. Preserve it clear and sincere so that I neither deceive myself nor deceive others.

Heavenly Father, I would adore thee this day with my heart and soul, asking from thee thy gift of Love whereby the beauty of thy presence and the wisdom of thy ways are revealed to us in the commonplaces of daily life.

Grant, I beseech thee, thy gift of Faith, that in doubt, darkness or despair I may work forward into light and peace, leaning on thee.

Grant also thy gift of a strong moral will, so that putting aside all slothfulness and false fear of the vain opinions of men, I may do thy discovered will with all my heart, with all my mind and with all my strength. Amen.[5]

A more personalised section of one of the notebooks is headed 'Think Of Living'. In three words that is precisely what McOmish Dott set himself to do throughout his own long life. On 22 December 1878 he constructed a check-list of virtues necessary for good and proper living. These he divided into descending categories of gold, silver, bronze and earth, following the old philosophy, as follows:

I	Truths fashioned of pure GOLD:	1. Faith
		2. Reverence
		3. Love
		4. Moral Will
		5. Truth
II	Talents fashioned of pure SILVER:	1. Creation
		2. Imagination
		3. Beauty
		4. Delicacy of sense
		5. Critical
III	Arms fashioned of BRASS and STEEL:	1. Will
		2. Obedience
		3. Earnestness
		4. Concentration
		5. Silence
		6. Dignity
		7. Speech
		8. Tolerance and Sympathy
		9. Discipline
		10. Enthusiasm
IV	Qualities of EARTH:	1. Sound (system)
		2. Vital energising functions & senses
		3. Bodily health[6]

Somewhat schematic as it is laid out, but with a background of reading behind it and a burning application to the future. A decade later he was still keeping a check on his progress. Towards the end of November 1886 he laments: 'Not much gold gathered throughout this month'. His problems are, he records, that his faith relies too much on intellect, he is behind in reverence, the moral will is too feeble. He has collected more silver but his creativity and imagination have not been used. In the realm of Brass and Steel he is under par and has gone backwards in every direction. 'An advance *must* be made.' Nor is he at all happy with the humble earthen qualities of his own body. Here too he has fallen behind and notes that some kind of advance is 'very necessary'.

So not only did Peter Dott organise his own moral life, he devised for himself a set of physical rules to ensure his bodily well being and so provide a decent house for the soul. This involved, for example, walking: fourteen hours in the course of each week; practising weight-lifting with dumbbells: three times daily; and taking Rebecca Dott's good wholesome porridge for breakfast. Rather like a physician conducting a self-examination, he kept detailed case-notes on the progress of his own body. On 8 January 1887 he records: 'Body in heavy, stupid condition—tendency to piles. Must reduce diet to simple things.' On the same day he notes more positively a distinct increase in his ability to tolerate his neighbours' weaknesses, based on an observance of his own shortcomings. He is pleased with the advance in self dignity but awards himself low marks for self discipline and concentration. His conclusion for that day is that more positive joyousness is necessary:

> a determination not to trouble others with my own deficiencies, the sense of which lowers my physical condition and makes the expression of whatever God there is in me meagre and insufficient.[7]

By the end of this month he records a falling-off in all the golden qualities. He is paying far too much attention to business, and though he is exercising his critical faculties usefully on pictures, he admits a failure in health and a lack of exercise. As the year wears on the notes become impatient and self-exhortative, lapsing into exclamatory denunciation, earnest prayer and frenetic appeals to greater effort:

> Deeper in degradation in all directions; poor, cheap and flimsy living—weak, weak, weak![8]

He adopts as his motto the commandment to love the Lord thy God with all thy heart and with all thy strength and with all thy soul and with all thy mind, and he prays continually for the necessary strength and guidance.

But by the autumn of the year he still claims no real overall advance.

Work and money-making are constantly getting in the way, the base, external trasheries of living. On the business front he regrets (September 1887) the loss of five or six years accumulated capital, equalling some £700. This resulted, he says, from 'foolish trust in another man' and absorbed a great deal of his time, thought and feeling. Now that trouble is past however, and leaves him, in a sense, a richer man with a priceless lesson on the vanity of riches. Plain living and high thinking are the things that matter, the worlds of work and love. Wealth is insubstantial and fleeting—and so, for that matter, is poverty. So the entry goes on, ending with his heartfelt prayer: 'Dear Good God and Father, help thy Son to live and love.'

The prayer was not answered at once. In April of the following year (1888) we find that the world has come yet again between God and his thirsting soul:

> I have found that owing to the illness of John McQueen and the consequent extra labour thrown on me, that business has absorbed far too much of my attention and time. Determine this month to enter on a fresh covenant with God, to reduce the hours given to worldly concerns and concentrate more power on education in art, and generally in forming my mind for higher things.[9]

Peter McOmish Dott was a bear with a headache.

His notebooks show that he found no cure for it—that intellectual ague of the bear's brain—at least not inside his own skull. The cure came from without, when he met the squirrel. By 1893, at the age of thirty-seven, he had met and fallen in love with Rebecca Morton, who was then in France. Into his notebook he entered a poem for her. He had composed it himself to an air of Beethoven's.

> Thou star of Love, from heaven high down gazing,
> Pour forth on me thy kindling ray,
> Thou wondrous orb, so pure, so distant shining,
> Draw near, make clear my dim and mist-filled way.

> And Thou, my Love, my true and only dear One,
> Though dwelling now in distant lands,
> Send forth thy love, so rich, so warm, so radiant,
> Burn on these lips, grasp firm these faithful hands.

> Dear God, beneath whose stars I stand adoring,
> Make pure my spirit while I pray,
> That our two loves be yet on earth united,
> One mutual flame to guide us on our way.

> Ah then, my Wife, my faithful and adored One,
> Our lamp of love aye burning clear,
> Life's evil fortune never shall divide us,
> Yea, Death itself shall draw us still more near.[10]

He framed pictures more successfully than words.

But the following year, when a greater wordsmith, his literary hero, died in Samoa at the age of forty-four, his prayer of love was granted. On 2 April 1894 the squirrel gave herself in matrimony to the bear. Very soon afterwards he became a free thinker. He never lost his profound admiration and respect for the Bible, and, judging from his later letters, never lost his faith either. What he did lose was his spiritual headache. Marriage cured him of that. The chained bear was released from bondage to the tormenting hounds of God and settled down happily with his squirrel. The honey of love and the nuts of wisdom were to be theirs.

They were married at Wester Brig o' Turk in the Trossachs, in a thatched cottage on the west side of the river Finlas, the cottage belonging to Mr and Mrs Ferguson. It was to be the start of a long association with Brig o' Turk both for themselves and for the yet unborn Norman.

Their honeymoon over, Mr and Mrs Dott, as they now were, moved into their house five miles outside Edinburgh in Colinton Village, at the foot of Spylawbank Road. No. 6 was known as The Nest, on the very doorstep of the Dell and it was in The Nest that all their children were born: Kathleen a year after the wedding; Jean eleven months later; Norman on 26 August 1897; Eric in the following year, shortly before Christmas; and Margaret in 1900, when the century had only several weeks left to run.

They were born during those years when the Scottish infant mortality rate (the annual average number of deaths under the age of one per 1,000 live births) actually rose to 130. In other words, at the time the young Dotts were being born in The Nest, the rate of infant deaths was thirteen times higher than it is today. And yet Cathy Morrison's father, who sprinkled the Colinton kirkyard with little villagers, did not put a single dead Dott into the ground. The Nest was a far cry from the housing circumstances endured by half Scotland's population, whose families still lived in one or two rooms.

They were also born into a time of exciting change. Shortly after the last of Peter and Rebecca's fledglings appeared, Oscar Wilde died in a Paris hotel, remarking of his room's wallpaper, 'One of us had to go!' Those less flippant spirits, Tennyson and Browning, were dead; Kipling was in his imperialist throes; the careers of Wells and Shaw lay largely before them. As the Boer War broke and the first airships probed the atmosphere, Hardy had abandoned the novel and was settling down to almost three decades of verse; Elgar's *Enigma Variations* ensured his forthcoming fame in 1899 and Peter and Rebecca held hands to the haunting *Salut d'Amour*. Picasso was poised to enter his Blue Period. The world nosed into the first year of the twentieth century: Queen Victoria's days were numbered. As were the days of rural tranquillity. The first motor cycles had appeared on the roads and frightened rabbits and hedgehogs heard ancestral rumblings, prophesying war. Thirteen years later Norman Dott would be ripping up Colinton Road on one of these new motor machines, to keep his appointment with destiny in Lothian Road. The Wright brothers were also hard at work, but Dott's destiny ensured that he would never fly a plane.

So: as the old earth left the long safe nest of the past for the unknown changes and challenges of the new future, Peter Dott took all his pretty chickens and their dam from The Nest and moved them less than a hundred yards up the brae to a house he had prepared for them. Hailes Brae was at No 18 Spylawbank Road. The land on which it was built had been sold by the Caledonian Railway Company to James Gillespie's Hospital. In their Disposition of 23 August 1876 in favour of the Gillespie Governors, the Company reserved the right of access through the land in order to maintain the tunnel. The Feu Charter whereby Gillespie's sold the land to Peter McOmish Dott is dated 7 June 1900. Building was completed and the house ready for occupation by 13 June 1902, when Mr Dott signed a Bond for £1,500 which was, effectively, his mortgage. The Dotts moved up the Kirk Brae beneath the summer sun.

In building this new home for his family Peter Dott would have had the words of the Order of Matrimony much in his mind: 'Except the Lord build the house they labour in vain that build it.' The new abode did not have a marriage lintel above the front door but the fireplace lintel in the main sitting-room served the same purpose. In the centre of the surrounding woodwork stood an interlinked pair of initial letters, M and D: Morton and Dott.

And on either side of the mantelpiece, carved into the lovely natural wood, were a squirrel and a bear.

CHAPTER FOUR

Aureum Milliarum—Colinton Village

One impulse from a vernal wood
Can teach us more of man,
Of moral evil and of good
Then all the sages can.

(*Wordsworth*)

Had there been a choice in the matter I should still have chosen Colinton as
my birthplace

(*Norman Dott*)

What a piece of work is a man: the beauty of the world, the paragon of
animals, and so on. And yet what is it that makes this quintessence of dust?
There is no single or final answer to the ultimate human mystery. The Child
is Father of the Man, says Wordsworth, as though that explained all. Behind
a single biological act lie the influences not only of childhood, parentage and
upbringing, but added to these the folded intricacies of history and genetics,
the trailing roots of evolution. God or the absence of God, education or the
lack of it, destiny or accident; friends, isolation; comfort, adversity, and so
on endlessly.

In his essay on the Manse of Colinton Parish Church, Robert Louis
Stevenson carries the question to the point where it teases us out of thought.
What, he asks himself, did he inherit from his grandfather, the Spartan-
blooded minister of the place, and, through him, from other people and
places? Beginning with their mutual love of Shakespeare, port and nuts,
Stevenson moves to his own fondness for the local parish gravestones and
the water mills of Colinton, back to the doings of his remoter ancestors, the
Picts, fleeing from Agricola's legions, and so on backwards to those
'marchers in Pannonian morasses, star-gazers on Chaldean plateaus', until,
boggling our brains, he finds himself peering through primeval branches at
his remotest ancestor of all, another muncher of nuts and sleeper in green
trees, who completes his pedigree. Thus he ends:

And I know not which is the more strange, that I should carry about with me some fibres of my minister-grandfather; or that in him, as he sat in his cool study, grave, reverend, contented gentleman, there was an aboriginal frisking of the blood that was not his; tree-top memories like undeveloped negatives lay dormant in his mind; tree-top instincts awoke and were trod down; and Probably Arboreal (scarce to be distinguished from a monkey) gambolled and chattered in the brain of the old divine.[1]

So 'our conscious years' concludes RLS 'are but a moment in the history of the elements that build us'. And although Stevenson allows himself a large helping of poetic licence and to us a wide degree of latitude in speculation as to how far those influences may stretch, the most obvious influence on a child after his parents is that he imbibes the atmosphere of a place and is affected by it just as surely as a nation's character is determined by its topography and climate. Norman Dott, addressing the Literary Society at Colinton in 1962, laid firm emphasis on the character-forming influence upon him of the old village of Colinton, acknowledging its salutary effects so far as saying that he could have desired no other cradle for his childhood years.

What kind of place was it?

Peter McOmish Dott's choice of name—Hailes Brae—for his new home was an apt one. Colinton wound itself round the ancient church of Halis or Hailes, which began life for a certainty as far back as the eleventh century, and most probably found its origins centuries before Macbeth had provided Shakespeare with a play to please the king.

The word Hailes is a form of *hale*, the Celtic for moor or hillock, and in the plural may suggest the miles of undulating moorland that swept the land like a wine-red sea long before man raised his civilising banner in Colinton. Surfacing as *Hala, Halis, Halys, Heallis* and *Hales,* the name Hailes was applied for generations to the parish now known as Colinton. Over the green whalebacks of the Pentland hills, turned to white whales by winter, came the earliest travellers, the grasshoppers of history, following the Water of Leith; paving the way for the pilgrims, cattle-drovers, fleers and adventurers who came later. They came down 1,500 feet from the windy heights to the river ford, where the water does a wide loop before turning off northwards to seek Edinburgh and the Firth of Forth. Four hundred million years before them the massed ice of the Southern Highlands and Uplands had already shown them the way. The two great ice-sheets, bent on conquest by division, had joined forces and travelled eastwards across the Midland Valley. Nudged east-north-east by the colossal stumbling blocks of the Pentlands, the great glacial flow had come grinding and gouging a passage through what was to be Colinton Dell. The way of the Water of Leith was chiselled by geology and in turn the water worked its softer effects on the landscape.

The earth-steppers stopped at the old ford, exchanging a few syllables among the water-worn rocks and the river chatter. Some of them paused in their journey, sharing food and drink, finding rest for the night; others gravitated naturally to this trysting-place of history. A sheltered valley, a river crossing, a meeting of peoples—it was not long before a Pictish temple would be raised nearby, and in time a Christian church on the west bank of the water, as in thousands of similar places throughout the land. And spiralling upwards and outwards in slow, snail-like whorls from this lowly heart of habitation, came Colinton village, its small cottages climbing the brae, looking up again to the Pentlands, from whence came their old beginning. Grander houses followed. The Edinburgh gentry wanted to live out their pastoral myth among foxes and kestrels and the lower orders of man that worked the snuff mills of John and James Gillespie, rustic props and stooges to boost their classical egos. Towers and battlements arose, bosomed high in the tufts of trees. A manse, a school, and in time a railway. Thus the conditions were created for the building of houses for the middle classes, some of whom, like Peter McOmish Dott, would spend their working lives commuting to Edinburgh.

Hailes Brae was just such a house.

It was built high on Spylawbank Road, commanding a magnificent view of the Water of Leith and the Pentlands. The land in front had been bought to preserve the view. From the great slope of hill the ground fell sharply from the main part of the house all the way down to the river several hundred yards below and beyond. Dr Eric Dott fondly remembers it nearly ninety years later with photographic precision.

> We were perched there and looked down eastward, the river lying on the east of us, and this made the house have different levels, which made it more interesting. The east side of the house had three stories and the west side had just two stories, and that made for an irregular level of rooms within the house. So the spacious central hall had its further back part (its northern part) higher than the front, with a couple of steps you had to go up halfway along.[2]

Like one of those massive manses that must have made many a bewintered Scottish minister, writing his sermons among draughts, contemplate new conceptions of Hell, Hailes Brae was a large house of twelve rooms, well designed to be convenient, but which ran on vast quantities of hard work and coal. A cellar took ten tons through a side hatch and this was entirely what kept the family warm. There was a large kitchen with a spacious larder, a scullery with washing tubs and sinks, and beyond these ten rooms, including an airily extensive basement, later fitted out with benches and tools for the practical young Norman. Here he made fishing rods and took his bicycles to bits; here his first operations on metal and wood were carried out by gaslight.

A tightly self-contained family group inhabited this eyrie above the trees.

13 Hailes Brae, Perched at the top of Spylawbank Road and overlooking Colinton Dell, this was the house Norman Dott was brought up in from the age of five.

There was no maid to wait on the master and mistress of the house or to pamper the children, whose efforts to help keep the home in order earned them their scant pocket money. A kindly eye was kept on them by Miss Annie Quibell, who passed muster as a nanny. Though not occupying the educational rôle of a governess, she did live in during the children's early years and took some of the pressure off the industrious Mrs Dott.

By and large the children's days were not mapped out for them constrictively. They were allowed to pursue their own inclinations: reading, drawing and painting—which interested their father because of his work—exploring the surrounding countryside; and playing in the magnificent garden designed and laid out by Peter Dott himself. The garden completely engirdled the house, running away down southwards and eastwards, the furthermost lowest part of it beetling over the railway tunnel so that the children could look right down on it and on the trains chugging along from Slateford.

Undoubtedly the chief occupation of these last day Victorian youngsters, so shortly to be Edwardians, was their pets. Norman Dott's love of animals, inherited from his father, began in the garden of Hailes Brae, which in the

14 An Edwardian childhood. From left to right are: Eric, Jean, Margaret, Norman and Kathleen, together with Jackie the crow and Paddy the terrier.

15 An earlier family grouping without the infant Margaret. Annie Quibell, nanny, props up Eric, while two year old Norman reacts to the tickling of his father's bushy beard.

16 Kathleen holds the bridle of Mailla, lord of the family pets, while Jean holds the reins.

17 Norman with old Nurse Leach, the midwife who looked after Mrs Dott in all her five confinements.

1900s resembled a miniature wild life park. An Irish terrier called Paddy suffered a long line of cats to purr beneath his watchful eye, the most notable of these cats being a big, strong Manx called Spunkie. Just as Paddy suffered the cats, so Spunkie tolerated the crow. At Hailes Brae the lamb lay down with the lion, resembling the apocryphal scene Peter Dott had read of in the Book of Revelation, and the Garden of Eden was just off Spylawbank Road, a haven and hospital for all God's creatures looking for succour. Norman's first patient was the crow. There was a big rookery in the woods on the far side of the river and on windy days the sky was strewn with harsh black rags. One bird had hurt its wing so badly it came flapping down into the Dott garden. It liked its treatment so well it decided to stay and in time became quite tame. Another unexpected visitor came from the railway tunnel. This was a black harbour for bats and when one of them strayed straight into the Dott front room the children immediately made a pet of it, feeding it on mealworms. It roosted hanging in the heavy curtain drapes, a pocket of wildlife inhabiting Edwardian plushness, and was quite one of the family. Here it stayed for several seasons before Norman finally released it into its tunnel again: doubtless a culture shock to be returned to the steam-filled noise and fury of those dark arches after the fireside chatter of the family Dott, with the gentle gaslight bubbling at their backs.

Almost as though Kenneth Grahame had written the script, the mole also came to stay. This glossy-coated intruder made himself at home in house as well as garden, and when running around the skirting boards of the rooms would demonstrate his great strength by pushing aside the heavy chairs with his front paws and putting his earth-shouldering weight against bulkier objects. He did not mind being lifted and dandled by the children, whom he soon got to know pretty well. They fed him on worms, though he fended well enough for himself in the earthy anchorages of Hailes Brae.

The king of pets was the donkey, who came somewhat later, just as Norman was entering his teens. He was a costermonger's donkey, retired from work in London and brought up by their father after one of his business trips. Each day Jean took the donkey down to the village and loaded it with shopping, encouraging it with a little rod to climb back up the steep Spylawbank Road. It was christened Mailla by Jean and her sister Kathleen. The name is the Romany word for donkey, reflecting the girls' reading. They were fascinated by the romance of the gypsy world and had read all George Borrow had to say on the subject. Borrow's wordbook of the English-Gypsy language, *Romany Lavo-Lil,* was published in 1874. There is something reminiscent of the Brontë circle in these children's absorbed projection of themselves into their own worlds.

Norman however was not so prone to this kind of imaginative identification. His concern for the pets, though kindly, was practical. He was chiefly interested in making things for their care. Ask him to build a hutch or alter

18   Eric and Norman with cat and dog at Hailes Brae.

19   *Dark brown is the river, golden is the sand.* Norman and Eric in Colinton Dell in April 1905.

a harness and he was in his element. The best example of this is the ingenious bell he made for Spunkie to ring. From the scullery an outside window looked out onto the garden and it opened only from the top. Norman rigged up an old Swiss cowbell inside the house, connecting it through the woodwork of the window to a little lever outside. The cat was trained to press his paw on this lever when he needed in from the garden, and this would ring the bell and the children would open the window and allow him inside.

Dr Eric Dott recalls how the bell probably saved Spunkie's life.

> The cat had gone missing for several days and we had given it up for dead or lost. But one evening the bell suddenly rang. We all rushed to open the window but to our surprise the cat did not jump up and in. So my brother Norman ran round the house to see what was the matter—and there was Spunkie caught in a wire rabbit trap that was tightly enmeshed about his body. He was terribly thin and bedraggled and near to dead. Obviously he had lain for days after having been caught in this, until finally he had summoned the strength to tear the snare from its attachments in the ground and crawl to safety, where he promptly rang us and was discovered. He was so far gone and exhausted at the time I think he would most certainly have died that night had it not been for Norman's bell.[3]

If Norman Dott's first patient was a crow, the first life saved seems to have been the cat's. Years later a grateful patient was to comment that Norman Dott gave some people nine lives.

The time comes when all children must leave their secret gardens and be exiled from the innocence of their respective Edens. Nowadays anxious parents dread the moment when the fledgling flies around the corner and disappears from view for the first time. As we approach the end of a millenium we have seen or read too many horror stories of abductions and accidents to want to inspire too much confidence in our own children concerning the world outside Eden. It was not so in the day of Norman Dott's boyhood. To him the Hailes Brae garden must have seemed merely an ante-room to the Elysian fields without, and the garden gate opened onto paradise unbounded.

Colinton was at that time a country village in Midlothian, five miles out of Edinburgh and well out of sound or sight of the nearest tram. The old village consisted largely of the main street, Spylaw Street, running from the high ground down to the Water of Leith bridge. On the south side of the street were the old harled cottages, timber-porched, where James Gillespie had earlier housed his mill workers, and now occupied by deserving pensioners of Edinburgh. The high street met the major roads to the city and it contained the main shops and several dwellings. These two streets formed the kernel of the old Colinton. Beyond them were a growing number of villas like Hailes Brae, standing in their own grounds, fine buildings with good gardens, owned mainly by people who worked in Edinburgh and shuttled between Colinton and the metropolis. But the heart of the community was where the water busily beat the stones, beneath the bridge and beside the parish church.

Norman Dott's first forays out of home were on missions of great importance: to run down the kirk brae (as Spylawbank Road was familiarly known) and enter the little corner shop at the bottom of Spylaw Street. The shopkeeper sold sweets and newspapers and cigarettes. The assignment was to buy Peter Dott's Gold Flake, which in those days he was never done chain-smoking. By the time the small boy who had been sent for his father's cigarettes was himself a famous surgeon, he had developed a taste for another well known brand of cigarettes, Three Castles, and the wife of the celebrated neurosurgeon would come down from their Marchmont home, crossing Princes Street to the branch of Menzies in Hanover Street to buy her husband's tobacco. Norman Dott characteristically appears off surgical duty with a cigarette between his lips or fingers. It is a pose which he took on from his father.

Just past the cigarette shop and on the other side of the street close to the water was Frail's Dairy, where the children went for dairy produce, though frequently they wandered down there simply attracted by the animals, the pigs being fed and the cows milked. A pastoral beauty spot it was even in the middle of this country village: a heart of hearts.

The quest for eggs often took them even further than Frail's Dairy, deep into the Dell itself and across the stepping stones and the whirling water to the genial Mrs Hutton's little poultry farm. Picture a troop of young Dotts, of varying heights, stepping gingerly in shaky single file across the Water of Leith, to buy eggs at a penny each, one shilling a dozen, and returning led by Norman, clutching the precious cargo in a brown paper bag. In those days there was no rustic bridge below the weir and egg-buyers simply struggled across those very shaky stones, polished and gleaming wetly in the dappled sunlight that danced on the water. A picturesque scene out of which the children usually came with wet feet but no broken eggs.

Some of the shops and trades were of particular interest to Norman alone. His father had not only recognised his skill with his hands by kitting him out with tools and a workroom at Hailes Brae: he also allowed him to go to the local joiners at weekends and holidays when he was still quite a young boy. The joiner was Sandy Thomson. His premises were at Allendale, close to Frail's Dairy and hard by the water. There Norman soon made himself at home, not just with wood but with the men who worked it, learning to apply their techniques and to speak their language. He was still a very young child when he made his first wheelbarrow there. Such a 'kent face' did he become at Sandy Thomson's that during their sing-song one Christmas the tradesmen tried to persuade him to sing a number. He flatly refused, but instead recited for them Burns's *Tam O' Shanter* in its entirety, a feat which earned him their loud applause.

By association, and when addressing the Colinton Burns Club six decades later, Norman Dott treasured for himself this fragment from the Colinton of the past and held it up to his audience in words.

> I remember so well the rustic smithy forge, the smell of burning horse hoof, the flying sparks; the thrill when the smith shrank the hot iron tyre onto the wobbly wooden barrow wheel that I took up to him from Sandy Thomson's joiner's workshop, where I had hand made it, and as the bubbles died away and the steam cleared—lo! a perfect, firm, round wheel.[4]

Sandy's daughter wrote to Professor Dott to congratulate him on the conferment upon him of the Freedom of the City of Edinburgh, and Dott replied with characteristic warmth.

> Yes, I remember Sandy Thomson and his joiner's yard at Colinton very well. He was a gentle, kindly soul, as I remember him. Yes, I worked as an apprentice with him for a few months and became proficient in making coffins, wheelbarrows and farm carts. The wheels were very tricky work in those days of hand craft.[5]

A little older and further afield, Norman continued to display this faculty of getting to know people of practical interest to him in a somewhat unorthodox way for a youngster. He came to know Alice Thorburn, for example, a renowned fly-tier with premises in George Street. Very soon a skilful assistant in her shop, he was making fishing flies for her at weekends. The same pattern repeated itself when Peter Dott bought his children their bicycles. Norman's immediate response was to dismantle his machine, get to know how it worked and put it all together again. He then sought out Willie McLeod in Juniper Green where he found he could buy bicycle parts. Like all those adults befriended by Norman in his early days, Willie proved to be something of a character, and like all the other characters he recognised and acknowledged the boy's skill by taking him on as an unofficial assistant. Soon he was also a friend. Before too long he was carrying out repairs for customers in the back of the shop and learning all he could in the process. Later still when he graduated to the world of motor bikes he was similarly drawn in to the world of Mr Leggat's shop in Slateford. And in this way he progressed with inescapable orchestration towards his eventual accident in Lothian Road.

Meanwhile he followed his safer pursuits in the sheltered cradle of innocence out at Colinton, making fishing rods out of the stems of wild roses and haunting the local blacksmith's. The sparks flew out the door in fierce fiery constellations, carried by the quick winds of March down to the kirkyard, where they buzzed among the gravestones like bright spring bees to kindle the dead. But Norman Dott's eyes were riveted on what was happening inside the shop. Fascinated by the manipulation of the metal, he was acquiring the engineering bug even then.

It might seem a trifle as though the boy Norman Dott was little more than an old man cut down.

The truth lies the other way.

Advanced as he was with his hands, he was still a boy and was tremendously popular with the local children on account of his ability to make and do for them and his willingness to oblige.

One winter he made a sledge.

As we might expect of Norman Dott it was no ordinary sledge but was a jumbo jet of sledges, a long, strong contraption which carried no less than ten children. Miss Cathy Morrison, she who used to deliver the morning milk to Hailes Brae from Frail's horse-drawn float, is still alive in Spylaw Street and deep into her eighties, having lived in Colinton all her days. One of her earliest and most vivid memories of life is riding on Norman's sledge.

> Norman was the nicest and kindest of them all. When I was ten he made this long sledge for sliding down the hill. But he would never run it down unless he found ten children to pack onto it—he had to have the ten passengers. As it happened there were a lot of mill workers' children in those days, so there was never any bother filling it up. It used to be a great thrill going on the back of the Dott sledge. The kirk brae was very steep, but down it would go—all the way from Hailes Brae round to the bridge, packed with its ten children and Norman steering them. And there was never once an accident . . .[6]

Those were tranquil times before the days of traffic congestion, when the bucket cart and the milk cart, both horse-powered, were all the traffic for the day in Colinton. Reflecting in the year of his retirement on those Arcadian roadways, Norman Dott recalled:

> As schoolchildren we sometimes walked the four miles of country roads to Craiglockhart, where we met the horse-drawn tram cars at the city boundary. We had the exciting experience of witnessing the introduction and operation of the cable-drawn trams and later the electric trams. The first electrified section was that from the Post Office to Musselburgh and we were much impressed . . . The thrilling speed of the electric tram was interrupted every few yards when the driver and conductor met to lift a prostrate reveller from the lines and lay him gently on the grassy verge.[7]

Nowadays such prostrate revellers would stand little chance on the murderous hurlyburly of the Edinburgh highways. When he made the sledge the traffic accident in Lothian Road was one year away from Norman Dott. He could not have foreseen it as he captained his two handfuls of screaming youngsters safely down Spylawbank Road, his young strong arms confidently steering his own handiwork. The sledge sped like a ship through the winter whiteness, woods and water birling behind it, and came to rest on the eighteenth-century bridge at Colinton's inmost core, where the earliest travellers had met and a gathering of tongues forged the first link in the old community.

The excited children who disembarked from the Dott sledge were the young of the mill workers. Robert Louis Stevenson, who played among these same mills less than fifty years before Norman Dott, speaks for all children who ever played by water when he recreates in verse the delight experienced by the youngsters of Colinton, Norman Dott included.

> Over the borders, a sin without pardon,
> Breaking the branches and crawling below,
> Out through the breach in the wall of the garden,
> Down by the banks of the river we go.
>
> Here is the mill with the humming of thunder,
> Here is the weir with the wonder of foam,
> Here is the sluice with the race running under—
> Marvellous places, though handy to home!
>
> Sounds of the village grow stiller and stiller,
> Stiller the note of the bird on the hill;
> Dusty and dim are the eyes of the miller,
> Deaf are his ears with the moil of the mill.
>
> Years may go by, and the wheel in the river
> Wheel as it wheels for us children today,
> Wheel and keep roaring and foaming forever,
> Long after all of the boys are away.
>
> You with the bean that I gave when we quarrelled,
> I with your marble of Saturday last,
> Honoured and old and all fairly apparelled,
> Here we shall meet and remember the past.
>
> Home from the Indies and home from the ocean,
> Heroes and soldiers we all shall come home;
> Still we shall find the old mill wheel in motion,
> Turning and churning that river to foam.[8]

That river as Stevenson fondly recalls it, (variously referred to as 'that willing drudge', 'that dirty Water of Leith'—by RLS in less romantic vein—and as a 'silver thread in a ribbon of green' with dangerous overtones of McGonagall to come) powered in its halcyon days nearly ninety mills. This was remarkable for a river which, in comparison with its bigger Scottish brothers, is something of an insignificant little driblet, a mere twenty miles or less from the Pentlands to the Firth of Forth. Yet it was still, at the turn of the century, one of the most important stretches of industrial water in the country, providing the energy for the processing of a variety of products: spices, wood, leather, flour, paper, And of course snuff. Tobacco became a Scottish passion just as the D'Otts were leaving the continent, so enabling James Gillespie, born with a bumper of a nose himself, to make his fortune in the following century. Long after he lay down in the Colinton kirkyard under his pedimented mausoleum, snuff continued to be made on the river and was still being made there when Norman Dott was taking his own brand of tobacco in the way that suited him best. And the breakfast smells of porridge that went round the heart of Cathy Morrison as she took the Dotts their milk, originated in one of these mills, West Mills, which at that time was run by A & R Scott for Porage Oats.

Put a kirk in a valley surmounted by the green crests of hills; surround it with moss-pantiled and porched cottages, winding streets, long gardens and dykes dripping with stonecrop; provide it with a smiddy, a dairy and a Thomas-the-Tank-Engine railway station and trains; camouflage it from the wider world with woodlands and watercourses that offered haunts for the roe-deer and fox, badger and vole, heron and dipper, and many a migrant come to rest among cedars of Lebanon and ivy-bound sycamores. The lesser celandines and wood anemones marry the March winds and come early to blossom; wild hyacinth runs riot in May and June; dog-roses bewilder the pink hedgerows of July and August; and the fading frogs croak among elderberries and rose-hips before going off to their dark slow sleep. In winter the dells fill up with snow. You might just wonder if any more could possibly be done to place a young boy in heaven.

In the case of Norman Dott the answer is: yes.

Add to all that natural beauty the busy sound of mill machinery—and wilderness is paradise enow. Quite simply the mills were a fascination that the boy could not resist. Leading his young brother by the hand he followed the Water of Leith through miles and miles of mills, exploring and trespassing as he pleased absorbing the irresistible work rhythms of men and machines. The scents and sounds of woodcraft crowded in upon him. One of the images that remains with Eric Dott is of how Norman used to enjoy twirling a rope that ascended through a series of hatchways, intrigued by the way the wave process he had thus set up would return in reverse from top to bottom. They came home covered in sawdust and flour.

Time and again Norman Dott, when reminiscing about his childhood, returned in imagination to these scenes, forever citing his and his father's favourite author, Stevenson, who has encapsulated the spirit of boyhood nostalgia for all Colintoners, as for all men and women, in his passage on the Water of Leith.

> Often and often I desire to look upon it again; and the choice of a point of view is easy to me. It should be at a certain water-door, embowered in shrubbery. The river is there dammed back for the service of the flour-mill just below,

so that it lies deep and darkling, and the sand slopes into brown obscurity with
a glint of gold; and it has but newly been recruited by the borrowings of the
snuff-mill just above, and these, tumbling merrily in, shake the pool to its
black heart, fill it with drowsy eddies, and set the curded froth of many other
mills solemnly steering to and fro upon the surface.[9]

Such was the scene Norman Dott saw as he explored the pristine world
of his childhood. Here he put a hook into the water for the first time; here
he sailed his first ships, liners of leaf-covered boughs that the current swept
away. No wonder RLS was his pride and joy. After Rebecca Dott had read
to him out of *A Child's Garden of Verses* he went out and played in the very
places that inspired the poems.

> Dark brown is the river,
> Golden is the sand.
> It flows on for ever,
> With trees on either hand.
>
> Green leaves a-floating,
> Castles of the foam,
> Boats of mine a-boating—
> Where will all come home?
>
> On goes the river
> And out past the mill,
> Away down the valley,
> Away down the hill.
>
> Away down the river,
> A hundred miles or more,
> Other little children
> Shall bring my boats ashore.[10]

Well, there is a poetic licence at work in the statistic of a hundred miles,
but to Norman Dott as to Robert Louis Stevenson fifty years before, the
Water of Leith seemed to wind and twist into the ultimate unknowns of
Edinburgh and the Forth, north-east of Eden. We see him in the old
photograph, standing with Eric in Colinton Dell, and lines from another
great favourite of Peter Dott's come naturally to the pen.

> The world was all before them, where to choose
> Their place of rest, and Providence their guide:
> They, hand in hand, with wandering steps and slow,
> Through Eden took their solitary way.[11]

The road out of Eden leads, as we all know, to the graveyard, where the
Angel of Death glowers among crossbones and scrolls and skulls, the sower
and reaper stone, hourglass reminders of mortality. In Colinton kirkyard
the sternest of all reminders existed, as it still does, in the form of a great iron

20 Colinton Parish Church. The Dotts played barefoot among its ancient gravestones.

mortsafe, to beat the resurrectionists. In this fresh bodies were interred long enough for an effective degree of decomposition to have set in, rendering the corpse useless to medical science. Little did Norman dream then that the bodysnatchers of old had served a profession he was destined to enter with dissecting hand.

Antiquity scented the atmosphere like powdered lichens from the tombs.

> HEIR LYIS ANE
> HONORABIL VO
> MAN A HIRIOT
> SPOVS TO I FOVLIS
> OF COLLING TOVN
> VAS QUHA DIED
> AVGVST 1593

The *memento mori* trumpeted its bleak messages even to the most casual reader

> Death's a debt
> To nature deeu
> I have paid her
> So mon you

But kirkyard humour never cracked a smile in the place. Perhaps there were too many headstones testifying to early graves and infant mortality.

Cholera had swept the village in 1886, sprinkling infants like daisies over the green. Cathy Morrison's father had wounded the turf for many a life cut short, stitching it back again in neat squares over sorrows that had not yet touched the Dotts. Even as the children played in the kirkyard, flitting among the stones with butterflies and bees, even there the sound of the busy mills filled their ears. One of the mills actually occupied the cemetery site itself, now encroached upon by the slow but sure-moving greenbelt of the dead. In the already quoted essay on the Manse—it was built on the banks of the Water of Leith, slightly lower than the graveyard—Stevenson evokes the atmosphere in lines that Norman Dott came to love, sharing his passion with unnumbered others.

> It was a place in that time like no other: the garden cut into provinces by a great hedge of beech, and overlooked by the church and terrace of the churchyard, where the tombstones were thick, and after nightfall 'spunkies' might be seen to dance, at least by children; flower-pots lying warm in sunshine; laurels and the great yew making elsewhere a pleasing horror of shade; the smell of water rising from all round with an added tang of paper-mills; the sound of water everywhere, and the sound of mills—the wheel and the dam singing their alternate strain; the birds on every bush and from every corner of the overhanging woods pealing out their notes until the air throbbed with them; and in the midst of this, the manse.[12]

The manse, that 'well-beloved house' that had stood so long amid bird-song and stones and the clattering of mill-winding water, was inhabited by the Thomas Marjoribanks who had welcomed the Dotts to church in 1909, and who was to speak up for Eric Dott eight years later during the war, when on Christian grounds he became a staunch conscientious objector. In Stevenson's day the manse's occupant was the writer's maternal grand-father, the Reverend Dr Lewis Balfour, that Spartan divine who sat alone, sermon-writing in his 'library of bloodless books'. To escape his chill sermons and psalms the young Louis scaled the old yew tree, from the crow's nest of which he looked out on scenes of piratical adventure. Perhaps inspired by Stevenson's imaginings and by his own reading of *Treasure Island*, the fourteen year old Norman built himself a crow's nest in one of the trees in the garden of Hailes Brae, from which point of elevation he wrote letters to his holidaying parents, penning the words, he says,

> on a little piece of planed wood which is conveniently fixed to a convenient branch in this convenient bower. It serves as writing desk, book rest, head rest or pillow, and innumerable other purposes. I can lie my full length and rest here without the slightest fear of falling.[13]

He goes on to describe a diet of bananas, strawberry jam and custard, hoisted to him on a rope!

A warm-blooded boy.

Dr Lewis Balfour was no colder as he lay in the kirkyard than his famous grandson had pictured him in life. Near him lay his predecessor, *in tyrannos atrox*, according to his tombstone, the Reverend John Fleming, who had turned the manse garden from a botanical wonderland into a potato plot. If learned divines are inclined to turn in their graves, there is not doubt that this act of vandalism would have stirred Mr Fleming's own predecessor, the Reverend John Walker. The 'Mad Minister of Moffat' had been considered demented by the Colintoners on account of his botanising obsession, the insect net peeping from his pocket believed by the ladies of his congregation to be curling tongs.

Alive or dead, past or present, human, natural or inanimate, the various influences of Colinton instilled in the young Norman Dott a deeply abiding love of Scotland and the Scots. When he first lifted his eyes to the Scottish hills he was obeying the injunction not of Psalm 121 but of the Scots poet Allan Ramsay:

> Look up to Pentland's towering tap,
> Buried beneath great wreaths of snaw,
> O'er ilka cleugh, ilk scar and slap,
> As high as ony Roman wa'.[14]

No energetic and curious youngster, looking on the scene Ramsay describes, could brook much waiting. Norman's feet began to itch and it was not long before he was leading Eric up and out of the valley, off once again in the haunted footsteps of RLS, his literary love, over by Bonaly and Torfinn and along to Swanston. Perched high on Caerketton, the boy's mind and eye could turn in all directions, round the compass of the world, travelling far into future and past.

Caerketton is the foremost wave in the green sea of hills that comes rolling up towards Edinburgh—frozen almost as it prepares to crash downwards on the crags and steeples of the city in its path. This was for Norman Dott, as for his esteemed author, the *Aureum Milliarum*, The Golden Milestone, measuring the distance between his Pentland perch and the village in the valley a kirkward mile off. And just as Stevenson's home-sick yearnings reached out from distant Samoa to this famous Scottish panorama in which he could visualise Auld Reekie

> Spring gallant from the shallows of her smoke,
> Cragged, spired and turreted, her virgin fort
> Beflagged;[15]

so the boy born to be a great surgeon never failed to acknowledge the first fount of his inspiration and the effects on him of that writer's words.

I saw rain falling and the rainbow drawn
On Lammermuir. Hearkening, I heard again
In my precipitous city, beaten bells
Winnow the keen sea wind.[16]

Norman Dott reaches the Pentland ridge for the first time and looks about him. The air is laden with history. Prehistoric peoples, Picts and Scots, here pitted their forces against one another with sound and fury, their bones now lying quiet beneath the peewees and the bee. Friars with naked foot came this way from Holyrood to St Katterine's Chapel to sing their vespers, and monks after matins to collect wax-monies and tithes, down in Colinton Dell. Kings and cattlemen, reivers and smugglers, shepherds and plough-men, all have left their aura, mellow, mysterious: a diaphanous haze about the hills. Prince Charlie's Highlanders came foraging, Walter Scott came fishing, and Henry Cockburn sat 800 feet up behind Bonaly, steeped to the very lips in Tacitus. Here he made his way thorugh the Latin from cover to cover. Most of all the mind turns to those bloody clashes between Covenant and Crown, when the hills hurled from one to another the echoing thunder of the king's dragoons and the cries of the Conventiclers, who stood for their beliefs in the spirit of Dott's Huguenot forebears, spurning the royal kirk command. The stones remain, to commemorate their stern stress.

Grey recumbent tombs of the dead in desert places,
Standing stones on the vacant wine-red moor,
Hills of sheep, and the homes of the silent vanished races,
And winds austere and pure.

Be it granted to me to behold you again in dying,
Hills of home! and to hear again the call:
Hear round the graves of the martyrs the peewees crying,
And here no more at all.[17]

The view from the Pentlands does not stop there. A young boy could see all too clearly both with the external eye and with the inner eye of contemplation just what wonders lay beyond Colinton Dell and Hailes Brae; what untold challenges were on offer when the wider world lay at his feet like a thrown glove.

Trains crawl slowly abroad upon the railway lines: little ships are tacking in the Firth the shadow of a mountainous cloud, as large as a parish, travels before the wind . . . The city is as silent as a city of the dead: from all its humming thoroughfares not a voice not a footfall reaches you upon the hill . . . You have a vision of Edinburgh not as you see her, in the midst of a little neighbourhood, but as a boss upon the round world with all Europe and the deep sea for her surroundings. For every place is a centre to the earth, whence highways radiate or ships set sail for foreign ports; the limit of a parish is not more imaginary than the frontier of an empire; and as a man sitting at home in his cabinet and swiftly writing books, so a city sends abroad an influence and a portrait of herself.[18]

Turning from the west and the comparatively new Forth Bridge, Norman Dott could see the islands of the Forth, Inchkeith, Inchcolm, its medieval abbey shut in by the bolts and shackles of the invading sea. He could view the Fife coast, where his people had landed from France, the Sidlaw and Ochil hills to the north, the Grampians, blue with distance; and turning north and east, the Castle, Arthur's Seat, the Braid hills, the Bass Rock and Berwick Law and the colder pulses of the North Sea heard in the mind's ear. A magnificently bewildering variety of impressions to accept in a single turn of the head, and an infinite penumbra of possibilities.

The time had come to open the oyster world and steal its pearls of learning.

Chapter Five

The Art of Education

I still had loved
The exercise and produce of a toil
Than analytic industry to me
More pleasing
                    (*Wordsworth*)

Of making many books there is no end,
and much study is a weariness of the flesh.
                    (*Proverbs*)

Education, it is often said, but not often enough, begins in the home. Our parents begin the educative process not simply by imparting information in reply to our first curious questionings, but by instilling into us the values they hold dear, and by raising the rafters of intellectual, moral and spiritual culture which carries the roof above our heads.

The Dott children were fortunate in being brought up by a mother whose Christian virtues of humility and strength were like the pillars of the Book of Kings, surmounted by their iron lilywork: an image that stayed with them all their days. Kind, gentle and concerned for others, she taught them that the paths of righteousness lead not into the pews but *out* from them: she taught by example and not merely by precept, though as we have already seen, she picked up the secular tools of poetry, the classics and song and passed them on to her children, who in time were to place them in their own children's hands. If they had never gone to school the Dotts would still have learned more from their mother in a decade than some people garner in a lifetime.

The same is true of their father as a teacher. His son Norman never forgot his civilising influence.

> I joined the human race at a house known as The Nest, just at the entrance to the Dell, in 1897. My father was an ardent reader and student of Burns, and the family at The Nest and later at Hailes Brae, near the top of Kirk Brae, was brought up on the Good Book, *The Pilgrim's Progress,* Walter Scott and Robert Burns . . .

My father brought us up on *Tales Of A Grandfather* and later the Waverley novels. He would read to us 'Wandering Willie's Tale' on Halloween and we knew our Burns from him.[1]

Similarly, Eric Dott, now in his nineties, remembers him with undimmed affection.

In himself he was gentle and kind and had a keen sense of humour. He loved all the old Scottish stories—he had a distinctive Scottish accent himself—and he read and recalled these to us frequently, adding many of his own. He was just full of these anecdotes illustrative of Scottish life and character. A great favourite of his was Dean Ramsay's *Reminiscences,* and, quite apart from his wide knowledge of the classics, he had thoroughly read Carlyle, Walter Scott, and, of course, Robert Louis Stevenson. He quoted these authors to us again and again, over and over, and naturally we came in time to read them ourselves . . . All this came through to us with the gentle kindness of a father for his children, because he was a tender-hearted person. And for so intelligent and intellectual and indeed widely-read a man, you would hardly think he could be so gentle and tender, but that he was. The portrait of him done by Jean in Hailes Brae represents him so very well—a commanding but kind presence with that warm expression of his.[2]

Dr Dott's reference to the portrait serves as a reminder of the most palpable of all the educational agencies that presided over Hailes Brae.
Art.
Having taken over the firm of Aitken Dott & Son, Peter Dott zealously set about the business of educating himself in the study of the fine arts. He travelled to the Continent and saw the leading art galleries of Italy, France and Spain—the Louvre, the Prado, the Uffizi, the Peti. Having enjoyed no formal education of that kind himself and lacking a college or university degree, this meant that his self-acquired knowledge of art tended towards the practical and pragmatic. It also helped to kindle and keep alight a living enthusiasm for his subject transcending mere business interests. According to Eric this affected life at Hailes Brae in a rather dramatic way.

My father's interest in art had a tremendous effect on the atmosphere in which we were brought up. He influenced us by bringing into the home a highly cultured view of life. The house itself was just hung with pictures by recent and living Scottish artists such as the elder McTaggart, Sir James Lawton Wingate, Edwin Alexander the fine watercolourist, and many others of the notable artists. And of course Peploe. Father bought these paintings direct from the artists with a view to selling them. If he liked the pictures however, he wouldn't sell them all at once but brought them to live at Hailes Brae for a while. Then, if he had a customer who wanted a McTaggart or a Peploe, say, he took it back to the shop again and brought another in its place. So we had in the house a permanently changing gallery of the finest art of the time. Not only that, but our father would talk to us about these matters, about the books he was reading, about the paintings and artists he was dealing with, and naturally we imbibed his feelings about them.[3]

Thus exposed to the finest accomplishments of contemporary art, and living in a picture exhibition on which business rang its fascinating changes, Norman Dott would have little idea that he was sometimes looking at genius on display. Nor did Peter McOmish Dott, interestingly enough, always know for certain when he was dealing with an artist of genius as compared with one whose pictures were engagingly executed and sold well.

This is illustrated by the case of Samuel Peploe, who at the time Peter Dott was buying his paintings was certainly not considered a genius. He was nonetheless an excellent commercial prospect for Aitken Dott & Son, at least in the beginning. In his book, *Three Scottish Colourists,* T J Honeyman corrects the earlier biography of Peploe by Stanley Cursiter.

> Cursiter seems to indicate that his (Peploe's) first one-man show at Aitken Dott's was in 1909. Actually it was some years earlier—in 1903. The records show that twelve paintings were sold, one of them to T J Ferguson for £15 ... At the 1909 exhibition Peploe had 48 drawings and 63 paintings, comprising still-lifes, flowers, figures and landscapes, a retrospective survey of his formative years ... This 1909 exhibition must have given the art-interested public the first chance to see what might be the significant trends in Scots painting arising in the new century.[4]

The established facts are that Peploe's first-ever one-man exhibition was at Dott's in November 1903 and that he sold nineteen pictures. Peter McOmish Dott befriended the young artist and warmly encouraged him in his work. Still, it was not until March 1909 that the reticent Peploe launched his second one-man show at Dott's, accepting £450 for his sixty paintings, thirty-five of which sold, in addition to a quantity of drawings. It was this success that put the writing on the wall for the Dott-Peploe symbiosis. With the 1909 money Peploe was able to marry and move to Paris with his bride, Margaret Mackay from South Uist. Guy Peploe, the artist's grandson, tells us, 'Peploe was bored with Edinburgh, perhaps a little alarmed by his increasing popularity, and sick of having "Wingate and McTaggart crammed down my throat" '. Peter Dott, a little alarmed by the recent changes in Peploe's style, wrote to Mrs Peploe a long letter of advice, urging her to keep her husband on what he believed to be the right commercial rails. It was agreed that another one-man show would be put on as soon as the Peploes returned to Edinburgh. Little did Peter Dott realise what he would bring back with him.

Three years later he came bearing his French fruits, a substantial collection of exotic oddities, at least in the eyes of the art dealer. Mr Dott was shocked and horrified. From his point of view the material was unaesthetic and unsellable, an attack on true art. In spite of his instinctive and generous desire to help the artists he did business with, he simply could not bring himself to exhibit Peploe's new work. The dismayed artist moved to the New Gallery in Shandwick Place and subsequently to Alexander Reid of Glasgow. It was not until Peter McOmish Dott retired from the business in 1916 and Duncan Macdonald came to Aitken Dott & Son that the firm once again brought back Peploe into the fold.

There is no slur on Peter Dott's behaviour here and no censure of his aesthetic perceptions if we understand the position of a dealer at this time. A revealing letter of Peploe's tells us how, in 1911, he returned briefly from France to try to raise some ready cash to keep the French sojourn afloat. He went down to Castle Street to see Peter Dott but as he was out at the time he spoke to George Proudfoot instead. He was offered £50 for twenty-two canvases and told it was more than he would earn if the pictures were put on sale. The artist had no option but to accept. A score of Peploes went for £50! By contrast Mr Dott mentions to Eric in a letter that Wingate has just done fifty canvases in seven and a half weeks, earning himself £1,800, twenty times the rate offered to Peploe. This was several years later, however, and Wingate was then aged seventy. A shrewd art dealer might be excused for adopting Feste's motto that youth's a stuff will not endure. And if a man's work endures only after he is safely dead— well, that is as common as the wind and the rain.

It should be stressed that the climate of painting and exhibiting in the early years of the century was very different from today. The few galleries were highly selective and disinclined to speculate by blazing a trail for unacknowledged genius. There was not, as there is now, any widespread public buying of paintings. Instead a number of wealthy collectors controlled the market and their custom was eagerly competed for by the dealers. The large public exhibiting societies like the RSA were discouraging of younger talent—established artists who are secure in their membership privileges are notoriously ungenerous to up-and-comers— and it was necessary, as it still is, to run the gauntlet of their selection and hanging committees. Serious painters tried to interest one of the prestigious galleries in giving them an exhibition and hopefully agreeing to buy their work regularly for re-sale to clients. Ideally a retainer or agreed sum annually would be paid to an artist in return for the exclusive rights to show his work. Peploe had struck a bargain with Alexander Reid in Glasgow and Aitken Dott in Edinburgh that they would tap his output in return for not less than £600 per annum. Sometimes the dealer allowed the artist to sell privately to patrons but would claim his usual commission on these pictures. An artist, if he were successful enough, could live like this, run a home and bring up a family, but it was a precarious and mostly under-remunerated way of doing so, especially if the painter wished to experiment in his work. His art did not normally buy brandy for the glass. The dealers and gallery owners were therefore powerful people, but at the same time in showing the work of a particular painter they were laying their own reputations on the line.

Peter McOmish Dott had his own wife and family to consider. He liked Peploe in the way that he was painting when he first saw his work and he had clients for that work. Peploe was then working in a painting tradition which came down the line from Velasquez and Goya to Monet: carefully analysed tones, broadly and boldly put down with great skill and with characteristic brushwork. The colour tended towards the monochrome, with small areas of brighter colour thrown into prominence by being set off among lots of subdued neutral colours—off-whites, all kinds of greys, greyed browns and greyed greens, with black used as a colour. It was not Impressionism: it lent itself to the still-life, with dazzling white tablecloths, napkins, sparkling glasses or silver, black bottles and dark backgrounds, all rendered in virtuoso brushwork and luscious, tactile paint. These were the Peploes that looked out at Norman Dott from the walls of Hailes Brae, and they were all very elegant.

Peploe came back from France with his vision transformed; it was the period just after the Fauves and the Cubists, of Matisse and Braque and Picasso. He had been in the south of France, in Royan and Cassis, where the intensity of the light and the colour of the landscape force painters to pitch up their tones and hues. Peploe was now thinking colour and his old style had disappeared. There is a well known portrait of his wife, for example, where she has a light green face, like a Matisse of the period.

So: although nowadays it is hard to see Peploe's painting as being 'over the top', it is not at all surprising that seventy-five years ago Peter Dott was appalled. From Dott's standpoint his gallery's reputation was at stake and his clientele for Peploe's work could vanish and the constant security of a sellable supply of paintings from this artist be gone overnight. He genuinely felt Peploe to be misguided and also felt personally let down by the artist he had succoured and encouraged. If only—Peter Dott thought—Peploe would put Satan behind him and just get back to painting the nice flowers and things . . .

It is again easy with our hindsight to wonder at this and call it crassness, but in 1913 Peploe was not considered a genius. Look at two Peploes from the pre- and post-France periods, set them side by side and imagine them turning up at the same time and you gain some sort of idea of Peter Dott's perplexity. Another pause for thought is that the RSA had turned down Peploe for membership around 1908. When Peploe was later dealing with George Proudfoot in Dott's during the 1920s the world of art appreciation had caught up with the developments of twenty years before and Peploe's position was acknowledged. Even so he made no real fortune: enough to keep bread in his family's mouths and little enough in comparison with the absurd price-structure of paintings today.

A precarious life for an artist then. A less precarious but careful line to be trod by a dealer. Eclipsing all that, surely, a great privilege for any youngster to be brought up in that area where the two lives met: the tide of artistic genius hitting the hard shore of business acumen. One can but speculate how many dazzling roses and teacups and wine bottles and dishes and jugs from the brush of the earlier Peploe might have offered themselves like the nectarines and curious peaches of art to Norman Dott as he passed daily through the rooms and hallways of Hailes Brae on his way to the basement workshop, to take his bike to bits.

If Peter McOmish Dott thought Peploe had derailed himself, his dismay contrasts with his undying enthusiasm for the work of William McTaggart, and to appreciate the late works of McTaggart in the 1890s and perhaps into the first decade of the new century *was* advanced taste. Bearing in mind that Mr Dott had no formal training, it may well be that a highly academic knowledge of art history and conventions tends to put the brakes on advancing taste. Perhaps it was precisely because Dott was self-taught that he was able to value McTaggart, even in his latest and most incomprehensible phase. It is well worth glancing at Peter Dott's 'Notes Technical and Explanatory on the Art of William McTaggart, as displayed in his Exhibition of Thirty-Two Pictures, 1901'. Here McOmish Dott's thinking reveals that philosophy of art which, according to Eric Dott's testimony, he communicated with great articulacy and frankness to his young children, educating them at an early age in the ways of his adult mind.

McOmish Dott was in no doubt that the pictures exhibited in the said collection (1878-1900) showed the mature powers of 'an original and forcible genius'. If you discount Turner, says Dott, and except Corot, William McTaggart's is probably the greatest living art force in landscape or marine painting. In a footnote to his notes he tries to allay any doubts as to a onesided fanaticism on his part by listing his favourite painters. The list comprises Titian, Tintoretto, Rembrandt, Raphael, Velasquez; then, among landscape painters, Corot and Turner above all. Now, he goes on, imagine the walls of the exhibition gallery to be covererd with Corots. Compare his works with those of McTaggart and what do you find?

> The main theme of both artists is similar in spirit—to set forth in colour and form songs of pure and joyous beauty. McTaggart chooses the *democratic and realisitc path* (our italics), extracting beauty from the *simplest and commonest scenes* by the passionate and direct intensity of his emotions; Corot takes the *aristocratic* path of classic tradition—transforming the actuality of Nature into scenes of ideal beauty.[5]

Next imagine the walls hung with the landscapes and seascapes of James Maris—so Dott continues. The McTaggarts are poetry beside prose, revealing a greater intellectual and emotional power. It is the art of McTaggart which 'exhilirates the soul by its ardent courage and high emotional beauties'.

Rising to his theme, Dott now proceeds to hang his gallery with Constables—no less. And what are his judgements? In both masters there exists the same 'manly courage' and in Constable 'a greater sense of the solidity of Nature and a more careful modelling, especially in the skies'. Comparing them as draughtsmen he finds neither of the very first order and Constable 'more substantial but less graceful'.

> But in nearly all other qualities the Scottish painter excels—as for instance in wealth, beauty and melody of colour; in force, truth and loveliness of lighting; in fullness of natural beauty. Lastly, there issues from McTaggart's productions a stream of emotional energy which thrills us with the joy of life— a radiant face without a parallel in the more staid and sober character of Constable's work. I prefer therefore the art of the Scottish master. Imagine for a moment 'The Hay-Wain', 'The Cornfield' and 'The Valley Farm' in the National Gallery replaced by 'The Storm', 'Hawthornden' and 'Playing in the Surf' exhibited here, and draw your own conclusions.[6]

Proceeding to points of a more technical nature and arriving at illumination and colour, Dott hammers home his own conclusions and convictions.

> I know of no landscape painter, British or foreign, past or present, who has achieved an equal success in these respects. I affirm *simpliciter* that neither the canvases of Turner, Corot, Constable nor Maris contain as much of Nature's vigorous colouring or approach so nearly her pitch of sunlight. Monet indeed might render certain aspects of illumination with equal truth but never charged with equal emotional beauty.[7]

Here is an art dealer of passionate beliefs, and one who discussed those beliefs fully with his youngsters. It is hard to see how the boy Norman Dott could have escaped having the genius of Scotland borne in upon him in a number of impressive ways. Born in one of her loveliest villages on the doorsill of her capital city, surrounded by some of her finest scenery and nurtured on her best loved authors, we need have no doubt that he was also assured of the superiority of McTaggart to one of the great ikons of English landscape painting. The boy who had seen the beckoning world from Pentland's towering top never answered the call; never saw the need to leave Scotland or to work farther afield than Edinburgh. Can we wonder?

It was of course Corot who made that famous pronouncement that there was nothing worth painting after nine o' clock in the morning: the best part of the day had gone. 'Noon arrives, everything is seen; there is nothing left to paint. Work on, my friends, but I go in to enjoy my siesta and dream of the morning's landscape;—afterwards I will paint my dream.' By contrast the more robust McTaggart rejects this muted and chimerical version of reality and attacks the world when it is alive and active and a man can see to do his work. The Dott temperament found itself greatly at home in this particular art house.

McOmish Dott ends his Notes with some general remarks which are fascinating in their revelation of the world view derived from the art view, both passed on to his offspring.

> It may be argued that McTaggart's works show over emphasis and exaggeration in affirming certain of his personal predilections—for instance movement in light and colour. Well, Shakespeare, Victor Hugo, Tintoretto, Turner, and all the anti-classicists sin in the same way! McTaggart's art will be found to have certain *elements in common with the songs of Burns*. Each artist lacks that idealism which carries us away from simple nature into the region of lofty imagination. Each artist depends on the sincerity, intensity and directness of his emotional statement; and by the *sheer force of his ardent sympathies* commonplace Nature becomes re-interpreted, vivified and glorified for all of us. Throughout McTaggart's pictures runs a vein of *kindly democratic sentiment*. Therefore in landscape he prefers *homely and human scenery,*—leaving untouched the solitudes of Nature, however sublime. And, in figure subjects, his heart is tuned to depict the *simple adventures* of child life or the joys and struggles of the fisherman's lot,—*others must illustrate the history and charms of 'blue blood and high breeding'* . . .
>
> Speaking of McTaggart's present art, Mr Arthur Melville, A.R.S.A., made this shrewd remark. 'His art is thoroughly modern and up to date. It reflects the influences of steam-power, telegraphy and modern life. The fact is, to produce his work, he does not require to retire from the stream of everyday life, like Burne-Jones, Rossetti, Matthew Maris, even Corot. On the contrary *he is in sympathy with the manual labourer, the engineer, the trader and the merchant*; he holds himself for a thread in the warp and woof of life that is being woven around him.[8]   (Our italics throughout)

The religious strain in McOmish Dott's fatherly teaching has already been highlighted. What his remarks on McTaggart bring out are those broad, warm political sympathies of his, consistent with his love of Burns and Scott, Stevenson and Carlyle; political beliefs which remained for a long time unlocalised and ideal. He did not at first interest himself or his chilldren in practical politics.

This was later to change as the country prepared itself for war and his political persuasions focused and hardened in those years during and following the war. He became even more detached from the church and affiliated to Socialism. 'It is quite a puzzle to me how the Churches have supported wars all along,' he writes to Eric in 1917. To Peter Dott, as to many other thinkers, the First World War was a scramble of powerful nations for markets and wealth and supremacy at sea—and not an idealistic defence of Belgium, even in the beginning. That at least is how he saw it. The war did not destroy his belief in God but it certainly weakened his respect for his Church and fanned fast and hard his passionate socialist convictions. In his will Mr Dott left a considerable sum of money, £3,000, to be put to work for Labour in the widest sense of the word and not to any one organisation. It was left to Eric Dott to administer the money for the benefit of the Labour Movement and Socialism generally and it was Eric who formed the idea of founding the Peter McOmish Dott Memorial Library. Books were purchased with a bearing on socialist education and to begin with the library was run by the young Jack Kane, subsequently a Lord Provost of Edinburgh after being a Labour Councillor for a long time. As Secretary Mr Kane ran the library originally from Grosvenor Crescent, but the genteel neighbours objected to such an egalitarian educative venture sprouting its groves of Academe in their Conservative midst and it moved several times. The longest and most successful site was a flat in George IV Bridge, currently occupied by the Junior and Music Departments of the Central Public Library. After that it moved house again and again until the funds finally ran out and the books were given to a Workers' Educational Association.

All this lay in the future.

In the early years at Hailes Brae Peter Dott's political teaching was not of a polemical or party-spirited ilk and indeed on such matters he waited quietly to be drawn out; he was not given to stuffing *ex cathedra* value judgements down his children's throats. The sympathy for ordinary humanity instilled into his offspring in the most indelible fashion was too universal, too ideal to be termed political in the narrow sense of that term. Norman Dott carried with him into later life and after his death the reputation of being a left-winger of the same dye as his father. The truth is that his credo, insofar as it was ever articulated, was even less directed to a specific socialist idol than Peter McOmish Dott's.

Dr Eric Dott denies the myth vehemently.

> Norman never had a left wing tendency himself. He was interested, as an intelligent man would be, but was always far too busy to take an active interest in practical politics. He didn't think that the Labour lot were really all that clever. Walking on the Blackford Hill with him one time, I happened to remark in conversation that I'd be voting Labour in a forthcoming election, and he said: 'Oh Eric, the Labour folk have great ideals but they don't understand human nature really well enough and they'll never be effective!' [9]

Successive governments may have made Norman Dott as cynical about politics as his father had become about the Church. The fact is that reputation is a shadow which often sews itself to a man's heels and dogs him without his deserving. Sometimes it is a cloud of ignorance trailed in his wake. It is another popular theory that Norman Dott's leftist beliefs militated against his ever being offered a knighthood. Yet another story is that he was in fact offered the knighthood and refused it because of his political leanings. Apocryphal though this would appear to be, it would be a tedious impossibility to determine how far a false reputation might have wreaked its inimical effects in high places in keeping the offer of the honour from him. In his heart's core he did not in fact care one scrap about the knighthood which many people felt he deserved and it has been left to other folk to cloud the issue. What we can be sure of is that he was brought and taught into an easy liking for all good people whatever their status or trade. If he had an axe to grind it was more than anything else a Scottish one. He followed his father's early teaching and example to the point where he became, quite simply, a man of his own people.

By contrast Jean and Eric were much more visibly moulded by their father's enthusiasms and ideologies. Jean turned out to be an extremely gifted artist herself, the Hailes Brae portrait of her father being done when she was very young. After a short time at Art College however she gave up her artistic activities, much to Peter Dott's sorrow, and sought out a more socially beneficial vocation in nursing, before going on from there to the Labour College in London, to work for people on an even larger canvas, as she saw it, through Socialism.

Eric assimilated the tutorings of both his parents most readily of all. Converted to the Church, as we have already noted, at quite an early age, and responsible for the rest of the family's joining the local church, he took his Christian stand early in 1917, soon after he had turned eighteen. Called up to active service, he became instead a conscientious objector, and was sent to Wormwood Scrubs and later Dartmoor. He entered prison as a staunchly pacifistic Christian and emerged an entrenched Socialist but with his original religious beliefs intact. Norman on the other hand, in spite of the fact that he had enrolled as a medical student, would have joined the forces willingly and dearly wanted to enter the Royal Flying Corps. Fighting quite apart, the lure and lore of machines drew him like a magnet. In the event he limped off, a rejected volunteer, and so never served. Unlike father and brother, he had no religious or political scruples whatever against the war and was rather sorry about the line Eric took, but he was also far too sensible to interfere with such ardently held beliefs and gave his brother his full moral support.

So did McOmish Dott. Voluminous letters of moral endorsement to Eric throughout his year in prison illustrate the teacher in him par excellence. The Hailes Brae philosophy of education takes on more flesh. Scattered throughout these epistles are lists of recommended reading for one to whom stone walls would not a prison make. 'Books', he says, 'are after all good talk between you and someone worth listening to.' Among poets he suggests listening to Wordsworth, Tennyson and Browning, but above all Burns. Among prose works he cites Ruskin's *Unto This Last, Time and Tide: Political Economy of Fine Art,* Charles Reade's *The Cloister and the Hearth* ('a very bracing book'), *Don Quixote,* Scott's novels, Jack London and almost anything by Carlyle. Of paramount importance is the Bible, and outside the Bible and Jesus his heroes are Socrates, Buddha, St Francis and Beethoven. But in an interesting passage he advises his son that books are not the ultimate aim in life.

> Action is what a man fundamentally exists for. For some men preaching and talking and book writing may be their natural and best vocation, but these men are few. I was struck with the passage in Zachariah, 13th Chapter, where, after inveighing against useless, foolish and untrue prophets, he says: 'In those days the prophet shall be ashamed every one of his vision,' and they shall no longer pose as the salt of the earth etc. Today crowds of clergymen, bookwriters and journalists should repeat that verse till they modestly become what God and Nature wanted of them: *husbandmen*—commonplace, quiet, daily workers who *make* some useful thing or *do* some useful or helpful action for their fellows.[10]

Such is the robust and practical philosophy of education that produced Norman Dott: surely the prize rose of all Peter McOmish's spadework and careful cultivation. If it seems a strange principle of life for an art dealer, he excuses himself in the same letter.

> Pictures are basically 'goods' for people. Well, any common, useful occupation is much more healthy than pretentious prophesying, pharasaical clergyising, political windbags and quacks etc. 'And upon the bells of the horses (ploughing) shall be *Holiness unto the Lord.* Yea, every pot (porridge and jam!) in Jerusalem shall be *Holiness unto the Lord.*' Good—the common things can be and should be consecrated by being used as He wants for the common good of man.[11]

Art and religion are compounded in a letter headed 'Art as a Guide to the Problems of Man's Life', where he stresses the need for unity. A man's life is his whole self and not a part of it. This includes the bodily part. He has no time for those diseasedly religious folk who in their selfishness are interested only in eternal life and not in *this* life—God's gift to us. God gave us stomachs and brains and senses. Though man's chief end be to glorify God he can only do that fully through his body as well as his heart, mind and soul. Shakespeare and Beethoven glorified God, but not by writing dry treatises. Their whole selves were involved in the process of glorifying the creation. So although in the highest art we must leave the worm and the cow in us, we must never forget that the worm and the cow are part of the universal struggle, part of the hymn to creation. In our efforts to reach the angels we must not leave the beasts behind. He does not actually quote it, but he has drunk the philosophy of Schiller's *Ode to Joy*, perhaps through the final movement of Beethoven's Ninth Symphony: 'Even the worm can feel contentment, And the cherub stands before God!' McOmish Dott's art is not divorced from life: that is why he says he enjoy's McTaggart, who 'enjoys God and his own living powers and recreates the scene as he feels best able to produce an interpretation of all these factors.'

This leads him to his definition of a work of art:

> It is a monument enclosing the best gifts of a powerful human life used in an orderly and masterful way; it signifies that Man has the power to recreate what is given from without and to recreate it on the pattern supplied from within and to recreate it from first touch to last under the guidance of the laws of beauty—i.e. melody, harmony and the reach to perfection.[12]

In a letter a fortnight later he quotes a definition of art formulated forty years previously:

> A work of art is any expression of harmonious human energy; and the measure of its value is the quantity and quality of human energies and faculties displayed in it. Thus I might say Wingate has a fine emotion and beauty of colour as McTaggart, but the latter has more energetic force.[13]

There is no subject on which Peter McOmish Dott will not touch if the argument suits his fiercely philosophic bent. There are notes on Materialism, Agnosticism and Evolution; there is a long letter on An Industrial and Trade Community Board based on Democratic Election or Selection as a Solution to Lock-Outs and Strikes; there are notes Concerning Idols; notes on St Paul's Solution, and so on. It is not hard to see why a young serving-girl in the Trossachs confessed she fled from the sight of the curious-questioning Peter Dott. Here he is writing to an eighteen year old son. But in doing so he is simply continuing in the rôle of a loving father who saw himself as responsible for moulding the minds of his young.

The main thrust of the letters is religious and philosophical. At the same time there is a backdrop of social happenings. He mentions meeting Ramsay Macdonald and speaking for more than two hours with him: 'a black Highlander and a good subject for the artist's pencil'. Mr Proudfoot of Aitken Dot & Son has joined the Volunteers and is busy drilling on the Castle Esplanade. The newspapers are full of pathetically foolish anti-German nonsense, the Germans being portrayed as 'our inferiors in all things'. Here he cannot resist a quotation from Burns: 'I never met a man, even in the lowest society of thieves, who was not my superior in something.' All peoples of the earth are our fellow creatures and we must keep the fire of love burning so that the world stays beautiful.

To the end of his life Norman Dott's father never stops teaching, exhorting, offering a criticism of life. The last extant letter in his hand is dated 11 March 1930. It was written from Madrid when he was on his last visit to Europe, seeing again some of the great picture galleries.

> I back sensible, good-hearted Socialism more and more against present chaotic competitive rush. If one goes up in an aeroplane and looks down at the mad push and struggle of human ants, it makes a cynic laugh and a wise man becomes sad. The shout and cry over 'Religion in Danger' shows how little people believe in God and His laws and His Religion and how much they fuss over their own particular symbolical idolatry . . . It is droll and sad to see the idolatry of the Immaculate Virgin. The Holy Ghost seems out of fashion and should get short skirts to bring him in. Then the plain, holy, suffering Christ is made into an impossible God-Man concoction. [14]

When he wrote these words he was in his seventy-fourth year, little changed in spirit from the earnest young student who had kept notebooks on his own moral and religious life. He never ceased to learn; never ceased to pass on his vision to his family. Long before Norman Dott had been handed one syllable of formal education he had plucked the fruits of a mind that never ceased to ponder the universal questions of society and nature, morality and religion, philosophy, politics, literature, music and art. Norman himself, though much more practically turned than his father, had the mind to understand it.

It was a highly liberal education.

Education in the formal sense begins with Primary schooling. A new school was opened in Colinton in Thorburn Road on 1 September 1891. The Dott Children were never sent there. Instead Peter and Rebecca Dott formed a little private school of their own in Hailes Brae quite soon after the turn of the century. Indeed house and school began life together. There were about a dozen pupils, five of whom were Dotts after the youngest, Margaret, was old enough to take part; the others were the children of neighbours. It was a happy and successful project, but took off in a much more memorable way when a new teacher arrived in 1904.

Her name was Miss Catherine Fraser Lee.

She was the last and best and made a strong impression on the Dotts. Later she became the Headmistress of the famous (and, courtesy of the cartoonist Ronald Searle, undeservedly notorious) St Trinneans, which opened at 10 Palmerston Road in 1922. The Belles of St Trinians, celebrated in film, perpetrated dastardly deeds upon their mentors, and indeed the real St Trinneans allowed its girls a considerable degree of latitude in planning and arranging their own study time. But that was as far as things went. There is a world of difference between latitude and laxity, between freedom and fantasy. What Miss Lee did was to foster her pupils' ability to cope with the freedom which they would later encounter at colleges and universities and in the world outside the sheltered towers of learning. The venture she began in 1922 was, in fact, revolutionary, and it is little wonder that Eric Dott, though only six years old when she arrived at Hailes Brae, remembers her so vividly.

> She had a fine, kindly, strong face, with a fairly long, well-pronounced nose and firm, close-set lips. She could have a very friendly expression and was indeed a very warm and friendly person, but there was also a great deal of strength behind her expression that was unmistakable. She was a most strong-minded character, very firm in her ideas and views, and this came across to us. But we got on so terribly well with her because she was such a gifted teacher.[15]

The photograph of the Hailes Brae School, taken in 1904, matches Eric's memories perfectly. Miss Lee was to be photographed again with Norman Dott nearly sixty years later during the ceremony in the Usher Hall when the Freedom of the City of Edinburgh was conferred upon her former pupil. Up to the day she died she was still the proud possessor of a handsome mahogany bookcase made for her by her not yet famous pupil—and inscribed 'Norman—Joiner'—just before he left her at Hailes Brae for secondary schooling in Edinburgh.

All five Dotts were enrolled in October 1908, his sisters at St George's School for girls and Norman and Eric at George Heriot's.

This entailed a five mile journey by train, for there was no other means of transport in and out of Edinburgh unless by private vehicle and school-children travelling into the city joined the commuters at the Colinton Railway Station. The little spur line, formerly known as the Balerno Branch, which had opened on 1 August 1874, was run by the Caledonian Railway Company. It followed the main line from the Caledonian Station out past Merchiston and Slateford, then there were points and it turned off and worked its way out past Colinton Dell and through a tunnel to emerge at Colinton Station. From then on it travelled through Juniper Green to Balerno.

Hailes Brae overlooked this line from its high vantage point, the lowest part of the garden hanging directly over the tunnel, to which the Railway Company was still entitled to access, via the garden, for maintenance and repairs. The arrival of the train, its quill of smoke inscribing the sky, brought the Dotts runing down to the overhang. Eric Dott looks back on it through a long tunnel of his own remembering.

> There were four or five carriages and the engine had water tanks at the side and a small tender. It was one of those short sturdy little engines. There was a fair gradient on that line and sometimes in wet weather they had some

21 The Hailes Brae School in 1904. Annie Quibell (left) looks on while Miss Catherine Fraser Lee (later to become headmistress of St Trinneans) commands her first school. Of the twelve pupils, five are Dotts. Margaret and Jean are in the centre, Eric is wearing a sailor suit, and Norman aged seven, is seated between Kathleen and the dog.

22 Norman at the age of twelve. Taken from a Heriot's class photograph.

23 Two of Norman Dott's former teachers share his moment of triumph as he is awarded the Freedom of the City of Edinburgh: Miss Catherine Fraser Lee and Bill Gentle, Norman's Physics teacher at Heriot's and a former headmaster of the school. Courtesy of *The Scotsman*.

24 Peter Dott was an ardent reader and an important personal influence on his family's education. This striking portrait, the product of his daughter Jean's consummate brushwork, shows him in one of his characteristic attitudes, as he might have looked, reading to his children. Courtesy of the National Portrait Gallery of Scotland.

difficulty in coming out. I can well remember when they were approaching our house, by the tunnel, there was this very steep bit, and we'd hear the wheels start to skid. I remember so well the regular puffing giving way to the skidding sounds. Then there was a moment of silence—and then came the sound of the whole train being allowed to drift back several hundred yards by its own weight, to get another go at it. It would get this fresh start, and eventually, after gaining more speed, it would make it! Sometimes we were in the train when it did this and Norman and I thought it was great fun.[16]

Peter Dott used this line regularly for going to business in Castle Street. Being so close to the station and having the advantage of a bird's eye view of that plume of smoke whitely feathering the sky towards Balerno, Mr Dott often used to sail clsoe to the wind when it came to timing his departure. He had the additional advantage of a short cut to encourage him in taking risks. A little way down Spylawbank Road a footpath and then a flight of steps known as Jacob's Ladder led directly to the station and he always went by that footpath, hurrying down the fifty-two steps to catch his train. The guard became used to the sight of the burly bear in the Inverness cape flying down the steps two at a time, sometimes holding up the train so that Aitken Dott & Son would have its director at his desk by nine in the morning.

Norman Dott soon learned to imitate his father by taking the steps at a headlong run, Eric and the girls trailing behind him. The Station-Master would not suffer any nonsense, however, from the schoolchildren who were milling around on the tiny platform. The stentorian-toned, florid-faced John Kerr was a man of mettle and pepper who emerged from his wooden booking office, his backside roasted by a roaring fire, to administer correction to madcaps. A demon with the sling, he was known to prowl the platform at night picking off rats. His reputation for dead-eyed accuracy as an executioner soon stilled the unruly scholars. Nor was he a man to suffer adult fools gladly. He achieved fame in Colinton by putting an end to the pernickety antics of a city-bound local business man who was a stickler for time, and who would stand by the train, fob-watch in hand, refusing to enter his first class compartment until his time-piece told him the proper hour had come. John Kerr decided one morning that his own station-master's watch was the one reading Greenwich Mean Time, while the city gent's was several seconds slow. He simply slammed the guard's door, waved the green flag without warning and sent the train on its way, leaving the pedantic punctilio gaping.

A maelstrom of bankers and brokers, tradesmen and teachers poured itself along with the uniformed youngsters into the dirty carriages—single compartments with no corridors—for the twenty-minute run to the Caledonian Station. The train was no sooner off than it entered the tunnel underneath the garden of Hailes Brae. At this point horseplay usually erupted, especially if Herioters and Watsonians, or, worse still, the red-stockinged boys of the Edinburgh Institution, later to become Melville College and later still Stewart's-Melville, had tumbled by accident or design into the same compartment. Eric Dott smilingly recaptures his brother Norman fearlessly throwing his weight about with the best of them and sometimes with considerable violence, as the tensions and rivalries that existed between schools were settled in the rumbustious darkness of the loud echoing tunnel.

As soon as the train emerged into the leaf-chequered light, the passengers were given an enchanted view of Colinton Dell for a mile or so. Norman was always intrigued by a stream which seemed to be running the wrong way, uphill, whenever they passed it at the exit from one of the mill lades. It was the banking tilt of the train on that part of the line which created this illusion on which his eyes fed, fascinated. There was no stopping however between Colinton and Slateford, until Hailes platform was later built to allow the golfers to disembark at Kingsknowe, the train halting there by request only. Then, just before Slateford Station, where the branch line joined the main Glasgow line, the train stood steaming, clothed with its own breath, until a mainline train went by. After Slateford, Merchiston, and finally their destination: the Caledonian Station at the junction of Lothian Road and the West End of Princes Street.

From the Caledonian the Dott boys footed it to Heriot's a cobbled winding and plunging along King's Stables Road into the end of the Grassmarket, and so up the steep Vennel near the old City Wall to arrive at the side entrance to Heriot's. There was no need for them to go round to the front of the school off Lauriston Place.

In the year that Norman Dott came to Heriot's Dr D F Lowe's tenure of office as Headmaster came to a close and his place was filled by John B Clark, who was entertained to dinner by his friends and colleagues on the staff in Edinburgh's Royal Hotel on 12 December 1908. Mr John Alison, Head-master of George Watson's College, was present—(the two Heads collaborated in the production of Alison & Clark's Standard Arithmetic)—and spoke of Clark's outstanding ability, firm will and great determination, his calm self restraint, his abundant energy, his wide and accurate knowledge, his judicious mind and his thoughtful consideration for others and courtesy of manner. It sounds rather like a panegyric on Norman Dott himself in the eminences of his later career. Certainly none of the boys could fail to be impressed and affected by Clark's example.

There were other influences waiting to work on him.

In the first volume of *The Herioter,* the newly formed school magazine, for the session 1907-8, T A Clark, the Technical Subjects Master, strongly advocated engineering as a profession. From the beginning Norman came under his wing and was ear-marked as a natural. In the third volume of the magazine, March 1909, is an advertisement for Aitken Dott & Son, Castle Street. Peter McOmish Dott, who placed this advert, and who was paying ten shillings per term for Norman's education in the Lower Department of the school (Primary 7) would have been delighted to read in the same issue, brought back to Hailes Brae that spring, an ardent defence of Socialism by John McCallum.

Addressing himself to the young, the author attacks the present social system as 'chaotic, brutal and immoral' and by way of proof offers a few blunt statistics, e.g.:

(1) One half of the area of the country is owned by 2500 people.

(2) Of the people who died in London in 1904, one in every three died in the workhouse, the hospital or the lunatic asylum.

(3) One-eighth of the people of Scotland live in single-roomed tenements.[17]

Socialism, the author says, 'challenges the modern world on the ground that it is the only way out of this welter of waste and suffering'. The bulk of the article then goes on to define precisely what is meant by Socialism. Following a lengthy and closely argued analysis comes this stirring conclusion:

> The gospel of Socialism is the new religion of the world. It has awakened throughout the nations the troubled, unquiet stirrings of another spring. No such wind has blown across the world since the French Revolution.
>
> Like all religious movements Socialism has produced its great men, and Scotland has given the movement one of its strongest personalities in Keir Hardie. It is an ill omen for our country that it has failed to appreciate the greatness of this Socialist leader.
>
> Keir Hardie, who commenced life as a pit-boy, has forged a weapon, in the Labour Party, which has revolutionised British politics.
>
> Keir Hardie's career is not unworthy of the high tradition of our land, yet the well-dressed youth of our city promenades has only a cheap contempt for the man and his work. From the meanest of the shrubs comes the fire upon the cedars of Lebanon.[18]

As he sat in the garden of Hailes Brae looking at the cedars towering across the Dell, Peter McOmish Dott, a man of his political time and future, would clearly have had ample cause to rejoice that he had sent his boys to Heriot's.

Norman Dott walked through the portals of the imposing seventeenth century building on Thursday 1 October 1908, and with the Class Teacher of 7L, Mr Carnon, entered upon the study of English, History, Geography,

Scripture, Writing, Arithmetic, French, Latin, Drawing, Nature Knowledge and Singing. When he moved into the Middle Department (S1) the following year, he found, as do all children making the transition from Junior to Secondary School, a varied battery of teaching talents waiting to assail him. In his case it entailed for his father a further 3s.6d. per term in fees added to the ten shillings he was already paying: a grand total of thirteen shillings and sixpence per term, or £2.0s,6d. a session—roughly equivalent to the price of a Peploe, or, if times were hard for the artist, four Peploes! How many art treasures of tomorrow are disappearing in today's school fees?

An imponderable sum.

For this comparatively humble price Norman Dott was taken under the jealous wing of Mr Thomas Clark for Technical, Mr W L Thomson (nicknamed Welt because of his initials) for Mathematics, Mr Andrew Lee for Geography—fondly known as Pan Lee from his habit of making himself a cup of coffee in a pan at each interval—and Mr William Gentle for Physics. Among others. It was Bill Gentle the Science Master, later to become Headmaster, who meant most to the boy at Heriot's. In his well established tradition Norman was soon helping him in making apparatus and in setting up his experiments. He was not so keen on the theoretical side of Physics but flourished whenever there was practical work to be done. As a matter of fact he spent too much of his time on practical affairs, neglecting his other subjects and areas of study. This did not prevent him from getting good results and he began to win numerous prizes with very little effort. Sport never interested him in the slightest and he avoided rugby where he could, inventing all kinds of excuses to shun Goldenacre. His one concession to physical exercise while at school was swimming. Heriot's had its own baths at that time and Norman struck out with ease, ploughing away many lengths and even enjoying the water polo contests. Otherwise he was happiest with bench and bunsen burner, hunched at the drawing board, or manipulating metal and wood, the work familiar to him since long ago.

When he entered Heriot's Norman Dott had just turned eleven. He left suddenly in his 4th Year, not even bothering to complete his third term in Class 4D. His marks are an impressive set of statistics, bearing in mind that he simply did as little study as he could possibly get away with.

English	78%	1st
History	82%	1st
Geography	62%	4th
French	77%	1st
German	75%	1st
Maths	58%	10th
Physics	65%	4th

Chemistry	74%	2nd
Drawing	85%	2nd
Handicraft	83%	1st

First in five subjects, second in two and fourth in two, with Mathematics his weakest subject: an easy harvest of achievements in his talented hands. The year was 1913. He was destined to become an engineer.

Or so he thought.

CHAPTER SIX

Holidays and Holocaust

Shall they return to beatings of great bells
In wild train-loads?
A few, a few, too few for drums and yells,

May creep back silent to village-wells,
Up half-known roads

(*Wilfred Owen*)

Once more the good old sunset's glowing red.
In thirteen days I'll probably be dead.

(*Alfred Lichtenstein*)

The counterpart of school is vacation and the Dotts made a great occasion out of holidaying.

Carlops was a favourite place in the early days when Norman was just turned five. There was a hotel there called the Allan Ramsay, run by the characterful Mrs Veitch. The whole family sometimes travelled to it in the back of the Aitken Dott picture van, such was the limited transport situation at the time. The railway went out to West Linton but not to Carlops and the bus routes did not extend so far. Motor cars were few and far between in the days when the Hailes Brae school had just broken up for its first summer vacation. Norman's earliest experience of the private motor vehicle was at Carlops, when a friend of Peter Dott came out to the Allan Ramsay in a fine green car and took the family along the road and back. Those were the vanished days before the fall of car-corrupted man, when only Toad of Toad Hall terrorised the rural roads for the price of a few shillings licence fee—and no driving test necessary.

It was not at Carlops but at Edzell that Norman, between a decade and a dozen years on his back, experienced another mode of transport which, along with the motor car, football, socialism and contemporary literature, had taken its share of the blame for the decline of the church and the deterioration of religious faith among the population of Britain. This was the humble bicycle. Peter Dott bought bicycles for all the children on their first summer holiday from Heriot's and St George's and these new-fangled iron horses were taken up to Edzell by train. Eric Dott marvels at how Norman took to cycling so quickly.

> He soon learned and was off at once, completing fifteen mile journeys that seemed extraordinary to us, who never dreamed of travelling such distances. But he was quite fearless in leading us off on those epic itineraries of his, and before we knew where we were, we found ourselves in Buchan and Montrose and places we had never even heard of. Norman was always so adventurous that way.[1]

By far the most important holiday place for the Dotts though, was the Brig o' Turk, in the Trossachs, where many an artist came and set up his easel, and where Peter and Rebecca had first become man and wife. It was their Mecca and Medina and the whole family went there every September with hardly a break, from the very beginning of the marriage right up to the 1920s. They had been wed in the Fergusons' thatched cottage west of the River Finlas, and as the Fergusons had been married in that same year, it was noticed that each autumn the Dotts returned for their holiday there would be anther Dott child and another Ferguson child.

Over the years they went to stay in a number of different cottages at Brig o' Turk. The custom was that during the summer and early autumn the local folk gave up their substantial cottages for the benefit of the well-to-do tourists and moved into shacks. There was quite a scattering of cottages around the area and the Dott family moved about a bit from year to year. As a family they first stayed at Mr and Mrs McDiarmid's cottage and a year or two later went to Mrs Macfarlane's of Mill Cottage, returning there repeatedly most Septembers. Sometimes they took with them the Schlapps, a family of Germans who had been made welcome at Hailes Brae during the wash of anti-Germanism that prevailed before and after the war. Otto Schlapp was Professor of German Literature at Edinburgh University. Later his son Walter was to marry Kathleen Dott. Some of the Brig o' Turkers surveyed the German visitors with narrow-eyed suspicion, but their pursuits were as peaceful as the paradise to which they had come.

They went on walks and hill climbs, wandering the fields and woods, picnicking and gathering mushrooms. One of the chiefest among their pleasures was boating. The Dotts kept a boat moored on the river, the Black Water that comes out of Loch Achray, and they rowed about contentedly on the shining lochs, hazy with September. Norman, who had fished the Water of Leith with his wild rose stems when little more than a toddler, now took to fishing in a bigger way. He first fished the burns and then, as he grew, the lochs—Lochs Vennacher, Achray and Katrine, catching trout and sometimes pike and becoming quite a canny angler.

> Oh yes, the Trossachs are still very dear to my heart, and I know the older folk about there very well. I have not fished there for two or three years. Loch

Drunkie—by the hill road over to Aberfoyle—is quite good, Loch
Vennacher is earliest and has best fish. Drunkie next. Achray is better than you
might think. Katrine is at least a month later and can be excellent, though most
days the average size is fairly small. I know every stone and corner of them.[2]

So Dott wrote in 1953. He knew his fishing.

He was aided in this by an ancient ghillie whom he had predictably
befriended. Old Parlane Macfarlane was a relative of the Macfarlanes of
Mill Cottage and used to camp out in summer in the fields beyond the Mill.
Parlane was an independent old eccentric, his white beard nicotine-stained
from constant pipe smoking, a browned old kipper of a man, and just the
sort of character the boy was in the habit of adopting. Season by season he
squeezed him dry of his fund of natural wisdom until in the end there was
nothing left to know. Typically Norman would wander over to old
Parlane's tent and gossip away with him for hours and days set end to end,
getting to know him on a much more intimate basis than was ever achieved
by any of the gentlemen he was ghillie to. Quite soon he was helping him
with rods and flies and all the practicalities of the fishing, becoming in time
a fast friend. And this unlikeliest of alliances—the very young middle-class
boy from near Edinburgh and the ancient boatman of the Scottish lochs—
lasted up to Parlane's death. From his self-acquired store of knowledge he
taught the boy the whole lore of the fish, everything he knew, sometimes
lapsing absent-mindedly into the Gaelic. They simply sat and sat and talked
fish for hours and went off on their own in Parlane's boat, working with
their lines and totally absorbed in what they were doing and in one another's
company. It was one of the old man's favourite forecasts that one day
Norman would be wearing a top hat. Along with his Gaelic he may have
had the second sight: more likely he simply realised how clever the boy
really was.

Parlane was uncle to Katie and Meg Macfarlane whose parents owned
Yew Cottage on the east side of the Finlas. When the Dott family stayed
there the two nieces used to look after them and see to the cooking. Katie,
now like Eric Dott dipping her toes in her nineties, was struck by how
Norman would prefer to leave the posh parlour where the holiday guests
were taking their meals and eat instead with Parlane in the rougher confines
of the kitchen, or out in the old man's tent. Like all the local people left alive
from that far era, she recalls Norman Dott with eager affection, growing
from a boy into a young doctor and still coming back to Brig o' Turk for
his holiday to be looked after by her.

> He was very fond of fried fish, especially if he'd just caught it himself, and he
> was a terrible man for tea, the worst man for tea I ever knew. He'd sit and just
> drink pots and pots of tea, long-brewed stuff—tinker's tea, he called it—and
> chat away to us. He was the easiest man in the world to get along with.[3]

25 Brig o' Turk, January 1921.

26 Glenfinlas from Brig o' Turk. The cottage in the centre was lived in by the watercolourist Edwin Alexander, one of the Dotts' many artist friends. Eric married his daughter, Sally.

27 Parlane Macfarlane, the ancient ghillie from whom Norman learned the lure and lore of fishing the lochs.

When Katie was a child she did not find all of the Dotts equally approachable. She was the very lass who was terrified by Peter McOmish Dott in his huge Inverness cape, and when she saw him approaching she used to run and hide, so disconcerted was she by his habit of always asking questions. Questions to which she never knew the answer, they were of a strange nature! 'He was a most inquisitive man under that great big cloak!' Mrs Dott, on the other hand, was as quiet as a log. Norman himself, boy or man, was simply the nicest person alive.

> I said what I liked to him and even told him off if I felt like it. I remember once giving him a row for clapping down an enormous pike he'd just caught, right down on my clean, freshly scrubbed dresser. He never minded. But I can remember his black eyes. He used to look right through you with those piercing black eyes . . .[4]

She was impressed too, as were the other country people, by the way Norman Dott, when a doctor on leave, received a telephone call at Brig o' Turk at midnight, to say that one of his patients in Edinburgh had deteriorated—and left at once to drive all the way back to the Royal Infirmary, telling Katie to have the tea in the pot for him at breakfast time. And back he came on time next morning for his pot of tea.

Katie's mother was such a flamboyant dresser that she was known locally as The Queen. Her Majesty's two daughters, Katie and her sister Meg, followed in their stylish mother's wake, sallying out at nights in long tartan skirts and plumed hats. Inevitably they were nicknamed The Princesses. A brace of handsome wenches, they never married, for all their nightly paradings and glamorous attire. While they were growing tall and beautiful with the turning years and going into Callander for the night, Norman Dott was sitting in a boat on Loch Vennacher, a solitary statue under the moon, or whispering to the wispy silhouette of Parlane Macfarlane, grown ancient as a ghost, while the seasons turned over like the tide and the fish glimmered to the stars in their cold soundless legions. It seems that Norman Dott's romantic impulses were stirred more by a leaping trout than by the sight of Meg and Katie going out in all their glory.

So: it was the lure and lore of the fish and the peaceful solitudes of the lochs and hills that brought back Norman Dott time and time over to stay at Brig o' Turk, well into the late 1920s and early 1930s when everyone else in the family had stopped coming or could come no more. Norman was the very last to remain faithful to this focal point of the old family holidays, haunting its soothing solitudes like a revenant from the old ballads.

Long after Parlane had lain down with the summer dust, Norman would go and stay on his own at Mill Cottage. In a nearby cottage, The Sheiling, lived another boatman, Peter Macfarlane, and he would often row out Norman onto the lochs when he came on holiday at The Mill. After fishing

the summer stars round the sky, the two of them would come back to The
Shieling in the small hours of the morning and drink their pots of tea and
talk about a fish from the point of its nose to the tip of its tail until there was
nothing left to dissect. It was Parlane all over again, an avenue back to the
earth and its mysteries. Then, with dawn whitening the lochs, Norman
walked the few yards to the Mill Cottage and fell into his sleep. Mrs
Macfarlane, Peter the boatman's widow, remembers him coming to Brig
o' Turk 'always dressed in old clothes and relaxed, sincere and plain, with
no affectation whatsoever'.

A warm and kindly memory.

Another visitor who made a striking impression on the whole Brig o'
Turk community was Mailla the family donkey. His arrival is recounted in
an article entitled *Travels With A Donkey,* written for the St George's
Chronicle, No. 53, July 1911, by Jean Dott, then in her 4th Form. The year
to which she refers is 1910, when Norman was thirteen.

Travels With A Donkey

If you had been in Colinton on the 1st September you might have seen a
singular procession trudging slowly out of the village in the direction of
Corstorphine. If you had asked who those children with the donkey were,
you would have been told, 'Oh, that'll be the Dotts' donkey.' But why is the
donkey loaded with those bags and why is their father with the children? Ah!
No-one in the village could tell you that—you will have to ask them.

The donkey does not know where he is going but he does know that things
are not as usual. He is allowed to walk and no-one jumps on his back. The
children are talking very fast and seem to be continually asking questions.

'Dear me, can this donkey of yours go no faster? I'd like to know when we
shall get to Linlithgow', says father.

'He's going splendidly, father,' says Norman. 'If you only saw the rate he
goes at generally, you wouldn't say he was slow.'

We have soon left Colinton far behind; we are determined to reach
Linlithgow by night, but we only started at half past two and we have sixteen
and a half miles to walk. Mailla must buck up or we will not be at our
destination till midnight.

Once out on a quiet road Mailla settled into a steady walk twenty minutes
to a mile. We stopped at the roadside about halfway to eat our sandwiches and
chocolate while Mailla grazed. We felt as if we could walk any distance after
the rest and Mailla evidently felt the same, and we felt more hopeful about
getting to Linlithgow that night. By the time it was getting dark we were
within six miles of the town. Mailla showed no signs of weariness until we
were entering the town, when he began to yawn. We found a hotel where
there was stabling and led Mailla up a narrow street to the stable. It was quite
dark, so a lantern was brought, but nothing, not even hay, would induce
Mailla to enter this new stable. He followed the hay to the door but no further.
The ostler was evidently accustomed to the behaviour of donkeys, for he

made a sign to another stableman and they joined their hands behind him and lited his hind legs off the ground and pushed him in.

Once in he was quite satisfied with the appearance of things, as he was not tied up.

'And what about the dog?' I asked.

'Oh, he'll be all right in the empty stall in the other stable,' and the ostler led the way to a comfortable looking stall with a bed of straw. Paddy was soon chained up with a biscuit to keep him company.

Next day we started off again early. The road passed through fields of corn where the workpeople were gathering the sheaves. All stopped to watch the donkey.

It is peculiar that people, horses and dogs all look at the donkey with wonder while he plods on taking no notice whatever of their attention.

As we approached Stirling after a long day's travel we were determined to go and see the stone in which Bruce placed the Scottish standard at Bannockburn. We had to go a good deal out of our way but we arrived in Stirling at length after a walk of about twenty-four miles.

About a mile from the town of Doune we met another donkey whom Mailla took a fancy to and would not leave. At length we got him in front of it, but he was constantly looking back to catch a glimpse of his friend.

It was terribly hot next day but the scenery was beautiful and for the first time we saw the Highland hills close at hand. We kept beside the River Forth for some time and we longed to jump over the wall and get a drink, but we had to stay with the donkey.

We rested on a wall, watching the cattle grazing and the river sparkling in the sun. It was delightful lying there but we had to reach Callander for dinner.

When we reached Callander Mailla was tethered with a long rope in a little corner below the hotel, where he could get a little grass, but he preferred to get his rope mixed with Paddy's chain till we were disturbed in the middle of dinner by Paddy's squeals as Mailla pulled at the rope.

We had then seven miles to go and then we would join the others at Brig o' Turk.

How interesting it was to see the old places again and how we rejoiced at passing each well known milestone, till at length we marched through Brig o' Turk with half the village following.

JEAN DOTT (L. IV)[5]

Quite a charming picture.

On that occasion Peter Dott clearly accompanied his children. But there were at least two future occasions when the two older girls were allowed to do the journey without their father, led instead by Norman. Peter and Rebecca Dott had gone ahead to Brig o' Turk, taking Margaret and Eric with them, and Norman and the girls set out from Colinton to join them. From Colinton Village to Brig o' Turk is sixty miles. On the first occasion they took three days to accomplish it, stopping as before at Linlithgow, at the Star and Garter Hotel, and the next night at Dunipace near Denny, where some farm people put them up. At first they looked askance at the bedraggled three, but when they noticed the donkey's harness and saw the beautiful condition in which it had been kept, they calculated on their being a respectable enough trio. On the third day it became clear they would never reach Callander by six in the evening in order to send the agreed telegram from the Post Office there to Brig o' Turk, to reassure the parents that the party was safe. So quite a number of miles from home Norman carried out a marathon run all the way to Callander and reached the post office just in time to send the telegram.He then collapsed exhausted on a house step and a policeman tried to move him on, thinking he was a vagrant child. The intrepid Norman managed to convince him of the true state of affairs.

The following year the same three did the same thing again but this time using a donkey trap and so they succeeded in doing it in two days. At Brig o' Turk it was considered a great occasion when the Dott children arrived at the village school with Mailla to take home those youngsters who had miles to walk. They had to share out the transportation honours on a rota basis however for there were a great many children who came from far-flung homes.

On another occasion the older children, Norman, Kathleen and Jean stayed at Hailes Brae, from which they trekked to Carlops by donkey while their parents went to Edzell with the younger two. In April 1911 we find them so split up and a bouquet of letters passing between the two house-holds, every member of the family writing to every other member. The letter from Norman to his mother is an interesting revelation of his thirteen year old mind.

The wind made the boy anxious. It filled his sister Kathleen with exhiliration. That same day she also wrote to her mother, 'The wind! the wind! the glorious wind! It howls in the key-hole and rushes over the hills!'

Two years after penning this letter Norman Dott left Heriot's. The following year his sisters left St George's, Margaret in April and Kathleen and Jean in July 1914, just as they had all begun in unison in October 1908. Jean went to the Edinburgh College of Art that autumn and rented herself a little studio nearby. Her talent as an artist can still be seen in her portrait of her father which now hangs in the Scottish National Portrait Gallery. She also exhibited a little in her teens. Her self-portrait in pastels, 'Laughing', appeared in the Royal Scottish Academy in the year she left school. (So far the picture has not been traced.) Next year she appeared in the Catalogue of the Society of Women Artists, her picture 'Autumn Sunshine in our Garden' being sold in 1915 for the benefit of the War Relief Fund. It was greatly to her father's sorrow that her art was not to last.

Hailes Brae.

Colinton. 18th April 19..

Dear Mother,

I am greatly please to receive your letter it gave me much pleasure I am in the house by my self. Kathleen & Jean are out with the donkey and will be for 1½ HRS.

This is my first day to miss the early walk, but I shall be out for yrs in the afternoon. Although the day is not a minute longer it seems to be several hours more. — (It is really a little shorter as I go to bed in time now.)

The washing up is very odd:— BREAKFAST 3 spoons, 3 plates, 1 saucer etc. Likewise dinner & tea.

This morning I wished to make a record in my work. I got up at 5.30 down at 5.35, fire roaring. 5.50. porridge boiling 6.a porridge out 6.40 The girls started 7.15 they will (or should return) at 9.15)

THE BATTLEMENT TEA-STRAINER PATENTED 18th Apr. 1911

A DURABLE AND HANDSOME XMAS GIFT

GUARANTEED PURE COPPER. DOUBLE GAUZE. FINEEST JAPANESE CHINA WITH NATIVE INSCRIPTION ON IT.

PRICE 5/- NET

P.S. This piece of work is finer and stronger and neater than anything else I have done in this line if such a thing is possible The fine gauze is nearly as fine as a silk handkerchief N

yesterday I gave Mr Wood 3 gunwells of my best & neatest dressing as samples I also lent him my rod in place of his which I wished to splice and varnish. I am making webs like frogs webs for my hands to swim with The cloth covers the palm of my hand and extends to the tips of my fingers, where it is secured by elastic bands. There is also one round my waist.

I have become a gormondiser. yesterday I had a large plate of porridge and an egg for breakfast. For lunch 2 slices of bread that is 4½ slices and a wafer. Dinner. A lot of tongue, and bread, 1½ bowls of curds. Tea 5 slices of bread IE 10 half slices with treacle honey etc. So do not imagine I am starving Please. The tea strainer is complete and looks very pretty in the little jar; like a round tower with battlements.

YOUR LOVING son N.

P.P.S. The girls have not come home and it is half an hour past their time; so I am rather uneasy I can imagine hundreds of thing having happened to them. The wind is whining dolefully round the house— Why have they not arrived?!!!!!!!!!!!!!!

P.P.P.S. Here they are, Hurrah !!!!! Everybody is quite whole & sound. We three are in the house very happy the cat is on a chair, doubled up very close. The Maila is in its his stable. And Paddy in the wash house. xxx N xxx I mean " tub—

Dear Eric do not break your neck in your efforts to reach the witches cave. Thank you very much for your letter. X Your Sincerey, N. Coll.

Kathleen Dott, as Head Girl of St George's, was a classical scholar and was offered a place at Girton College, Cambridge. Girton has no record of her having taken up the offer and it is recorded in the St George's Chronicle that she was unable to enroll there 'for family reasons'.

Margaret Dott too left school without an academic destination and is described in the Chronicle as 'leaving to help at home'. She was just thirteen and a half. Rebecca Dott's health was beginning to fail.

Eric completed his time at Heriot's and enrolled at Edinburgh University to study medicine, but not until he had done hard labour in Wormwood Scrubs and Dartmoor as a Conscientious Objector.

For these schoolchildren who had holidayed happily at Brig o' Turk, fates lay in store that neither they nor their parents could have surmised.

Perhaps Norman's was the strangest destiny of them all.

For on that fateful day in August 1913 he suffered a terrible injury which not only shattered his leg but altered his career prospects violently, and at the same time lamed him to such an extent that he was declared unfit for active service.

Active service for Norman Dott would certainly have come in the second year of the Great War. Peter Dott would have been appalled to read the December 1914 issue of *The Herioter* brought home by Eric at the end of the winter term. In an unashamedly if understandably jingoistic piece of writing, Norman's Headmaster, J B Clark, encouraged his boys to go out and get themselves killed.

The article is worth quoting from at some length.

The Great War

The 24th day of June of the present year saw the celebration of the six hundredth anniversary of the Battle of Bannockburn. How eager we all were to share in that celebration, and how proud to feel that the men who, on that far-off June day covered themselves with glory, deeming 'fredome mar to prise than all the gold in warld that is', were men of our own Scottish blood.

And now within a few short months that same spirit of Freedom, which six centuries ago found so doughty a champion in Robert Bruce, has sounded her clarion call to Britons the world over, summoning them to assist in the defence of small nationalities against a powerful, aggressive and unscrupulous militarism, and to show that Britain regards her plighted word as a sacred and binding obligation. This urgent, appealing call of the Spirit of Freedom, Mr Balfour has well described as the call 'to a task as great and noble, and as intimately connected with the progress, prosperity and morality of mankind as there ever was in the whole long history of human effort'. To such a call there could be but one response, and a truly heroic response it has been. The cruel outrages committed under the plea of military necessity in Belgium and the prospect of even the bare possibilities of similar doings within our own shores, have fired British blood as it has not been fired for many generations, with the result that already considerably more than a million of men have voluntarily placed themselves at the disposal of the War Office for service on the Continent. This does not include large Expeditionary Forces consisting of men of the very finest quality from Canada, Australia and New Zealand, which are vieing with each other in a noble rivalry of devotion to the Mother-land. Nor does it include even the first of India's contributions. The coming of the magnificent Indian contingent, which is already serving with the British army in France and Flanders, and the many and lavishly generous offers of assistance both in men and money which have been made by the various Princes and Rulers of the Native States, constitute one of the most inspiring episodes in connection with the war, and are a most eloquent testimony to the fervent loyalty of our great Eastern empire.

With the causes of this appalling European conflagration it sesms scarcely necessary to deal. The immediate or proximate causes may be gathered from a study of the admirable Government Blue-book on 'Great Britain and the European Crisis' and the sequence of events beginning with the tragedy of Sarajevo on 28th June of the present year is sufficiently well known. The effective determining causes of course lie deeper, but their setting forth is a task for the historian. It is indeed possible that when the verdict of history is ultimately given, there may require to be some revision of the present popular view which places the entire responsibility for the war on Germany, in favour of another view which will regard the war as having been almost if not wholly inevitable, and as having been due to the fortuitous co-operation of a variety of causes . . . Whatever weight the future historian may attach to any one of these possible causes, and whatever may be his verdict as to the ultimate responsibility for this war and for all the untold sorrow and misery and horror which must be its fruits, we in this country have at least the great satisfaction of knowing that our own hands are clean.[6]

Having quietly and cleverly changed gear from Scottish patriotism ('Wha wad be a traitor knave?') to British Nationalism ('If I should die think only this of me') and washed his hands with Pilate, he ends with this stirring paragraph:

One word in conclusion to the boys. I should like to say how proud and pleased I am of their bearing at this time of national stress. They have shown how fully they realise the seriousness of it all, both by the enthusiasm with which they are devoting themselves to assisting the various war-relief funds, and by the ardour with which they have taken up the additional burden of military drill. May I venture to put into words a thought which I feel sure is already in the minds of very many of the boys? It is this, that just as the nation is now calling on her manhood for sacrifice—aye, even for the sacrifice of life itself—so is she calling with a voice of no less earnest entreaty on her boys to train themselves to be educated, brave and God-fearing men. And if I can speak with admiration of the boys, what am I to say of the 'Old Boys', of whom, as the Roll of Honour shows, considerably over six hundred are now serving with the Forces of the King? Surely that is a record of which all who are in any way connected with Heriot's have every reason to be proud. Our Roll of Honour is a proof that Herioters are of 'the right stuff', and it will be an inspiration to all who work within the walls of the Old School—masters and boys alike—for generations to come.[7]

J B C

The Herioters answered the call to arms.

They joined the Royal Engineers, the Royal Artillery, the Royal Scots, the Gordons, the Argyll and Sutherland Highlanders, the Scottish Rifles, the Royal Navy, the Royal Flying Corps . . .

And they joined the Roll of Honour of which J B Clark spoke so proudly and where it says of them 'Their bodies are buried in peace, but their name liveth for evermore'.

Of the two and a half thousand Herioters who served, just under 20 per cent were killed and many more were wounded, some to die later of their wounds. Of those boys who were schoolmates of Norman Dott during his four and a half years at Heriot's, 225 were killed in action.

A more startling statistic is that of the thirty members of the Norman Dott class of 4D—not all of whom actually served—twelve were killed or wounded.

Take three fatalities from that 1913 class, as reverentially catalogued in *The Herioter*.

> Alexander Maxwell Bisset. Born 1897. Attended Heriot's 1909-15. 1st XI. 1st XV. 10th Seaforth Highlanders, Private, May 1916. Killed in action on 9th April 1917. Only son of Alexander Bisset and of Mrs Bisset, 3 Bernard Terrace. He went straight from school into the army and was drafted to France and killed at 19 years of age.

> Francis S. Howell. Born 1898. 1911-16. Played rugby and cricket for the school. Prefect. 3rd Gordon Highlanders, 2nd lieutenant, March 1917. France, May 1917. Wounded and missing in action since 2nd August 1917. Killed in action on that date. His body has since been found near the Ypres-Roulers Railway and was buried in the Ypres Town Extension Cemetery. Eldest son of Mr and Mrs G. A. Howell, 100 Montgomery Street. Killed at 19 years of age.

> Robert Drysdale McLean. Born 1898. 1908-15. He studied music and was a fine pianist. RFA and Royal Flying Corps, 2nd lieutenant, June 1917. France, July 1917. Killed in action near the Ypres-Poperinghe Road on 26th October 1917. Only child of Mr and Mrs Robert McLean, Levenhall House, Musselburgh. His death, which was instantaneous, was caused by a bullet from a bursting shell penetrating his head during the attack on the Passchendaele Ridge. An enthusiastic Herioter, he was also an accomplished musician and played at school functions. Letters from the Colonel and Major of the Brigade tell how excellent an officer he was and how well he did his duty. He was buried in the military cemetery near the Ypres-Poperinghe Road. He was 19 years of age.[8]

29   The Schlapps on holiday with the
Dotts at Brig o' Turk in 1929. From left to
right, standing, are: Otto Schlapp
(Professor of German Literature at
Edinburgh University), Norman Dott,
Peter M Dott, Mrs Schlapp and her
daughter. Eric kneels in front with Walter
Schlapp, who later married Kathleen Dott.

They never made it into their twenties, never left their teens.

Unlike Norman Dott, Alexander Bisset enjoyed rugby, and unlike
Norman Dott, he stayed on at school and was in the 1st XV Rugby Football
Team of 1914-15. Of these fifteen boys, fourteen of whom are pictured in
the Rugby Team photograph for that year, six were killed on the field:
Bisset, Fulton, Bell, Maxwell, Brand and West were all dead before the end
of the war.

The December 1915 issue of *The Herioter* refers to the photograph of the
5th Royal Scots Rugby Football Team, fourteen members of which were
Herioters, and mentions with a touch of pride the fact that only two of the
thirteen who went out were left unwounded in Gallipoli. The phrasing
almost invites the researcher to feel some compassion for the unlucky two
who did not collect a wound and who had nothing to do on their St
Crispin's Day, no sleeve to strip, no scars to show in token of their valorous
exploits in that campaign.

30a The George Heriot's Rugby Team of Norman Dott's year. He had left school by this time and these 1st XV former schoolmates were now in 6th Form.

30b The six boys from the 1st XV Rugby Team photograph who died in the war shortly after leaving school.

The names of the 1st XV rugby players of Norman Dott's year—now dead rugby players—are listed with even greater reverence on the Roll of Honour, the *Sancta Sanctorum* of those who see any glory in war. Alex Bisset has already been described. Here are the others:

BELL, JAMES. born 1895. 1911–15. 1st XV. O.T.C. Cadet, 1913–15, Sergeant. 11th Royal Scots, 2nd Lieutenant, November 1915. France, August 1916. Killed in action on 11th January 1917. Second son of Mr Richard Bell, Holmhead, Newcastleton, and the late Mrs Bell.

BRAND, WILLIAM MARTIN. born 1896. 1907–15. 1st XV, 2nd XI. Prefect; Prizeman, Heriot Club Essay. 14th Argyll and Sutherland Highlanders, Private June 1915. France, June 1916. Severely wounded, December 1916; died of his wounds on 19th January 1917. Eldest son of Mr and Mrs George Brand, 1 Comely Bank Terrace.

FULTON, ANDREW. born 1897. 1911–15. 1st XV. Captain, 2nd XI. O.T.C. Cadet, 1914–15. 6th Argyll and Sutherland Highlanders, Drill Instructor; 2nd Lieutenant, November 1915. France, October 1916; attached 2nd Battalion. Killed at Fontaine-les-Croisilles on 23rd April 1917. Elder son of Mr and Mrs Alexander Fulton, West Craigs, 5 West Barnton Terrace.

MAXWELL, ROBERT. born 1897. 1906–15. 1st XV. O.T.C. Cadet, 1912–15. Started work in his father's firm, the Westfield Autocar Company Ltd. Royal Army Service Corps (M.T.), March 1916. France. Died in a military hospital at Rouen on 11th June 1916. Elder son of Mr and Mrs William G. Maxwell, 1 South Oswald Road.

WEST, WILLIAM ANDERSON. Born 1897. 1910–15. 1st XV. 1st XI O.T.C. Cadet 1912–15. 14th Argyll and Sutherland Highlanders, Private 1915. France, June 1916. Wounded. In hospital, France. Attached 8th Royal Highlanders (Black Watch). Wounded. 3rd Royal Scots, 2nd Lieutenant. May 1917. France, August 1917. M.C. 28th March 1918. Killed in action near Arras on 21st June 1918. Only son of Mr Charles M. West, Register House, Edinburgh and of Mrs West.[9]

All of Norman Dott's class stayed on to complete their schooling. James Bell stayed on to become School Captain in October 1915. The paragon of Norman Dott's year, he went to France to do the work of war and was highly praised as an officer by his Captain and Lieutenant-Colonel. On the night of 11 January he was out with a working party and was struck by a whistling shard of minenwerfer bomb. He died instantaneously and joined the ranks of the fallen in a military cemetery, his grave registered: 'He sleeps with the great army of the noble dead on the fields of France.'

Norman Dott did not stay on with the rest of them. Had he done so he would not have been lamed and would have willingly gone to war. There, in France, he would have stood the same chances of injury or death as taken and suffered by his classmates. The history of medicine in Edinburgh would not have been the same. As he embarked on his mission of learning to save lives, however, not destroying them, his thoughts can only be guessed at as he saw the flowers of the Heriot's forest so cruelly weeded away.

The archivist's saddest experience is to turn back several volumes in those rows of gilt-spined and embossed chronicles and read the names of the fallen in the 1914-15 annals of school sports: the games they played, the tries they scored. Brand and Bisset and Bell, captaining their sides to victory, booted and jerseyed and floundering in the touchline mud—playing at war. More than eight million men were to die in the mud of the Great War, and higher figures have been offered up. For a truth we may quote that life expectation for officers at the front, shortly after Norman Dott enrolled as a medical student in 1914, was about five months. For a truth it is recorded that at the Battle of the Somme on 1 July 1916, when Norman Dott, student doctor, was already injecting his first patients, the British Army was losing fifteen men killed and twenty-five men wounded per minute for twenty-four hours continuously. Courtesy of the Haig plan of attack. They left Goldenacre, Myreside and Inverleith for Flanders Field, Joe Soap's army, to play the game for their country as king and kirkmen asked of them: *Dulce et decorum est pro patria mori*. The boys who a few months previously were facing Watson's and the Royal High, The Academy and Stewart's, were soon facing the Germans on the Menin Road. Officers and gentlemen, they led the pack from the class of 1913 and their leaders cheered them on.

The addresses of the dead tell their story: Bruntsfield Terrace, East Mayfield, Warrender Park Road, Gilmore Place, Brunswick Street, Comely Bank Avenue, Montpelier Park. A city with hearts holed in nearly every street. And in time all streets were visited. They went from Morningside and Marchmont and Musselburgh to the Vimy Ridge, to the Dardanelles, to Ypres, Arras, Passchendaele and the Somme. They were seed merchants, bankers, doctors, shop assistants—or, from Dott's year, just plain schoolboys. They went to hold their Heriot's heads high and were killed by snipers and shells, bayonets and bullets; they were drowned in seas of mud and choked by gas, with froth-corrupted lungs; they were buried in woods and on beaches, in windy war cemeteries and in quiet back gardens.

They all had one thing in common: they were too young to die. And they left behind them bitter ashes in the grates of Blacket Place and Grindlay Street and Polwarth Gardens.

So: the Dotts came from Flanders—and but for an accident of history, Norman Dott would very probably have returned there, and indeed remained there, in a war grave, a foreign field become his home again and always. One of the sentinels in those armies of white crosses whose sheer size numbs the brain, sweeps and swathes of human corn, imitating the endlessness of death. The celebrated neurosurgeon could so quickly have become a name inscribed on the archway where soldiers' names become nearly anonymous. Or, shot down in his paper aeroplane and covered by the sea, he might easily have joined the ranks of those lost souls known only unto God: one of those who have no memorial and are perished as though they had never been.

In Norman Dott's eager young mind there was no such thought. He simply wanted to get into the Royal Flying Corps and operate machinery: he wanted above all to be a pilot.

At one point during the conflict his life expectancy as such would have been thirteen days.

PART TWO

The Wicket Gate

Give me that man
That is not passion's slave, and I will wear him
In my heart's core, aye, in my heart of hearts.
(Shakespeare *Hamlet*)

CHAPTER SEVEN

Gaudeamus Igitur

God and the Doctor we alike adore,
But only when in danger—not before!
(*John Owen*)

In 1917 or 1918 I did what was probably the first cardiac massage in
Edinburgh.

(*Norman Dott*)

Sow a character and you reap a destiny.

They are pleasant, but not remarkable, the fading photographs of the
young Dotts reproduced in this book. Most of us can match such a family
group: the parents, five children, and animals caringly introduced here and
there. Always the air is of unity and comfortable middle class, enhanced by
these somewhat diffident intruders, culled from the Colinton countryside,
slightly more numerous perhaps than the usual quota of family pets.

Study the pictures more closely, identify the parents, the pets, the three
sisters, the two brothers. Each time you are drawn inexorably to the small
boy sitting there—Norman McOmish Dott. Former patients and staff will
try to expunge from their minds all previous knowledge of the 'Chief' and
his extraordinary career and attempt to join this small boy in the garden of
Hailes Brae. He is a fortunate child. The scenes are redolent of the peace and
prosperity in which the family has entered the new century. The First
World War is still a decade away.

Non-medical folk will point to the hands and comment on their sensitive
activity, which even a fading still photograph fails to mask. A doctor will
at once disparage, with some gentle irony any idea of prediction. More
nonsense has been uttered about surgeons' hands than about almost any
other subject, so he will say. Surgeons in the operating theatre do not walk
around with these sensitive extremities raised and apposed like a priest.
Screen a dozen rubicund local butchers with a clutch of eminent surgeons
and who would allocate all the exposed hands correctly?

And yet.

And yet there is something about those particular hands; the face too. It is not the chubby countenance of a contented child placidly waiting completion of another cliché for the family photograph album; it is small, well-cut, and already bears the architecture of the commanding, thoughtful surgeon that many were to recognise so well in later life. It would be an extravagant abuse of the imagination to suggest that the eyes conveyed the message which had been enunciated so clearly by another small boy, a carpenter too, many centuries before: know ye not that I must be about my father's business? At least they seem to say in practical Scots terms: finish your photograph, will you? I must be about my own purposes.

What these purposes were has already been described in some detail. By now there seems little room for doubt that such a small boy, whatever fortune held hidden from him, would forge for himself an independent career in which, though intellect was overriding, manual skills would come into vital play. It is no surprise that he was apprenticed as an engineer with McTaggart's of Loanhead, though it is questionable whether such prospects would have satisfied him in the end. However capable he was of managing his own affairs, the dramatic event took place which abruptly terminated his engineering apprenticeship and altered the tenor of his life.

Two months earlier a Suffragette had killed herself under the pounding hooves of the King's horse. In avoiding a horse Norman Dott suffered the permanent injuries which were, indirectly scanned, to save the lives of many of his fellow creatures.

The interpretation of this event depends largely on personal persuasion. With deep religious conviction you may invoke a deity who, with an eye to firming up Christian apologetics, stepped in with an immediate catastrophe to preserve Norman Dott from the slaughter of the 1914–18 war and turn him to the achievement of undoubted benefits to mankind. More cynically it may be regarded as a chance happening which hastened and ensured a reasonable outcome. Whichever view holds, the speculator must pause for considered wonder, for curiosity if nothing else, at this pivotal happening, which thrust him savagely and suddenly into the Edinburgh Medical sphere.

This was represented mainly and massively by the grey stone façade of the Edinburgh Royal Infirmary and the Medical School hard by, separated only by the windy walkway of the Middle Meadow Walk. Few hospitals in the country are so large and so imposing, a somewhat fearsome fastness against illness and pain to the timid eye of the lay person who comes for succour. The central clock tower and turreted surgical wings on either side house a vast entrance hall, sweeping staircases and unusually long corridors, dwindling into distance as far as the numbed eye can reach. From these awesome aisles the wards and operating theatres radiate unseen. The public areas are embellished with a sedate decorum, a gravity and hauteur which

31 Edinburgh Royal Infirmary from George Heriot's. In charge of Ward 20, Dott later occupied the little room under the clock.

imparts confidence and anaesthetises fear. Wall scrolls display in fading gold the names of past benefactors and benefactions, from Elie to Indianapolis. There is a sense that the goodwill and wishes of the world are present in a vast crowd of witnesses, all the more real for being unseen. Some busts and plaques, discreetly placed and commemorating royal visits, enhance this stately aura. George IV on his plinth, guardian of the age of elegance, guards also those wide steps conducting you to monumental wooden doors, secured at nights against intruders, while the casualties and emergencies filter in at all hours through the ever open East Gate, leaking yellow lamplight onto the meadow walk. The steps are lit by crowned globes and from above the entrance the golden words of scripture proclaim Christ's gospel, trumpet-tongued: *I was sick and ye visited me . . . I was a stranger and ye took me in.* Here indeed stands the medical peer of castle, cathedral and palace: from doctors and nurses an answer to Holyrood, St Giles and the Edinburgh citadel itself, sufficient to satisfy soldiers and churchmen and kings that Scotland's capital leads the field against all that makes us perish.

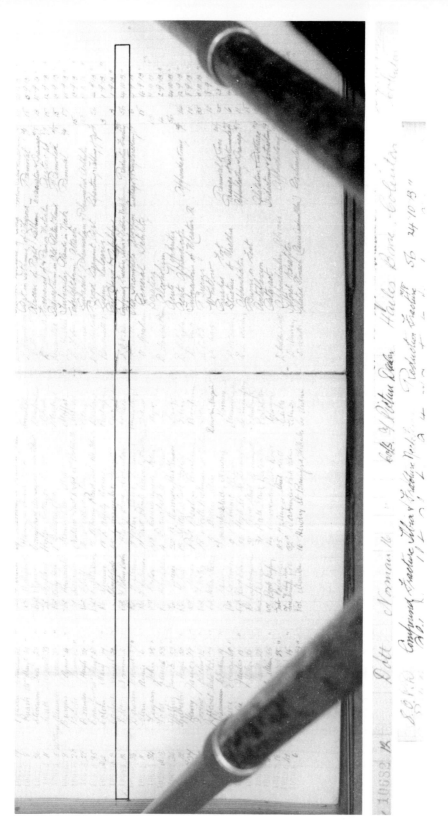

32   The entry for Norman Dott in the Royal Infirmary General Register of Patients 1912-1914.

When David Bryce designed and began to build this familiar and enhancing feature of the Auld Reekie skyline in 1870, it is said that he was receiving advice from Florence Nightingale. If so, she advised him well.

Lauriston Place is the street which runs in front of the Infirmary and separates it from a similarly celebrated Edinburgh building in characteristic-ally dour grey stonework, but surrounded and lit by well-planned open grounds and gardens; yet another bastion of its kind. The bequest by Jingling Geordie, the Court Jeweller to James VI, predates the Infirmary by over two hundred years. It is George Heriot's Hospital, Norman Dott's old school.

So the badly injured boy was not on altogether unfamiliar territory when he was picked from the dust and debris of Lothian Road and hurried through the East gate of the Royal Infirmary on 29 August 1913. This is the crucial date, because although it was not until October 1914 that his name was officially inscribed on the roll of medical students, it was then that in spirit at least he joined the Edinburgh medical fraternity.

The bald but undeniable facts are recorded in the Royal Infirmary General register of Patients 1912-14. This large impressive volume with leather spine precariously preserved can be picked from its place on the sixth floor of the modern Edinburgh University Library overlooking George Square.

There, by a strange coincidence of modern storage problems, it keeps place not far from the records of hundreds of Dott patients and their complex brain and spinal operations. As you turn through the 1912 pages, slowing a bit in case you are to be disappointed, you pause and ponder in your delving to try and visualise who made these matter-of-fact entries.

A sister more than likely, at the end of the day's work and with most of her more immediate concerns of patient care behind her; bound now to the clerical chore of taking up pen, avoiding ink on her starched cuffs, and entering these routines in the allocated colums. If there was some irritation on her part, at least in those days she was spared the toil of having to arrange nurses' off-duty lists.

As the pages turn through 1913 the researcher is not disappointed. There, along with all the other unadorned entries—Edinburgh's entire casualty list since Adam, so it would seem—is recorded an accident which at the least assessment worked its far-reaching effects.

Date: 29/8/13. *Number*: 10862. *Ward*: 12. *Name*: Dott, Norman. *Age*: 16. *Marital Status*: Single. *Religion*: Church of Scotland. *Occupation of Patient or Head of House*: Picture Dealer. *Address*: Hailes Brae, Colinton. Recommended by S.O.P.D. (This meant that as an accident case he had been admitted directly from the Surgical Outpatient Department).

Compound Fracture Tibia and Fracture Neck of Femur. *Operations*: Reduction Fracture, 29/8/13. *Residence*: Surgical 56 (He was detained in a Surgical Ward for 56 days). *Date of Discharge or Death*: 24/10/13. *Results of Treatment*: Cured. *Remarks*: Blank.

Even the most gifted writer cannot recreate in words the actual physical sensation of pain, though he can evoke memories of pain past and work upon the empathy of the imagination. This entry, on the other hand, is a clinical reduction of human distress to a cold jumble of data. It draws a mundane graph; no more. There is no sense in it of the sheer scourge that had fallen on the boy three days after his sixteenth birthday, three days after he was legally entitled to ride a motorbike—a freedom from which he had great expectations. Nor any sense of the sweet uses of adversity.

For a nursing sister is neither poet nor prophet.

His injuries then are as starkly described in this Register. No clinical case notes remain. These gaunt entries are the mere syllables of recorded time; they are not detailed from an absorbed or pensive hand. The side of the injured limb is not given, though we know it was on the left side that pain made its first massively brutal intrusion into the life of Norman Dott as he was brought by motor ambulance past his old school and down the East Gate entrance into the Surgical Outpatient Department of the Infirmary.

Dott's subsequent history suggests that he would have been stoical. But after his identity had been established, was the catalogue of questions really necessary before his wretchedly painful leg was attended to? I'm sixteen. Yes—of course I'm single. Religion? Is that going to make any difference to my treatment? Actually I haven't been to church lately. My father never goes. He's a Free Thinker but believes in God: so what? My mother and younger brother go to church most devoutly. Will Church of Scotland let them get on with the job?

Ah, but these entries are for record and classification only.

Even so *Compound Fracture Tibia and Fracture Neck of Femur* by no means indicates the severity of the injury for which the duty registrar wanted to carry out an immediate amputation. *Reduction of Fracture 29/8/13* does not tell of Mr (later Sir Henry) Wade's special return to the hospital and his decision that with particular operative care the limb could be saved.

Was Dott particularly fortunate in coming under the care of Mr Wade?

A son of the manse in Falkirk, he had graduated with honours in 1898. Already for two years after graduation he had been on active service as a surgeon with the Royal Scots Fusiliers in the South African War, so that his reputation as a rapid operator with a fine aseptic technique was combined with a wide experience in the care of wounds and injuries. He served again in the First World War, now less than a year away, and by his work at Gallipoli and in the Middle East firmly established his reputation as a military surgeon.

By fortune or fortuity Norman Dott was saved from mutilation. Under *Results of Treatment* he is billed with unjustifiable confidence as 'cured'. Of course he was not cured. His bones may have knitted and his wounds healed but he was left for the remainder of his life to contend with pain and disability which were the direct sequel of these injuries. He never allowed these complaints to interfere materially or for any protracted length of time with his care of others, but they subtly turned him to pay particular attention to the rehabilitation services and the relief of intractable pain. An ex-patient wrote of her surge of confidence on simply seeing him, a total stranger, limp into her ward for the first time.

> He walked awkwardly and looked as if at some point in his life he himself had known great pain. I knew at once that he would understand mine.[1]

So there are no detailed medical records of any kind. The entry does however indicate one important fact not found elsewhere. By the time of his discharge on 24 October 1913 he had been in a surgical ward at the Royal Infirmary for fifty-six days, during which he could absorb, according to his passion for devouring new experience, the whole atmosphere of a busy surgical ward. The long 'Nightingale' wards with beds down either side and, if a waiting day has been busy, beds in the middle, are virtually the same today as they were at the time of Norman Dott's first admission in 1913 and subsequent stay in the 1950s.

It is easy then to picture him after he had recovered from his operation and the first few days of pain and discomfort. This slightly built youth lies in his bed immobilised by the complex system of splint, beams, pulleys and cords designed to exert traction on the injured leg, and—so it would seem—tribulation upon the newly qualified young doctor whose interests are not, as Dott's were, mechanical. Many a promising resident, constrained to set up such a system on a patient, has left the bedside not daring to look back for fear that his interpretation of the ordering of weights, ropes and pulleys had projected the patient clean out of his bed instead of retaining him in relative comfort. With what contrasting glee would Norman Dott have set his mind to the workings of his traction apparatus and confirmed its principles of action. There is no telling if his old Physics Master, William Gentle, was among the visitors at his bedside, but if he did appear, in an initial spirit of concern, there is no doubting what conversation would have been struck up between the old head and the young.

It was not long, in fact, before Norman Dott was offering the resident doctor at first tentative and then more confident advice on the maintenance of the traction system—an adjustment of the splint, the tightening of a cord. His brother confirms that during the regular visits of his parents the conversation rapidly turned from family matters to reports on ward activities and even the condition and progress of various patients. Through Eric Dott's remembering eye you can see this kindly pair sitting at the bedside, at first consumed with anxiety about Norman's condition and whether his leg was to be saved from amputation; and then, as progress continues satisfactorily, a little more relaxed and joined by other members of the family and friends. Norman, forgetting his own discomforts, tells them all eagerly of the day's routines and of the operations of the day. It emerges that what has captured his imagination most is the bedside teaching of the Chief, Mr Wade, later Sir Henry.

What was it that appealed to this injured young apprentice engineer? Was it the electric anticipation of the Chief's round, as sister supervised her nurses in ensuring that the ward and its patients were immaculate and bed charts charged with the latest information on human function? For these were the disciplined days of 1913. Was it the appearance of Mr Wade himself, white-coated, godlike, austere but kindly, as he entered the ward at the head of his entourage? We would expect a military bearing but a contemporary student magazine tells of him as a popular teacher. He would stride in with hair waterfalling down over his right forehead like the Ancient of Days. He spoke with a sonorously strong Scottish accent, interspersed with colloquial phrases. The hard glitter of granite and the tang of peat was on his tongue. He did not patronise: he inspired confidence.

The retinue in those days was impressive, Olympian.

Sister, with that wonderful starched and frilly cap; her penguin badge worn like a military decoration and indicating that she had trained at the Royal Infirmary of Edinburgh, the only place, so she thought, that such a nurse could be trained; the spotless apron, more a badge of office and asepsis than any protection of her glorious blue uniform of sisterhood. She is attended by a nurse in case there is any fetching and carrying to be done, for sister must not leave Mr Wade's side. Nurse's uniform, though equally immaculate, is a pale shadow of sister's, but she bears the priceless asset, which the surrounding doctors and students readily endorse, of being more approachable and several years younger than sister.

The students are a varied group. The eager ones are to the front, ready for the cut and thrust of question and answer; the less fervid are glad of the back row, appalled at the thought of active participation, or drifting into a dreamy contemplation of nurse's ankles. On some may be discerned a fairly recently acquired stethoscope stealing self-consciously out of a white pocket. The house surgeon or resident has only lately left the student group, has more in common with them and wears the anxious expression of one who will be expected to answer immediately on any factual details of his patients. The remaining doctors, senior registrar, registrar or postgraduate student, are committed to a surgical career, will take part in this impromptu symposium and hope to catch the Chief's eye or ear with a point of surgical erudition.

The varying facets of this scene Norman Dott will have observed. Which influenced him most is mere entertained conjecture. Less tenuous a supposition is that even at sixteen he was too mature to be unduly influenced by any superficial glamour and that he had already begun to follow the rational arguments and deductions which he could overhear, and which led to diagnosis and the relief of suffering.

What we do know is that at the end of these fifty-six days he had decided to become a doctor.

In October 1914 Norman McOmish Dott entered the University of Edinburgh as a medical student. By this time Britain was already two months into the war against Germany. Norman Dott waited impatiently on the touchlines of his late teens, anxious to take the field.

There was much bustle at the beginning of things to fire the blood of a youthful spectator. In the days before the outbreak of war the builders of Redford Barracks came out by train on the little spur line and walked up from Colinton Village to the site of the barracks. Before long the quiet roads and fields were noisy with guns and horses and men, the steeds going down to the Colinton smiddy by the hundred to be shoed, perhaps even the humble horse aware that his hour had come again, like the battle-mount of the Old Testament. *He sayeth among the trumpets, Ha! ha! And he smelleth the battle afar off, The thunder of the captains, and the shouting* . . . Rural tranquillity heard the din of war well away from the front. And in 1914 the primitive planes flew low over Hailes Brae like angry autumn wasps, droning displeasure till they came to a shuddering halt on the small landing-strip at Redford.

In the city itself the knowledge of war was inescapable as the air with its wasps of war. The soldiers were never off the move. A present inhabitant of Colinton, born in 1903 and delivered by Elsie Inglis herself, remembers the drama.

> I saw the men of the 4th and 5th battalions infantry go off to Gallipoli to make the sea red with their blood—that was old Churchill's mistake. I saw the Territorials, the Lothians and Borders Horse, who were quartered in St George's School for Girls—the Princes Street Lancers, we used to call them. From Melville Street I saw them coming down to Charlotte Square to parade for inspection. All the Royal Scots, from the 1st Battalion and the Dandy Ninth in their kilts all the way down to the Bantams. And I can remember when the 1st Battallion Cameron Highlanders left Edinburgh Castle for France in August 1914 . . . I recall the soldiers marching four abreast out of the Castle, down the Mound and along Princes Street, thousands of them going

off to die, and when they were coming over the Dean Bridge the men bringing up the rear of the procession were still at the West End . . .[2]

Then came the air raids.

On the second night of April 1916 Edinburgh received its first ever attack from the sky. Ironically one of the bombs just missed the Infirmary—an event of which Dr Alistair McLaren, then a boy, has graphic recollections.

I was born in Lauriston Place where now stands the new extension of the Royal Infirmary, which I am pleased to say still carries my old address, 39 Lauriston Place. This short terrace of Georgian houses between Archibald Place and Chalmers Street, each house consisting of three storeys and a basement, stood virtually back to back with the then George Watson's Boys' College.

On the night of 2nd April 1916 my elder brother and I were lying in bed reading, when the electric light suddenly dimmed once or twice. I did not realise what this meant, but my brother cheerfully said, 'Oh, that means there's going to be an air raid!' Just then our parents came upstairs to see if we had noticed the lights, and I immediately said I would not stay in bed on the top flat. My brother and I moved down to the middle flat, to the spare bedroom, where we promptly went to sleep.

Sometime later we were rudely awakened by an explosion and realised that a bomb had hit the house. Zeppelins had, for the first and only successful time, crossed the North Sea, reaching Edinburgh, where their objective was said to be the Castle; one bomb did actually hit the Castle Rock. On their way, bombs were dropped on Marchmont, on Watson's School, on our house in Lauriston Place and in the Grassmarket.

The 100 lb. Zeppelin bomb exploded on hitting the roof, causing extensive damage throughout the house, particularly to the roof, top landing and staircase, also blowing out all the windows. The nose cap travelled down through the middle landing, then the sitting room, and was finally stopped by the stone floor in the kitchen pantry.

My father and mother had heard the noise of the Zeppelin engines and had gone up to our top floor bedroom overlooking Lauriston Place and the Castle, and, kneeling at the open window, were calmly watching the Zeppelin overhead when the bomb struck.

As soon as the noise stopped my father called out to everyone in the house to ask if all were well and we were all happy to find that everyone was safe and unhurt. My sister, the eldest of the family, in her bedroom on the top flat, shouted that she was alright and was lying looking at the stars! She added that she could not get out of bed as the roof was on top of her. My father warned us all to stay put where we were until he could find out if the floors and stairs were safe. As the electric light had gone he called to the maids, also on the top flat, to light a match and a candle, but they shouted back that the could not do so as they had no matches with them, having dived under their beds—very wisely, as it happens.

My father then called down to the street and asked someone to go to the Fire Station nearby and ask for a fire-escape. This was done, but the escape went to the house next door and took some people from the top windows there, though the damage there was slight apart from the windows.

However firemen did come to the house and made their way upstairs, finding that the stone stairs were safe, as were the landings, but the banisters had disappeared and stairs and landings were piled with debris.

While we were waiting to be told what to do, my irrepressible brother amused us by drawing cartoons on the spare bedroom floor in the thick lime dust which covered everything. He depicted the Zeppelin dropping its bomb on our house and also a caricature of the Kaiser. These drawings were photographed by the press, and I understand were published abroad as propaganda showing how even youngsters were not frightened of German Zeppelins.

Firemen extracted my sister from her bed. When the bomb had exploded her wardrobe had been blown across the room and leant across her bed, so preventing the rafters from actually falling on her. She was unhurt apart from a scratch on her leg! They assisted the maids to come from under their beds and found what a wise precaution it had been, as the door of the bedroom had been blown on top of one of the beds. The bed where my brother and I should have been sleeping was deep in heavy plaster and debris from the roof and we undoubtedly would have been injured had we been there.

The next day, Monday, my aunt took me round to see some of the other bomb sites—Marshall Street and the Grassmarket—and I remember how embarrassed I was as the leg of my pyjamas, which I was still wearing, would persist in coming down below my shorts.[3]

That other reminiscer, safely delivered by Elsie Inglis, was a thirteen year old when the bombs came down. His brightest image is not of the Zeppelins over Stockbridge, or the noisy batteries on Craiglockhart Hill and the Torphin Golf Course—but of being in Lothian road, almost on the exact spot where Norman Dott had had his accident three years earlier.

The Caley cinema was a hotel at the time and folk ran down into the cellars as fast as they could. But as a confectioner's windows had been blasted out, I helped myself to some bars of Duncan's hazelnut chocolate before making good my escape from the Germans.[4]

Manna from heaven.

The following year he left Tynecastle school on a Friday and on the Saturday morning was in a screaming sawmill making bomb boxes—but not before he had been taught poetry by Wilfred Owen, who was rehabilitating at Craiglockhart Military Hospital, and whose treatment for the psychological injuries inflicted by war included this kind of therapy. Valuable therapy, not just for Owen but for the boys of Tynecastle school, who found him inspiring as well as kindly, and a welcome change from the bunned and bespectacled old maids who taught them, most of the men being away at the war.

It is strange to picture the medical student Norman Dott, roaring up and down Colinton Road on his motorbike and past Craiglockhart, oblivious to Wilfred Owen who was sitting inside the medical retreat yards away, mulling in his mind the best poetry to come out of the war, and some of the greatest poetry of all time. Both fine young men, the greatness of each in his own sphere to be confirmed by a later age.

But Owen was destined to die young.

He met Siegfried Sasson at the Craiglockhart War Hospital on 17 August 1917. Less than three months later he was dead, killed in France at the age of 25, one week before the Armistice; one of those who died like cattle, but whose passing bell still rings.

A casualty closer to home was Norman's cousin, Alasdair Geddes, the eldest son of Patrick and Anne Geddes, Anne being Rebecca Morton's sister. Peter McOmish Dott heard of his death in action from his daughter Kathleen, while on holiday in the West, and wrote to her a typically uncompromising response, in the course of which he laments bitterly that, after two thousand years of Christ, his fellow creatures have not progressed beyond the level of savage head hunters.

> This is sad news—it brings things home to one, as it might as well have been Norman . . .
>
> You have a stake in the future and I hope you will become a Wilsonite and promoter of peaceful settlements and not look with pride on your son going forth in uniform to kill some other body's son for a 'good cause'. Not one soldier out of a thousand has the time or opportunity even to know whether his cause is good. They just follow their leader in the spirit of patriotism . . .
>
> Alasdair was a splendid fellow, so modest and manly, pure and kindly, and this is his end, to die for his country's 'cause', and to form one of eight millions of dead, raised as a monument to the nations' stupidity, selfishness and want of mutual love.[5]

Alasdair Geddes had joined the Royal Flying Corps.

Thus saved from the conflict which made a singer ask in another war where all the flowers had gone, Norman Dott graduated in December 1919, six days before Christmas.

A carefully preserved leather-bound volume, embossed '1919 Medical Graduates' may be taken from its series and studied in the Special Collections Room of the Edinburgh University Library. At first it seems to be another ledger of dry data, but as the pages are turned, illuminated here and there by verbal vignettes, something of the picture of medical student life in those catastrophic war years is faintly etched. Each graduate is there in alphabetical order: *Davidson, Davison, Deane, Denham, Dingwall, Dott, Dunderdale, Erskine, Fox, Galloway, Gill, Gillis,* and so on, up and down the line. Each has several pages allocated to him, but it is the first page that evokes the strains of grim-visaged wartime studies and the vile incurable horror of those years. This page is almost blank except for the student's name and a stamp giving his date of admission and the earliest date for qualification.

Against each one of them however, except for the women, is pencilled or written in ink a note of the wartime status: *Surg: Prob: R.N.V.R. allowed to study till wanted; Captain 6th Gordons, served in France, wounded, returned to Medicine March 1917; Sub Lt. Hood Batt: 63 RN Division B.E.F. France, wounded and gassed; Trooper Scottish Horse—Lt: 11th Scottish Rifles, wounded 21st May 1916 Hohenzollern Redoubt.*

One pencilled word appears on Dott's page: *Lame.*

Lame.

Many years later a patient's wife was to write that Professor Dott always seemed to take special care of his soldier patients. The lameness that kept him from participation may have left a subtler scar, one that neither time nor the doctor cures.

The remaining allocated pages tell of the proposed curriculum, its successful completion and marks awarded in the final examinations. Attention focuses in passing on the printed programme of the Graduation Ceremonial in the McEwan Hall, Friday 19 December 1919. From 9.30 to 10.00 a.m. there is a programme of music on the Grand Organ, the usual floodtide of chords flowing round the great dome and pulsing over the frightening tightness of all those seats in their serried splendour, to help create something of the pomp and dignity of the occasion. The platform party, looking infinitely wise in that splendid backwash, process down the aisle to take their high places. The sobriety of their suits and black gowns is flecked by the multicoloured hoods. From these the knowledgeable can identify the source and nature of their particular wisdom. The less enlightened observe or acquiesce that it makes a rather pretty sight.

Prior to the first organ notes these spectators have gathered outside in small groups. The recipients of today's honours are looking a little self-conscious in best suit, or occasionally a kilt. The shirts, wing-collars and ties and the odd blouse gleam whitely against the new sweep of black gowns, the swaddling clothes of just born medical babes. There is no doubt about the pride in the eyes of the attendant families, mothers and fathers especially. From all airts they are honouring the occasion; some of the ladies with ill-afforded new outfits; some of the men with suits that rarely leave the silent arena of darkness and mothballs.

The degrees are awarded, the recipients capped. First come the degrees of Doctor of Medicine and the titles of the theses are recorded in the programme. Again the First World War blows its broken bugle as a reminder, lest we forget. One recipient holds the Military Cross. There is a Lieutenant Colonel of the Indian Medical Service. Captains and a Major of the Royal Army Medical Corps are there.

The theses are even more revealing of the carnage which has just closed its last chapter over Europe. *Observations on the Effects of Gas Poisoning During the War 1914-1918; Trench Fever; Medical Work and Prevailing Diseases in a Destroyer Flotilla; Some Medical Aspects of the East African Campaign.* Thus medical scholarship grows out of the graves and stretchers of the war that should have ended wars. And here too is a lady who has secured her M.D. with an *Account of Medical Work Among Refugees in Russia during the War.*

No sterile theses these.

The recipients of the qualifying degree MB ChB follow on. They are forty-nine in number. Thirty-seven are men and twelve are women. Twenty-eight are from Scotland but it is noticeable that even among these several stem from families serving abroad in the colonies. Three come from south of the border. The rest are gleaned from Africa, Egypt, Malta, British Guiana, Australia, India, Ceylon, New Zealand, British West Indies. Edinburgh's reputation for a cosmopolitan intake of students and for training women doctors is preserved. The printed names are in alphabetical order. Strangely, only one name figures in Antique Capitals indicating First Class Honours and only one in Antique small type showing Second Class Honours.

Norman Dott is not among them.

He is fifteenth in the alphabetical list—but he has become a doctor.

Turn now to the details of Dott's curriculum and marks achieved in the Final Examinations. He attended the lectures and practical classes in Physiology of Professor E A Schafer, who was to play such an important part in advancing his career within a few years. For Practical Anatomy he went to the Royal College of Surgeons under Dr Whitaker and for this he had to pay a fee of two guineas. In later years Dott was to describe this as 'having my own cadaver on the black market at Surgeons Hall in addition to the dissection provided for at Old Bristo Street'.

Dr Robertson was the lecturer in Mental Diseases and after returning from America Dott would be corresponding with him about setting up a Surgical Neurology service in Jordanburn Nerve Hospital. Forensic Medicine lectures were from Professor Littlejohn and Dott was to recall even into old age how kindly he had been treated by him when, as a student, he had been involved in an anaesthetic death. Harsher treatment might well have deterred the promising conscientious trainee. So Dott was to be fortunate in a gradual transition from student to qualified doctor in familiar

33 Norman Dott as a 2nd Year medical student. Because of the wartime shortage of medical manpower he had already administered numerous anaesthetics and was sole Resident of the Deaconess Hospital.

34 The children's ward, Deaconess Hospital, Edinburgh.

surroundings and with the assistance of eminent and helpful mentors. His initiation into the basic practices of surgery was from the lectures of Professor Alexis Thomson and the Clinical Surgery Practice and Dressership with Mr Dowden.

Oddly, when you consider Dott's subsequent experience and pioneering work with endotracheal anaesthesia (this involved placing a tube down through the vocal chords and into the trachea) a tick is all the comment on a satisfactory completion of his undergraduate anaesthetic appointment. But all that was necessary in 1916 was a course of six lectures and six personal administrations!

The Dott family still have in their possession ageing and discolouring Certificates of Merit of the University of Edinburgh Faculty of Medicine awarded to Mr Norman Dott. Four, Diseases of Larynx, Ear and Nose; Diseases of Skin; Experimental Physiology and Histology are First Class. They are followed by nine Second Class Certificates for varying subjects but not one is for surgery.

As with the other graduates the examination marks achieved by Norman Dott between 1915 and 1919 are still there to be read as recorded in the volume already described. It seems somewhat unfair that seventy years later a critical eye can scan these figures without knowing anything of the hard work put in to gain them, the stresses and anxieties involved at the time, and, perhaps of greatest import, the personality and mood of the examiner. It would be tedious to detail each of Dott's marks. They are good, and the percentages are usually well into the sixties and seventies, and there is an 80 per cent for oral medicine. However, they were not considered good enough for an Honours Degree and therefore did not suggest the brilliant career which was to follow.

Two sets of marks catch the eye as being contrary to the average described. In October 1917 he obtained only 35 per cent in the written Materia Medica and Therapeutics examination and there is no record of his attending the oral examination. All was set right by March 1918 when he gained 72 per cent and 70 per cent respectively in these examinations.

But 1917 was far from a good year.

A letter from Peter Dott to Eric on 13 June mentions that Norman and his sister Jean are off to Brig o' Turk for ten days following Norman's three weeks of pleurisy and pneumonia, caused in his father's opinion by his intense studies, followed by overwork in the heated surgical theatres and exposure to draughty corridors down which the east winds of Edinburgh whistled grimly. As a result he had to drop out of his two demonstrations and to give up half of his professional exams. Better news in the same letter is that the Chief has adopted Norman's new surgical clamp and an order has come for one from an English surgeon.

A similar letter two months later refers to the failure in Materia Medica and gives as the reason the fact that Norman put off cramming until the last ten days and then found these precious days broken into by his other work. He was required to assist Mr Dowden in some dozen private practice operations, for a fee of two sovereigns for each operation, and in addition was appointed pro tem (during other men's holidays) to be Resident Surgeon to the Deaconess Hospital. All this happened just as the exams came on and he failed to take the hurdle.

> His wise old Father told him months ago that a few days' illness or anything might spoil his time and that he should not run it too fine. It means he will have to pass before his Finals two years hence and as likely as not will have to put aside something he really likes to tackle . . .
>
> We all think that since his pleurisy he has not been quite so magnificently strenuous but that he would pass if he did not overwork. He has not only work to do as Resident Surgeon but books to keep and write up at night and then his classwork besides . . .[6]

So there were great pressures on this young medical student in 1917. In themselves they would explain why he faltered where it might be expected that he should have firmly trod.

Had they been all in all.

But a greater shadow than this fell over the year 1917.

Rebecca Dott had not been well for a while, and by the time cancer of the womb had been diagnosed in 1916, it was too late even for Mr Dowden, one of Norman's great heroes, to do anything except parry it. She returned from the Royal Infirmary to live for just a few more months. The last photograph of her—still wearing her squirrel brooch—suggests the calm, gentle and thoughtful woman who was at the centre of her young and united family, but there are also deep tracks of resignation and suffering in the face. She lay in an upstairs room and heard the harsh voices of the rooks in the wood, requieming the fields of Colinton into autumn.

The year closed in.

In a faint hand she pencilled a note for her children and passed it to Kathleen.

> It is best to have a serene, clear faith in the future life. I trust in the mercy of the All Merciful. What is best for us we shall have, and life and love are best. Our friends have all passed into the great shadow of silence, or rather into the great world of light, and we alone are lingering here. I shall soon follow and I wait the call with a calm trust in the Eternal Goodness.
>
> I have been ill all summer but the world is still very fair to me, my friends very dear to me. I love and am loved . . .[7]

The Dell filled up with snow; the year turned.

35 Norman Dott in his final year with
Sister Anne Dickson. She is seated in the
long sidecar where at other times Norman
is reputed to have kept bodies for
dissection!

36 Rebecca Dott's workbasket lies open
and the cat lies contentedly on her lap.

37   Rebecca Dott. See the squirrel on her brooch.

Rebecca Dott never left Hailes Brae again except to take the last journey. She died there on 17 February 1917, not to experience a mother's pride in seeing her son Norman qualify as a doctor, let alone achieve the fame that was later to be his.

The heart of the house was cracked.

They took her down the kirk brae, down the old sledging route to the old kirkyard, where Cathy Morrison's father had prepared a place for her and the family stood stiffly in a black huddle—Norman the most reticent but the most deeply hurt of all, on that cold harbinger of the spring she was never to see.

> *Earth to earth, ashes to ashes, dust to dust; in sure and certain hope of the Resurrection to eternal life, through Jesus Christ our Lord.*
>
> *He that believeth in me, though he were dead, yet shall he live. And whosoever liveth and believeth in me shall never die, but shall have everlasting life . . .*

Rebecca Dott believed.

She knew she was passing into a spring that knew no autumn. But all that Norman Dott saw was his mother lowered into a cold hole in the ground, where he had played barefooted as a boy. The sexton shovelled in the clay and replaced the turf in neat squares that time would stitch with a seamlessness unmatched by any surgeon.

Then Peter McOmish Dott led them slowly, decorously up Spylawbank Road, leaving their loved one in an unmarked grave.

On the drawing room of Hailes Brae, where bats and moles had listened blindly to the conversational stream of philosophy and art, the blind came down.

> *In the room the women come and go*
> *Talking of Michelangelo*

Not any more.

The woman who was the gentle lynch-pin of the home had gone out of their lives for good. And the talk of Michelangelo—or Peploe— grew cold on the hearth.

The squirrel had left the fireplace.

'Once my squirrel—and now my friendly angel,' her bereaved husband called her in the first of many letters that resurrect her in a sharp-scented bouquet of words in the year following her death. In his idealist's mind she was always the Old Testament ideal of femininity, the virtuous woman whose price was above rubies. 'Mother was a very beautiful woman—a work of Art made through God by generations of fine forefathers and mothers.'

That autumn he went up to the Trossachs for the first time without her, to revisit the early haunts of their courtship and honeymoon and all their holidays together. At the Fergusons' cottage, where they were wed, the bear found his squirrel again and spoke to her in language strange. It was a retreat to a holy place.

> I had a private pilgrimage to Wester Brig o' Turk and other places where I talked with mother. She was greatly interested in hearing how you were growing up, and all her chickens who could not at first get their heads above the grass in flower were prospering and mighty cocks and hens now. I saw all her old smiles: from the arch-teasy one to the tender sympathetic ones. What a music she carried about with her![8]

A year after Rebecca's death, her son Eric was still in prison. Peter Dott wrote to him on the fifteenth of the month so that the letter would arrive at Dartmoor on the anniversary of their saddest loss.

> On the 17th February one year ago mother died. I will keep her in my thoughts all Sunday. What a wonderful gift you got in such a mother. My own sweet mother (a great carer of the poor and suffering) died six days after I was born. I have no personal memories about her and missed the wonder and beauty of a real mother's love.
> Give thanks to God for yours![9]

Much of the crushing melancholy of her mother's death had fallen on Kathleen, who attended her in her last illness. Robbed of her own immediate prospects of study and career, worn out by constant nursing and managing the house, and bowed down by the emotional strain of the sick woman's suffering, Kathleen was sent to an old friend of her mother's in Surrey for a much needed rest. This was in the summer of 1917. When she returned to Hailes Brae in the autumn she tried to assume the rôle of the new mother of the house. She even took over what had been one of her mother's most joyful tasks: reading aloud to Norman to relax him when he came home from hospital or medical school at his weariest. Giving Eric the latest news in a letter, his father mentions that Kathleen has just finished reading to Norman Gorki's 'The Man Who Was Afraid'.

But there was to be no real replacement for Rebecca in Norman Dott's world, though later he found a wife who turned out to be more of a mainstay than could conceivably have been expected. Already seeing the dangers and necessities of his son's ways, Peter Dott spelt it out in a letter to Eric in the spring of the following year.

> Norman is an honest worker but it is a pity he has no sideline (music or art) to vary the stringency of his close avocation. If he lives and keeps health he will be 'a credit tae us a'', but unless he hits on a very fine mate he will have more labour than joy in his life.[10]

Perceptive words. Fortunately the father's implicit wish for his son was to be granted. In the meantime Norman was cut adrift, and, though he kept his own counsel, cut to the core. It is little wonder that his marks in that Third Professional Examination, which he finally passed in March 1918, are his weakest.

There is something different too about the only other set of poor marks which catch the eye. In July 1918 he scored 44 per cent in the written Public Health Examination and 45 per cent in the oral. He had to re-sit. In December all was well again with 64 per cent and 55 per cent respectively. In 1960 Dott looks back with the words, 'I too as a youngster thought I knew just what I required of formal education at school and at medical school and kept it to a minimum.' Doubtless the young Dott over economised on the less appealing subjects so as to devote his energies to the glamour of practical work, diagnosis and therapy. All that apart, the fact simply has to be faced that an educational system does not always succeed in setting its sacred seal on a potentially great man.

These are the records and figures which sketch Dott's life as a medical student and his early medical career. A little light and shade enter the picture through Dott's own words and those of his family and colleagues. The few remaining photographs are slats in a not quite shuttered period. 'Of course he was different—he had this motorbike,' said a colleague who had returned from active service. Consider the group that graduated with him. Was he slightly apart from them, this slim young man with the wavy hair who limped towards his machine? From one of the photographs and his own recollections it is clear that he had soon achieved this distinction: that he enlisted the aid and captured the imagination of a nursing sister who travelled about with him in the side-car and eventually came to live at home with the Dotts. 'Here I am,' he says in one of his talks, while showing a slide, 'as a medical student in 1918 with Sister Dickson of the Deaconess Hospital who helped me so faithfully with early experimental surgery.' Clearly he showed initiative and independence in his studies. In later days, whenever he dwelt on the history of neurosurgery, he would proudly relate how a pioneer in brain operations had been a Scotsman in Glasgow: Macewen. Equally proudly he would relate how he and another second year Edinburgh medical student had succeeded in 'sneaking into the theatre at the Western Infirmary in Glasgow to watch Sir William Macewen operate—a superbly conducted pneumonectomy'. The situation could only have been bettered had it been a craniotomy. Brain or lung however made no essential difference—this young man was going to go a long way down his own particular road.

In those war years, as again in 1939–45, students were thrown early into medical practice and responsibility. Dott recalls this in his address to the Royal Medical Society.

> In 1914–18 medical manpower for the civilian population was increasingly insufficient; medical students were in demand for hospital work. I had administered innumerable anaesthetics by the end of my second year. In my 4th and 5th years I was sole resident at the Deaconess Hospital with its multiple activities.[11]

In 1965 a colleague contemplating a history of anaesthesia with particular regard to developments in Edinburgh wrote to Professor Dott. He received the usual courteous consideration which the professor offered to any such enquirers. Again he referred to the countless anaesthetics he had given as a student. He went on:

> I took some part in anaesthesia in my early days, yes. I made improved air pumps, vapourisers, laryngoscopes etc. They were made by a fine old craftsman over whose shop in Lauriston Place the words 'Philosophical Instrument Maker' appeared, and whose back shelves were littered with prototypes of carbolic sprays that he had been making for Professor Lister in the 1870s.[12]

Only in a modest postscript to his letter does Dott recall an incident which surely reflects outstanding courage and initiatve in a third or fourth year medical student:

> I recollect that in 1917 or 1918 I did what was possibly the first cardiac massage for cardiac arrest in Edinburgh.[13]

He goes on to describe the administration of an anaesthetic for a dental operation when the heart stopped during induction. Incising the upper abdomen, he immediately started manual massage of the heart through the diaphragm. Unfortunately his efforts were unavailing. It is here that he mentions that Professor Harvey Littlejohn, the forensic expert necessarily involved, was 'not unsympathetic'. Well he might be at this courageous effort of a medical student at a time when there was no space to stand and stare.

The post-war influenza epidemic struck Edinburgh in full force in 1918–19 when Dott was in the final year of his student days. There were hearses in every street, sometimes gleaming blackly in the kirkyards at midnight as folk buried their dead at the witching hours by the light of naphtha flares. In the public houses the war song took on its inevitable variant, *Napoo, take the flu and di-ee*. Once this 'pestilence eased', as he put it, he was able to combine research work with the early years of apprentice-ship in surgery.

Thus in those hard times in which disability, war, pestilence and personal loss all played some part, Dott passed by gradual transition and increasing responsibility from medical student to qualified doctor, although the date on which he formally graduated was 19 December 1919.

By this time the grass was blowing greenly over Mrs Dott's unmarked grave. A citizen now of no mean city, she needed no monument but the memories of her that her children would carry into their future.

Her eldest son was now able to consider his future career and obtain relevant appointments. At first between 1919 and 1920 he was resident house surgeon at the Royal Infirmary Edinburgh. Little word of this appointment now remains, except his own irony that he 'early formed a good conceit of myself'. He also found—and there is no irony here—'that I had the manual dexterity necessary for a surgeon'. He became clinical tutor in surgery at the Royal Infirmary and lecturer in the Department of Physiology. By 1923 he had been appointed Assistant Surgeon at Chalmers Hospital and at the Deaconess Hospital.

It was at this point that either chance or some inscrutable workmanship again intervened to alter the whole course of his life and to direct his career.

CHAPTER EIGHT

A Crowded Time

Strait is the gate
(*Matthew*)

Should you scratch deeply enough a man of pioneering spirit, the chances are
that you will draw Scottish blood.

(*Harvey Cushing*)

Looking back after a well spent lifetime practising and teaching the arts of
Surgical Neurology, Dott said to the Foundation Meeting of The Scottish
Association of Neurological Sciences: 'I hope young men will continue to
join surgical neurology from all sorts of backgrounds and experiences.' This
was a favourite theme of his to encourage young enterprise and to caution
against too firm adherence to the rigid training and career programmes so
beloved of many medical planners. 'I myself,' he said, 'found a wicket gate
through endocrinology'. We do not quite know how he found this wicket
gate for Professor Sharpey-Schäfer was a world-famous physiologist. Dott
always said that although Banting and Best had promoted the therapeutic
use of insulin, it was Sharpey-Schäfer who had recognised and named the
hormone;[1] Dott was unknown. Although he had as a student been awarded
first class certificates of merit by Sharpey-Schäfer in Histology and
Experimental Physiology, only the former is signed by the Professor's
hand; the latter is rubber stamped. There is a clue in one of Peter Dott's
letters to Eric in 1917.

> Professor Schäfer has offered him £50 to do research work for him this year
> and he thinks it such a splendid chance to work for such an eminent man that
> he will go in for it.

Nevertheless, once through the wicket, Dott's enthusiasm and skill in
experimental physiology was fully recognised.

It is interesting to pause and consider how Dott reconciled the love of
animals developed in him at Hailes Brae with the experimental operations,
not without some suffering to canine patients, which he now undertook. He

would proudly illustrate later lectures with pictures of the animal operating theatre in Sharpey-Schäfer's physiology laboratory where the operations were carried out. The results of his experiments were published in the medical journals. There we can read and see illustrated his 'Apparatus for Insufflation Anaesthesia'; read of 'Experimental Jejunal Ulcer' in the dog carried out with co-worker R K S Lim.[2] Of greatest import, though, with regard to Dott's future career are his observations on the endocrine status after ablating the pituitary gland in dogs, using carefully planned approaches, among which was a formal craniotomy. Dott's meticulously scripted report to the Medical Research Council on these Pituitary Experiments by himself and co-worker Fraser and dated October 1922 is still available for study. He is careful to point out:

> As regards general treatment, we make it a rule never to manipulate the animal in any way it can resent. Its natural confidence must remain undisturbed—if the animal is nervous morphia is used.[3]

Sister Dickson, whom Norman had first met as children's ward and theatre sister at the Deaconess Hospital, helped him with this work and with the care of the animals. She subsequently became a firm family friend living at Hailes Brae and it was she who christened three of the dogs Charlotte, Emily and Anne. The 'Three Brontes' were brought home to the kindly sanctuary of Hailes Brae, where they enjoyed much more luxurious kennelling and care than in the University Laboratory; until a Home Office Inspector pointed out that it was illegal to keep experimental animals on unlicensed premises and they had to return by way of red tape.

In later years, too, Professor (subsequently Lord) Adrian, the renowned physiologist had written to Professor Dott to enquire about his wife Hester's phantom limb pain and its possible management by surgery. Dott, who was actually a patient himself at the time in Manchester Royal Infirmary having his painful hip arthrodesed by Sir Harry Platt, nevertheless replies in a most relaxed and friendly letter on 19 July 1948, which confirms both his care for and involvement with animals. With advice on the management of phantom limb pain goes an invitation for Adrian and his wife to visit him at his home in Edinburgh. He describes the family pets amusingly but, as befits communication with such an eminent physiologist, he also describes in serious detail some informal—almost Pavlovian—observations on them. He has fitted up a cat door and bell. When his cat wants entry, he will ring politely and wait watching through the window for action. If there is no move to open the door, politeness is cast aside and the bell is rung imperiously until admission is afforded. Shades of Spunkie! His description of his dog's reaction to his daughter Jean's tuning of her fiddle tells of a deep knowledge of music and acoustics as well as of his fondness for the two participants. In addition he has taught his Samoyed

'Aymer' to guard a rag until summoned to bring it by a particular note on a whistle. However, it is the sense of smell, he relates, that predominates in dogs and even 'in humans retains a very strong emotional appeal and through it many intellectual associations. The smell of pine woods recalls in me scenes of childhood much more vividly and forcefully than any other stimulus.' So from his sick bed in Manchester, he summons up remembrance of things past—the scents of the Trossachs surely predominating?

At any rate, in helping us to trace the start of his career and in describing fond exploits with his pets, Dott reveals a facet of his personality which was also to become evident and so necessary in his subsequent practice of surgical neurology. An innate kindliness subtly but firmly inscribed on his character was blended with an intensely disciplined, far-seeing outlook which defined the ultimate benefits. Mankind was to profit from his experiments as a physiologist; as a surgical neurologist he never flinched from advising and carrying out an unpleasant procedure if he knew it was for the ultimate benefit of the patient.

A minor though important piece in the jigsaw of Dott's career is that in 1908 Professor Sharpey-Schäfer travelled to Baltimore to deliver the Herter Lectures at the Johns Hopkins school. One of these concerned the pituitary gland. Lying deeply and centrally in the cranium and inaccessibly at the base of the brain, this small structure, as its name implies, part gland part neural tissue, had long been a challenge to doctors. Today, despite considerable advances in which Dott has played his part, there is still much to be learned of its function, its pathologies and their therapy. Dr Harvy Cushing attended these lectures and following them pursued his important series of experimental studies of pituitary function and became a regular correspondent with Schäfer.

Who was Cushing?—A rhetorical question for anyone remotely connected with the study of the brain and its diseases. For Dott, strangely in an independent Scot, he became a hero, friend and the inspiration of his subsequent career. There is no doubt about it: Cushing was the source of the great Dott tide that was destined to flow fast and far out of Edinburgh. Always interested in the lessons of history, Dott was, at a later date, invited to address the Royal Society of Medicine on the History of Surgical Neurology in the Twentieth Century. He brought Cushing into the forefront of the following picture

> Since Neolithic times there had been instruments and skull operations either ritualistic or for fractures, headaches, epilepsy, blindness. But these were operations on the scalp and skull and rarely was puncture or transgression of the meninges, the lining membranes of the cranium, described. This was altered by the advent of Listerian asepsis, subsequently assisted by anaesthesia

and from 1879 Sir William Macewen in Glasgow, (whom Dott, as a student, was to watch) was pioneering successful surgical attacks upon tumours of the brain and spinal cord, brain abscesses and blood clots. In London too, Victor Horsley, despite having achieved one of the most prized chairs of surgery sacrificed it in order to concentrate on neurophysiology and clinical surgical neurology. He had been helped in his early work on cerebral cortical localisation by the young Sharpey-Schäfer, before the latter's transfer to Edinburgh. It must not be thought that others over the continent of Europe were not turning to pursue similar advances into this hitherto unapproachable territory.[4]

Sadly Dott comments, 'Horsley and Macewen were individuals and left no disciples.' Would the eager student from Colinton, so Scottish in his loyalties, have preferred at an early stage in his career, to apprentice himself to Macewen in neighbouring Glasgow?

No, there is no evidence that Dott had then made up his mind to pursue surgery of the brain and spinal cord and there is no hint of retrospective regret in his next words 'But Harvey Cushing had come!' Working under the famed Halstead at the Johns Hopkins School in Baltimore, Cushing was one of the young men whom Halstead was encouraging to pursue specialised fields. By 1899 he had decided to specialise in surgical neurology. In 1912 he transferred from Johns Hopkins School to be Professor of Surgery at Harvard in the Peter Bent Brigham Hospital in Boston. By dint of inherent brilliance and the application of an extremely disciplined character, into which Dott later builds us a revealing window, he had by 1914 and still more by these early post war years established an international reputation in his chosen field, and with a particular interest, amongst others, in the relatively unexplored country of the pituitary gland. Wryly, when this promising trainee of Halstead was given a year's European study leave in 1900-1, he found Victor Horsley unable to accommodate him and when he travelled to Glasgow he failed to see Macewen. Had each lost the chance of an eminent disciple?

Return then to 1923. Harvey Cushing, now renowned and established, is attracting a highly selected group of postgraduate trainees in neurosurgery to his practice at the Peter Bent Brigham Hospital in Boston. Across the Atlantic in Edinburgh his correspondent Sharpey-Schäfer has working for him as a lecturer in physiology young Norman Dott. Dott has completed his necessary residency at the Royal Infirmary and acquired the Fellowship of the Royal College of Surgeons of Edinburgh. He has been awarded a Syme Surgical Fellowship and been appointed as a Clinical Tutor at the Royal Infirmary. In 1923 he secured the appointments of Assistant Surgeon at the Chalmers Hospital and at the Deaconess Hospital. Thus he was making his way as a surgeon and 'had just put his plate up,' as doctors did in those seemingly less complicated medical days.

In addition to these responsibilities, arduous enough in themselves, he had completed, as well as other physiological research, an excellent study of the functions of the pituitary gland. It was, as he said himself, 'a crowded time.' The detailed report of this study had gone to the Medical Research Council in London which had been responsible for funding. The secretary of the Medical Research Council, Sir Walter Fletcher, came up to Edinburgh to visit Schäfer's department and see the experimental pituitary surgery that was being carried out. Let Dott continue in his own words.

> Afterwards I chanced to meet him in the quadrangle. He, this tall medical aristocrat, said that I should go to work in Boston for a year with Harvey Cushing, the pioneer of pituitary physiology and surgery, and of brain surgery. I demurred; he said he would arrange a Rockefeller Fellowship, which was at the Council's disposal, to enable me to go. I protested; I was newly on hospital staffs, I had just put my plate up. He argued that the importance of working with Cushing would be much greater in ten years and still more so in forty years than these small matters. Sir Walter prevailed. I went.[5]

And so Norman Dott set sail westward from Liverpool, in the *Aquitania*, on the bounty of Rockefeller, for a year (1923-4) with Cushing. Never again was he to question the correctness of Sir Walter's judgement on this issue. Always he acclaimed Rockefeller and other charitable foundations for the opportunity for travel and international exchange of ideas. He used to recall that, as he travelled west to study under Cushing in Boston on the bounty of Rockefeller, Penfield, another eminent neurosurgeon to-be, was travelling eastwards on the bounty of Rhodes to study under Sherrington at Oxford.

But if you stand in imagination—or even in your own shoes in the quadrangle of the Medical School at Edinburgh University you can gauge more keenly the feelings and reluctance of the young Norman Dott at his chance encounter with Sir Walter; feelings which he dismisses somewhat light-heartedly many years later after a most successful outcome. The buildings surrounding the quadrangle, close set, are tall and grey stone granite. As you hurry across, unless you are very resilient and confident, the wisdom and learning of the ages or the personal lack of such commodities may bow you down, however fleet of foot you are. Dott was confident; he must have thought that Fletcher's visit had gone well, but he was not brash.

The clock, to the east has a friendly face but to a doctor few faces are friendly that have time written across them, and perhaps it merely reminded Dott that he should be well on his way from the physiology laboratories to his surgical duties. Now comes this chance encounter with the rather awe-inspiring figure and his unexpected suggestion of travel to America. Although, fortunately, he is persuaded to go, Dott is honest about his initial reluctance. Confident—not extrovert—but travel to America? His family did have some background of travel, his mother had spent a few years in Russia and journeyed to China, his father had visited the Art Centres of Europe. Perhaps, too, the scope of travel had broadened since the recent war; but essentially they were a close knit Edinburgh family. A close weave they had been, none tighter, but the strands were loosening. For this very reason, Norman, the elder son, might have felt that he had increasing responsibilities at home. Despite the care of Mr Dowden, who was his surgical tutor as an undergraduate, his mother had died of cancer in 1917 leaving his father bereft at Hailes Brae. As he sat lonely by the hearth did he ponder on the squirrel who had vanished so fleet of foot, leaving only her fond image inscribed in the bark of the mantlepiece? Then there was Sister Dickson who had served him so faithfully and was a family friend. On his return from America he was again to set up home with this dwindling family at 8 Grovesnor Crescent—premises more convenient for an Edinburgh surgical practice but a ground floor flat so cramped that one room doubled as a waiting room by day and Eric's bedroom by night. Already however his sister Margaret had said farewell to Hailes Brae on her marriage to Arthur Millward in the previous year, and his artistic sister Jean, who had gone to work in London, had just married Percy Sephton. Kathleen was to marry Walter Schlapp a year later in 1924. Eric would soon be ready to put up his own plate. But above all there was his surgical practice, which, with promising hospital appointments and private work, was just beginning to burgeon. There is more than one tide in the affairs of men, which taken at the flood leads on to fortune—but which to take? Nevertheless, Sir Walter, undoubtedly working on that disciplined, far-sighted streak in Dott's character prevailed.

Boston, 1923; how sad that no letters remain to give the young man's first impressions of Boston and the United States. How revealing they would have been if his mother had still lived! The nuts of intimate description would have been carefully gathered in the squirrel's store, this mother who had ensured that her family's childhood drawings were preserved for us to see over seventy years later. Dr Eric Dott's recollections fill the gap.

> I remember him telling me that it seemed to go too slowly for him at first, there were too many showy, talkative young men there, who liked to push themselves into prominence, whereas Norman just worked quietly and patiently away. Cushing soon discovered his real talents though, and gave him work to do.[6]

There is no doubt that Cushing did discover the talents of this slight, quietly spoken Scot whom we see posed among Cushing and his trainees in a photograph taken at the time. Having encouraged Dott and Percival Bailey in the monumental task of reviewing all his pituitary tumours, he

38 Norman Dott as a young doctor aged twenty-two.

39 Harvey Cushing. Dott became his disciple and apostle.

40   Norman Dott in Cushing's team.

wrote the 'prefatory note'—a veritable neurosurgical 'imprimatur'—to the
resultant important paper, when it was published in the *British Journal of
Surgery* in 1925.[7]

When Dott returned to the United States in 1929, intending a brief visit
to Cushing's amongst other clinics (for he was still practising as a paediatric
surgeon and wanted to see work in connection with congenital dislocation
of the hip) he found himself pressed into major clinical responsibility. Dott
was to write in later years describing a photograph of Cushing that the latter
gave him on this occasion.

> It is an excellent picture of Cushing in his dressing-room after an arduous
> operation sketching his observations. The subscription reads 'For Norman
> Dott—from his greatly obliged co-worker—Harvey Cushing—P.B.B.H.[8]
> Aug. 17th 1929.' On that occasion the writer had planned other visits in the
> USA but on his arrival at Boston, Dr Cushing at once sent his first assistant
> Gils Horrax on vacation and set the former to work, which continued until
> the day his ship sailed for home. The subscription 'from his greatly obliged co-
> worker' is still [40 years later] sweet music to the ear of one of his assistants.
> It probably comes as near to an apology as we could expect from the Chief![9]

More revealing is the correspondence which developed between Cushing and Dott in the years 1924-38. This, initially showing mutual respect and admiration developed an increasing affection and familiarity. Indeed, in as much as it was possible between two reserved characters, Cushing appeared to assume an almost father-like rôle in his relationship with the young Scottish doctor. This is perhaps also suggested by Cushing's frequent greetings at the end of his letters to Norman's true father, whom he met on his visits to Edinburgh. Much has been written about Cushing, his life and achievements, but let us turn to Dott for a sketch of this famous man, whom he so admired and who, he repeatedly acknowledged, was the prime influence and pattern for his career.

Should any Dott trainees, dubbed by him 'Cushing grandsons'[10] read the following words, they will soon wonder if they are not reading a description of Dott himself, so closely must he have taken his mentor as his own model. However, his was no empty flattery for Cushing, godlike, had good Scots clay to mould—perhaps Scots granite to sculpt is an image which does apter justice to both men.

> He began to employ and to educate that series of assistants who were to form by 1932 a large international body of truly inspired disciples. In the devotion to himself and to his ideals, that he inspired in them, he resembles the great religious founders more than any medical man so far appearing on the pages of history. The Chief was small, slim and dynamic with an unexpectedly bass voice, stern and puritanical in demeanour. He rose betimes and ordered his day with iron self-discipline, which he also imposed without difficulty on all associated with him. By 11 a.m. he was 'scrubbed up' and supervising final operating room preparations and the operation started. He usually conducted the whole affair from skin preparation to the last stitch himself. The last stitch and dressing did not complete the operation. The Chief would retire to his dressing-room where full notes of the procedure were dictated and these were often supplemented by beautiful sketches. He did no formal teaching of his staff. We learned from him by watching his face and hands and by absorbing his casual remarks. We learned so thoroughly that it has amused and impressed the writer in later years to observe some of his disciples displaying unconsciously but most faithfully the Chief's personal attitudes and character-istic utterances in their own operating rooms as well as observing his technical routines with religious exactitude—such was the imprint of the hero worship that he evoked.[11]

The sketch is completed by reference to family life, the support of his wife, his children:

> He was a good father, theirs was a happy family life, he had an ability to throw himself whole-heartedly into domestic activities or festivities for brief periods while maintaining his own iron discipline for the rest of the day.

A prototype of the Dott professional and domestic regime.

This then was the Cushing with whom Dott was to correspond for several years after his brief stay in Boston. It was a surprisingly brief stay when we consider the influence and knowledge imparted and the subsequent achievements but by these well culled, descriptive phrases Dott has also relieved us of a search for an adequate picture of himself. His very being is faithfully mirrored—reflects him too most admirably. There is only one exception. Dott's voice was not deeply bass. Slowly spoken, a Caledonian drawl, every word considered before it was uttered, the slightly high-pitched lilt was a surprise and, if one had not known better, might have been taken for diffidence. The letters between Cushing and Dott reveal much of the character and relationship of these two men with perhaps the greater illumination of the younger man's enthusiasm and progress than the older established surgeon's paternal guiding rôle. On 13 September 1924 Cushing writing from the Peter Bent Brigham Hospital to 'My dear Dott' at No. 8 Grosvenor Crescent, Edinburgh, appears to acknowledge a letter from Dott because he refers to Dott's paper on Pituitary Adenomas and is 'glad that he has had the opportunity and enthusiasm to go over the material.' He concludes with various greetings to Edinburgh surgeons and Sharpey-Schäfer and the words, 'I shall hope to have frequent word from you and to keep in touch with you. Always sincerely yours. Harvey Cushing.'[12] So the correspondence develops until 1938 when one of the last of Cushing's phrases is, 'I rejoice at the great success you are having in your work and of which I hear on all sides. It fills me with pride to have had even a small part in it.' Cushing's opening address changes from 'My dear Dott' to 'Dear Norman' and his conclusion equally becomes warmer and more informal even to 'My very best to you'.

Positively enthusiastic, considering the epistolary formality of that stern epoch.

Dott initially addresses Dr Cushing formally, but latterly writes 'Dear Chief.' The subjects covered range from technical neurosurgical topics, planning of neurosurgical services in Edinburgh to kindly concern for Dott's family affairs. Frequently there are words of encouragement and praise for Dott from Dr Cushing, perhaps, indirectly, the greatest being an offer in a letter dated 13 May 1925 of a further year as Cushing's first assistant. Dott tells Cushing of an abstruse spinal case, which he diagnosed because he had seen a similar case with him in Boston. He describes a large benign intracranial tumour, which he has successfully removed and also tells of gratifying improvement in vision in patients upon whose pituitary tumours he has operated by the transphenoidal route. Cushing writes back encouragingly and mentions that he has abandoned the transphenoidal approach in favour of a transcranial approach; he had not realised his results from the former approach were so good!

(In surgery of the pituitary there are essentially two routes, by which the gland may be approached. These are referred to here. Opinion used to be divided as to the better method. In the transphenoidal approach, the surgeon works through the nose and broaches the base of the skull at the sphenoid bone thus reaching the gland. In the transcranial approach, a formal craniotomy is fashioned in the frontal region and the brain gently elevated to expose the pituitary.)

Then Dott sorrowfully reports the death of a patient upon whom he had operated for an enormous pituitary tumour. He starts to entertain doubts as to whether he should have operated:

> Do you think it is unwise of me to attempt such cases, where the risk is obviously very great, at my present stage? I feel very unwilling to deny those people such chance as lies in operation and feel that it is humanly and scientifically the right thing to do. At the same time I feel I ought not to risk shaking public and professional confidence too much at present. I should be very glad of your advice on the subject.

Cushing must have had similar experience and feels for the young surgeon anxious to offer his skills in this new discipline to a public, including referring doctors, who can so easily be frightened away:

> I am distressed that you lost that big pituitary adenoma, it is very high-spirited of you. I know you are not a person to shirk responsibilities and you will have to use your own judgement in the matter. I am sure no one could have done more in this case than you did.

On another occasion Dott asks for similar guidance because he is being asked to see numerous neurological patients whose conditions have no surgical bearing. Cushing advises him strongly not to burden himself with such work which would only impair his efforts to set up an efficient neuro-surgical service. Sometimes more technical discussions are interspersed with family affairs. There are detailed considerations of the functions of the pituitary by both writers. It is fascinating to read Cushing's letter of 14 December 1936 in which he discusses the set of signs and symptoms associated with a small basophil, blue staining, tumour of the pituitary or with carcinoma of the adrenal cortex, a syndrome to which he puts no name but which the world, now for many years, has recognised as 'Cushing's Syndrome'. There are requests from Dott for advice on such varied matters as suction apparatus and preparation of post-mortem specimens. In 1931 Dott has not been able to confine himself to neurosurgery and is still practising paediatric surgery at the Royal Hospital for Sick Children. In a letter dated 29 September he writes:

> I think Neuro-Surgical technique, as I learnt it with you, has been extremely valuable to me in the more general surgery of young children. A week ago we had a very distressing case of intussusception (this is a condition where part of the small bowel enters the large bowel to block it and cut off the blood

supply) in a baby of seven months. We had to resect from the middle of the pelvic colon to the lower ileum. With careful deliberate technique and fine interrupted stitching to conserve blood supply, all has gone well and the baby will be going home in a few days.

Eagerly too Dott reports steps taken in the setting up of a successful neurosurgical service and receives encouraging advice. Soon he is requesting that his anaesthetist, Miss Wood, and surgical assistant Henderson be allowed to visit Cushing for training and is readily accommodated and encouraged:

> I am so glad to know about your cases and learn of your excellent results and to feel at the same time you are going at it slowly and patiently and carefully. You being a Scot need not be reminded of John Hunter's dictum, 'It's dogged as does it.'

This quotation must have crossed Dott's mind when in later years he delivered his 'Dr Harvey Cushing MD—Memoir for the Centenary year of his Birth'. He draws the oration to a close on the theme 'Scotland played a not inconsiderable part in pointing the path of this great man.' He suggested that Cushing's visit to Glasgow in 1901 and study of the Hunterian pathological collection there inspired his own collecting zeal and his setting up of a similar collection. Again he refers to Cushing attending Sharpey-Schäfer's Herter lectures in 1908 and their subsequent correspondence particularly on the pituitary. In 1924 Cushing gave the Cameron Prize Lectures at the University of Edinburgh and his titles were 'The Third Circulation', which referred to the cerebrospinal fluid circulation; 'The Pituitary Gland as now Known' and 'Intracranial Tumours and the Surgeon'. On this occasion he dined at the house officers' mess in the Royal Infirmary of Edinburgh and enjoyed this somewhat boisterous youthful company. He also visited the Trossachs and had the good chance fortune to witness a dress rehearsal of a Black Watch pipe band at the pier by Loch Katrine. It could have been no-one but Norman Dott who arranged this visit and was forever 'gladdened that the beautiful scene had been so suitably enhanced by Highland Warriors and Pipers.' So '1927 again found him in Scotland,' continues Dott, 'when he gave the first Macewen Memorial Lecture on Surgical Diathermy, which he was pioneering.' In his introduction Cushing graciously remarked, 'Should you scratch deeply enough a man of pioneering spirit, the chances are that you will draw Scottish blood.' It is unlikely that Dott was entirely absent from his thoughts as he composed this tribute. Finally Dott concludes,

> Scotland is deeply indebted to this great man and she can also bask in his reflected glory with the knowledge that some of his principal directions in life were of Scottish origin.[13]

Thus Dott, with the names of Cushing and Rockefeller ringing in his mind, emphasised the firm Scottish-American bond, not entirely one-sided, which cemented the development of modern Scottish Neurosurgery among other joint ventures.

From this knowledge of Edinburgh, Cushing recommends to Dott those who will be most helpful in the clinical field. Thus in 1924:

> With Wilkie's appointment to a full-time chair, I am sure that there will be a new spirit aroused in your surgical group and this will give you a most excellent opportunity.

And in 1927:

> Edwin Bramwell (neurology) and Traquair (opthalmology) are such sterling fellows to have back of you that I have no worries about you.[14]

In his letter of 28 December 1927 Cushing appears to encourage a Dott, somewhat daunted by lack of progress, 'I do hope that the neurosurgical post at the Royal Infirmary will be made, but then, if it is not, the worse for the Infirmary.' This introduces a concern as to where to site his hard-gained neurosurgical services which must have challenged Dott until the problem was finally satisfactorily settled in the last years of his active surgical life. Should the unit he was determined to achieve be part of a large general hospital, namely the Royal Infirmary, or should it be a separate component more closely associated with other neurological and psychiatric services?

On 11 March 1929 Dott writes to Cushing mentioning the possibility, which actually came about, of re-visiting Boston in the same year! Almost casual is the piece of news which follows.

> A new Neurological Hospital has been started here in Edinburgh under the auspices of the Asylum people (*pace* present-day psychiatrists!) It is supposed to deal with organic neurological cases and borderline mental cases. I have been asked to go on as a surgeon and I think there should be a possibility developing here of a real Neurosurgical Clinic—probably a better possibility than one would have as a department of a large general hospital.

This draws the response on 21 March 1929:

> I am so glad to hear about the prospects of a neurological hospital with you as the surgeon-in-chief. I feel great pride in your development and progress and am sure that Edinburgh will come to be one of the leading neurological centres, if, indeed, it is not so already.

However this hope was not realised and indeed was not to come to full fruition until 1960. On 1 April 1931 Dott writes to Cushing:

> As things are working out here, it would seem for local, politic and other reasons, best that I should presently establish my headquarters at the Infirmary with arrangements to take out my team for private cases in a Nursing Home.

I do not think this could ever develop into an ideal neurosurgical clinic. I feel
that it is quite essential to get a new place going for that. However, I think it
is a step in the right direction and will alleviate some difficulties meantime.

Again on 29 September of that year,

> Things are well in train now for starting at the Infirmary and we should be
> in order for actual operating there within a week. As I think I told you, I have
> obtained permission to take my Infirmary Staff out for private operations and
> for these cases I have the good fortune to have found shelter with Mr Wilkie
> and Mr Wade at their Private Clinic which is a better equipped and more
> stable institution than the average Nursing Home.

His first hurdle is behind him when he writes a month later, 'I got actually
started at the Infirmary about three weeks ago and have been pretty busy
doing three or four cases a week.' Perusal of Dott's papers leave little doubt
that, even if he did on occasion stray towards the pedantic, he loved correct
English and its descriptive powers. Therefore in his cumbersome phrase, 'I
got actually started' he may well by the contiguity of 'actually' and 'started'
be emphasising the stuttering frustration which preceded the final delayed
start.

This concern for the English language cannot be better illustrated than by
a page of one of Dott's characteristic notepads. He always carried one with
him for jotted memoranda. Typically it would be of the cheapest quality,
though the cover ironically bore the resounding description 'Memorandum Tablet—For Pen or Pencil—Containing Superfine Ruled
Paper—Any Leaf Can Be Detached Without Loosening the Others.' Dott
carried such miracles of modern paper technology to any scientific meeting
that he attended, and he could be seen sitting concentrating and jotting
down points from the papers being delivered, whether scientifically
exciting, tedious, or offered by a naive tyro. On this occasion he is listening
to a paper on 'Subclavian Steal'. (In this condition an obstruction in the main
subclavian artery to the arm leads, when the limb is exercised, to reversal of
flow in its vertebral tributary stealing blood from the brain to supply the
needs of the inadequately perfused arm.) We see that Dott has pencilled on
his pad, 'Masterly and highly informative presentation', 'Subclavian Steal'
Scottish Language Steal=Verb—corresponding noun is theft, derive
'Subclavian Theft'. Unfortunately others are not so pedantic, and the
syndrome remains 'Subclavian Steal'.

As 1936 comes to a close, on 28 December precisely, Dott writes to
Cushing:

> This year I have been lucky in getting some Rockefeller help to keep the good
> team together and also in getting local professional and financial support for
> a new department at the Infirmary. The plans are all through and construction

in the Infirmary begins early in the New Year. So I think I am about to realise my ambition to settle down to work in one place with a good team and decent facilities for scientific aspects of work. This did seem pretty impossible for a long time but Sir David Wilkie has been very helpful throughout. Whatever good may come of my schemes here, I owe it to you.

Thus are the serious matters of neurosurgery debated, but respect and then friendship is cemented by lighter exchanges. Many of Cushing's letters carry warm regards to Dott's father; there is an enquiry after his sister's health; he is delighted to receive a Christmas card; he recalls their first meeting at 305 Walnut Street; he thanks Dott for a delightful picture of him and his dog. (In this Dott shows obvious affection for his Cairn and looks far too young for his position on the surgical ladder). He congratulates Dott on his engagement, saying that it is quite evident that his fiancé is going to have her hands full. On 26 September 1933 Cushing is 'perfectly delighted with your letter particularly with its news of the arrival of your first offspring' and later in 1936 he acknowledges an entrancing photograph of daughter Jean. Dott mentions, 'Peggy and I are both well, Miss Dickson and our good little scoliotic maid, who were both with me when you visited are still with us.' So Cushing had visited Dott's home, by then at Chalmers Crescent, and had been introduced to the household. Strangely there is no mention of Cushing's family.

So with these events and this correspondence, as the pieces of circumstance, is built up the mosaic of the forces which sent Dott back to Edinburgh in 1924 fired 'with missionary zeal' to set up neurosurgical services compatible with Cushing's standards. Only one piece of advice which Cushing gave him, did Dott completely ignore, fortunately, as far as we can ascertain, without major ill-effect. It concerned smoking. In his letter of 2 February 1936 Cushing, who by now is suffering from the painful condition of intermittent claudication in his lower limbs, tells of being advised to have an amputation because of a persistent ulcer on his right toe. 'With great mastery of spirit,' he says, he gave up smoking and the ulcer began to heal in three days. 'If you are a smoker', he advises 'you may take warning by my misadventure and become a nicotine teetotaller, which I would recommend to all neurosurgeons.' All those associated with Professor Dott in his work will recall the characteristic posture; sitting leaning back in his chair, stiff leg outthrust, the silver cigarette case drawn from his waistcoat pocket and the plume of smoke quietly inscribing the air as he pondered a problem or chose his words to answer your question.

CHAPTER NINE

Scheme of Things Entire

And your old men shall dream dreams,
and your young men shall see visions.
(Joel)

Exegi monumentum aere perennius—
I have built a monument more lasting
than bronze
(Horace)

Norman Dott was only twenty-seven when he returned to Edinburgh in 1924 inspired with his vision of setting up neurosurgical services there. An uphill struggle faced him. 'Edinburgh was not particularly forward in this limited field in early days,' was his own understated description of the state of affairs,

> Mr Joseph Cotterell, surgeon to the Royal Infirmary of Edinburgh 1883 to 1912 and Mr Alexander Miles 1898-1924, were well known for their efforts in cranial surgery, which however were largely confined to the operative treatment of head injuries and their complications. They were great surgeons but better known in other aspects of surgery.[1]

Norman Dott too in the early days was not in a position to confine himself entirely to neurosurgery, although colleagues were increasingly seeking his opinion in neurological cases. In 1925 he was appointed honorary surgeon to the Royal Hospital for Sick Children. Occasionally he was irked when pressure of work, such as by absence of a colleague, seemed to interfere with his neurosurgical efforts but essentially he found this work stimulating and rewarding. Over half a century later nurses from these days contributed their memories by letter about Dott's fondness for the sick children and how they adored him. The writing may come from a shaky hand but the memories are clear and loud and tell of the children crying out joyfully for 'Dr Dott, Dr Dott!' The walls of one lady's mind are still ringing with their cries, as the walls of the Children's Hospital did years ago, when

138

the slim young man with the limp was so sought after. The letters tell also of dolls from Dott for Christmas—'my first real doll'; of dolls being plastered by Dott because they also had to have congenital dislocation of the hip like their sympathetic owners. Dott applied a lot more than the neurosurgical techniques he had recently learnt to the care of his infant patients.

At all times he was to commend paediatric surgery as a valuable discipline and training ground for other branches of surgery and speak of the 'thrill of setting on his feet again one who has stumbled on the threshold of life.' Thus Dott addressed the Scottish Surgical Paediatric Club, of which he was Chairman for a period of years from 1955, with the words:

> Such success as I have had I owe very largely to my little patients. I would commend paediatric surgery as the first training ground in surgical technique and management.

Even to the end of his active neurosurgical career Dott took a special interest in his juvenile patients. It is a pity that he retired before world neurosurgical opinion confirmed the importance of paediatric neurosurgery by developing departments devoted to this speciality and founding Societies such as The European Society and the International Society for Paediatric Neurosurgery. There can be little doubt that but for this unfortunate error of timing there would have been further accolades for Dott in this sphere.

There was never any question that Dott's participation in paediatric surgery was passive or grudging. Pondering on distressing cases in the newborn of anomalous rotation and herniation of the gut, he clarified and described the normal developmental intrauterine hernia which is followed by orderly rotation and return of the intestines to the peritoneal cavity. This allowed a better understanding and care of infants afflicted in this way. The observations were published in the *British Journal of Surgery* in 1924 and this contribution remains one of the classics of all time.[2] Furthermore it was illustrated by some outstandingly detailed and artistic diagrams in Dott's own hand. The tale is told that Dott's unravelling of this knot was Archimedean. Possibly, but 'Eurekas' surely did not spring from those lips, rather the quiet smile of satisfaction and pencil put methodically to paper. When, in 1956, a request came from the Royal College of Surgeons for the drawings so that they could be preserved in the museum, he even had to reply that he no longer had them. Fortunately he did confirm that, 'The drawings were done by myself and not by a professional artist.'

At this time too he was making useful modifications to intestinal clamps and describing an ingenious original method of aseptic intestinal anastomosis. His own disability must have led to a particular affinity for children with congenital dislocation of the hip and he pursued this problem with numerous observations on the operative care. How proudly he told in later days of being tended himself by a nurse whose brisk gait showed no sign of a limp but whose warm care gratefully acknowledged that he had operated on her in early childhood for this condition. Mouth gags and techniques of anaesthesia allowing freedom to operate in mouth, nose and cranium had always captured his attention. When he was asked about the modified Davis mouth gag, which still bears his name and is used in cleft palate surgery, he replied:

> The story of the gag is quite simple. In 1923 and 24 I was with Dr Harvey Cushing in Boston. There I learned the technique employed by him of Transphenoidal Hypophysectomy, after Hirsch of Vienna. Cushing used a Davis gag for this procedure. It was an American instrument. I brought one home with me from Boston in 1924. I had a smaller lighter one made for small cleft palate children, replacing the flange by hooks to hold on to their gums and making them adjustable round the arc of the mouth frame to act also as lip retractors. The earlier ones had a tube incorporated with the tongue depressor to deliver anaesthetic vapour. After about 1926, this was replaced by intratracheal intubation which I adapted from my monkey work in Professor Sharpey-Schäfer's experimental physiological laboratory.[3]

Always, however the surgeon, he adds a modest post-script:

> In cleft palate surgery, my main contribution was transverse converted to vertical pharyngoplasty. This did compensate remarkably for an otherwise too short palate.

He is here referring to the concept of making a transverse incision in the posterior wall of the almost tubular throat and sewing it up vertically to narrow the tube and allow the repaired but short palate to close it off intermittently as necessary in swallowing and phonation. Thus did Dott, apart from his surgical duties at the other Edinburgh hospitals, make maximum use and expand the boundaries of his 'training ground' in paediatric surgery. All the time though his vision was set on the development of an Edinburgh neurosurgical service second to none; no effort was too great and he never relaxed his energies to this end. But the tireless planner was also the compassionate healer and his fondness of and concern for children never left him. Age did not dim the brightness of that indulgent smile, as by then he had a healthy brood of grandchildren to administer to. And when all was young a child with illness or disability amenable to neurosurgical care would quickly capture his heart and undivided attention. Not that there was any emotional display; all was done with calm and efficiency but the acts spoke with feeling.

There were times he could barely bring himself to speak at all, such was the pathos of the situation. The little boy propped against pillows in his cot with huge head and large, appealing, unseeing eyes, has eventually been referred to Professor Dott. But it is too late. Dott examines him, re-

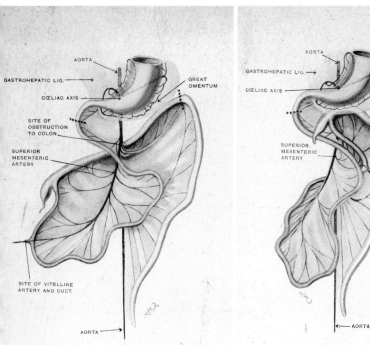

Fig. 1 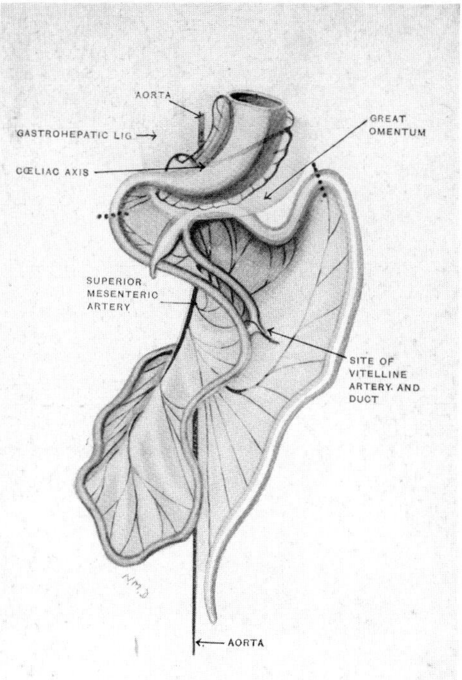   Fig. 2

DIAGRAMS OF CHIEF ANOMALIES OF ROTATION

OF THE MIDGUT LOOP. (Mr Dott.)

Fig. 1. Reversed rotation of midgut loop. The midgut loop has
rotated in a clockwise direction through 90°, from the
original sagittal plane. Thus the colon is brought to
lie behind the mesenteric vessels and the duodenum in front
of them. These are the only noticeable defects, the
viscera otherwise attaining normal positions, though of
course their anterior and posterior surfaces are reversed.

Fig. 2. Mal-rotation of midgut loop. Reversed rotation of the pre-
arterial segment through 90° in a clockwise direction.
Arrested rotation of the post-arterial segment. The mesen-
tery is folded over, as on a hinge, at the line of the
superior mesenteric artery.

41   Diagram from a series drawn by Dott to illustrate his Paper on Rotation of the
Gut and its Anomalies. He was not lacking in the family's artistic talents.

42 Commander of the Most Honourable Order of the British Empire: Dott and his staff celebrate his award for wartime services at Bangour Hospital in 1948. Dr Kate Hermann, his loyal neurologist, just enters the picture on the left of the party. Dr Tony Donaldson, neuroradiologist, is next to her.

43 In command from an early age: Dott with one of his early surgical teams.

examines him. He calls in his senior colleagues for independent opinions. Few words are spared. It is too late to save vision and useful development. And yet the tumour, which is there, could have been removed so satisfactorily at an early stage. Dott cannot hide his distress and he does not shirk from his responsibility to press, in appropriate quarters, for more and wider teaching about neurological syndromes which are amenable to surgery—surgical neurology. Sorrow was the briefest luxury he ever allowed himself.

On a much happier note, William, another infant is admitted with a large head. Is this not another case of the relatively common condition of hydrocephalus? Some fluid is removed, examined and reported to Dott. No, this cannot be a straightforward case of hydrocephalus; the protein content is too high. He studies the X-rays at length and with care. Time grew like moss on a stone and people simply stood and watched and waited in the inviolate silences of those occasions when Dott gave himself to X-rays. The X-rays would be placed and lined up on the stereoscopic apparatus so that Dott, with his slight forward stoop and penetrating eyes, would see focused in the mirrors the beautiful three-dimensional picture of the skull. Words were few, an occasional 'Uh, huh,' a brief comment, like pebbles in the sea, and the ripples carried learning to the attentive. The registrars nearest him crane forward to catch an oblique glimpse of the film, those behind take their weight first on one foot then on the other as time passes; none dares to allow concentration to lapse because it is inevitably then that a question is posed. The courteous tone is deceptive; it is certainly not to be brushed aside or answered in facile manner. In this case it is, 'Isn't that some calcification frontally?' followed by, 'Doesn't it look like a little limb bone, and a tooth there?' Dott has the diagnosis: a large, fortunately benign, developmental tumour centred deeply in the cranium and composed of fragments of nearly every tissue normally found in the body—a teratoma. A few days later Dott removes it successfully and is greatly intrigued to study under the microscope all the various tissues which have no established right to be in the cranium.

It is 1959 and on 12 January Dott is writing to that eminent Canadian neurosurgeon Wilder Penfield to invite him to participate in a joint meeting of the Canadian Medical Association and the British Medical Association in Edinburgh and to receive various honours. As is usual with any neuro-surgeron corresponding with a colleague, he mentions, somewhat casually, any recent case of interest. 'A 230 grm teratoma successfully removed from within the cranium of a five week old baby, I think it must be rather unique?' Back comes the reply in five days, Penfield readily accepts. And— 'two hundred and thirty grams of teratoma from the head of a five week old baby is rather a feat; a little like the extraction of Athena from the head of Zeus, which is said to have given the father of the Gods an awful headache!'

It was rather a feat; there was considerable press publicity; his first assistant was later able to claim, before a dental audience, to have assisted at a transcranial dental extraction! Dott received, in addition to these classical allusions, the commendations of his peers, none of which touched him so closely as little William's annual card, on his own birthday, which brought Dott greetings and conveyed his own, and perhaps more deeply and knowingly his mother's heartfelt thanks. The cards continued to arrive well past Dott's retiral and William's attainment of healthy manhood. Thanks to Dott, some men never forgot their childhood, and the fact that they had stumbled on that early threshold.

What were the plans Dott had before him for neurosurgery and to what ends was he working as he utilised his paediatric experiences in his development as a surgeon? They are revealed by their gradual realisation and final culmination in the opening, in 1960, of the Department of Surgical Neurology at the Western General Hospital in Edinburgh. How inappropriate it is that no eponym attaches to this department; no animated bust or commemorative portrait, within its walls, pays tribute to Dott's vision and struggles. Such images of success are not, however, so important as the sober satisfaction of this achievement, which he expressed with his own words in an address to Medical Laboratory Technicians in 1962:

> I consider that this is the best unit for inpatient care in elective surgical neurology in existence at the present time. It will not be so for long; others will soon emulate and surpass but it is a step forward.

After the opening of this department too, he continued, in lectures and addresses, in letters in response to world wide requests for advice on planning, to advocate the ideas which he had incorporated in Edinburgh. These involved the abolition of the artificial division between medicine and surgery, the encouragement of system medicine—neurology in this case, with its surgical and medical therapies. Within this concept, he argued, must be set up a first class complex with the most modern facilities for diagnosis and cross consultation, for surgical care, for pathological study of the conditions encountered and for adequate rehabilitation of the patient. To this complex must be attracted outstanding staff, who would also be offered facilities for study, research, and teaching.

Today with the enthusiasm of re-discoverers the term 'Holistic Medicine' has become popular and we are counselled to consider the whole patient and not just the treatment of his disease by modern technology. There is irony here, for Dott, essentially a technical surgeon, and undoubtedly advocating the study of system disease, had, from his early days, surrounded himself with other specialists for cross referral and insisted that the benefits of operation were incomplete if not followed by rehabilitation to restore the patient, as nearly as possible, to a rewarding position in the community. To this end he had insisted that his department be fully equipped, apart from nursing staff for the acute period, by staff and facilities for physiotherapy, occupational therapy, speech therapy and social work.

It is easy, with the hindsight of sixty years and from an era when such ideas have become commonplace, to look back with rather moderate appreciation of Dott's ideas and achievements. Return instead in spirit to 1924, realise what this young man of twenty-seven was formulating and preparing to struggle for, and his vision and calibre are thrown into bold and bronzed relief. He was certainly embarking upon a titanic struggle and Cushing was quite right in saying there was no need to remind him that 'It's dogged as does it.' In following these early steps in an Edinburgh that 'was not particularly forward' in the neurosurgical field, you fall upon a deeply human story.

Dott's first task was to establish himself as, beyond doubt, a competent surgeon in the neurological field. This he soon did with his disciplined and meticulous care in all aspects of the work, and his single minded and untiring efforts for the benefit of his patients. Superimposed upon these was his pleasant, friendly manner, a face and voice that warmed coldness from the clinic and chased fear from consultations. Medicine was a much more personal matter in those days and well he knew that any failures or mishaps would soon become known and diminish his chances of acceptance. This had been the theme of his letter to Cushing about the enormous pituitary tumour case, who unfortunately died. Nevertheless he did have some failures, as he was bound to, in this new and unforgiving branch of surgery; but he did not attempt either to dismiss them brashly or to sweep them out of sight and into fruitless oblivion. Each was examined in depth and detail so that, in the midst of death, the living might benefit.

This led to the abiding principle in Dott's work that a post-mortem examination must be obtained if at all possible. An assistant from this time writes, 'I have more than once gone with him to do the autopsy in a private house in the Borders, if a patient had died at home after discharge.'[4] That invaluable information was thus gained will be seen later. Permission was sought with the greatest sympathy and kindness and this sometimes involved Dott himself in prolonged interviews with hesitant relatives. One such relative has written to the authors confirming that, after many years, it is this aspect of Dott's concern and kindliness that comes to mind.

After such an interview with Dott, permission for autopsy on the dearly loved relative had been given with some hesitation and on condition that no disfigurement of head and face was incurred. After the autopsy had been completed, Dott had made it his business to meet the relative, who had granted permission, and walk with him to the chapel to confirm that his promise had been kept. Meanwhile he explained the exact mode of death and what information had been gleaned from the examination, which would be invaluable in the treatment of other patients with similar afflictions. Though these measures were all pursued with the greatest respect and concern for the bereaved, the comic mask forever hangs beside the tragic, and a slightly humorous aspect could not always be entirely excluded. In 1926 there was a post-mortem which was difficult to complete because it was on a low bed in a private house. One overworked resident doctor attached to Dott and who later became an eminent plastic surgeon, used to recount how, at some awkward hour, he would be telephoned by Dott with the information that a patient had unfortunately succumbed in the nursing home and would he 'just get along to remove the brain' and take it to the pathology department for subsequent study. The unfortunate resident, who by good chance had a lively sense of fun would set off on foot as he had no car. The outward journey was usually uneventful: the return journey, with the brain in a suitable receptacle, was a matter of concern as it frequently took place at a late hour and the nursing home was the other side of Princes Street from the Royal Infirmary. The young doctor was always worried in case he was stopped by enquiring police, who would not have forgotten those other night-running Edinburgh citizens, Burke and Hare.

Dott too realised with wry amusement that his fame for this invaluable discipline had spread beyond the medical fraternity and recounted the following tale of a lay conversation overheard in the hospital waiting room, 'Aye, the Professors dae marvellous operations noo; oor Jenny's awa intil Professor Broon's ward for gastero—something.' 'Hoots that's naethin, oor Jock's in under Professor Dott for a post-mortem!' Thus Dott regaled the Congress of Neurological Surgeons in Toronto in 1968 and this was just another instance of his readiness to illustrate an important point, on this occasion the value of autopsies, with a homely tale in the Scots vernacular, however erudite or important the audience.

In the Edinburgh University Library in George Square, it is possible to find one's way through well filed though ageing case record folders to Case I of Mr Dott. Read on from this point down those early years and it becomes luminously clear how Dott rapidly established his reputation as a caring and competent neurological surgeon. Number one, actually in 1923, is the son of a Spanish Dancing Master in Glasgow, a dying profession. This small boy has a depressed fracture of the skull which is righted at operation and he makes an excellent recovery to full normality. Number six is a most unusual spinal tumour, which Dott excised and like his mentor Cushing immediately drew what he had seen at operation. In fact the year is 1925 and the initial examination findings have been recorded on Peter Bent Brigham

Hospital diagrammed notepaper. The disciplined surgical skill is evident but an added kindly charm can be deduced from these old records. It is a spinal case with paralysis; extensive physiotherapy and rehabilitation would have been necessary and there is a copy of a letter from Dott to the physiotherapist thanking her for all her help.

The sheets at the back of the folder take us on to thirty-seven years later. It is 1962 and the patient, now elderly, has made her way very diffidently into a seat at the Usher Hall in Edinburgh. Perhaps in the back of her mind and from her school days lurks a parable about touching the hem of a garment but she now has no need of healing and just wants to see, from a distance, her surgeon of old, as the Freedom of the City of Edinburgh is conferred upon him, with all the civic dignity which this ancient Burgh, his birth place can so royally muster on the appropriate occasion. She is warmed when Dott, in his address of thanks, characteristically pays tribute to courageous patients who have ventured with him into unknown dangers, and realises that she, anonymously, is numbered amongst them and has found her life's memorial. She makes her way home having paid her small tribute. Before the ceremony though, the man in the next seat has engaged her in conversation and she has casually mentioned the reason for her presence. This kindly, titled gentleman, with some social acquaintance of Professor Dott, immediately sees the spirit of the incident and writes to him describing the lady and her presence at the ceremony. Straight away Dott pens to her his warm regards and wishes for the future. He recalls every detail of her case of three decades previously and rejoices with the words, 'You and I,' (mark that; no vaunting first or only person) 'got rid of your tumour.' And he thanks her for her help in this scientific advance!

Another case from 1925 bears some resemblance. This is the very large benign intracranial tumour, in a young woman, which Dott successfully excised and mentions in his correspondence with Cushing. Again Dott refers to patient and surgeon as co-equals in getting rid of this life-threatening tumour. The friendly correspondence, on these lines, and with family details, continues for nearly forty years. Sir Thomas Browne tells us in *Religio Medici* that the world is a hospital rather than an inn: a place not to live in but to die in.[5] Norman Dott was a doctor who did not share his view. He never forgot that his patients went on living after they went out of hospital and back into the world.

So with each triumph or hurdle surmounted the referrals increase, the range from which patients are taken expands and doctors recommend seeking Dott's opinion with increased confidence. By 1931, in support of his application for further facilities, he is able to cite that, in the months June to December 1930, seventy-four cases were recommended to him, eleven from Edinburgh Royal Infirmary Staff and sixty-three direct referrals to him from Edinburgh, Glasgow and Aberdeen. But this runs ahead; earlier more sporadic referrals tell their tale. In 1925 Dott is called in to a case in coma because the London surgeon, already involved, cannot get up to Edinburgh in time. Eminent though the London surgeon was, it is questionable whether he would have brought across the border, in the proposed dash by train, the expertise and skill, which was already waiting in the Scottish capital. In 1926 there is a somewhat backhanded referral, 'Dear Mr Dott I would be much obliged to you, if you would see him for me, knowing as I do that the brain is a great specialty of yours. He will never be of any use as he is.'

The experts however know full well what a force has entered their field. Dr, later Professor, Edwin Bramwell writes 'Suggest that young Dott should do the operation—first rate fellow—technique excellent.' In 1927 a letter comes from Kuala Lumpur, 'It's a far cry from Kuala Lumpur to Auld Reekie but when we want your advice and help we don't hesitate to send a message across the twelve thousand miles—I hope you are fit and not killing yourself with overwork.' Dott takes the patient under his wing and writes back:

> Here things are going very much as usual. I enjoy the Children's work greatly and am getting more and more central nervous work, the results of which are more gratifying than one is usually led to suppose.

The means by which Dott achieved these gratifying results and the constraints under which he worked in these early days are remarkable. That he overcame the difficulties is the greatest accolade. Patients there undoubtedly were but one can sympathise with the hesitancy of his colleagues in referring them. No one knew exactly which cases were suitable for surgery nor what surgery could achieve. Dott was so young. It was incumbent upon him to secure every patient of any promise to prove the merits of surgical neurology. These were the days before the National Health Service when surgeons, although they had hospital appointments under which they treated the less well off, relied for their incomes, in the main, on private practice. Dott at this time had no official appointment as a neurological surgeon. Specialised investigations, so vital in neurological cases, were complex and time consuming. The operations were very lengthy so that a theatre might be occupied for nearly a whole day before it was finally cleared for the next case. It is not surprising that colleagues were in no hurry to share facilities on these terms until results could be proved. To prove his results Dott had to undertake each and every case whether they were private patients or hospital patients. For a time, like many of the pioneers of the past, he seemed to stand completely alone, unsheltered from the sceptical winds of the 1920s. However, fortune smiled and he was taken in and offered operating facilities at number 19 Great King Street.

Most Edinburgh citizens will be able to direct you without hesitation to Great King Street. Lined by elegant Georgian façades, it is one of the parallels of the New Town as it slopes downward towards the glinting Forth and the quiet coasts of Fife. At No. 19 Miss Muir, a fine and far-seeing woman, ran a most efficient nursing home and gave Norman Dott, who it must be stressed was still so very young for a surgeon, every facility to operate. One of Miss Muir's nurses, now eighty-one years of age, still has clear memories of those days.[6] She confirmed that Miss Muir was very accommodating as she would have to be to accept this young surgeon, who operated all day and had to be screened off so that other surgeons could also complete their less lengthy procedures. Accommodating and far-sighted beyond measure, for according to nurse the first two patients, both elderly, died. Dott was very upset; it was an awful blow to him but he was intrepid and knew he must not be daunted by initial failure. Soon the next patients, fortunately somewhat younger, were recovering satisfactorily and confidence grew in Dott's lonely furrow.

Nurse continues with her recollections:

> Sister Keith was his theatre sister and went with him to the Royal Infirmary, when he became established there. Many of the procedures were carried out under local anaesthetic with Sister Keith's assistance. If an anaesthetic was necessary he brought his own anaesthestist, a lady, Dr Wood.

Sister Dickson, Miss Muir, Sister Keith, Dr Wood, it is invidious to select these names from the early struggles. They are among those from his earliest school mistress to his latest secretary which moved him in 1946 to address the Glasgow Women Medical Students with the words: 'Like most males, I suppose, I have derived support, encouragement, inspiration and comfort mainly from females.'

That nurse, in her youth, had lovingly contributed her own whit to this support was clear as she continued to conjure and focus her sixty year old memories of Great King Street. 'He used to bring his own instruments too, including a box which was plugged in at the wall and he would ask for cutting or coagulation.' Nurse is here referring to Dott's pioneering work in surgical diathermy, which is indispensable in modern neurosurgery. Confined by her vital duties of readying theatre, she cannot detail the preparations which take place away from the nursing home and the trek, usually on a Sunday, down to Great King Street. Dott's car and a taxi are both being loaded with instruments, the design of each having been carefully checked or modified by Dott himself. The diathermy and the cumbersome operating table headpiece follow. The latter, he has specially designed for immobilising the head while the cranium is operated upon. There ensues the anxious last minute check that all is on board for this voyage into the human brain. Kindly Dott might be to patients but no foolish omission would be tolerated on the part of the assistants who climb into the taxi.

It is these assistants who have left us the picture. They and the experience of others complete the scene. Among them was the late Mr A B Wallace, the plastic surgeon already referred to. It was always a delight, particularly to current Dott assistants, after a strenuous perhaps slightly abrasive day, to see his smiling spectacled face and receive from him the emollient of his experiences with Dott in his early days now so well recorded in Ross's *The Edinburgh School of Surgery after Lister*.[7] The taxi driver puzzles at first at this unusual call and bustle on a Sunday morning, but after several repetitions the Edinburgh cabbie is soon feeling pride at his part in Dott's Sunday operating routine. Perhaps he even comes to recognise and name the precious diathermy box; loads it into a privileged position by his side. What picture has he formed of the unseen Chief who inspires such devoted concern as the swathed packets, hidden by their outer cloth wrappings, are checked and stowed to weird chants such as 'Gigli saw and guide', 'perforator and burr', 'clip gun'? Surely he sees a large, flamboyant surgeon in butterfly collar, black coat and pin-stripe trousers, the trappings and costume of a hectoring manner, instead of the small, quietly spoken young Scotsman in a tweed suit and with the eyes of a visionary.

Down the Mound they go and across Princes Street. The city is almost deserted for the operation has to be underway by 9 a.m. on the Sabbath before the beaten bells have begun to winnow the keen sea-wind that sings along its streets. A few soberly dressed citizens are hurrying to an early service in the name of one who also had the temerity to heal on the Sabbath. Perhaps the assitants in the taxi may have time for a moment of spiritual reflection of their own. Perhaps they give thought that, when they finally peel off their gloves at about 5 p.m. after a day of unremitting concentration (any lapse from which will earn a telling rebuke) the citizens they have passed on the road will be sitting down to tea, having managed, according to preference, morning service or a visit to the local hostelry and Sunday dinner, rounded by a sleep or gentle walk. More likely the Dott team are going over in their minds the exact steps of their part in the operation and checking that their preparations have been complete. The repetition of this drill is halted by the taxi drawing up at 19 Great King Street, where the whole loading process is repeated in reverse. Tensions there undoubtedly are, but overall there is the undeniable bonhomie, which seems to generate among assistants submitted to intolerable demands by a Chief, who, together with his aims, is a source of admiration.

Through the door of the nursing home step back again into nurse's memories of a strange little part of Edinburgh's medical history. Perhaps she didn't follow the stages and technicalities of the operation but she knew great advances were being made and loyally she switched from cutting to coagulation and back to cutting again when Dott demanded it of his new machine. In the ward after the operation she remembers that each patient required a special nurse; injections were given if they became restless and sandbags also were used to prevent harmful movements. If the temperature rose dangerously, Mr Dott had to be informed by telephone and then the patient would be wrapped in sheets wrung out in cold water and nursed by an open window. Well she recalled these technicalities of her profession from prior decades. Professor Dott too would frequently point out what advantages Edinburgh, with its east winds and cold air, offered her neurosurgeons in combating this dangerous complication of brain damage. What had evidently impressed her most though, was Dott's courtesy and care for his patients.

> He was always very courteous when we telephoned and impressed upon us that we must never hesitate to ring and he came in to see his patients every day, twice a day, sometimes more.

Thus with stealing steps, was surgical neurology established as a viable specialty in Edinburgh. But, however helpful and forward-looking Miss Muir was, with her first class nursing home at Dott's disposal; however enthusiastic his assistants and grateful his recovering patients; and although his colleagues were increasingly encouraging, still the service had to be paid for. Dott knew that, although he had made an effective start, he could not possibly conduct an improvised symphony for the rest of his life however faithful the players. He must forward further plans.

At this stage hospital patients were investigated from the beds of referring physicians and surgeons in the Royal Infirmary and then transferred by Dott to the nursing home for operation. Private patients were obviously admitted directly to the nursing home. The latter he could charge appropriately. This he did, with perhaps a slight weighting for the benefit of his poor patients. His own requirements were almost ascetic. Plain living and high thinking was the style he had adopted from his parents. In seeking support for his work Dott, in 1930, issued a *Statement re Surgical Neurological Work in Edinburgh*. Here he illuminates his almost monk-like philosophy:

> I am not an extravagant person. The necessities of my work have trained me in methods of economy in dealing with it and personally I spend a minimum, having re-visited America last year on a steerage passage and having worn the same evening dress clothes for the past 14 years, and they are still perfectly good![8]

The less endowed hospital patients had their stay in the nursing home paid for partly thus. The astonishing evidence exists, however, that some of these poorer patients had their expenses paid for them by Norman Dott himself from his own resources. Peter McOmish Dott made an arrangement with his son that he should have his portion of the anticipated family legacy, at this time before his own death, so that it could be used in this way? In these days when the prevailing cry is for higher wages and mounting income such genuine altruism seems almost unbelievable. Genuine it was and although largely fostered by an urge to prove that there was, here in neurosurgery, a benefit for mankind, as yet untapped, its deep rooting in a compassionate upbringing defies denial.

In later years Dott was publicly though unassumingly to reveal a small part of his philosophy of life, 'Philosophers tell us that happiness is proportional to our contribution to the weal of our fellow men.' In later years too a colleague was to ask him why, with his somewhat socialistic attitudes, he was so insistent upon preserving his rights to private practice. He was said to have replied, with that amused look his eyes sometimes assumed, 'You have heard of Robin Hood, haven't you?' He must have had these early struggles in mind. Hadn't he, in some degree, bought for Edinburgh, and an even wider field, a neurosurgical service from his own hard-earned resources and by his own untiring efforts? This last was a sterling bargaining counter in his long term plans, which were always focused on a single complex of neurosurgical excellence with facilities for public and private patients, where a surgeon could retain some independence from an employing authority but concentrate all his efforts on his patients without needless and wasteful travelling to and fro.

The final accomplishment of this was not to come until 1960. However in returning to 1929 to follow his struggle, it can be seen how, along the way, Dott has to employ some pragmatic change of direction to achieve his ends. It is in this year that he starts his correspondence with Professor Wilkie who, Cushing has already suggested will be helpful. Ross[10] describes Wilkie as the son of a well-to-do Kirriemuir jute manufacturer who got from his parents a nature that was radiantly happy and imperturbable. In 1924 he was appointed to the Systematic Chair of Surgery in the University of Edinburgh. In this, although he continued with practical surgery, he moved into an academic environment and was involved in setting up a new research department, which, to this day, flourishes as the Wilkie Surgical Research Laboratory. Unfortunately he died in 1938 at the early age of fifty-six. Sir Charles Illingworth,[11] who worked with him in various capacities, considered that his greatest contribution lay in the influence he exerted amongst his colleagues and assistants. His genius was in his ability to foster cooperation and inspire enthusiasm. Such was the character to whom Dott turned and from whom he obtained invaluable help.

In his letters to Wilkie, Dott emphasises the unsatisfactory conditions under which he is working and repeatedly returns to the theme. His irritation destroys his usually meticulous phrasing and the deficiencies tumble out in rapid sequence.

> The nursing home regime is most inefficient. The burden of arranging initial consultation at my own house, X-ray at another place, perimetry at another, assembling these data by personally going to these different places, managing secretarial work at irregular intervals at home, not having records conveniently available at the Nursing Home, arranging for possible donors of blood, blood testing, sufficient nursing staff and assistance at operations; impossibility of having immediate pathological investigation, conveying and arranging examination, photography and recording of pathologic material in separate laboratories visiting these laboratories to study pathology in odd moments.[12]

Despite this drudgery, he held on to his humanity, a patient from this era wrote telling of Dott's kindness to her. When he drove her home from the nursing home, after a successful cranial operation, she asked about her tumour and said that she would love to see it. Amused by this, Dott interrupted the journey to visit the laboratory with her and request the technician to produce the specimen for inspection. These were the unsophisticated but far from golden days when a pathology technician would become used to the slight, unassuming figure of Dott regularly presenting himself at the laboratory with a brain wrapped in oiled silk to be prepared for examination. Much more demanding than Dott in those days was a certain Irish porter, whisky loosening his step and tongue, who would cross from the Royal Infirmary and emerge from the top of the Meadows Walk like a bearer of Crown Jewels—holding an uncovered bedpan for appropriate examination![13]

But Dott's torrent of troubles continues.

> Visiting these laboratories to study pathology in odd moments, having to stay at the Nursing Home with critical cases for hours by day and night in default of a resident surgeon; for reporting cases, having to prearrange day and hour suitable for perimetrist, self and possibly radiologist. With increasing work these difficulties are wasting two thirds of my time and worse still I know that the work is suffering. Valuable material is being wasted for lack of time to arrange photography etc. I have certainly lost some lives from absence of a resident, difficulty in arranging transfusions etc. A complete department in a General Hospital would meet the case but I can see no such prospect as at all probable at the R I E within even remotely measurable time. I should like to develop such a place at Jordanburn as formerly mentioned to you. I have worked quite hard and got to a certain standard on a very small scale by individual effort and by sacrificing nearly everything to it. I find myself wearing a bit thin in physical endurance. The matter cannot progress now without better organisation. So far as I am concerned personally however I am 33 now and I do want a chance to advance the matter a bit in the next twenty years.

However there is one note of triumph at the end of the letter which is dated 3 June 1931. Almost as an after thought Dott adds, 'Mr Colin Black's tibialis anticus seems to have stuck well to his internal carotid—he has gone for a holiday.' He is referring to the operation, later to become world famous, in which he made the first successful intracranial approach to a bleeding cerebral artery aneurysm, arresting the haemorrhage by investing it with a piece of the tibialis anticus muscle in the leg. The pioneering operation will be discussed in greater detail in the chapter on Dott's surgical achievements.

What high ideals, what unstinted effort, what frustrations, Dott expresses. Was this the nadir of his career, fortunately to be surmounted at an early stage? We do not know but certainly from this man who, in a long career was never to allow his own pain, suffering and disability materially to interfere with his aims or the care of patients, the phrase, 'I find myself wearing a bit thin in physical endurance', was unusual and never to be repeated. What he now conceived as the optimum was the setting up at the Asylums' Board's new Jordanburn Nerve Hospital of a suitable complex serving the integration of psychiatry, neurology, neurosurgery and neuropathology. He felt this would improve the old 'Asylum' image, as well as improving all the neurological services and their teaching. He obtained the plans of the hospital and although, superficially, there may not have appeared to be sufficient room for his ideas, he inspected and found to the contrary. His report in a letter to Professor Wilkie, 'I have had a look at the place and observe that there is plenty of room for building expansion,' conjures up the picture of 'seeing for himself' to be repeated on so many occasions and for so many causes throughout Dott's career.[14]

The time, typical Dott time, is probably when others have ceased work, late, or at a week-end. He advances quietly but purposefully, his cheap scribbling pad and pencil ready for the notes and measurements of an inspired project. As he paces about the arena his mind fills with those dreams of the surgical Utopia, which he eventually brought about. His visionary spirit conceives, his practical hand jots down the measured constraints. He produces the most forward-looking ideas with detailed plans of exact requirements for operating theatres, recovery rooms and other facilities. Unfortunately the Board and its funds cannot implement his schemes. Refusing to admit defeat Dott has to change tack and is soon writing to Professor George Robertson, who is a medical manager of the Royal Infirmary, pointing out that he is operating at the nursing home on many public hospital patients and suggesting as an initial move an official position as a Neurological Surgeon at the Royal Infirmary.[15] He and Dott himself know well that the Infirmary is overcrowded and all facilities fully stretched. Professor Robertson replies expressing great interest but suggesting the possibility of the Rockefeller Foundation funding a conjoint scheme of research laboratories, psychology, psychiatry, neurology and neurosurgery at the Jordanburn Hospital. Dott is quite prepared to accede to these suggestions and to approach the Rockefeller Trust.

His papers give a measure of his determination. Dr Gregg the secretary of the Rockefeller Trust is in London. Dott proposes to travel to Gullane, that sedate seaside village nineteen miles from Edinburgh, to see and enlist the aid and advice of Professor Wilkie, at his home, during the evening of Saturday 6 June 1931. On Sunday 7 June he will go to London, arriving at 7.20 p.m., to put his case before Dr Gregg at his hotel before leaving again to return on the 11 p.m. train to Scotland. Arrived back in the Scottish capital, Dott would again take up his normal arduous Monday morning round of neurosurgical duties.

And all, it seems for nothing. The Rockefeller Trust proves unable to support him on this occasion although it was to do so most generously in the future. His worth, however, was by no means unrecognised. The National Hospital for Diseases of the Nervous System in Queen Square London, so familiarly abbreviated to 'The National' or 'Queen Square' had and still has an outstanding international reputation in matters neurological. During the year 1930-1 the appointment of a neurological surgeon was under consideration. Dott was lobbied to apply and a correspondence to this end with one of the consultant neurologists ensued. He encouraged Dott by telling him that, 'London is the centre of Medicine and Medicos from all over the world come to London,' though he had to own 'admittedly, as a city, London does not compare with Edinburgh!' Then sensing that Dott was loth to sever his firm roots in his native city, he continues, 'Quite frankly should you decide to stay in Edinburgh and the schemes you speak of come true then I think that Queen Square will suffer severely but it might act as a stimulus to the staff.'[16]

Dott hesitated but did prepare and forward an application for the post, accompanied by a detailed curriculum vitae and the names of his Edinburgh sponsors, who included Professor Wilkie and Mr Logan Turner. It was a considerable tribute to Dott to be sought at the age of thirty-three for the most outstanding neurological hospital in the United Kingdom if not the world. Nevertheless very little time elapsed before he withdrew his application and an undertow of relief and strong feeling can be felt in his explanation to his sponsors:

> The application is not a very serious one, I have withdrawn my application mean time. So far as I can judge, from what I have seen, Edinburgh is the foremost Medical School in the world at present, taking things all round. I am proud to belong to it and mean to stay here if I can.

Was this the final stimulus to his colleagues to urge his appointment to the staff of the Royal Infirmary and to Professor Wilkie to offer him facilities in Wards 13/14 of the Infirmary? In 1931 he was appointed Associate Neurosurgeon to the Royal Infirmary of Edinburgh and in June 1931 he writes to Professor Wilkie accepting his offer of facilities but pointing out that it was 'going to help but only to a very limited point.' This was because he was being offered operating theatre time and some four beds for postoperative recovery but no beds into which he could admit patients referred directly to him. Mainly his patients were still to be admitted and investigated, in the first instance, under general physicians and surgeons. Letters between Dott and Mr (later Sir Geoffrey) Jefferson throw interesting light on Dott's feelings at this time.

Mr Jefferson was the consultant neurosurgeon in charge of the neurosurgical unit at Manchester Royal Infirmary. Since 1926 he and Dott had been associated as founder members and protagonists of the Society of British Neurological Surgeons. Indeed, at the subsequent celebration of the fortieth anniversary of this foundation, Dott described Sir Geoffrey Jefferson as 'the creator, midwife, nurse and guide of this Society.' Already in 1931 a firm friendship had been established by this common interest and a relaxed friendly correspondence was taking place, though many a serious topic was also explored deeply. Jefferson wrote to Dott agreeing with him that a clinic 'set up' (comparable with Dott's ideas for Jordanburn Hospital) is better than a department in a general hospital. Dott wrote back saying:

> I may have to compromise. The staff at the Royal are rather pressing me to start work there. I have held out long enough to be able to secure fairly good conditions but to hold out longer might be misunderstood. What I hope to be able to do ultimately is, that having secured a hold on the Royal here, I can get a more ideal clinic going in the next few years and then quietly and unobtrusively transfer all the work there!

Little did those who were privileged to work with Dott in the unique Edinburgh Department of Surgical Neurology, when it opened in 1960, realise that this was the culmination of a young man's vision of twenty-nine years previously. The only part of his stated aim which he was not able to achieve was to, 'quietly and unobtrusively transfer all the work there.'

By 1960 Dott was so famed and his new department was arousing such interest, both neurosurgical and lay, that the press was full of detailed descriptions before and after the opening. Numerous enquiring and admiring visitors had to be diverted. The unique aluminium domes for the twin theatres made a royal progress on monster lorries from Glasgow one Sunday, accompanied by police and press. The patients already under Dott's care in beds at Bangour Hospital, were, under the auspices of the ambulance services and 'commanded' by Lt Col John Fraser, the physician superintendent of the Astley Ainslie Rehabilitation Hospital, transferred to their new and luxurious quarters in quasi-military convoy. Finally the opening ceremony was performed by Secretary of State John Maclay (later Viscount Muirshiel) and the occasion was also planned to coincide with a joint, almost congratulatory, scientific meeting of the Society of British Neurological Surgeons and the Société Neurochirurgie de la Langue Française. No it was not quiet and unobtrusive it was a public triumph for Dott: a pealing of bells. The Society of British Neurological Surgeons made it the occasion to present Dott with his own portrait by the Queen's Limner in Scotland Sir William Hutcheson—that portrait which captures so well the man and his restrained triumph after years of struggle. It now looks down from an honoured position on the walls of the Royal College of Surgeons in Edinburgh, where also rests that other token of Dott's fame the silver casket and Freedom Scroll of the City of Edinburgh. As surgeons both eminent and apprentice pass along those quietened corridors, the familiar face still speaks a message of resolve for the diffident and caution for the confident. Characteristically, however, he appeared outwardly unmoved, though his mind must have been ranging back over those nine and twenty years of struggle through which we must now return.

Dott wrote again to Jefferson on 3 November 1931:

> I have just come through a rather difficult stage of commencing work at the Infirmary and of shifting my private work to another institution. (This refers to his change from Great King Street to the nursing home at Drumsheugh Gardens.) I have just got things well going and am very satisfied with arrangements and equipment so far as actual operative work goes. Facilities for investigation and observation of cases, pathology etc. still require to be worked out probably eventually on the lines of a separate clinic. Anyhow the primary thing is the establishment of really good operative facilities and I think that I have got everything that man can reasonably desire in that direction now. I hope then that when you are able to come I shall be in a better position to entertain you as you would wish than I was in October.

Thus towards the end of 1931 Dott is able to pause in his relentless pursuit of 'a separate clinic' and to agree that he has 'really good operative facilities.' These he now uses to the full as Associate Neurosurgeon to the Royal Infirmary. Those days still live in the memory of a Royal Infirmary nurse who writes in 1988 from Western Australia, relating what must have been common gossip among the nursing staff.

> I had the great privilege of seeing Mr Dott's work and of nursing a few of his patients. The royal Infirmary almost lost this brilliant surgeon as there was nowhere for him to operate and only by Mr Wilkie, Chief of Wards 13-14, giving up his plaster room near his operating theatre was Mr Dott able to continue his work. Many patients came from overseas especially South Africa—a long journey by sea. As one of the probation nurses in the ward, we

had to take the patients on the trolley to theatre early in the morning. They usually didn't return to the ward until late evening. A screened off area in the centre of the ward was where their beds were situated.

Later, as nurse in charge of Ward 13 on night duty, I was responsible to Mr Dott for his patients. He would always pay a visit late at night to check on his patients for the first few nights following their operations. He was always kind, gentle of manner and unassuming.

Beneath the cloak of that gentle young man with the unassuming manner, there brooded the far-sighted planner pressing forward to his goal. Understandably it was not long before, helpful as Professor Wilkie was, the small theatre and the beds, screened off in the middle of the ward, failed to satisfy Dott. Soon, he was again producing those succinct but readable memoranda about surgical neurology, which capture the imagination and outline the defects of the system under which it was then worked. They are scattered amongst his colleagues who were helpful and undoubtedly anxious to see a properly constituted neurosurgical service for their patients in the Royal Infirmary. Dott felt added confidence because of the backing of the Society of British Neurological Surgeons which was steadily gaining in strength. Again he approached the Rockefeller Trust and this time he obtained substantial aid to develop his team. Emboldened too, Norman Dott called on Sir Alexander Grant Bt of Glenmoriston to elaborate on the memorandum which he had already sent. From the letter received by Dott on the day after this interview we can only assume that there was mutual recognition of worth between the practical Scottish Industrialist from the famed McVitie and Price Biscuit Company and the Scottish surgeon with his vision and carefully detailed plans.

As a 'down to earth' Scotsman, Sir Alexander wrote on 9 June 1936, not from his impressive estate, but from the St Andrew Biscuit Works Edinburgh. His letter with its decision to assist Dott financially, his wry suggestion of reluctance overcome, and his final placing of the whole matter in Dott's hands surely underlines an understanding and trust which had developed between these two Scotsmen.

> With reference to your letter of 3rd inst in which you state that you require £5000 to complete and equip a suitable department in Edinburgh for the surgical treatment of diseases of the brain, spinal cord and nerves. I now write to confirm having told you at our meeting last evening that I would give £5000 over a period of seven years to the Royal Infirmary of Edinburgh to expend on a Department for this new work of yours. As I explained to you I am really not in a position to give the full amount all at once and, frankly, I would not have been willing to have parted with it for any other object, but the scheme you explained to me appeals so much, I cannot help it, even although I have to go into debt. If the Infirmary Authorities accept my offer, I leave it in your hands to send me the Bond of Annuity for signature. With my kinds regards and all good wishes, I am yours sincerely.

It was sad that Sir Alexander died before the new department was completed. Patients were first admitted in October 1938, and, fittingly, Lady Grant performed the official opening ceremony on 16 March 1939. Even today, as you reach the top step of your climb through the Infirmary and push open the swing door to enter Ward 20, your first sight on the wall opposite is a plaque commemorating Sir Alexander's generosity and the opening of the Department by his widow. Catford, in his *The Royal Infirmary of Edinburgh*, also reminds us that others, no less willing, supported the project and even Dott and his friends contributed £600.[17] Thus by October 1938 the Department of Surgical Neurology at the Royal Infirmary of Edinburgh was caring for patients afflicted with disease or injury of the brain and spinal cord amenable to surgical therapy. But it was Ward 20; and as Ward 20, Dott's Ward or even 'Dott's Workshop' it was known and gained recognition and affection. It was in Ward 20 that Dott pursued the major part of his established surgical career and from which his prowess gained him widespread renown and numerous honours.

Ask colleagues, trainees, staff or former patients for their recollections of Dott over half a century later and it is, in the main, of Ward 20 that the images come flooding back from all quarters of the globe. Memories are of the slight figure, usually in a grey suit and belted dun coloured raincoat, walking with a limp. The first warning of the Chief's arrival is the long bonnet of the Alvis, later the Bentley, nosing into the forecourt of the Royal Infirmary. Someone, even if not a deliberately posted 'watch-dog', warns so that last minute tasks are completed and patient data assembled for any ward round. The lift door scrapes open; ascent by lift and not the long main stairway is his only late and grudgingly conceded allowance for his lame leg, Dott steps out. He leaves his mackintosh in the cupboard at the foot of the spiral stone staircase leading to the turret. If he is needed in the ward he will go straight in and will respond to such a call at any time of day or night. If the need is not immediate he will grasp his attaché case and a little awkwardly mount the old worn spiral steps to his room under the turret, there to absorb himself in deskwork, undeterred by the ancient clanking of the clock mechanism just above his busy head. Thus symbolically the instigator and pilot of the whole affair bends to his tasks beneath that familiar clock face, which is so reassuring to the citizens of Edinburgh as it lends living and timely emphasis to the welcoming mottoes emblazoned below: *Patet Omnibus, I was sick and ye visited me, I was a stranger and ye took me in.* Symbolically too he could look across at his old school Heriot's. Equally by a reverse glance, if the lights of Ward 20's operating theatre were on, any Herioter or passing Edinburgh citizen could deduce that, under Dott's tireless guidance, someone was being given vital succour from a head injury or similar condition.

It is of operations, ward rounds, distinguished visiting surgeons, anxious newly qualified residents, courageous or rowdy patients, events amusing or sad, all in 'Ward 20', that memories are sent. But Dott had struggled hard before, as he put it in his own words, 'The Royal Infirmary made room for us and encouraged us to follow the ladies of doubtful virtue into exalted Ward 20.' For Ward 20 had been the Female Venereal Diseases Ward. 'The City Fathers even countenanced an alteration in the Edinburgh skyline there.' He was here referring to the small wings which were added to each side of the central tower without materially altering the imposing façade of the Royal Infirmary. Once again the picture is of Dott stamping round these dust-ridden areas, with his notebook, devising his plans long before the Royal Infirmary invited him to follow upstairs the night-strutting strumpets of Auld Reekie.

On a more serious note he wrote to Cushing in December 1936,

> This year I have been lucky in getting some Rockefeller help to keep the good team together and also in getting local professional and financial support for a new department at the Infirmary. The plans are all through and construction in the Infirmary begins early in the New Year. It will give us 22 beds, good outpatient facilities, a good operating suite, clinical laboratory next to the operating room for acute observations, artists' and photographic room and reasonable comfort and facilities for the medical and nursing staffs. Best of all we have got through plans for the accommodation of private patients so that I think I am about to realise my ambition to settle down to work in one place with a good team and with decent facilities for scientific aspects of work. This did seem pretty impossible for a long time but Sir David Wilkie has been very helpful throughout and recently it has been great fun working the various elements into it.

His reference to private patients is interesting and cannot be judged by present day standards with the possibility of full time commitment to salaried National Health Service employment. In 1936 a surgeon's income came largely from private practice and although Dott would always acknowledge the benefit of such independence from an employing authority his main concern was that he be allowed to care for private patients, an established necessity, and hospital patients in one place, to the very best of his ability, without the distracting and harmful need to move himself and his specialised equipment from place to place. There was considerable resistance to the idea of provision for private practice in the Infirmary. Nonetheless Dott stood out for his aim, 'to settle down to work in one place' and who could deny that his work with private patients and in private nursing homes had not materially contributed to the development of this Department in the Royal Infirmary? He fought, he accepted delay but eventually won his point and started work in one place in October 1938.

'Great fun working the various elements into it,' as Dott wrote to Cushing, might be seen as ironic understatement from other standpoints. From contact with Professor Dott as he brought his second and ultimate Department of Surgical Neurology to fruition in the years leading up to 1960, members of his staff will have no doubt that this phrase meant that he had planned everything accurately down to the smallest detail and seen that his requirements were carried out. 'We are going in for an air-conditioning plant and also a system of lighting from a reflector-vaulted roof,' he wrote in a subsequent letter to Cushing, who replied with interest, 'I don't know of any other surgical plant that has been air conditioned, and I trust it will lower your incidence of infection.'

The 'reflector-vaulted roof' was culled fro m France. Had he gleaned the idea when he visited Paris so enjoyably in 1926 with that other Cushing trainee, Percival Bailey and Mrs Bailey? Mr Moffat, an Edinburgh old age pensioner in 1988, gives a better and more human description of this exalted fitting than many an expert might.

> Part of the building under the clock had been damaged by fire so they renovated it into an operating theatre for Professor Dott. Another worker and I were sent to do some cement work. There were also two men putting up a silver coloured dome hanging from the ceiling. I asked them what it was for and they explained that when Professor Dott operated on his patients he would not cast a shadow. There was a panel on the wall with a switch and when it was switched on, a beam of light struck the dome and shone down on the operating table. When I had been working there a couple of days, a gentleman came in and was looking around the place. He asked us how we were getting on and shook hands with us. He also did a lot of talking to the two Frenchmen about the dome as they were erecting it. Later on that day we were surprised to learn that the gentleman was none other than Professor Dott himself. He was a very nice man and made us feel at home.[18]

Workers with cement and high-tech medical engineers—Dott made no distinction. Never haughty to the humble nor humble to the haughty, he was remembered by all men alike. Leap ahead to the year of his retirement and a greetings telegram dated 4 October 1962 tells how these attitudes persisted and what warmth they enngendered. 'Sincerest respects and good wishes for a long and happy retirement. God bless you, sir. From the porters and the technicians, ground floor, Department of Surgical Neurology, Western General Hospital.'

Before Norman Dott, now established in Ward 20 leads us on to his next goal, glance again at the 1936 letter in which he so enthusiastically reports his plans to Cushing. It opens by wishing his old Chief well for 1937-8 but can barely contain the next paragraph, 'Here is a portrait of the most

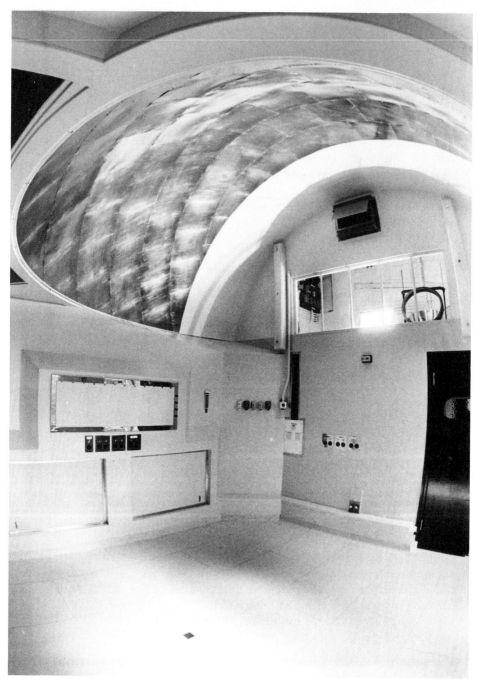

44 Ward 20 Theatre showing 'silver coloured' reflector vaulted roof for shadowless lighting of operation field. Courtesy of Lothian Health Board News and Capital Photography.

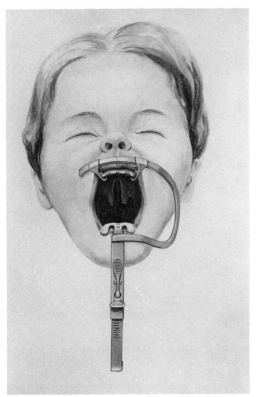

45 'I brought one home with me from Boston . . . and had a smaller, lighter one made, with modifications.' Dott's modified Davis Gag used in cleft palate surgery and still bearing his name.

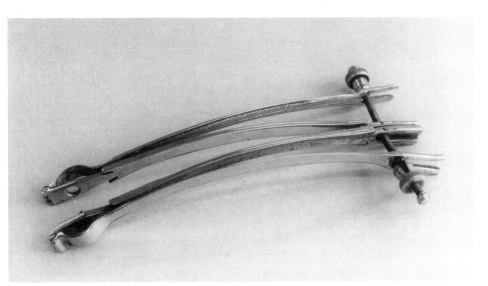

46 'A new aseptic method of Intestinal Anastomosis.' The spring clamps which Dott designed to this end.

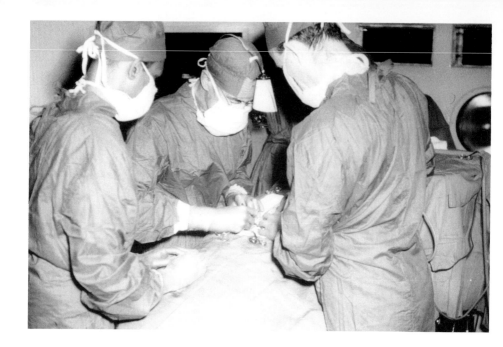

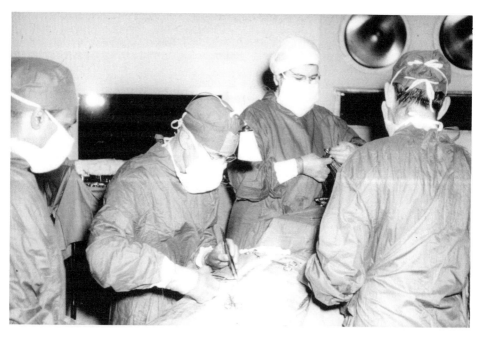

47 and 48   'I can get a more ideal clinic going . . . then quietly transfer all the work there'.
'He usually conducted the whole affair from skin preparation to the last stitch himself.'
Dott makes the first skin incision (above) and inserts the last skin stitch (below) during the first operation, 13 May 1960, in the new Department of Surgical Neurology at the Western General Hospital. His assistants came from all parts of the globe. Despite the sophisticated wall lighting to be seen above the assistants' heads, Dott prefers the trusted old headlamp!

important person in our establishment at the age of three. What do you think of her?' The portrait is obviously of his daughter Jean. His wife Peggy and the various members of his household, whom Cushing has met, are remembered to him before he goes on to discuss in detail some of his work on pituitary function and pathology. His plans are described as already recorded and finally with an apology for the length of his letter, he ends, 'Let me conclude by acknowledging that whatever good may come of my schemes here I owe it to you.'

Lady Grant opened the Department of Surgical Neurology in March 1939 but in September 1939 the war was upon the country. The place that Edinburgh would play in it was unknown. Dott had now moved into the sphere of 'elder statesman' of surgical neurology. His father, we know, abhorred war. Norman himself had been anxious to serve in the first war but had been prevented by his lameness. Maturity blended with this experience and the experiences of medical student colleagues, returning to resume their studies after periods in the trenches or at sea, appears to have instilled in him the futility of war. But, if war were not avoidable, he had also assumed a very personal responsibility to provide the highest standards of specialist care to those injured, particularly if their injuries were received in the course of battle.

In 1926 Dott had been a founder member of the Society of British Neurological Surgeons. From 1927 he was listed as the Honorary Assistant Secretary and Librarian. The secretary was Mr (later Sir Geoffrey) Jefferson. It is little surprise that correspondence and a genial liaison sprang up between these two surgeons dedicated to the highest standards of Surgical Neurology. This was cemented by letters and meetings in London, Manchester and Edinburgh and subsequently, in the course of a life-long friendship, in other parts of the United Kingdom and the globe. They have peace in mind when Dott writes to Jefferson on 31 January 1939. They are discussing the possible foundation of a European Society of Neurological Surgeons. Although there is hesitation, in view of the troubled times, Dott ponders:

> I am not sure but what a European Society of Neurological Surgons is more urgently desirable now than in more normal times. I suppose the only thing likely to avert the catastrophe of war, in the long run, is a degree of mutual respect and trust between the peoples of different nations and I should suppose that science generally and medicine in particular constitutes one of the best international bridging systems. Possibly we should not lose the opportunity to do what we can in that direction. No doubt in the present international situation, it would be a very small matter but it would be always telling in the right direction. I should incline to do our bit by showing rather exceptional friendship in medical matters to those whose national policies we find so disagreeable at present.

However the war was looming inexorably and they are concerned about neurosurgical services should it break out. Dott writes to Jefferson:

> It might be a good thing if our society collaborated with the British Medical Association in their attempt to obtain a survey of the available medical profession in case of national emergency. I think it would be rather important for the authorities to know where those with neurosurgical experience are, what their teams consist in etc. Neurosurgery would be quite important in case of war and I should think the proper distribution and the proper holding together of trained teams would fall to be considered.

They approach the British Medical Association and the deputy secretary Doctor Charles Hill, later Lord Hill and famed as the war time 'Radio Doctor', writes back:

> Dear Mr Dott, thank you very much for your letter of September 30th 1938. In the breathing space, which follows the emergency (The Munich crisis had just been resolved) we are reviewing the whole of the arrangements for the allocation of personnel in the event of war and any help you can give us in regard to those surgeons, with special knowledge and experience of brain surgery would be most helpful.

Dott and Jefferson, presumably with some amusement, decide that even their privileged positions as deputy secretary and secretary of the Society of British Neurological Surgeons do not entitle them to comment on the competence of the surgeons concerned. The best they can do at present is to send the Society's booklet with the names and appointments of members. This they do.

In this way Dott, while consolidating his own services in Edinburgh, was taking an increasingly active part in the overall direction of neurosurgical services. A 'Brain Injuries Committee' was set up under the auspices of the Medical Research Council. The minutes of its first meeting at the London School of Hygiene and Tropical Medicine on 7 March 1940 show that the eminence of its members was going to exert great authority in matters concerned with injuries of the central nervous system. Professor E D (later Lord) Adrian was in the chair, Professor (later Brigadier) Hugh Cairns, Mr Norman Dott, Dr J G Greenfield, Professor (later Sir Geoffrey) Jefferson, Dr A Lewes, Dr (later Brigadier) George Riddoch, Group Captain C P (later Sir Charles) Symonds, Dr E A Carmichael, were members; Sir Edward Mellanby also attended. Thus every aspect of such injuries would receive expert attention, and advice and recommendations would be transmitted to both civilian and service authorities.

Dott attended the meetings of this committee assiduously and is very much to the fore in formulating the committee's recommendations for treatment and overall management of head injuries. In this he had confidence stemming from his well planned department in Edinburgh, already running efficiently and with emphasis, not only on the operative care of the acute head injury, but also on rehabilitation and the study of the effects of varying brain injuries. He was always to give credit to a further generous Rockefeller grant which enabled him to keep together his team of enthusiasts, who not only treated the head injuries but studied extensively the varying more subtle aspects of brain injury such as speech defects, personality disorders, visual defects and epilepsy. With some amusement he used to relate that news of the Rockefeller grant arrived on the same day as President Roosevelt announced the rather more major 'Lend Lease' Agreement.

Dott's Edinburgh Unit was working efficiently but as a precaution against air raids it had been moved to an emergency hutted hospital at Bangour 15 miles west of Edinburgh with only a relative foothold retained in Ward 20. All the operating was carried out in emergency theatres at Bangour and great emphasis was placed on rehabilitation, especially of service cases. Dott received official recognition which helped in organisation of services. In September 1941 he wrote to Geoffrey Jefferson, 'Our centre in Edinburgh is working much better since they have made me Consultant in Neurosurgery to the Army in Scotland and Consultant Neurosurgeon to the Emergency Medical Service.' Copies of letters from Dott to appropriate authorities encouraging early direct admission of Naval, Army, Air Force and civilian head injuries to this unit reflect his sage and enthusiastic planning. A letter from the Department of Health for Scotland approves his staffing which allowed for two surgical teams, for Mr G L Alexander who had been working with him since 1931, had been appointed assistant neurosurgeon in 1937. One of these was to be mobile based in the vulnerable Royal Infirmary. Among those listed and indicating the disciplines covered are D K Henderson psychiatry; G Maxwell Brown, anaesthetist; Elizabeth Batters, junior anaesthetist; Kate Hermann, neurologist; O L Zangwill, psychologist; C A Beevers, physicist; W Blackwood, neuropathologist.

With such a staff working with him Dott was enabled to read a paper 'The Importance of Psychiatric and Psychologic Assessment in the Management and Disposal of Organic Brain Damage' to the summer meeting of the Society of British Neurological Surgeons in London on 1 August 1942. In this paper he describes his very active unit in the following words:

> The Rockefeller Foundation, the University of Edinburgh, the Department of Health for Scotland and the Royal Infirmary Edinburgh collaborated to constitute the Brain Injuries Unit in Edinburgh. We deal with about a thousand cases yearly, five hundred from the armed forces and five hundred civilians. Two thirds are mechanical injuries of the brain, one third are cases of injury to the brain by disease.

For his work in setting up the Brain Injuries Unit and his wartime neuro-surgical service Dott was in 1948 awarded the CBE. If in the light of this subsequent award, you picture him as now being more the senior administrator, withdrawing from day-to-day contact with patients, you are soon disabused by reading the numerous letters, with memories of Bangour days, which poured in to the authors of this biography in 1988. They are hard to put down and they all tell of personal care and kindness remembered over forty years and more. Sister Cheyne recalls:

> During the war he operated on all the services but he insisted on his usual civilian lists as well. Operations lasted anything from two to eight hours. Time meant nothing to him. A glass of milk was his sustenance, when possible, given to him by theatre orderlies. He was such a wonderful man, but a very hard disciplinarian. His hand work was precise, his expectations from his team were of the highest. I had been his staff nurse in Ward 20 and wanted to join the Royal Navy. He sent for me and told me, 'That would be a waste.' I agreed to go to Bangour as a theatre sister on his staff. With his cold blue eyes staring at you, you could not say no!

The words of so many former staff clamour to be heard.

> Nothing was any trouble to Mr Dott, for staff and patients alike; he was a perfect gentleman. His 'thank you' to all concerned at the end of many long operations was greatly appreciated . . . One had to marvel at his kindly approach to so many young war-wounded lads . . . My training was early enhanced and my character indebted . . . I was a very junior member of his staff, but he never entered a room where a nurse was 'specialling' without first courteously greeting the nurse.

He also operated on German prisoners if necessary. A nursing auxiliary of those days still remembers:

> One operation that did cause a sensation was on a German prisoner who had a bullet removed from near the brain. Mr Dott called us all into the side ward, when he removed the bandages to reveal the naked brain.

If his staff remembered his involvement how much more did his patients and their relatives.

> My father was a captain in the Royal Engineers and developed a tumour of the brain. Unfortunately the operation was not a success. After five hours in the theatre and after completing his ward round, Dott, though obviously very tired, kindly explained things to my mother and then drove her home. Transport was difficult in those days and Bangour was fifteen miles from Edinburgh. So very weary himself, he still had thought for another in her distress.

So writes one on behalf of her 80-year-old mother who still cherishes the act of kindness.

Nobby Clarke had sustained a bad head wound in the desert.

> He was a really wonderful person. In addition to operations, he always seemed to be in attendance at the bedside. I, like many others, was having injections every four hours day and night, and although there was a nurse present, Mr Dott always appeared to be there doing the injection. He usually addressed his patients by their first or nickname. As a Clarke I always got 'Nobby'. He created a wonderful atmosphere in the wards. Among the nurses and patients, he was always referred to as Norman.

And another warm tribute:

> My husband Alf was wounded in the back in the Normandy D-Day landings, resulting in paraplegia. Kindness is the main thing Alf thinks of when remembering Mr Dott. He encouraged Alf in every way. After all, being a paraplegic at 19 in those days was like a death sentence. One day he said to Alf that I would be marrying a rich man with all the penicillin he had put in his back. Penicillin at that time was scarce and only used for war-wounded!

Let a 23-year-old soldier, who had been a bank clerk in civilian life, conclude these war time recollections:

> I was suffering from facial paralysis as a result of a crushed skull as well as other injuries and was finally discharged from the Army in 1945. On one of his Sunday evening ward rounds, Dott asked me about my job and whether I felt that I could cope with the work, after a few months' convalescence, and then, 'If you ever find it too much for you and you can't cope, come to see me and I'll see what I can do to find something to suit you.' (Writing in 1988 this same soldier is anxious in case we confine ourselves to Dott's technical triumphs and fail to illuminate, 'The man behind the scalpel and his great human qualities.') I hope you can imagine the effect that kindly word had on me; I was twenty-three and having always been fit, was finding it hard to accept my physical and mental limitations, but this gave me a safety net and I felt I could face the future with more confidence. I have never forgotten his kindness and the way in which he made even his services patients feel that he had a personal interest in them.

By the time the war comes to an end Dott has well merited his ensuing award of Commander of the Order of the British Empire for planning and organisation of the Brain Injuries Unit of which he was Director. He had also not spared himself in his care and compassion for his patients whatever their country, creed or station in life. What did Dott himself take from these wartime experiences? Undoubtedly he learned much from each case treated, and would be the first to point this out. This stood him in good stead with his later civilian patients and led him to be consulted internationally, especially if there were a sensitive political background to the injured. Stood him in good stead too when he had to turn his mind to the mounting toll of head injuries from road traffic accidents in the post-war period. Perhaps too his close involvement with young men and women shattered by injury to the central nervous system and with lives and very hopes disrupted, caused him to lay increased emphasis on rehabilitation. Never had he suggested that his task was completed when the wound was closed, but now, with peace, he increasingly encouraged the practice and teaching of physiotherapy, speech therapy, occupational therapy and all the skills of adequate rehabilitation.

Mr Frank Galloway formerly Sergeant Galloway confirms this,

> After completing my primary and advanced training in the Rifle Brigade, I was sent to the Army School of Physical Training and Remedial Training. On completion of these courses, I was posted to Bangour Hospital to work under Mr Dott My duties were to assist in the rehabilitation of army and civilian personnel suffering from injuries and diseases of the brain and spinal cord. I worked under Mr Dott for a period of four years 1942-45 and got to know him very well. During those years, I attended his staff meetings every Monday morning and he visited the gymnasium every Wednesday morning to watch, assess and discuss the progress of his patients. My memories of Mr Dott are those of an exceptional human being and doctor. He showed great interest and patience in his patients and staff. He had that rare ability to make one feel an important member of the team and engendered a true team spirit.[19]

The esteem is mutual and Dott gives Sergeant Galloway a glowing testimonial at the end of his period of service at Bangour. Perhaps more telling though are the letters they exchange. In 1948 Mr Galloway writes to Professor Dott to congratulate him on the award of CBE and receives the following reply from the Private Patients' Home, Manchester Royal Infirmary, where Dott has been having his painful hip fused.

> Dear Sgt Galloway (I can't think of you otherwise) thank you very much for your kind letter of congratulation. I am very pleased and more especially for my excellent staff, whose splendid endeavour and achievement is recognised in this way. You certainly have your part in this, in the good work and high morale you put into our unit. I used rather to envy you your light springy step at Bangour for I was then troubled by my hip and would have had it fixed earlier but for the war and the difficult period after it. Now I have had it fixed solid and am up on crutches in plaster from ankle to chest. Still I swing through in the proper style and make fair speed.

Dott is obviously referring to physiotherapy exercises in which he will have seen Galloway instructing.

With peace the emphasis passes from Bangour back to Ward 20 in the Royal Infirmary. The title Brain Injuries Unit lapses, the National Health Service is introduced and Dott takes up or continues his peace time work in the Department of Surgical Neurology. Rôles are reversed and now patients are prepared for operation and convalesce in Bangour, while operating, emergency and acute care all take place in Ward 20.

However the Department of Surgical Neurology did not sever its connection with Bangour Hospital until that Sunday morning in 1960 when the 'military' convoy of ambulances took the last patients to the newly opened Department at the Western General Hospital in Edinburgh. Many of the staff from Bangour took up new duties there too. Bangour will always be part of the history of surgical neurology in Edinburgh. A great deal of fine surgery and hard work was achieved there in those war and early post-war years. Each one who worked there will carry away particular memories, some sad and some amusing. There was the young Cypriot boy shot in the back and rendered paraplegic during the troubles in his island home and flown specially to Edinburgh to be under Dott's care. There was the old car which Dott had organised so that his resident could travel swiftly from his cases in T Block down the hill to Ward 32 in the event of need, for Bangour was a scattered emergency hospital on the Lothian hillside. There was the overseas resident who partly mastered this form of transport, sometimes in reverse but never higher than first gear before he ran it into the side of a ward. Perhaps the most well-known and even most characteristic story was of the resident, weary from long hours of very active duty, who went into the telephone kiosk to take Dott's not unaccustomed, late night call with detailed enquiries about each patient. It was only next morning when sister sought him out to start the fresh day's work that she found him in the kiosk propped against the instrument, still asleep!

With peace, too, Dott was able to turn to his ultimate goal, a separate clinic with all the facilities for the practice, advancement, and teaching of surgical neurology. His claims for such a department, founded upon his own reputation, were enhanced by the steadily increasing number of neurosurgical patients, brought about by the war time advances in the specialty, and the mounting toll of the road traffic accidents.

It was decided to continue treating patients with accidental injuries to the head and spine in Ward 20 and to treat other neurosurgical conditions, both elective and emergency, in a new unit, which was to be sited in the grounds of the Western General Hospital Edinburgh. Despite these changes, despite the seductive glamour of the latest equipment and unrivalled operating theatres, in the new department, neurosurgery in Ward 20 at the Royal Infirmary, of the ever open doors, neither halted nor slowed. Emergency care was offered to a wider range of head and spinal injuries. It was possible to study them in greater depth and advance to new methods of treatment. No longer was Ward 20's small theatre overstretched, with long elective cases postponed, at the last minute, because of the arrival of an urgent head injury. For twenty-four hours of the day and seven days of the week a surgical team was available to deal with the tragic harvest of injuries from home, industry and the roads, where those sinister reapers of the twentieth century the motor bike and car, propelled by their frenzied drivers, were hard at work. Rewarding results there were, but devastating and multiple injuries seemed to preponderate in this senseless slaughter. Some injuries were so bad or the effects so swiftly progressive that it was wiser for a trained Ward 20 surgeon to travel to the hospital of initial admission and operate there. A telephone call, a brief description of the injuries, by the surgeon at the outlying hospital, and Ward 20's registrar would be on his way.

One tragic night such a call was responded to by Bob Howatt. Bob, that tall loose-limbed Australian whose demeanour smacked more of the cricket field than the operating theatre, conscientious and hard working but unencumbered by the rigidities of the old country, a most genial and relaxed colleague. His old car took him with all speed to Dunfermline, where he operated through the night. Skilfully his unexpectedly gentle hands dealt with damaged brain and daunting haemorrhage and dawn was not far off when the last stitches were placed and the dressings applied. We know little of the return journey but deductions are all too sadly clear. It was a straight length of road. 'Do what I could, his headlights came unswervingly at me, on the wrong side of the road,' said the sorrowful lorry driver. There could be no doubt that Bob, utterly exhausted by his life-saving efforts, had fallen asleep at the wheel. It was unbearably poignant an hour or two later, when Bob's sister, with whom he lived, tears stemmed only by Aussie pride, reached gently out and removed the ignition key from the wreckage of her brother's unlit pyre. Thus with a devoted hand she seemed to consign to unknown realms the driving spirit of a beloved brother, a well liked colleague, and a most promising neurosurgeon.

Many times his patients had brought Dott face to face with death. He had seen elderly colleagues, his anaesthetist Maxwell Brown among them, lay down the baton, after a long and arduous course. But this was a new experience, not a young man who had faltered and chosen an easier route but a young man, of the greatest promise, who had been cut off, with devastating suddenness in mid course, while offering succour to others.

Naturally he took it personally as he led the stunned neurosurgical staff out of the brief memorial mass and back to that work, which to many was a more understandable memorial tribute to their colleague. Not unexpectedly he acted; and said little. He would not deprive patients of this service, which he had initiated, but never again was a registrar to drive himself on such a mission. The Hospital Board and the police responded to his insistent demands generously with contract car or high speed vehicle. Many a Ward 20 registrar, with hair still standing on end was to stutter an appreciation of the police driving skills after he, accompanied by scrub nurse and instrument drums, had been swept at breakneck speed and with lights flashing and sirens blaring through the Lothians or Borders on such an errand.

In this and other ways, Dott commanded and directed his service. With passing years he no longer undertook the long and arduous operations on head injuries frequently necessary at unplanned hours. Nevertheless he was always available for help.

One morning two young physiotherapists set out by car for their duties in Bangour Hospital. The cheer and noisy chatter as they reached the outskirts of Edinburgh are so easy to imagine. Suddenly they glimpsed two colleagues at a bus stop, about to make the same journey. Impetuous youthful generosity stamped on the brakes to offer a lift but did not look in the mirror. There was a rending crash from the vehicle behind, inflicting the most awful injuries on these two young girls. They were rushed to the Royal Infirmary and examined by the Ward 20 duty surgeon. Operation was futile; he could offer no hope. The parents, hastily summoned were distraught and unbelieving. Dott was told of the tragedy and immediately saw his rôle. He hastened to examine the young patients. His skill made him look unhurried and he spared no detail. He agreed, the outlook was grim beyond doubt; no treatment was of avail. He took the parents aside. With heartfelt sympathy he explained the situation. Their grief was no whit lessened but their anxious doubts were quelled. Those adored daughters, who had left home so full of cheerful anticipation a mere hour or two previously had, at least, had the care and concern of Dott, the best in the land.

But the whole Department of Surgical Neurology was to remain undivided under Dott's direction and encompassed both sites, with many of the staff undertaking duties at each. In this post-war period Mr G L Alexander left to take charge of the neurosurgical department at Bristol and Professor Dott was joined by Mr F J Gillingham, after his war time service as a neurosurgical specialist in the army. It was Mr Gillingham, who subsequently, when Dott retired, succeeded him in the chair of surgical neurology and in charge of the department. Mr P Harris, who had trained with Professor Dott, was also appointed as consultant neurosurgeon. Undoubtedly these two relieved Dott of some of the burden of arrangements for the new department but there was little that was not initiated and delegated by Dott. To quote again from Catford's excellent *The Royal Infirmary of Edinburgh 1929-1979*, simply increases consciousness that this bare statement of fact covers limitless effort and an immense amount of painstaking work by Professor Dott and Mr Holt, ably assisted by the two surgeons just mentioned and by others in their specialist fields.

Building at a cost of £500,000, a fully equipped surgical neurology block
which was opened by the Secretary of State for Scotland, the Rt Hon J S
Maclay (later Viscount Muirshiel) on 1st July 1960. It had been designed by
the Regional Hospital Board Architect Mr John Holt and his staff to meet the
exacting requirements of Professor Dott and his colleagues.

Exacting requirements they were. Who but Professor Dott could have
been expected to put his mind to the design of the most advanced operating
theatre suite, with its filtered, temperature-regulated air currents, its focus-
able shadowless ceiling lighting, its specially designed operating tables, its
facilities for X-rays and brain wave recordings during operation, and
ranged his attention down from these complexities to ward waste disposal?
The operating tables were made to his specifications, each surgical instrument was carefully checked. The most sophisticated neuro-radiological
services were installed. Physiotherapy and occupational therapy departments were carefully designed. Ward layout and nursing facilities were
discussed and planned. The residents' accommodation and facilities for their
refreshment and scanty recreation were secured. All bore the imprint of
Dott's impeccable attention. Registrars and residents from those days will
recall Dott expecting them to be familiar with the plans and layout of the
new department when the steel girders were barely rising from the foundations, so that they could show visitors round. They will recall the hordes of
visitors, from all corners of the globe, who used to descend to visit Dott's
wonderful new department and hopefully see him operate. They will
remember having to research and report in detail, for Dott's consideration,
such matters as staff paging and haemoglobin testing in the ward. Truly no
one would dispute Dott when he says, 'I consider that this is the best unit for
inpatient care in elective surgical neurology in existence at the present time.'
However with characteristic honesty and modesty in the words already
quoted he goes on: 'It will not be so for long; others will soon emulate and
surpass, but it is a step forward.'

And yet the department still stands and by the quality of its work remains
a testimony to the vision and achievement of Professor Norman McOmish
Dott. It was with the opening of this new department that his career reached
its zenith. If you bring forward the honours that were heaped upon him, the
patients he succoured, and the distinguished lectures he delivered, after this
date, as argument to the contrary, it still must be said that this was the zenith
of a planner, who could see the larger vision and yet to whom no detail was
too small to receive all his attention.

No detail was too small for this extraordinary man who planned his
whole life with care; fishing, travel, work . . . pipe lighter! Among his
papers we find a billet notifying him of a meeting of The Scottish Society
of the History of Medicine in Inverness before which Dott has arranged to
meet a member at 6.30 p.m. On the back is pencilled in his handwriting,

'Leave Edinburgh 1.00=5 hrs=160 miles at 32 m.p.h.+30 mins: break: Leave Inverness 2.30—arr. Edinburgh 8.0 p.m. i.e. 5 hrs driving at 32 m.p.h.+ 30 min. break.' Precise planning, except that in practice he would not have held the Bentley to 32 mph all the way there and back. Word has it that in Bangour days only an inexperienced officer would have held up the familiar speeding Bentley on that stretch of road and risked delaying the small figure on his missions of mercy between the two hospitals. More experienced police turned the other way and uttered a prayer for both patient and surgeon!

Most men, if their pipe lighter fails to function, turn it in with irritable comment to the appropriate expert for repair. Not so Dott. Mr Charles Gillespie sends a copy of a letter he received twenty-five years ago from Professor Norman Dott and headed 'Ronson Gas Lighter'.

> This lighter is used for pipe. It gets tarry. I clean it from time to time with nail brush and soft brass wire brush. I dare say the joints get a bit sticky, which may interfere with secure closure by returning spring. I have had trouble from this recently—incomplete closure and undue loss of gas. I think it might be cured by a stronger returning spring? I presume the spring gradually weakens from much use?—and may need occasional renewal?

From the pen of Dott himself, then, perhaps the best available comment on Dott the planner!

CHAPTER TEN

With Missionary Zeal

And for some their daily work is their prayer
(*Ecclesiasticus*)
So far as I know, this is the first occasion upon which the question of the
treatment of a leaking aneurysm by direct exposure has been brought before
a medical society, at any rate in this country.

(*Bramwell*) [1]

'I have given up neurosurgery and returned to my first love, general
surgery,' wrote Norman Dott to an American colleague just a year before
his death. He went on to describe the resection he had recently undergone
for carcinoma of the lower bowel and how he had set up a stoma clinic to
help those with colostomies like himself. Nine months before his death he
wrote a comforting letter to a young woman who had been attending this
clinic. Overcoming, with his help, many of the trials of ulcerative colitis, she
had triumphantly given birth to a daughter only to be dashed by the
discovery of a congenital dislocation of the hip in the hard won infant. Dott
writes:

> I was pleased to hear from you. My warmest congratulations on your splendid
> achievement, not forgetting your husband! What is her name to be? I hope
> you are liking your new home and have got over the settling in. I do not think
> you need worry about the baby's hip. When this is spotted at birth and treated
> by splintage, they grow up with no defect whatever. I do not think splintage
> troubles a small baby—I suppose they just take it for one of the facts of life.
> In my young days I was surgeon to the Sick Children's Hospital in Edinburgh
> so I know.

Such are the words that encompass a remarkable career; the confident
opinion, the kindliness; paediatric surgeon, general surgeon, neurosurgeon,
a surgeon for fifty-four years. Even more, because a year before he qualified
in 1919, he had as a student, performed a laparotomy to massage the heart
for cardiac arrest, believed to be the first such procedure in Edinburgh.

Who is entitled to assess such a life or even to claim an unbiased description? The aristocracy of the surgical world recall organisational achievements, fellowships and memberships, honours bestowed, prestigious lectures given; medical academics note advances made, scientific papers published. Practical surgeons give weight to techniques and therapeutic results; trainees may be accused of unjustified loyalty and not giving sufficient credit to other schools. Patients are untutored, some live simple lives, their opinions may be uncritical, but they and they alone have the intimate experience of pain relieved, and disability overcome. On occasion, they seem to understand just how closely they have faced death—though this is usually better judged by the surgeon himself and is one of the responsibilities and ironies of neurosurgical practice. The patient may dismiss a subsiding though moderately severe headache (of a type which the neurosurgeon has identified as stemming from a life-threatening intracranial haemorrhage) and resist the proffered operation. During such an operation, despite the greatest care, brisk haemorrhage or alarming brain stem dysfunction may have caused the greatest concern before being rectified by the use of every skill the surgeon could bring to bear. It is not unknown, on the subsequent ward round, for the exhausted surgeon to be greeted by a cheerful patient who firmly believes he has just undergone a relatively minor intervention.

A wise judge will call on all available opinions for a true and just picture of Dott the surgeon. That eminent doctor Lord Cohen of Birkenhead wrote, 'For to be quite frank your massive contribution to neurology, (I use this noun advisedly in place of neurosurgery) has been inadequately rewarded.' Sir Herbert Seddon, whose own reputation in the fields of orthopaedics and injuries and diseases of the peripheral nerves was second to none, utters equal praise in a context of concern that Professor Dott is needing yet another operation on his hip. 'He is one of our greatest surgeons and we cannot afford to have him laid up.' Sir Hugh Cairns, the neurosurgeon, writing at the same time when Dott himself is a patient, is trying to organise 'A Festival of Britain Surgical Symposium'. The British Medical Association was joining with the Royal Society of Medicine to put on international display the achievements of British doctors at the same time as British Industry was advertising its post war recovery in the Festival of Britain. Cairns writes: 'It was planned that Norman should do the Surgery of Cerebral Aneurysms because undoubtedly the preliminary pioneer work in this field was done in Edinburgh.'

If you turn to the *Bulletin of the World Federation of Neurosurgical Societies* Vol I No I published in May 1963, under a heading 'Page of Tribute' and associated with photographs of Professor Norman Dott and his 'Utopian' operating theatre, you read this paragraph: 'It appears fitting in this and future bulletins to pay tribute to a neurological surgeon universally respected and admired throughout the world. In this first issue Professor

Norman M Dott of Edinburgh has been chosen by your Editorial Board'. A great honour to lead the field in this way and the subsequent paragraphs, describing his achievements, give ample backing to this selection.

In 1968, accompanied by Mrs Dott, he was guest of honour at the Congress of Neurological Surgeons meeting in Toronto. This entailed the delivery of an inimitable series of lectures stemming from his long experience. They were subsequently published in *Clinical Neurosurgery*.[2] He returned to Canada in 1973 for the Honorary Fellowship of the Royal College of Physicians and Surgeons of Canada to be conferred upon him. The citation delivered on this occasion by the famous Canadian neurosurgeon Dr Harry Botterell sums up Dott's merits so succinctly and well that it merits quotation in full.

> The first Professor of Neurological Surgery of the University of Edinburgh, founder of the world famous Edinburgh school of neurosurgery, whose great distinction as a pioneer neurosurgeon, scientist, teacher and scholar has earned him international fame; in his hands great contributions to the science of neurosurgery have been matched by humane, exemplary care of the sick. The ward and operating room have been his laboratory. By way of example, he was the first person in the United Kingdom to demonstrate by angiography a cerebral arteriovenous malformation and a saccular intracranial aneurysm. His paper on 'Intracranial Aneurysms; Cerebral Arterio- radiography, Surgical Treatment', read at a meeting of the Medico Chirurgical Society of Edinburgh on 28th June 1933, remains a classic. Fortune smiles on the brave and this young neurosurgeon as long ago as 1930[3] successfully operated directly upon an aneurysm of the middle cerebral artery! This was no small feat, especially when the grateful patient was the powerful and influential Chairman of the Board of Governors of the Edinburgh Children's Hospital. His accounts of his original work are cautious, thoughtful and brilliantly clear, reflecting the patient scientist. His professional life of service to neurosurgery, to education and to his fellow man continues in what passes for retirement. His interest in rehabilitation has spread beyond the neurologically disabled. He is presently developing a stoma after care clinic for individuals in Edinburgh and south east Scotland with a colostomy, ileostomy or ureterostomy. Physicians and Surgeons the world over have been invigorated by visiting Professor Dott and the Edinburgh school of neurosurgery.
>
> In peace and war Canadians have felt extraordinarily at home and have been deeply touched by the warmth of the Scottish hospitality and the scholarly generosity of their neurosurgical colleagues. Professor Dott is a Freeman of the City of Edinburgh, a truly special distinction. The medical Freemen of Edinburgh have been and are few. There are only five other doctors, among whom are Lister and Simpson of chloroform fame. Mr President, I have the honour to present Norman McOmish Dott Commander of the Order of the British Empire, Professor Emeritus of the University of Edinburgh, Freeman of the City of Edinburgh, recipient of honours from countries the world over and courageous gentleman that he is, so that he may

receive from your hands the Honorary Fellowship of the Royal College of Physicians and Surgeons of Canada.

Such a warm, well merited accolade is at risk of being sullied by further discussion, but one phrase must be taken up, *recipient of honours from countries the world over.* Certainly this is borne out if an enquirer follows the list, (too long for repetition here without tedium,) as it carries him round Europe, from North to South America and back to the Middle and Far East. Norman Dott's reputation puts a girdle round the globe. Most proffered honours are accepted with grace, courtesy and enthusiasm, but not always: he is not greedy for distinctions. Just before he retired, further honours for him were contemplated at a European neurosurgical meeting. On hearing of this from a British colleague, he writes back:

> I'm sure it is most generous and courteous of them to wish to honour me; ungratefully I find these things a little embarrassing and boring.[4]

Courteously he excuses himself to his prospective hosts:

> As well as fulfilling my commitment duty here in Edinburgh, I shall be 'holding the fort' and enabling my younger colleagues to join you. This is perhaps as it should be that the old promote the young.[5]

Strange as it may seem, this was the entire truth. Full of honours and rapidly approaching retirement age, Dott was always still prepared to take his part as duty surgeon, a task which might be regarded by many others of similar seniority as tedious and to be avoided. Of the honours he did accept, it appears that those promoted by former trainees were most dear to him. There can be no doubt about the quasi-paternal enjoyment of his trips to South Africa, Thailand and India.

Academically, the list of papers published is as long as the list of honours conferred and must also be banished to the Appendix for detailed study.[6] However just as the honours list took us on a brief world tour so does the publications list cleave a passage through the jungles of surgery. Within two years of his qualification 'A New Gastro-Enterostomy Clamp' and 'Cardiac Massage in Resuscitation' have appeared. Then follow his days of physiological study with observations on 'The Isolated Pyloric Segment and its Secretion', 'Hydrocephalus', and increasing attention to the Pituitary. 'Apparatus for Insufflation Anaesthesia' in 1923 reminds us of Dott's early work on endotracheal intubation and anaesthesia. The classical paper on 'Anomalies of Intestinal Rotation' with its practical applications follows also in 1923. In 1925 Dott and Percival Bailey published their monumental review of Cushing's pituitary tumour cases under the title 'Hypophyseal Adenomata'. Gradually the papers became confined to neurosurgical topics. After his description of the famous operation on the intracranial aneurysm, which was published in 'Intracranial Aneurysms,

Cerebral Arterio-radiography, Surgical Treatment' in 1933, there is a particular, life long, interest in cerebrovascular topics. Other neurosurgical problems which also capture his attention are lesions of the optic nerves and optic chiasm, facial neuralgia and intractable pain, head injuries and tuberculosis of the spine. There is little that escapes his study.

He was invited to address innumerable societies and to give not a few prestigious lectures. Of these the following fistful are selected as examples of the most outstanding. The Sir Victor Horsley Memorial Lecture was delivered at the British Medical Association in London in 1960, his title being 'Brain Movement and Time'. In this he discussed his own observations on the various pathological displacements of the brain within the skull.

With his experience in paediatric surgery, he was a fitting choice, in 1960 too, for the Alexander Simpson Smith Memorial Lecture at the Hospital for Sick Children, Great Ormond Street, London. He chose for his subject what used to be a somewhat depressing topic: 'Medulloblastoma Cerebelli', the malignant brain tumour of childhood. However, he encouraged renewed efforts and summarised as follows: 'I am old enough to have quite a large anniversary correspondence with these patients who have done credit to our profession.'

In 1966, based on his personal acquaintance of Sir Hugh, he was invited to deliver the 'IIIrd Sir Hugh Cairns Memorial Lecture' to the Society of British Neurosurgeons, and described his ideas on 'The Training of the Specialist Surgeon'.

In 1967 the fortieth anniversary of the introduction of cerebral angiography was celebrated at an international meeting in Lisbon. What was more natural than that Dott with his early application of this wonderful diagnostic advance should be asked to pay tribute to the pioneer. This he did in 'The Life and Work of Egas Moniz'.

In the same year the Royal College of Surgeons of Edinburgh honoured him with the Alexander Welsh Memorial lecture. He responded with a far sighted review entitled: 'Surgical and Medical Neurology: Disintegration and Re-integration in Specialist Surgery and Medicine'.

In 1969 a panel of Distinguished Lecturers was elected and the members invited individually to address 'The World Federation of Neurosurgical Societies'. Dott complied with 'Medical, Psychological and Surgical Neurology'.

The Syme Surgical Fellowship in 1921; the Rockefeller Surgical Fellowship in 1923; the Liston Memorial Jubileee Prize for advances in neurosurgery in 1932; election as a Fellow of the Royal Society Edinburgh in 1936; the Honorary Fellowship of the Royal Society of Medicine (a roll containing Royalty and only the most distinguished doctors) in 1968 illustrate the spectrum ranging from academic prizes won to academic honours conferred. Thus the academics did not find him wanting and his own University of Edinburgh created for him and appointed him to the Forbes Chair of Surgical Neurology in 1947 and as its final accolade conferred upon him the honorary degree of Doctor of Medicine in 1969.

What judgement of their surgeon do his patients offer? When a biography was tentatively mooted fifteen years after his death, many letters poured in from all parts of the United Kingdom and from abroad, amply reinforced by telephone calls. They told of operations covering a span from 1921 to 1962. Significantly and adding value to these testimonies, they are not all of successful operations and some describe carefully taken decisions not to operate. How kindly though was the disappointing lack of success or the unavailability of operative care explained to the relatives.

> He examined Linda carefully, then sadly told me there was nothing he could do to help her. I was young and couldn't understand. Then the next time, shortly afterwards, he came through to Glasgow to my mother's home and explained to us my baby's condition and why he couldn't help her.

The elderly write in with memories from his early surgical career among children: 'the sinews of my toe corrected', my wry neck cured so that I could look like others': 'tuberculous glands of the neck excised': 'a burst appendix dealt with so that a full life ensued'. Some of these older patients were operated upon so early in their lives that they have no personal memories of what happened. But they were told later that the great Dott himself was the surgeon and they have taken fast hold of this instruction and not let go, for they consider it their life.

> I am now 55 years of age. Professor Dott operated on me at the age of six weeks for cleft palate and hare lip. I have been in hospital many times during my life and great interest has been shown at the excellent job. I am always proud to inform people that it was all due to Professor Norman Dott.

Through all the letters runs the vein of his kindness:

> As a very, very, young thirteen year old, you can imagine how I felt about going to him for treatment. I was absolutely terrified. On meeting him, how quickly that fear disappeared! He had a way with children, so much so that you really looked forward to any future visit.

If repeated recollections of his kindness are in danger of cloying, it had better not be forgotten that it was sincere and that Professor Dott was equally capable of showing the steel in his character. Was someone unnecessarily standing in the way of his plans for the benefit of his patients; was some instrument badly made or carelessly treated; did some member of staff fail to carry out a request; was there a clumsy movement or lapse of concentration whilst assisting him to operate; did standards not quite come up to those expected by Dott—the wrong doer experienced, if not the terror of that thirteen year old, at least something not far removed, all administered with the soft voice and penetrating gaze, never a sudden outburst.

One former patient relates his unusual entry into Dott's orbit at several ages of man.

> I was the victim of a motorbike accident with, among others, head injuries. Our family doctor brought Professor Dott to see me. In that little boy's mind he was a very kind and gentle man.

He then goes on to describe how as pupils at Heriot's School in the 1930s they received with great pride the news that a girl with a cerebral tumour had travelled from South Africa by ship, for there were no routine air services in those days, to consult their eminent former pupil Norman Dott and how this pride had spilled over into the hearts of other Edinburgh citizens. One would not have anticipated further contact but regretfully this patient's mother was admitted to Dott's new Department of Surgical Neurology in 1960. Unfortunately the diagnosis was of a malignant brain tumour but his mind was cast back to his meeting with Dott as a boy and he had no doubt that the informed kindness with which the sentence was made known to him stemmed from Dott's hand on the working of the Department. Lastly, while getting over a difficult operation in the Chalmers Hospital in 1970, it came to his notice that there was a patient in a side room, who neither asked for nor received any special treatment. The discovery that it was Professor Dott instilled in him a marvellous sense of well being: 'If the surgeons on that ward were good enough for Professor Dott they were good enough for me.' His confidence was by no means misplaced, for Dott would only have chosen his surgeon after the most rigorous assessment of his skills.

So one turns over the letters, that form a vast human harvest, reads and re-reads the very moving stories and regrets that they cannot all be published in their entirety.

They tell of all walks of life and of wide ranging injuries and disease processes; of the small boy, who falls from a railway bridge; of soldiers wounded in battle and living to show their scars; of the mountaineer brought by rescuers to a cottage with the words, 'There's no need of your bed, he's gone', who yet recovered under Dott's care to a full life into old age. They tell of tumours removed, pain relieved, sight restored, of joy and sorrow.

> I was born on 6th September 1938 and was operated upon on 8th September. The operation was between my spine and brain and only a hair breadth to

work on. I was fourteen years old before I stopped my yearly visits to see him. That day each year he always treated my mum and me to the price of our dinner in town.

Another had emotion in her voice which trembled audibly when she confirmed over the telephone the events, of over fifty years ago, about which she had previously written. She was only nineteen at the time and her boy-friend had been diagnosed as having a tumour of the cerebellum. In those days knowledge was less complete about the effects of operating on the cerebellum. Would he survive? Would he walk again? Dott advised operation with the words, 'Have courage lass because he has got plenty of it.' And so—as Dott would have had it—they *together* got rid of his tumour and nursed him through a prolonged convalescence to a normality which had scarce been hoped for. She continues:

> I was young and an ardent theatre goer. I attended every Edinburgh première. I had two tickets for a very special show when Douglas received a letter asking him to attend a lecture by Dott on the same evening. I said, 'Phone Mr Dott and ask if it is really necessary for you to be there.' Douglas came back crest-fallen, 'Mr Dott asked why I didn't want to go, sends his apologies, but says that the success of the lecture depends on my presence.' Three days later an envelope arrived with two of the best tickets for the Lyceum and a note, 'To Len (my name Helen was always shortened to Len) with Norman Dott's compliments.'

They married and Douglas was fit enough to serve in the Merchant Navy during the war, only to be tragically lost when his ship was torpedoed two months before the armistice. When he heard of this Dott wrote expressing his great sorrow but saying he was glad that he had saved Douglas's life for the five years of happiness, which he felt sure they had shared. 'How proud and privileged I still feel to have known him,' writes Helen, fifty years after her first meeting with Dott. 'It took Edinburgh a mighty long time to recognise him but I feel sure he is now a Freeman of a bigger and better city!' Half a century has not dimmed the memory of that awful year of anxiety capped by the gesture of the theatre tickets, which Helen still describes, with unwarranted harshness towards herself, as 'from a very busy and great man to a stupid selfish teenager'. How Dott must have pondered about the promised achieved by courage on one part, and hard earned skill on the other; promise which could be wiped out in a moment by the touch of a button in war.

These are all moving personal experiences but are they to be dismissed as merely important episodes to the individual and not offering any reliable evidence as to the character and skill of the surgeon? Patients do not always report with scientific exactitude or in the jargon of science. One soldier wounded in action remembers:

I had heard lots about double vision, in my case I had treble vision. I was put
to sleep at 9 a.m. and came to at 4 p.m. with a nurse sitting beside me. 'Bloody
hell!' I recall saying when I opened my eyes, 'There's only one light bulb!'.
Nurse shot off and returned with Professor Dott. 'Hello! awake are we?' he
said, 'How many lights do you see?' 'Just one Sir,' I replied. 'Fine' said he, 'a
good job, I think.'

As befitting another soldier came an even more succinct report of therapeutic success. 'I'm back in the green beret,' wrote Colonel Denis
O'Flaherty in a letter to Professor Dott, wishing him well in his retirement.
With this descriptive phrase he was telling Professor Dott that he was back
on full military duties in command of the 29th Commando Regiment
despite a life-threatening fracture of the cervical spine which he had
sustained in a Commando raid in Norway in 1941. Professor Dott and he
had achieved this result over a period of two years of rigorous treatment
including reduction, immobilisation and grafting of the injured spine. With
soldierly precision he had condensed that wonderful war time saga of
bravery on a foreign shore, near mortal wounding and succour from the
persistent and unparalleled skills of one who had himself been prevented
from serving.

Let the last words at this stage come from the ladies. Jennifer was seven
and a half years old when a rare tumour of her cervical spine was diagnosed
and Professor Dott operated on it successfully. This she acknowledges
gratefully thirty-five years later. Of course she does not know the technical
difficulties involved in excising this tumour in front of the spinal cord.
What she does recall vividly is her hatred of hospital porridge, which the
nurses tried to make her swallow, and her relief and admiration when Dott
entered the ward, perceived her distress and, in no uncertain terms, put an
end to these sessions.

Miss Grace Allison does not waste words. 'I was a patient of his when I
was a child; he was very, very kind to me and also, I know, to my parents,
who had implicit faith in him.' We have to go to her records to learn that
in those days of her childhood she was operated upon by Professor Dott
because of a pituitary tumour. It was life-threatening and also hazarded her
vision. The passing years have shown that the first of these dangers has been
overcome and Miss Allison went on to demonstrate that the visual
deterioration had been arrested and sight effectively improved, by taking
some of the best photographic portraits of Professor Dott that are available.
His staff agree that she has captured to an artistic nicety various characteristic
expressions of his. He was greatly gratified when she presented him with
copies of these and several are still in the possession of long standing
members of his staff. No, it's not scientific, but how deeply his patients
loved and admired him and that is a matter which cannot be determined by

science. His reputation, which now lives after him, formerly went before him and created equally unscientific preconceptions.

> My first recollection of him was in Ward 20 among his patients. I remember the lightly built unassuming gentleman with the limp and thinking Professor Dott, never! I think I expected him to be ten feet tall with a halo on his head!

We have seen that Norman Dott's active surgical career spanned fifty-four years, for it appears to have started as a student before qualification in 1919. He retired in 1962, but he was still giving advice as a surgeon shortly before his death in 1973. As he himself says:

> In retirement I have attempted to assist some of those, whose condition I could not help sufficiently during active practice, by taking part in relevant medico social voluntary organisations as for Epilepsy, Paraplegia, Spina Bifida of Children and Cancer.

He had seen great changes many of which he had pioneered himself. 'Indeed in the earlier part of the present century, I myself have frequently assisted at major operations carried out on the kitchen table in and around Edinburgh,' were the words with which he described some of his earliest surgical excursions. This contrasts strikingly with the description of his last operating theatres, by fellow surgeons, as 'Utopian'. Certainly Dott was more sanguine labelling the advanced design of the theatres in the Western General Hospital's Department of Surgical Neurology (a design for which he had been in no small part responsible) as 'a step forward'. Many a knowledgeable visitor came to inspect this 'step forward'. They left praising the twin theatre suite, each theatre of specially designed ovoid shape so that the filtered air with its pressure gradient would not cause eddy currents, which predispose to infection. They saw the domed roof with inset shadow-less lamps focused from a magnetic panel on the wall and with observation windows interspersed. They saw the operating tables specially designed for head and spinal work, the X-ray and electroencephalographic installations, the large anaesthetic recovery rooms and many other carefully considered facilities. Many went away to plan departments and theatres on similar lines.

Stemming from his early engineering experience Dott had an abiding interest in the instruments and mechanical aspects of his craft. But 'abiding interest' is too casual and abiding passion would be too emotional a description for the unrelaxing and critical concern with which the tools of his trade occupied him.

Here he was fortunate in his early anaesthetist Dr George Maxwell Brown, who was a superb precision engineer. In his spare time he made delightful models. For himself he made modifications and additions to his anaesthetic apparatus. For Dott he made ingenious original instruments.

Best known are the Dott slow occlusion carotid artery clamp used in aneurysm surgery, which he made in 1935. This small metal clamp could be placed around the main carotid artery in the neck with its milled edged, screw top protruding through the surgical dressings. Slowly this was tightened, with the patient awake and under careful observation in the ward. Thus gradually was the artery occluded and the pressure of blood flow into the aneurysm reduced without the deleterious effect of too sudden a diminution of cerebral blood flow.

The other instrument which will be referred to again, was the fine needle holder used for anastomosing the facial nerve in the depths of the cranium. Dott also acknowledged another quality of Dr Maxwell Brown. 'His paternal good nature saw the unit through many a stressful period during the war.' In later years, especially when the new department was being equipped with theatre instruments, Mr George Newell took his place and admirably fulfilled Dott's exacting criteria. What memories Mr Newell has of Professor Dott.

> I first met Professor Dott during the late 1950's in his garret office in Ward 20, his neurosurgical ward at the Edinburgh Royal Infirmary. I have pleasant memories of this quiet unassuming man, his great personal charm, his infinite patience, sincerity and a total dedication to his patients. I was a young engineer and he arranged the meeting in order to introduce me to a colleague of his, Dr Maxwell Brown who for some years had been assisting him with the development and making of various surgical instruments and accessories. Maxwell Brown had a home workshop with several small machine tools, which he used with considerable skill. At the time of our meeting he and the Professor were working on the modification and improvement of some brain retractors originally designed by de Martell, and had reached a point where their small workshop capacity was quite inadequate. It was at this opportune time that the facilities in the University Genetics Department workshops were put at their disposal through an agreement with Professor C H Waddington.
>
> At this time a new momentum was gathering in neurosurgery in Edinburgh. Ward 20 was becoming cramped as increasing numbers of young neurosurgeons were coming to learn from the internationally known Professor. The new neurosurgical unit at the Western General Hospital was about to be built. For a year or two Dr Maxwell Brown made increasingly frequent visits to our workshops, mainly in the role of intermediary, but sadly he became ill and died. From then on I had an increasing personal contact with Norman Dott and assisted with the development of various instruments.
>
> Prior to studying medicine, he was an engineering student, so he was a very mechanically minded person. His ideas and innovations were usually very well thought out and sketches made before he approached me with them. Often he would come to our workshops during an afternoon, arriving over in his black Bentley car. This was a two door sports saloon and the very wide doors enabled him to get in and out more easily, since he was unfortunate in

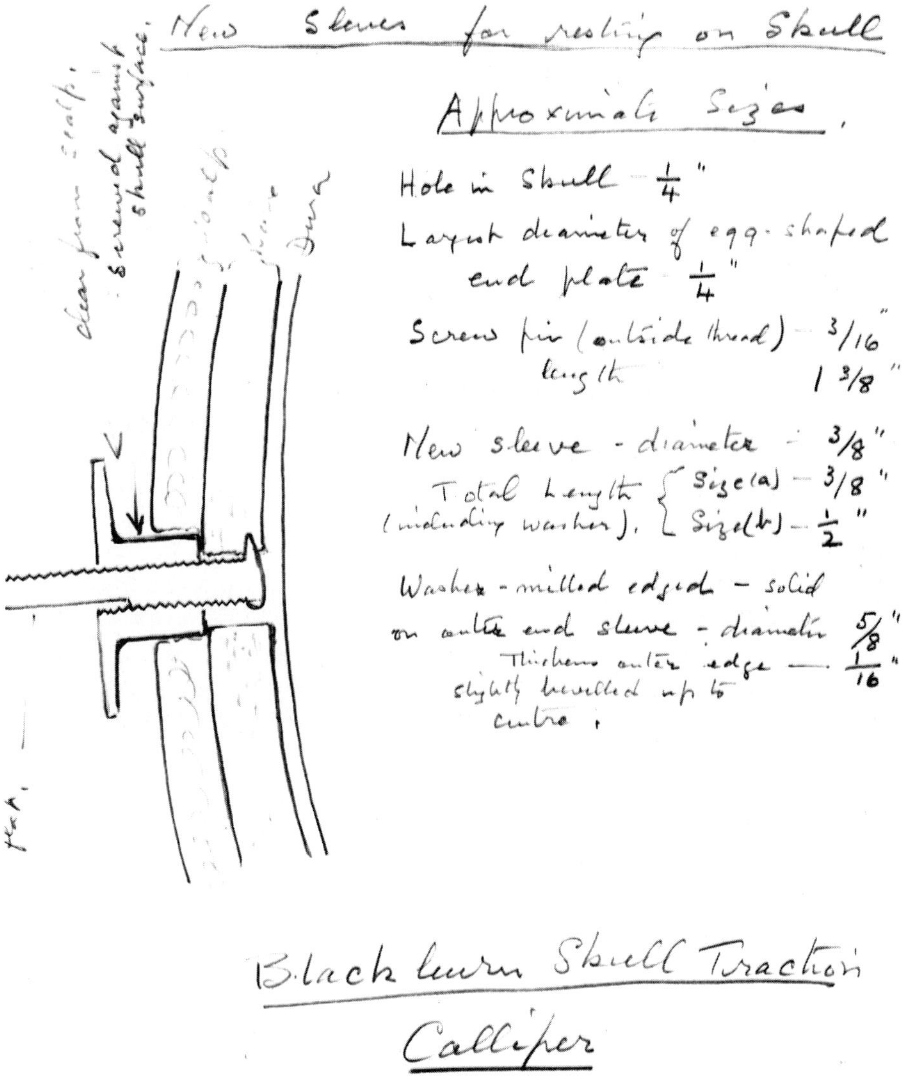

New Sleeve for resting on Skull

Approximate Sizes.

Hole in Skull — $\frac{1}{4}$"

Largest diameter of egg-shaped
end plate $\frac{1}{4}$"

Screw pin (outside thread) — $\frac{3}{16}$"
length 1 $\frac{3}{8}$"

New sleeve - diameter — $\frac{3}{8}$"
Total Length { Size (a) — $\frac{3}{8}$"
(including washer). { Size (b) — $\frac{1}{2}$"

Washer - milled edged — solid
on outer end sleeve - diameter $\frac{5}{8}$"
Thickness outer edge — $\frac{1}{16}$"
slightly bevelled up to
centre.

Clean from scalp.
Screwed against Skull surface.

Blackburn Skull Traction

Calliper

49 Blackburn Skull Traction Calliper: with characteristic detail and engineering
skill, Dott orders an instrument exactly to his requirements.

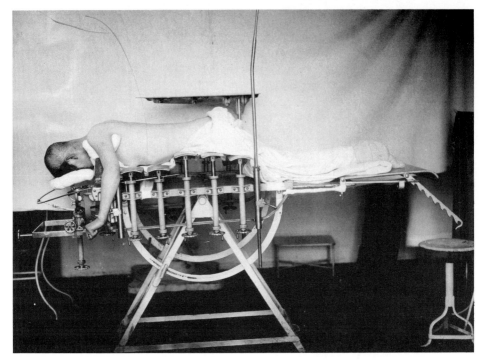

50 Engineering skills brought to Surgery: Dott introduced many novel designs into theatre tables, particularly the intricate headpiece for accurate positioning of the head during cranial surgery. This is one of the early theatre tables.

having a stiff hip due to an accident. Usually on his way over he would stop at Blackford pond for a short time to walk his little Skye terrier of which he was very fond. His dog would come into the workshop with him and I recall one amusing visit. That morning I had been to a butcher for bones that were of similar thickness to a human skull. These were to enable the Professor to evaluate some prototype perforators and burrs. They were clamped into a bench vice and Professor Dott drilled a number of holes with each cutter for comparison and evaluation. Much to our amusement the little dog sat under the vice and caught and ate most of the bone shavings before they even reached the floor!

He was a keen fisherman and I remember him telling me that one of his favourite areas was around Brora in Sutherland. Well before the start of the fishing season, he would come along to me with a leather bound attaché case containing a number of his reels, which he wished me to check over. In his usual meticulous way, he had labelled and numbered them and on an accompanying sheet of paper were details of specific points that he wished to have checked. Like most of his equipment, they were the best obtainable and

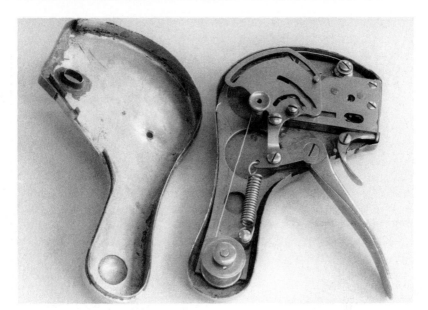

51   The Clip Gun: before the days of the ready supply of tiny metal clips for occluding small vessels, Dott designed this sterilisable 'gun' for making and delivering such clips, from a coil of wire, at the time of need during an operation.

52   Obsolete instruments evocative of the days of Dott: the old headlamp; Dott's Slow Occlusion Carotid Artery Clamp; Malleable Aneurysm Needles for passing ligatures round the necks of aneurysms.

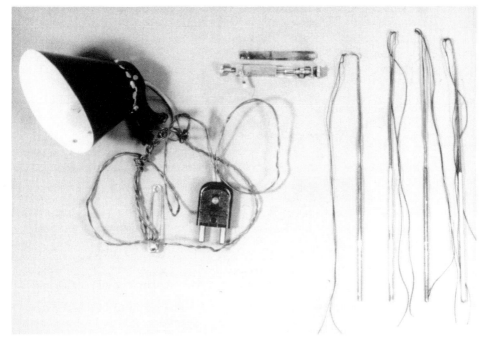

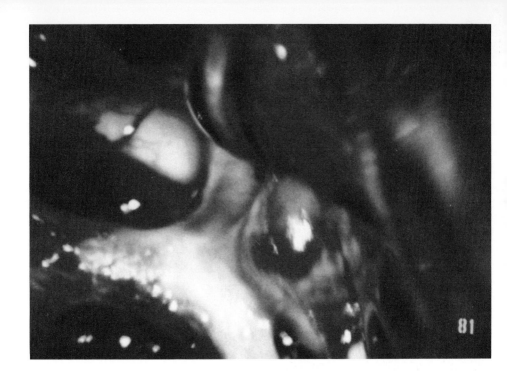

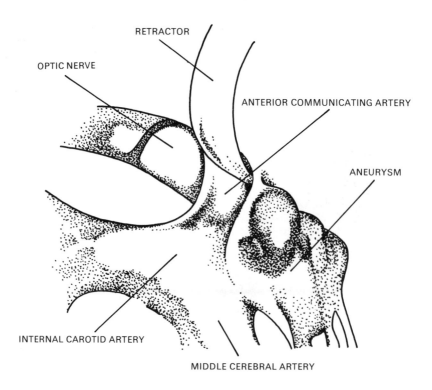

OPTIC NERVE

RETRACTOR

ANTERIOR COMMUNICATING ARTERY

ANEURYSM

INTERNAL CAROTID ARTERY

MIDDLE CEREBRAL ARTERY

53 'with a time-bomb in his head.' Photograph and diagram of Cerebral Artery Aneurysm of the type to which Dott gave the above description and for which he conceived the idea of direct operation.

rarely did anything need much attention, perhaps a slight polish up here and there and a modicum of grease on the pall and ratchet. He would, quite unnecessarily, more than amply reward me with a piece of smoked salmon.

He only once asked me to be present in the operating theatre in Ward 20 in order that he could demonstrate some problem or other. I was there only a short time during an operation scheduled to take several hours but during a lull in the procedure, whilst waiting for an X-ray plate to be developed, I asked him if he found standing for long periods a strain on his hip. He replied that most modern operations were not too prolonged but went on to say, 'In my younger days some operations could last seven or eight hours and you just had to cross your legs, hold your bladder and get on with the job. To-day (circa 1959) most young surgeons want coffee and biscuits every two hours or so!'

The only other recollection I have regarding Norman Dott concerns a shepherd whom I encountered whilst walking the hills south of Edinburgh several years ago. During conversation I was admiring his crook, a good example of the craft, which he said he had made himself. He had apparently taken up this hobby, in his late twenties whilst recuperating after a serious head operation by a surgeon named Mr Dott, of whom, he said, I had probably never heard! It was now about thirty years after the operation to remove a growth on or adjacent to the pituitary gland. Mr Dott had diagnosed the problem and said it required immediate surgery. He explained what was involved and went on to say that he would like to perform the operation himself but he was scheduled to leave for South Africa in two days' time. Therefore, if the patient wished him to do it, it would have to be the following day. This was agreed and a bed found in Ward 20 there and then. The operation was performed the following day and the shepherd told me of his deep gratitude to this wonderfully skilful man saying that he even visited the ward on his way to catch the train at the commencement of his journey to South Africa.[7]

On this moving note Mr George Newell concludes his memories but it deserves mention that this instance of working right up to the time of departure on Dott's part was by no means unique. Mr Gordon McNaught worked for a long time with Sir John Bruce, one time President of the Royal College of Surgeons in Edinburgh. He recalls that John Bruce used to emphasise the value of observation in clinical surgery and relate how in 1929 he had been Resident Surgical Officer at the Royal Hospital for Sick Children, when one evening Norman Dott was called in to see a small boy who was vomiting. He stood at the end of the cot for a period which was variously described as fifty minutes or 'a bloody long time' until he observed the abnormal abdominal movements which confirmed the diagnosis of pyloric stenosis. (In this condition, which usually affects male babies, the muscle encircling the outlet of the stomach thickens and obstructs it so that vomiting and life threatening fluid depletion ensue. A delicate operation, in which a carefully graduated incision is made into the muscle of the small infantile stomach, yet preserves intact the inner lining, will relieve the symptoms.) Thus satisfied, Dott completed the operation, drew sketches of his findings, had a shower, got into his car, one of the famous Alvis Speed 25's, and drove down to Southampton to catch his ship leaving at 7.30 a.m. for the United States!

Mr Newell made instruments; he checked instruments. Instruments from suppliers, which were not up to standard, were sent back with detailed criticisms and equally detailed demands for correction. There is copious correspondence, which, to a third party after this interval of years, offers an excellent picture of Dott's standards and precision but which to the recipients at the time must have been little short of humiliating.

> I have re-examined those instruments and I regret to say they are unaccept-able—the skull pins are rough and variable in thickness varying from two to three and a half thous from one end to the other. They are made of copper but should be of phosphor bronze.[8]

These are two random complaints which sent instruments back. And again:

> One small point about screw pegs. The taper is now correct and the thread correctly deep and sharp. In future however there should be no undercut next to the shoulder. The reason for this is use on thin infants skulls.[9]

Here was an unusual surgeon who knew his procedures and knew, to thousandths of an inch, the instruments with which to carry them out.

Some of this correspondence refers to the manufacture of 'The Edinburgh Self-Retaining Brain Retractor' or Dott's modification of the de Martell self-retaining retractor. How familiar will any Dott trainee be with this instrument, almost universally used in Dott's brain operations. The metal rods bearing the gentle malleable spatulae had to run smoothly through the small box joints and then lock firmly so that the lobes of the brain were parted gently and the exposure maintained without damage. How anxiously were these instruments prepared and their initial applica-tion watched! If there was any catch in their smooth running or the brain jolted, however gently, the icy, 'That won't do' emanated from an enraged and frustrated soul, part surgeon part precision engineer, and presaged a more extended reprimand in the quiet of the changing room after the operation with a full lecture on the mechanics and workings of box joints.

Another instrument which residents and registrars will recall as exer-cising Dott's engineering knowledge was the skull traction caliper. This caliper takes purchase on the skull by means of small flanges passed through a drill hole, one on each side. Weights are attached thus exerting traction on and correcting the position of a fractured and dislocated cervical spine. It was usually a very satisfactory system but on one occasion the flange slipped out of place and traction was released, offering some risk to the patient in the short interval before the resident re-positioned it. There was little that escaped Professor Dott and, as was his wont, he got to know of this episode which might have been dismissed as minor and soon rectified. Every aspect was examined; there was no technical error in placing the calipers. The calipers were exchanged and scrutinised. It was not long before they were dispatched back to the makers with detailed criticisms of the flange and screw, including micrometre readings. There is no doubt that Dott had an exceptional knowledge and command of his instruments.

A surgeon however, particularly in surgical neurology, does not achieve an enhanced reputation merely by his technical performance in the operating theatre. Diagnosis, assessment of the real needs of the patient, choice and timing of the operation, when alternatives exist, are equally important. Explaining to the patient and relatives measures to be taken, instilling confidence, and supervising after-care are no less vital. Above all he must know when not to operate. The overconfident surgeon, who feels that no problem is insurmountable when measured against his skills, is a menace. Dott excelled in exercising these necessary judgements and in teaching these qualities to others by example. Again and again he quoted from Cushing's example, saying, 'The watchword and the touchstone is what will help my patients most?' Again and again he warned medical colleagues not to reserve all the praise for pioneering surgeons but to pay tribute to the courageous patients who ventured with them into the unknown. When Edinburgh's mighty Usher Hall was filled to see the City Fathers present him with the Freedom of the City, when all had gathered to praise his achievements and long career of service, Dott still remembered his patients and drew towards the conclusion of his address with these gracious phrases:

> We pay insufficient homage to the great courageous pioneering patients. When I recall those patients, who, with implicit faith and unfaltering courage, have adventured with me into the unknown, I realise that they should be standing here rather than their surgeon. Their courage implies an apprehension of risk—it is indeed fear under control—their faith is in the properly constituted authority of the doctor. These are the heroes and the heroines, who in the nature of things must remain unsung; and in which Scotland is so richly endowed.

His patients' letters have told us how successful he was in instilling faith and thus gaining the properly constituted authority for the necessary operative procedures. Some forty years before administrative and legal authorities on each side of the Atlantic started warning surgeons that it was mandatory to detail procedures to the patient and obtain 'informed consent', Dott was lecturing, in 1930, in the following terms:

> The mental state; the significance of 'operation' to the lay mind is dangerous, fearful, painful, something quite apart from other therapeutic measures. It is usually most desirable that he should fully understand the nature of his malady, the general lines of any proposed operative treatment, the result to be anticipated, the part an actual operation plays in the general management of his case. When he shares the knowledge and the responsibility of his case with the surgeon, he approaches operation in a sensible way, as the best treatment available in the circumstances—with confidence in his surgeon and himself, without emotion. In most cases the patient has a right to be treated with such confidence. In my experience lay people are capable of appreciating very well general reasons for surgical decisions and of sharing any difficulties and responsibilities that may present themselves. The patient should be in a position to request operation on a reasoned judgement, the surgeon supplying him with the pros and cons of the particular case, for example the prognosis of the condition untreated, the degree of relief to be expected from operation, the risks of operation as a percentage.[10]

If these sentiments seem somewhat commonplace today, when the term 'informed consent' is familiar to the man in the street, and nearly every other television programme is devoted to medical matters, you must remember that Dott was lecturing students and junior doctors in 1930. In that era the medical profession was much more authoritative, the gulf between doctor and patient much greater. The emphasis was on diagnosis, and the tendency to offer treatment with paternal condescension. This was a kindlier attitude that Dott was advocating.

Such attitudes, however, were not lightly formed. They could only be based on sound knowledge of the patient and his ailment. Innumerable letters tell us that Dott got to know his patients, their work, their family background, their hopes and aspirations. For his aim, an aim he instilled in his trainees, was to return the sufferer to as near a normal and rewarding life as possible. He made as accurate a diagnosis as he could in order to plan his operation. This led him always to prefer the title 'Surgical Neurology' to 'Neurosurgery'. He did not claim originality for this, saying that he had heard Wilfred Trotter use the term, even if he was not the originator. In his inaugural lecture, when appoined to the Forbes chair in 1947, he made it clear that his department was to be called 'The Department of Surgical Neurology' and not the 'Neurosurgical Department'. He was to repeat on many occasions that the science or discipline was neurology and surgery was one therapeutic arm. He, and any one who completed his training with him, was to be a competent neurological diagnostician and was not merely to wield a scalpel at someone's else's diagnostic behest. It would be insulting to other respected pioneers of surgical neurology to suggest that Dott was unique in these high ideals but he was certainly in the forefront in promoting them.

X-rays played a large part in the preparation of the patient. Although years have passed, many in all quarters, whether of his staff or as doctors seeking an opinion from him, will still recall sessions with Dott reviewing X-rays. His slight figure stood in front of the lighted box, always the stiff left leg, always the grey suit. Time must have a stop if a problem was to be solved, although, having come to a satisfactory conclusion he might bring from his waistcoat pocket the silver watch on its chain to check on the timing of his next commitment. Even as he worked, his mind advanced in hidden progress. His face, leaning slightly forward would be illuminated by the lighted viewing box; finely cut with lines of concentration, you would see the occasional contractions of the muscles at the angles of the jaw, especially if someone in the retinue made an inappropriate remark or stated the obvious. Words were few.

The films were frequently produced by his long-standing and trusted radiologist Dr A A Donaldson, who would have carried out the specialised techniques. There might be a 'What have we here Tony?', an occasional 'Uh—Huh!' or, 'There's a thing!'. Usually the viewing box was the specialised one, whose angled mirrors threw up beautiful stereoscopic three dimensional images. The skull stood out miraculously and, if it were an angiogram, the intricate pattern of the cerebral blood vessels could be seen weaving in and out within the cranial cavity. Alice in Wonderland might have sprung to mind with her enviable power of foreshortening to explore the rabbit holes. Given such a gift, how gladly one would have entered and traced the paths of those vessels. Not far from this concept, Dott would be mapping his approach to the fateful aneurysm or arteriovenous malformation, for he knew well that to disturb, unnecessarily, any of the fine vessels might, at worst, be a matter of life and death and, at best, inflict avoidable disability upon the patient.

In this and many other ways Dott prepared his patient and himself for operation with detailed care. It is worth following him to the operating theatre before turning to describe some of his more famous operations. In his Ward 20 days, like his assistants, he would strip off his suit and outer clothes in the bathroom at the western extremity of the ward, put on the drab hospital dressing gown and make his way to the theatre at the other end before pulling on a theatre suit. However grand the visitor, he too, would have to follow the same routine, if he wanted to see Dott operate. As he limped quietly along the corridor Professor Dott had to pick his way between patients, nurses, auxiliaries and beds and trolleys too. He must have been mistaken for a patient on numerous occasions, especially as, garbed only in a dressing gown, his disability was rather more evident. Who was he but a small slight man with a limp?

With the opening of the new Department of Surgical Neurology, matters were more discreet. He would enter the changing room door. His assistants would have taken care to precede him into the theatre to see that all was ready. Mr Dunn was waiting. He undoubtedly owed his long-standing appointment as Professor Dott's theatre charge nurse to efficiency in matters neurosurgical. However his relaxed personality and tolerant sense of humour were of immeasurable help enabling him to ride over and correct, to Dott's satisfaction, the numerous storms over instruments and theatre tables, which are inseparable from a perfectionist. Like the bearer of some ancient royal office, he would assist Dott into his blue operating suit, and tie his fabric operating gaiters. Mark the blue, to match the operating drapes, in subtle distinction from the rest of the hospital, where they were green.

Once in the operating theatre, though words were few and teaching, from Cushing's precept, almost entirely by example, there was no doubt who was in command. Strangely, despite the elaborate and expensive lighting system, Dott still clung to his old fashioned headlamp with bulb and conical shade. This used to heat up and deliver the assistant a sharp stab of pain on the forehead, if he leant forward too enthusiastically. The myth of surgeon's hands has been dismissed. Still Dott's fingers were long and gave the impression of slight hyperextension as if, sensitive, they never relaxed their responsibilities. This was seen as he prepared the operation site with antiseptic solutions, using bare, scrubbed hands, and later as, gloved, he operated. In his earlier days, Dott was renowned for personally starting the operation by placing the patient correctly on the operating table and focusing the lighting. He also completed the operation, often after many exhausting hours, not only by tying the last stitch, but also dressing the wound with his own authoritative hand.

When he started operating in the nursing homes, this was a necessity; subsequently it was a regime of perfection; latterly it was relaxed somewhat but only after he had carefully assessed the performance of his assistant. The famous story is told of Dott exploring, for a tumour, the posterior cranial fossa, the back compartment of the skull, containing delicate and vital neural structures. Undoubtedly this operative approach needs care and skill for its wound closure. Unfortunately, in this case, it was not possible to remove all the tumour although samples were taken for histological examination. When this had been completed Dott turned to his assistant, a somewhat ebullient character, and said uncharacteristically, 'Now you close.' This he did with complete satisfaction and the patient was returned to the ward. The singularly favoured assistant, justifiably even a little more ebullient, made his way to report to Dott. He found him in his office bent over some writing. 'The patient is back in the ward, his condition is satis-factory and stable,' he reported proudly, 'but unfortunately the tumour,' which had by then been examined histologically, 'is a malignant glioma.' (This is a tumour of very poor prognosis.) Barely raising his eyes from his work, Dott replied with a characteristically drawn out, 'Ye-es! Why do you think I let you close?'

So we see Professor Dott in theatre with his confident gentle techniques and no trace of the flamboyant behaviour which is the picture that some lay people carry of a famous surgeon operating. His head is bent towards the wound in complete concentration. If you were first assistant, you were following towards the vital area of the wound the undistractible gaze of those eyes between his mask and the surprisingly small theatre cap, which was surmounted by the old headlamp. It was a surprisingly small head for all that knowledge and experience. If his hands did not entirely explode the myth of feminine-fingered surgeons, the cranium 'bulging with brains' was a notion certainly dispelled by Dott's head. As second assistant, you would be standing at Dott's side with, crane as you would, a very limited view of the field of operation. Nevertheless, your performance with the retractor or other instrument, which had been put in your charge, was expected to be without flaw. Sometimes the first intimation that you were falling down on this impossible task would be a slight twitching of those muscles at the angle of his jaw or an increased prominence as his well-marked neck muscles were tensed. But this was soon followed by, 'That won't do, doctor!' uttered in a tone of utter disbelief that you had ever achieved that status.

Sister too was in the same predicament, as she stood behind her table of instruments, for usually the neurosurgical operating field is small and the action is within the cranium or the depths of the spine. When he finished a manoeuvre with a particular instrument, without shifting his gaze from the vital field, Dott would extend his hand with the instrument in it, in the general direction of sister. It was her duty, without a word passing, to retrieve the instrument and to slap the next required instrument into his hand. Sometimes the manoeuvre was more intricate such as handing forceps holding a cottonoid pledget embracing wax for controlling oozing of blood from bone. Or an aneurysm needle, threaded in a specific manner to encompass the neck of an aneurysm, might have to be delivered. If there were a hitch and a delay, say ten seconds, a reprimanding plaint would be heard: 'Don't keep me waiting, sister!' rather as if he had been waiting at a bus stop for half an hour! It was of course extremely difficult to maintain Dott's standards with the wide range of finely balanced instruments submitted to endless hours of use and wear and tear. Despite this his theatre sisters served him loyally and stayed long. Sisters Keith, Ross, Cheyne, Hogg, Gaffney and several others equally loyal.

A consideration of Dott's general operating techniques would not be complete without returning to his 1930 lectures which still offer good advice to today's aspiring surgeons. We have seen how he advocated enlisting the patient's confidence and, with 'informed consent', leading him to operation in as tranquil a frame of mind as possible. He condemns apprehension and 'great speed in operating involving rough handling of tissues, sudden blood loss, coarse suturing'. He continues:

> Every cell the surgeon injures during an operation contributes to a post opera-
> tive histamine toxaemia. Clean cutting, delicacy in handling, prevention of
> drying, delicate suturing and absolute haemostasis are important. No surgical
> field is absolutely aseptic; our ideal cannot be absolute sterility but should be
> minimal contamination and minimal tissue injury. Delicately handled tissues
> will deal with minimal surgical infection with ease and with certainty; our
> whole faith in surgery is based on this proven fact. I find the time factor in
> operating almost negligible so far as immediate and ultimate recovery are
> concerned. A four or five hour brain case does quite as well as a half hour case.
> Careful technique and deliberate waiting for compensation of blood volume
> or waiting for clotting under a pack to control severe capillary oozing are
> much more important. [11]

Thus in 1930 was Dott enunciating most of the principles of operating to which he adhered for the remainder of his active surgical career—unending patience, meticulous respect for tissues and haemostasis.

Utterly unforgettable was Dott's first demonstration that a cerebral artery, however small, was functionally important and that, if it was damaged and bleeding, this did not immediately demand occlusion by a clip. Arterial bleeding could be arrested without blocking the lumen of the vessel and interrupting the vital blood flow, by sitting patiently with a small pledget of hammered muscle, pressed, with the aid of fine forceps, to the site of damage. Fifteen, twenty, thirty minutes passed thus were of no consequence, if flow of blood through the vessel was maintained.

And so Dott taught, largely by example, the patient, gentle handling of tissues. As he demonstrated this manoeuvre his mind must have ranged back to that singular operation in 1931, shortly to be described, which had established his international reputation; the first successful intracranial operation for a ruptured cerebral artery aneurysm. Like most advances in medicine and surgery the approach to this climactic operation was gradual, step by step. It is probable that previous surgeons had operated on the rarer large intracranial aneurysms by the transcranial approach under a mistaken diagnosis of tumour and with catastrophic results. More usually cerebral aneurysms are small and present themselves by rupturing and bleeding.

This syndrome of spontaneous subarachnoid haemorrhage was well known and had been fully described by Byrom Bramwell[12] and Charles Symonds.[13] Dott and other surgeons had attempted to treat such aneurysms by ligating the carotid artery in the neck to diminish the arterial pressure at the aneurysm. Dott too had taken up enthusiastically the pioneer work in Portugal of Egas Moniz on cerebral angiography and had been the first in the United Kingdom to demonstrate by this method a cerebral arteriovenous malformation in 1929. Later in 1932 he was the first in the United Kingdom to demonstrate an intracranial aneurysm. However his famous first craniotomy for aneurysm was, remarkably, based on clinical diagnosis only. The aneurysm was not visualised radiographically before the operation.

Let him describe in his own words his thoughts and the reasoning, which led to this courageous intervention. They seem to sum up his deep concern for humanity and the orderly care and deductive thinking, which were so characteristic of him, and which he applied not only to surgery but to all other aspects of his life.

A beloved wife and mother aged forty seven. As we watched her go, in company with her anguished relatives, we could hardly bear it; and then came the duty of persuading the stricken family that the dead have precious knowledge to impart to save the next generation. I remember that occupied three hours in this case. This had been a dearly loved lady with everything to live for, who had been in perfect bodily condition except for one minute defect on one of her arteries. Surely some surgical measure could be devised to meet such devastating minutiae? We answered by carrying out some 'blind' cervical ligations in cases that we could diagnose clinically.

This however did not always suffice.

It soon became apparent that in order to operate successfully for cerebral diseases, one had to plan things from an intelligent grasp of the nature of the lesion. One required a reasonable knowledge of neurological anatomy and physiology and of course of general neurology in order to distinguish surgical from non-surgical cases and in order to arrive at a diagnosis in the surgical group, which would permit a rational plan of operative treatment. It was essential to carry out one's own pathological work, gross post-mortem examinations to check up possible operative errors and to elucidate the causes of symptoms observed during life. For example, I observed a series of cases of the relatively uncommon condition of spontaneous subarachnoid haemorrhage. I became familiar with and confident of their diagnosis, noted that in some there were signs pointing to the site of the responsible aneurysm. Those which bled recurrently in rapid succession died. I watched them die and afterwards noted at autopsy, how accurately one could have exposed them during life, on the clinical facts. These were healthy subjects and it seemed too bad that they should be lost because of a weak spot in a cerebral artery. These considerations led me to attempt operative treatment and I had the privilege of repairing such a leaking aneurysm of the Circle of Whillis (that circle of arteries at the base of the brain) for a personal friend and benefactor. It required knowledge and confidence in diagnosis, an appreciation of the surgical possibilities, combined into a feeling of rebellion against letting these cases die.

These were the words with which Dott in 1932 described to a Women's Medical Society the steps which led him to operate.[14] Equally well chosen was the description to the Medico Chirurgical Society of Edinburgh on 28 June 1933.

From post-mortem observations, we saw how a leakage from one of these small aneurysms induces thrombosis within and around the sac, and inferred that if a haemorrhage or a series of haemorrhages is not fatal it is likely to result in a fairly secure healing of the aneurysm by thrombosis and organisation into a solid mass. Thus we decided that, if another patient should have recurrent haemorrhages, and there was evidence of the site of the aneurysm, we should make some attempt to reinforce Nature's attempt at healing. We were accustomed to deal successfully with quite formidable intracranial haemorrhages during operations by applying to the bleeding point a fragment of fresh muscle which formed a secure scaffolding for the clot and became organised into fibrous tissue with it. Why not expose a bleeding aneurysm and deal with it after this fashion? It is surprising how few of these haemorrhages from aneurysms of the large basal arteries are immediately fatal; the majority give sufficient warning to allow one to formulate a plan of treatment. A majority of these patients, moreover, are comparatively young and many are perfectly healthy apart from this one small defect on a cerebral artery.

We did not have long to wait in order to put these speculations to the test of practice, for, ten days after the death of the last recorded case another presented and began to run a similar course.[15]

This calm logic and the courage which 'put it to the test', still, after half a century, excites a most profound admiration. Pause and see if we can recapture the atmosphere preceding the operation before continuing with Dott's own beautifully modulated phrases and unemotional description of the event. Dott was young, thirty-three years of age. He had been Honorary Surgeon to the Royal Hospital For Sick Children since 1925 and although he had been appointed as Consulting Neurological Surgeon to the Jordanburn Nerve Hospital in 1929 it was not until 1931, the year of this operation, that he was to achieve official status at the Edinburgh Royal Infirmary as Associate Neurological Surgeon.

The patient was a well known senior Edinburgh lawyer, who also happened to be the Chairman of the Board of Governors of the Royal Hospital for Sick Children. In later years Dott described him as, 'an able, middle-aged, legal gentleman, who ruled the medical staff as with a rod of iron, sometimes with whips of scorpions.' How much easier would it have been to let this illness pursue its accepted course to unavoidable death. Others could have ministered to the headaches and brought comfort to the bereaved family. Fortunately a, 'feeling of rebellion against letting these cases die' was too much for Norman Dott. What did he propose to do? The young, unestablished surgeon proposed to tell this able lawyer, who was used to ruling his medical staff, Dott himself included, with a rod of iron, that he appeared to be heading for certain death and that his only chance of escape was an untried operation carried out by one of the younger members of his staff. So well did he impart this information to an analytical mind, so well did he impart confidence, that the operation was arranged for 22 April 1931.

Fifty-seven years later Dr Eric Dott related how Norman had, after the event, confided in him that an eminent and senior Edinburgh surgeon, whose name he did not want to disclose for its very familiarity, had warned him against operating on the Chairman of the Board of Governors of the Sick Children's Hospital, saying that it would not be successful and it would damage his career and reputation. Norman had replied:

> My career and reputation have nothing to do with it. He will die if I don't operate, he might live if I do.[16]

Fortunately this advice, undoubtedly given with the kindest intention, was disregarded. Fortunately for subsequent generations of patients, the world over, the effects of this disregard were the opposite of those predicted.

Dott chose his assistants for this important operation with care. Sister Keith was still with him, Ian Aird was later to become the Professor of Surgery at the Postgraduate Medical School in London; A B Wallace, as we know, also gained eminence. The aneurysm was eventually wrapped with muscle taken from the tibialis anticus muscle, and this is the meaning behind the modest reference in a later letter from Dott to Professor Wilkie, already referred to: 'Mr Colin Black's tibialis anticus seems to have stuck well to his internal carotid.' To A B Wallace was entrusted the task during the operation of incising the leg and removing the required piece of muscle. With his usual humour he recalls, 'The following day I meekly enquired of the important patient. "Oh! he's fine," was Dott's reply. "All he complains of is his leg where you took the muscle from!"'

If such a major innovative operation were to take place today, it would undoubtedly be recorded in speech and moving picture, much of the latter beautifully magnified with the aid of the operating microscope. What a pity that we do not have such records of Dott's first essay! Regrettable too that the assistants are no longer with us to bring the scene to life and describe the emotions more fully. Perhaps however, Dott's own unembellished account sets the scene more fittingly. We know that all preparations would have been made and checked with the usual thoroughness—or was there a slightly keener edge today? The anaesthetist and anaesthesia so frequently unsung, would have been of the highest order. Then:

> A left frontal approach was employed and it was a difficult matter to elevate the tense and oedematous brain and identify the basal structures, which were bloodstained and largely embedded in clot. The left optic nerve was found and the internal carotid artery was defined at its outer side. This vessel was closely followed upwards outwards and backwards to its bifurcation into the middle and anterior cerebral arteries. As this point was being cleared of tenacious clot a formidable arterial haemorrhage filled the wound. With the aid of suction apparatus, held close to the bleeding point, we were able to see the aneurysm. It sprang from the upper aspect of the bifurcation junction; it was about 3mm in diameter; blood spurted freely from its semidetached fundus. Meanwhile a colleague was obtaining fresh muscle from the patient's leg. A small fragment of muscle was accurately applied to the bleeding point and held firmly in place so that it checked the bleeding and compressed the thin walled aneurysmal sac. Thus it was steadily maintained for twelve minutes. As the retaining instrument was then cautiously withdrawn, no further bleeding occurred. The vessel was further cleared and thin strips of muscle were prepared and wound around it until a thick collar of muscle embedded the aneurysm and adjacent arterial trunks.[17]

So lucidly do these wonderfully chosen words describe the operation and give us a picture of Dott himself; the unhurried orderly steps, despite the difficulties of swollen brain and blood clot, which might have caused a less intrepid surgeon to retreat. 'A formidable arterial haemorrhage.' In Dott parlance that, if anything, would be an understatement. Dott would also know, that, in addition to the difficulties of bringing it under control, each moment of bleeding was dangerously depriving the brain of its essential blood supply.

As to whether there were any fleeting regrets at having undertaken the operation, any pictures disturbing his concentrated mind of having to tell distraught relatives that there had been no success, images of a surgical career, if not ruined, at least severely constrained as too reckless, this is an imponderable which cannot be dismissed, for Dott never denied fear. His own words present a laconic statement of his views.

> Surgical capacity is an attitude of mind, manual dexterity is a small but important adjunct. Sometimes courage is required. Courage implies an appreciation of risk—in fact it implies fear under control. He who knows no fear is not courageous but reckless.

If indeed, he did experience fear, he was certainly courageous and it was not allowed to paralyse the calm manoeuvres taken successfully to arrest the haemorrhage. When Dott described this operation to the Edinburgh Medico Chirurgical Society, he was able to tell its members that over two years had elapsed since it had been undertaken and the patient was, 'so fully recovered that he is able for the responsible legal and social duties on which he was formerly engaged and he is able to indulge in shooting, mountaineering, etc.' On the same occasion, in the discussion which followed the presentation, Professor Bramwell commented:

> So far as I know, this is the first occasion upon which the question of the treatment of a leaking aneurysm by direct exposure has been brought before a medical society, at any rate in this country.[18]

It was only at a much later date that the record was completed, how he survived actively for some twelve years after his operation only to die of unrelated cardiac causes while stalking in the Highlands of Scotland.

Dott lived long enough to see intracranial aneurysm surgery established and become the major interest of neurosurgeons the world over. Ever a conscientious attender at congresses, it must have amused him to listen to enthusiast after enthusiast describing ever more sophisticated techniques for approaching and controlling these small but lethal lesions; opinions often delivered with scant regard to the slight, unobtrusive figure seated in the front row, a position sought not out of any sense of his own importance but because it offered a more comfortable position for his stiff painful leg. He himself actively pursued improvements in technique and new methods. In 1941 he had the temerity to open a large intracranial aneurysm in a nursing sister and stuff its cavity with muscle to its successful treatment.

A story he was fond of relating was of another 'first'. Deep in the centre of the brain is a small artery which transmits blood from one side of the brain to the other, as necessary. For obvious reasons it is termed the anterior communicating artery. With increasing study of subarachnoid haemorrhage and intracranial aneurysms it became evident that this artery was a common site for aneurysm formation and, in those earlier days of aneurysm surgery, extremely difficult of access without disturbing the vessels and aneurysm to cause further haemorrhage. Dott conceived the idea that it would be a safer procedure to put a clip on the larger artery which fed this small vessel and was sending jets of blood at high pressure into the aneurysm. This could be done without disturbing the aneurysm, which had already ruptured, and would render the aneurysm safe at the same time as the brain was left with an adequate circulation by a slight variation of the blood flow. He determined to put this into practice after explaining in detail to the patient, as was his wont, the originality of the operation.

But this was 1944 and the first appropriate patient, with aneurysm confirmed by the relatively new technique of angiography, was the 4th engineer of a Dutch merchantman, docked in Leith, who spoke hardly a word of English. As Dott put it:

> No relations could be contacted in war time to share the responsibility of a new operation upon a man who was now well but with a time bomb in his head. It was then that we turned to the merchant cheese importer for help—The Netherlands Consul in Edinburgh.[19]

He goes on to describe sitting the Consul in front of the stereoscopic X-ray viewing box, showing him the aneurysm, explaining the situation and obtaining his decisive permission. The operation was completed successfully and Mr de Kok returned to further years of active service in the Dutch Merchant marine. In later years, as an invitation speaker, Dott delighted to describe this case to the Netherlands Society of Neurological Surgeons. He also mentioned it in an address to the Rotary Club of Edinburgh hence his emphasis on the help provided by 'a merchant cheese importer'.

However courageous and carefully planned this first aneurysm operation was, however far-reaching its effects, Dott's continuing and enhancing reputation was not dependent on it alone. No surgical task was too trivial to merit his fullest attention. He would give the same thought to the best material, the correct placing and the optimum number of drainage holes in the simple tube used to divert the cerebrospinal fluid, obstructed in hydrocephalus, as to the steps of a major craniotomy. Concentration was maintained throughout an operation, whatever its length. However stressful or haemorrhagic an aneurysm or tumour case had been, still there were the same disciplines down to the correct tension of the last skin stitch and the careful application of the wound dressing with regard to its tension and reliability.

Given such an artist, such a perfectionist, the memories, among staff and trainees, of Dott the surgeon, his disciplines and foibles, within and without the operating theatre, are legion. The lights can be turned on only a few of the operations, which seem so closely associated with Dott, and would certainly excite memories of that slight though formidable figure, should any Dott trainees meet or gather.

What an education it was to a young registrar surgeon to see Dott clear the cavity of the fourth ventricle, the floor of which was the vital brain stem, clear it of those unpleasant tumours of childhood. The child might be small, the tumour bloody, but Dott would work away deftly and confidently. He paused at the bloodiest point, when the registrar was wondering whether it would not be justifiable to withdraw defeated, and, as if defining what was in his assitant's mind, there was a suggestion of amusement in his eyes as he said, 'You have to get all of these away or else you never stop the bleeding.' So he continued and soon intermittent glimpses, through blood and tumour, of the pale brain stem were afforded as encouragement, and before long bleeding had been arrested, the fourth ventricle was free to the flow of clear cerebrospinal fluid and, forming its floor, could be seen, pulsating normally, that vital area of the brain where respiration, circulation, facial and eye movements, are all controlled. In later years when the trainees themselves were called upon to carry out similar operations and felt they had acquitted themselves well by removing the tumour leaving only a minor degree of transient imbalance or disturbance of eye movement, they would be put into perspective or 'cut down to size' by Dr Kate Hermann. This loyal colleague of Professor Dott, a German Jewish neurologist, who had fled from the Nazis and been accepted by Dott, used to approach the young surgeon as he secretly admired his own work and in her guttural tones say, 'Ach! but when Professor Dott did this operation I could only tell that it had been carried out because of the dressing at the back of the patient's head!'

In a lecture Dott once said that he entered neurosurgery through the wicket gate of endocrinology. If we accept this analogy then surely the latch that he undid was the pituitary gland. This and his training with Cushing left him an undying interest in operations on the pituitary. Dott returned to Edinburgh from Boston to publish with Bailey the review of Cushing's pituitary tumour cases and to continue operating on similar patients by the technique which he had learned in the United States.

This operation, termed a transphenoidal hypophysectomy, involved an approach through the nose to breach the floor of the skull at the roof of the nose or sphenoid bone, thus entering the pituitary fossa and affording access to the abnormal pituitary gland. Needless to say, such an operation takes place in the depths of a darkened cavity, frequently further obscured by bleeding, and with the use of long instruments needing skilled manipulation. Dott worked assiduously to improve his techniques and to gain experience in this type of surgery; he made modifications to improve malleable indwelling lights. Thus he achieved good results by removing as much tumour as possible and following with radiotherapy. These benefits and their documentation together formed merely another example of Dott's meticulous care for his patients.

Characteristically a pituitary tumour expands upwards within the cranium, to impinge on the optic chiasm, which is the junction of the optic nerves. This impairs the field of vision in a typical pattern, which varies somewhat dependent upon whether the tumour expands upwards directly in the midline or expands asymmetrically to one or other side. The art or science of perimetry is to map out these defects in the visual fields. This is done by exposing to one eye at a time and at a given distance, test targets of varying diameter and varying colour, usually white and red. The patient is asked to notify the examiner when they are first seen. From these maps or visual field charts, can be deduced the type of pressure that is being exerted on the optic chiasm and therefore whether the lesion is compatible with a pituitary tumour. If so, an estimate of the size and contours of the tumour may be arrived at. Perimetry was carried out with great care and expertise on all of Dott's patients both before and at intervals after operation. This too is why Cushing, in one of his early letters to Dott, commended him to cooperation with Drs Stirling and Traquair. Both had already established reputations in perimetry. Thus by perimetry and careful stereoscopic X-ray study of the contours of the pituitary fossa Dott would build a picture in his mind of the tumour to be dealt with. Of course endocrine assessment was also completed by the appropriate specialists and replacement therapy started as necessary. In those days, these were usually the only investigations carried out.

However Dott's clinical acumen was never blunted and the case presented to him as a pituitary tumour, with perimetry and skull X-ray seeming to confirm the diagnosis, is remembered by many. Dott rejected the diagnosis because it came to his hearing that the lady was still menstruating and his long experience had suggested to him that a lady harbouring a tumour of that size never continued to menstruate. The large intracranial aneurysm masquerading as a pituitary tumour was subsequently shown by the angiogram which he ordered. Present-day regimes are in marked contrast to those of Dott in the heyday of his pituitary surgery but his results still bear comparison and he played a telling part in advancing pituitary surgery towards its present sophisticated standards.

Today the pituitary gland, its pathologies and surrounding structures can be visualised as a routine by advanced imaging techniques such as magnetic resonance imaging. By the same method even very small pituitary tumours can be identified and defined from surrounding normal pituitary tissue. Circulating pituitary hormones can be identified and quantitated more accurately. Drugs have been developed which diminish pathological hypersecretion and can even 'shrink' some pituitary tumours. This all leads to better results and Dott would have been the first to describe his activities as merely 'a step on the way'.

Shortly before Professor Dott retired, a patient was presented to him for an opinion. She was an attractive young woman, whose complaint was of amenorrhoea or lack of periods and subsequent sterility. Skull X-rays showed minimal and equivocal changes in the pituitary fossa suggesting a microscopic tumour of the pituitary. Dott pondered deeply all aspects of the problem, painfully concerned that, at that time, he had no surgery to offer to alleviate her distress. The risk of damaging normal pituitary tissue while removing the minute tumour was too great for the attempt. Today her condition would be managed satisfactorily either by drugs or micro-surgery.

It is ironic how Professor Dott played his part in developing micro-surgery of the pituitary. When he returned to Edinburgh to practise and improve the transphenoidal hypophysectomy, which he had learned from Cushing, his old mentor had already given up the operation. In a letter written to Dott he confirmed this, saying that Henderson had reviewed the results of his transphenoidal operations and he, himself, had not realised that the results were so satisfactory. It is open to conjecture why, apart from this, Cushing had given up the operation. Had he encountered some diagnostic difficulties? Had he just found that a craniotomy with a transcranial approach to the pituitary was becoming so much safer? There is no knowing, but it is clear that, conversely, Dott, with his painstaking meth-ods, was establishing increasing confidence in the transphenoidal route in his own hands. Some years later Gérard Guiot, an eminent Parisian neuro-surgeon, visited Dott in Edinburgh and was so impressed with what he saw of Dott and the transphenoidal route, that he returned to Paris armed with details of the instrumentation and determined to practise the same approach. What would be more natural than that his assistant Jules Hardy should also become adept at the procedure? Hardy became established in Montreal and, with the advent of the operating microscope, pioneered and expanded the whole field of modern-day transphenoidal pituitary micro-surgery.

Now watch Dott carrying out a typical pituitary operation. The patient, lying supine, is covered overall by surgical drapes; only the nose and mouth are exposed. Dott leans over this area with a headlight on and every now and then adjusts the position of the long malleable light, held by the assistant. Anxiety lies in the narrowly exposed eyes of his assistant who is responsible for maintaining the correct position of this light but can only fleetingly see the deep operation site as he peers first one way then another around Dott's neck and hands. Sister too looks anxious, especially when she sees the light start to flicker and go out, which, test it as you may before the operation, seems unfailingly to occur at least once during that crucial period.

How Dott would have appreciated the convenience of transaxial illumination of the operating microscope which was denied to him by a matter of years. Sister can see even less of the operating field than the assistant and the confident way she slaps the instruments into Dott's outstretched hand comes only from years of experience and the ability to deduce the stage of the operation from sound and hand movements. She too, in company with the small group of hopeful postgraduate students, hovering behind the assistant, seeing little but hanging eagerly on any word or gesture, would have appreciated the modern microscope, with its television facility; all would have been shown so clearly, on a nearby screen. So approximately ninety minutes pass to the noise of the sucker, or of instruments against bone, the silence of soft tissues, the occasional, sometimes testy, interjection. Then Dott packs the nose and strips off his gloves. His assistants have been privileged by an occasional fleeting glance of the vital areas. The anaesthetist and sister clear the drapes and leave you thinking that the former never gets sufficient recognition for maintaining the unseen patient in admirable condition from the distance which sterility demands.

There is another operation, which though now consigned to history, was Dott's concept and reflects the character which achieved where others faltered. Imagine again that part of the back of the cranium, deeply hidden under the strong muscles of the neck, which forms a compartment harbouring the most vital parts of the brain. Within this posterior cranial fossa, and at its deepest part, two nerves leave the brain stem and run adjacent courses to a small orifice in the bony wall. One is the facial nerve which controls the muscles of facial expression, the other is the auditory nerve, which, formed of two divisions, subserves hearing and balance. On this auditory nerve a tumour may develop. It is entirely benign, grows slowly but if neglected destroys hearing and balance and threatens life by pressure on the brain. Today, doctors recognise the manifestations of such a tumour in their earliest form. Highly specialised hearing tests reveal a characteristic pattern of impairment by even the smallest of tumours, which may then be visualised by up-to-date X-ray and imaging techniques. Such small tumours are removed under the operating microscope by a specially trained neurosurgeon or otologist or by both working together. Thus the benign tumour is totally excised and, working with the finest instruments and considerable expertise, facial movements and even hearing may be preserved.

In earlier days, when Dott was striving to establish neurosurgery, and during most of his active surgical career, patients were less ready to trouble their doctors with symptoms which were tolerable, a buzzing or deafness in one ear. Doctors were less conversant with the syndrome, the effects of the tumour, if neglected, and what could be achieved. Methods of investigation were considerably less refined. So it was far more common for these tumours to reach a large size, causing considerable disability and deterioration in the patient's condition before their excision was attempted. Discussion used to rage as to whether total excision of the tumour should be completed, in which case the facial nerve was invariably damaged leaving the patient with that distressing deformity of a face, flattened and drooping on one side, and unable to smile or express emotion. Alternatively, it was argued, a subtotal excision was preferable to this curative operation with appalling deformity, even if it did mean re-operation at a later date when the residuum of his tumour, left protectively round the facial nerve, had regrown.

One day in 1936 Dott was faced with the removal of a very large tumour of this type. After many hours of operating, he successfully completed a total excision. The majority of surgeons would then have hastened to close the wound with self- congratulatory feelings of relief. Not so Dott. Always observant and anxious to improve upon his techniques, he noted that the tumour had been so large that it had compressed and displaced the neighbouring cerebellum to such an extent that a large cavity remained within the cranium. In the depths of this, issuing from the brain stem, could be identified with ease the severed facial nerve. Some 3 mm of the nerve remained. As Dott took in these appearances, he must also have pictured the unsightly disfigurement, due to facial paralysis, that was to be the patient's lot and legacy even although he had been cured of his tumour.

Pondering this, he realised that there was sufficient nerve 'stump' and room to work in, albeit at a most inconvenient depth to consider repair by nerve grafting, although it would be an extremely difficult manoeuvre. Recall how the facial nerve leaves the brain stem and runs a short course through the cranial cavity to enter an orifice or foramen in the bone. Having entered the bone it follows a tortuous route before emerging from the base of the skull to run another equally short course in the neck and then break up into fine branches supplying individual facial muscles. Dott realised that in the leg there was a dispensable nerve, the sural nerve, of an appropriate diameter to serve as a facial nerve graft. If he could join one end of a measured length of this nerve to the 'stump' of facial nerve adjacent to the brain stem he could lead the remainder of the graft out of the cranium and bury it in the tissues of the neck. At a subsequent operation, confined to the neck, he could identify the facial nerve as it left the base of the skull, section it, retrieve the distal end of the graft and unite it to the distal facial nerve, with its muscular branches. In this way he might anticipate some return of function.

Arrangements were set in hand. His talented anaesthetist, Dr Maxwell Brown, was allocated the task of making a very fine elongated needle holder, which could grip, manipulate, release and grip again the extremely small needle at the necessary depth. Whenever, on subsequent occasions, he described this operation, Dott always gave the fullest acknowledgement to the beautiful finely turned instrument that Dr Maxwell Brown produced. Many with considerable experience of operating in the posterior cranial fossa can scarcely credit that the manoeuvre was possible. This is how Dott described it:

> We used a fine lace needle and speared the nerve stump, then progressively broke away the pointed end of the needle until only approximately 7 mm remained with the eye, this allowed the needle to be turned and brought out of the wound.

Thus was the union or anastomosis of the nerves achieved and in 1945 Dott described the operation to the Society of British Neurological Surgeons presenting two successful cases. In one of these the facial nerve had been damaged by a gunshot wound of the mastoid region. The operation excited considerable interest and there was reference to it in more than one publication. Dott was also asked to speak on the subject at various meetings. He seemed somewhat reluctant; it was a very difficult operation for ordinary surgeons and his attitude is summed up in his closing words on the topic to the Second Workshop on Reconstructive Middle Ear Surgery in Chicago in 1963.

> If acoustic tumours were habitually diagnosed in their 'otological stage' that is when only a few millimetres in diameter, they could be totally removed every time, without causing facial paralysis. I am convinced that this can and will be done. Then my operation will be found only in the pages of history.

He did allow however that it might still have a place in severe traumatic disorganisation in the mastoid region. Was this then an operation overtaken by history and too difficult for ordinary mortals? Probably it was but it still seems to illuminate Dott, the surgeon and the man, with his ingenuity and painstaking application.

No description of Dott the surgeon would be complete without reference to his attitudes to pain and his attempts to relieve the pain of his patients, both acute and chronically intractable. Throughout his career, he himself suffered a great deal of pain stemming from his hip injury in youth. He was stoical about this and seemed able to divorce his dauntless spirit, with its impelling tasks for the welfare of humanity, from the lagging body in which it was entrapped. The latter he was able to study, as if it belonged to one of his patients needing now fusion of a joint, now a cordotomy operation for pain; describing accurately the nerve root distribution of his pain and finally amputating, himself by his own fireside and under local anaesthetic, a painful toe when he considered it too troublesome to serve any further purpose. No doubt his own suffering made him more aware of what others could be enduring. Not that he was sentimentally weak in this regard. He demanded an accurate assessment of pain, its causes and distribution. It had to be shown to be intractable to well planned simple drug regimes before he would undertake any operation specifically for its relief. Again his own words supply the best description of his attitudes to pain as he elaborates on the topic in an early undergraduate lecture.

> Pain, the most prominent and commanding of symptoms. It is a sensory perception but, more importantly, it is an affective experience. We know it only from our own experience; our attitude to it, as it affects others, is necessarily one of belief or faith. Remember this always when you listen to your patient's woes expressed with varying command of descriptive analogy. Do not dismiss his pain too readily as imaginary or exaggerated. After all, it is how the pain strikes your patient—not yourself—that matters.

Later in 1959, he was asked to address the Section of Neurology of the Royal Society of Medicine in London on 'The Treatment of Intractable Pain'. Again he made the point that 'it is the patient's own valuation of his pain that is of real importance.' He underlines this with telling humour by recalling the old limerick:

> *There was a faith-healer of Deal*
> *who declared, 'If pain isn't quite real,*
> *when I sit on a pin,*
> *and it punctures my skin,*
> *I dislike what I fancy I feel.'*

He refers to racial differences in pain perception—the Stoics—and describes a 'Scottish Stoic' he had recently encountered. A Scottish Borderer patient had consulted him because of severe spasms of facial neuralgia but had dismissed his own suffering with the words, 'Ye ken doctor, I could thole (bear) it, but it's the wife—she canna bear tae see me in them.'

In more serious vein, Dott continued to expose his balanced assessment of others' complaints.

> The Stoics are few nowadays; and I think the Welfare State rather favours the neurotic, dependent attitude—'I have a pain and it's somebody's duty to take it away.' I do not believe that a neurotic patient's over-valuation of pain is a contra indication to surgical treatment. Rather it is an indication in favour of it for ultimately it is the patient's valuation of his pain that is of real importance.

Based on these views Professor Dott undertook numerous and varying operations and injection procedures for intractable pain. Although he was not the originator, one that he made particularly his own and in which he developed a considerable expertise was the injection for trigeminal neuralgia. This was familiarly known as a Tic Injection from the French 'Tic Douloureux' given to the severe spasms of facial pain or Facial Neuralgia for which it was usually administered. The whole elaborate procedure merits description because it will stir memories in any grateful patients, who are still surviving, will serve wry recall to more than one old member of

Dott's staff and above all add another perspective to Dott's character and skills as a surgeon.

The patient, usually elderly, was admitted as urgently as possible because the pain was undeniably severe. He or she would be seen in the ward with the diagnosis self-evident because of the expression of profound depression or fear of the next spasm. Perhaps a handkerchief or hand would be pressed to the face on one side in an attempt to relieve the agony. Conversation would be limited for fear of initiating another spasm of pain; sometimes it was terminated in mid sentence by a spasm. Inspection might reveal that the patient had been unable to wash or shave the affected half of the face. At mid afternoon sister would attach a notice to the door of the room set aside for surgical dressings and injection procedures: 'Silence Tic Injection'. Mid-afternoon, because, when a senior neurologist asked Professor Dott about his technique for these injections his first comment was, 'They are all done after 4.30 p.m. and never followed by an inescapable engagement later in the evening.' He continued, 'I am rather horrified at you considering pain of injection a factor. I think I very rarely hurt mine more than the initial skin prick with a very fine hypodermic needle.'

Peace and undisturbed concentration were the main factors in a successful procedure. Sister would also make arrangements for her senior staff nurse to take charge of the ward for she knew she was to be closeted with Professor Dott and the patient for the next hour or two and no interruptions were permitted. The patient, worn down by pain and anxiety and wondering what the next hour held, would be brought in. Sister would carry out a last minute check of the sterile instrument trolley. This was always laid out precisely, each bowl, each syringe, each needle in its correct and accustomed position so that any could be reached without disturbing the concentration and without risk of mistake.

One and only one selected trainee might be allowed in to watch the procedure. He would be expected to learn by observation; he was certainly not expected to speak. If he were lucky he might glean a few comments from Dott. Then Dott would arrive, take off his jacket and put on the gown proffered by sister. Words were few. There might be an enquiry, directed at sister, about a patient in the ward. Garbed, Dott would make his way over to the patient who was now lying on a trolley with head towards the light of the window. Concentration lined his intent face as he limped forward and was barely relaxed as his eyes smiled some confidence to the patient. Reassurance loosened the taut features of the sufferer as soon as he heard that essentially Scottish voice speaking the same familiar language, 'Just a few wee lines on your face to help me get the needle in the right place.'

The complex lines were marked out with a special skin pencil. After anaesthetising the proposed line of injection with local anaesthetic, Dott would pick up the long fine needle, approximately 10 centimetres in length, puncture the skin near the angle of the mouth and deftly advance the point some 7 centimetres. A few minor adjustments ensued and then a relaxation and Dott would stand back from his semi-crouched position. You knew that he had successfully entered with the point of his needle the very small opening or foramen at the base of the skull, which transmitted the nerve, the cause of this dreadful pain. Sister, who had been standing almost to attention, at the patient's side, relaxed, also perhaps examining her arm and hand where the patient had been gripping her, digging in to relieve tension, though pain had not been great. The skill of reaching that small hole in the base of the skull, after passing through all the sensitive tissues of the face could only really be assessed by watching a tyro at the same procedure with his repeated painful ineffectual jabs. But to pass through the foramen was not sufficient; the needle point had to be placed within it, to an accuracy of millimetres, to ensure permanent interruption in the nerve's conductivity and relief of pain. Furthermore the needle point was now within the cranial cavity, within the cerebrospinal fluid pathways and adjacent to the brain where injection of sclerosing fluid even slightly misplaced could cause untold damage. Only if a small fraction of reversible local anaesthetic, on injection, caused immediate total loss of sensation over the side of the face, was Dott satisfied that the needle point was precisely located. Then ensued the injection of sclerosing alcohol with a very small syringe calibrated so that a tenth of a cubic centimetere of alcohol could be delivered at a time. Between each injection there was an unhurried pause in which the patient's response was noted, eye movements were tested and any irregularity of the pupils detected. Thus the injection of 2.1 cubic centimetres of alcohol was completed fraction by fraction.

The unusual quantity of 2.1 cubic centimetres was always related to a sister, fraying under the strain of standing silent for ninety minutes watching each meticulous step. 'You think you have injected two cubic centimetres,' she was supposed to have said, greatly daring, at the end of the procedure, 'but you have left some solution in the needle!' Dott was always ready to accept a well proven point hence, ever afterwards, sister's 2.1 cubic centimetres!

Even this precision was not enough. A dressing was wrapped around the needle, which was left in situ, and a transparent plastic cup secured over the orbit on the affected side, before the patient was returned to the ward. Observation continued for two hours. Only if careful testing at the end of this period revealed a persistent complete loss of sensation was the needle removed and the injection procedure accepted as successful. The plastic cup had been placed to protect the surface of the eye, for one drawback to this form of therapy was that the eye was deprived of sensation and therefore rendered more vulnerable to damage and ulceration by such hazards of day to day living as dust and splashing.

A further step had to be completed before the unsightly cup was discarded. On a visit to Toronto, Dott had been shown by the surgeon Kenneth McKenzie the beneficial effects on chronic ulcers around the nose of excising the nerve chain in the neck called the cervical sympathetic nerve. The understanding was that removal of this nerve chain diminished tone in the vessels to the area, increased the blood flow and thereby enhanced healing. Ever ready to learn from other surgeons' practice and apply to his own work, Dott not only conceived the idea that such an operation might be useful in ulceration of the cornea, after his injection procedure, but might, better still, be carried out routinely as a 'prophylaxis'. This he instituted.

Finally before the patient departed from the ward, usually pain-free and mightily relieved, it was the resident's duty to fit him with protective spectacles, with side pieces, to prevent dust entering the orbit, and to provide him with a typed sheet of simple instructions for the care of the anaesthetic eye. Not only was the resident usually asked by Dott whether he had provided the typed sheet but he would also be asked whether he had read the instructions over to the patient to make certain he understood them!

With this profound and characteristic attention to detail, Dott achieved excellent results in this miserable condition. Not unlike a golfer or a cricketer, who revels in his best shots, he undoubtedly gained satisfaction from these injections and was stimulated by carrying them out and teaching others. But he kept an open mind. He was prepared to operate and section part of the nerve under direct vision, leaving sensation in the eye intact, if pain was confined to the lower half of the face. Continually he searched among different techniques and different solutions for a means of permanent pain relief accompanied by some retention of sensation in the face. The years following his retirement and death have seen the introduction of a drug which simply and effectively controls the largest percentage of these cases of spasmodic facial pain. They have seen the introduction of new procedures for those cases resistant to drug therapy, new procedures which aim to abolish pain and yet retain sensation; ingenious operations to cushion abnormal vessels pulsating against the nerve, graduated thermo coagulation made possible by modern technology. No doubt Dott, had his time span been different, would have taken an active part in these arguments and advances.

It is evident that throughout his career, Dott was always ready to learn, even when others regarded him as a most senior neurosurgeon. He soon put into practice Moniz's advance of cerebral angiography and was the first in the United Kingdom to demonstrate an arteriovenous malformation of the brain and an intracranial aneurysm. He was early in the field of surgical diathermy and he wrote to Cushing in 1929 that he got Cairns, 'to come down here to help me with my first electrosurgical effort—a case of a huge angioma in the roof of the fourth ventricule.' In 1949 he wrote to Geoffrey Jefferson describing how he had taken up the technique of preoperative bleeding, storage of blood and reinfusion at operation as necessary 'and had done 15-20 cases without snags.' This technique gave way to the readier availability of blood transfusion services though strangely has, at the present day, returned for discussion in the light of the AIDS epidemic. He used to return from visits and congresses with his little notepads, covered with pencilled notes, ideas from the most junior as well as the most eminent speakers.

It is his trip to Norway in 1960 however that is surely unique for a senior surgeon seeking knowledge and new techniques. In that year a young Australian, the son of a doctor, an enthusiastic oarsman and with a university career before him, collapsed with his first fit. The ominous hissing and rumbling noise heard through the stethoscope pressed to his head, left little doubt that an arteriovenous malformation of the brain had bled. Angiography confirmed this and showed that it was so strategically sited that its excision might inflict disability; and yet to leave it would surely entail further fits and further life-threatening haemorrhage. The boy, accompanied by his mother, arrived in Edinburgh for consultation with Professor Dott. If a patient has travelled half way round the world for consultation, it takes a big character to step down from the position of ultimate oracle. But Dott had heard of Doctor Kristiansen's work in Oslo. Kristiansen by cannulating the main carotid artery in the neck was cooling the cerebral blood-flow to low temperatures thus shrinking any vascular anomaly and also rendering the brain less vulnerable to damage from disturbance of blood vessels and neural tissue. He was invited to Edinburgh to describe his techniques. Dott conceived the idea that they would be of benefit to his young Australian patient and should be pursued. With what must have been extraordinary powers of persuasion he was able to secure the Health Board's agreement to the funding, for travel to Oslo, for himself, a small group of younger surgeons and an anaesthetist. There the young Australian was operated upon most successfully, Dott actually excising the malformation, and the cerebral cooling techniques were studied. On coming back to Edinburgh (and his party recall with amusement how they nearly missed the return plane because of his insistence on breaking the journey to the airport for a final assessment of his young convalescent friend) Professor Dott set about plans to continue similar work. This was his introductory letter to Professor Michael Woodruff, in charge of the Wilkie Surgical Research Laboratory.

> As I mentioned, from the latter part of June 1961, I would hope to set aside one day a week from about 11 a.m. for laboratory work and my objective is local cerebral cooling; I have an idea that when I retire from clinical work in

August 1962, I might put in more intensive laboratory work for a year or two. I started professional life as an experimental physiologist—I would rather like to finish in the laboratory after too busy a clinical life.

Dott's skills in the operating theatre, the operations he conceived and carried out, would have been valueless if they had not been followed by equally detailed after care. The regime of the 'Tic Injection' illustrates this. Nurse, from his days of operating at the nursing home in Great King Street, recalls that Dott, looking so young, visited his patients daily, or even twice or more if necessary. Staff nurse from ward 13 and 14 at the Royal Infirmary remembers Mr Dott always calling in to see his patients late in the evening. There are recollections from Bangour days of the inconspicuous figure in the dressing gown moving down the ward to attend a particular patient, though one has to admit that there is probably a misinterpretation here: not Dott raised from his bed but Dott with a hospital dressing gown thrown over his theatre clothes after a late operating session. However lengthy the operating session, he never left the hospital without a final visit to the ward to see that the patient was recovering well. In addition there might be an instruction to the resident or registrar to, 'Just phone me at such an o'clock to let me know how he is.' His residents and registrars, too, knew that phone calls might come at any time of day or well into the night. The unfortunate resident was expected to answer Dott's queries on any patient in the ward immediately. Sometimes he had to answer questions on nearly all the patients. If he sounded hesitant on any point he was sent to confirm, 'Just go into the ward and find out!' Ward rounds were rigorous, and usually twice a day. Each change in the patient's condition had to be interpreted, action taken to correct it if it were a deterioration and all appropriately reported.

In addition to this detailed early after care Dott had, for those days, an unusually wide vision of rehabilitation. This, if not derived from, was enhanced by his wartime experiences in the Brain Injuries Unit and the necessity to resettle the war wounded. His weekly meetings, where the continuing care of those discharged from hospital was fully discussed, were termed 'Blitzes'. He had ensured that he was surrounded by specialists in after care, for succour of the whole being—today's 'holistic' medicine—neurologists, psychologists, psychiatrists, physiotherapists, speech therapists, occupational therapists. He always gave due credit to Rockefeller bounty for enabling him to set up this incomparable team.

Such was Dott the surgeon, acclaimed by his patients and peers; a martinet served devotedly by a disciplined staff. He was a skilled technician, yet a humane doctor of deep compassion. He was an innovator and pioneer, yet quick to appreciate and establish other's innovations. He relished diagnosis and operation, yet did not shirk rehabilitation. He taught and was taught. He lives in numerous trainees the world over and in their pupils and work.

CHAPTER ELEVEN

Fast Hold of Instruction

And gladly wold he lerne, and gladly teche
(Chaucer)

Only continuous learning can make a good teacher and Dott was not wanting in this respect. Early he gave evidence of this; in 1930 in the hope of gaining improved facilities he circulated a *Statement re: Surgical Neurological Work in Edinburgh by Norman M Dott*. At the foot of page two starts a paragraph of relevance:

> Some idea of the nature of the work, its value to suffering humanity and the actual results being obtained may be gained by reference to my *Recent Experiences in Intracranial Surgery* published in 1928, in which my first 50 cases are recorded. Since then by diligent improvement in methods and by increasing experience, the results in the next 100 cases show improvement e.g. the operative mortality has been reduced from 17% to 6%.[1]

Similarly all through his working life Dott was learning from an increasingly vast experience and it was characteristic of him, that, when an unusual problem was encountered or a distressing complication developed, a relevant case was conjured up from the past and its lessons applied. His memory achieved this so readily that one failure in teaching, of which he could be accused, was a failure to teach the value of modern data recording and reclaim. This was learning from his own experience. He was not too proud to learn from others, however junior. Already described is his conscientious attendance at symposia and congresses, and how the sheets of his little writing tablets would be covered by pencilled entries, however junior the speaker might be.

Nearer home, he was quite ready to learn from his junior staff, even to the extent of the extra 0.1 ml of alcohol in the injection syringe for facial pain. One day a small child of about six years of age was admitted complaining of severe sciatic pain. This was most unusual. 'Slipped Discs' are excessively rare at that age. Eventually a small cyst, composed of skin elements and pressing on one of the nerve roots to the leg as it lay within the spine was demonstrated and excised. One of Dott's junior staff, a Greek trainee, became increasingly excited as this girl's investigation and treatment proceeded. It appeared that because of restricted resources in Greece at that time, he was familiar with lumbar puncture being carried out using a needle without a stilette within it. This could, at the initial puncture, pick up a fragment of skin in its lumen, and carry it into the spinal column where, over the ensuing weeks and months, it could grow into a cyst and press on nerve roots. Dott was intrigued and encouraging so that it was not long before the Greek house officer had uncovered a history of the child having been treated in infancy for meningitis by repeated lumbar punctures. With Dott's backing, he exhibited a display, at the combined British and Canadian Medical Associations' meeting, of this case and the mechanism by which the cyst developed.

This eagerness to learn and to pass on his knowledge remained with Dott during all his active working life. The great lengths to which he went, to learn the techniques of cerebral cooling and to put them into effect towards the end of his career, as described in the previous chapter, is one of the supreme examples of his ceaseless quest for the grail of knowledge.

It has been said that Dott was not a great teacher; he was more a practical surgeon. This is a superficial assessment largely based on the routine lectures which he, as the incumbent of the chair of Surgical Neurology, was bound to deliver to medical undergraduates. His style, to a slight degree, was ironically pedantic. His subject was rarefied and remote for the average student with his mind on examinations and a very general practice. Delivery was too analytic for a student body, which, on the whole preferred the more flamboyant dogmatic teacher. Nevertheless he knew their needs and, at a very early stage, had recommended that they be not troubled by details of operations. Rather he concentrated on the diagnosis of more common life-threatening neurological conditions.

But no-one could fail to follow and be impressed by his gentle and rational unfolding of the problems of pain, its assessment and management; by his discussion of the preparation of the patient and his relatives for operation and, above all, by his description of the pathologies of rising intracranial pressure and his deductions from them of the correct therapies.

If Dott was not a dramatic lecturer he was still a good teacher. He taught patients, he taught nurses. Occupational therapists and physiotherapists were among the professionals, complementary to medicine, who learnt from him. He taught young doctors who did not contemplate a career in surgical neurology; he taught more senior neurosurgical trainees. Firmly and precisely, he made his views on medical education, hospital planning and surgical matters in general, widely known to senior colleagues in the profession and to administrators alike. He taught by simple routine lecture; but was well aware of the close liaison of the visual cerebral cortex with memory and used extensively, small 2″ × 2″ slides, each a photograph, X-ray or diagram, taken from his army of patients, to illustrate a point. Although he was a member of the University Senatus Sub-Committee on Teaching by Television and Broadcasting, although his work and his department was the subject of an early television programme 'Your Life in Their Hands', and he himself broadcast at least one charity radio appeal, his active career preceded the present almost universal use of videotapes and television in instruction on medical matters. He taught by careful arrange-ment of courses and lectures. He was instrumental in establishing a course and certification in Neurosurgical Nursing in the new Department of Surgical Neurology.

In earlier years he was responsible for the Neurosurgical component of the Royal College of Surgeons Postgraduate Surgery Courses. Professor Ritchie recalls Dott's care in ensuring that any course which he had arranged, should be of the best quality:

> He established a postgraduate course in what one might call applied neur-ology; several people took part and I had the job of doing some of the lectures. It was not entirely conducive to self-confidence to see the Great Man himself come in at the back of the Royal Infirmary lecture theatre to listen to the first run of lectures. He went to all of them, which he need not have done, but he wanted to make sure that the course was along the lines, which he had in mind.[2]

Above all he taught patients. This was always an outstanding feature of his practice. Perhaps influenced by his own disabilities, he was never content to administer the appropriate therapy, surgical or otherwise, and then consider that he had discharged his responsibility. He must encourage and ease the patient back into as rewarding community life as possible. In this he was well in advance of today's established concepts. And so before discharge, he would take the patient with an anaesthetic eye aside and instruct him in detail about the day-to-day care and precautions which were necessary. The same applied to a patient who had had pain in a lower limb treated by cordotomy. Here of course he had had very personal experience. But he was still learning. Dr David Bowsher, the well-known authority on Pain, writes from 'The Pain Relief Foundation': 'I was enquiring into the physiological aspects of cordotomy and wrote asking Professor Dott if I could perform various tests on post-cordotomy patients.' Instead of the anticipated formal reply, Dr Bowsher received an invitation to come and stay with Professor and Mrs Dott in Edinburgh. This he did, and when he explained to them his difficulty in investigating, reliably, whether cordotomised patients could be startled on their affected side, Professor Dott was most interested and volunteered himself as a subject.

> I showed Mrs Dott how I wanted her to creep up on him from behind and tap him sharply on a bony prominence in the affected region—and left

Edinburgh! Mrs Dott subsequently reported, with a confirmatory postscript from the Professor, that he had reacted too violently, abruptly and bad-temperedly for the experiment to continue. None of this prevented him from coming to stay with me next time he was in Liverpool for a meeting and being as kind and charming as ever![3]

This teaching of continuing self-care was exemplified by his reaction to his own colostomy and the encouragement and advice his patients received at the Stoma clinic. He even invited patients to his own home to advise them on colostomy care, helping them so much by this informality to overcome reticence. On a wider scale, in these matters, he taught by articles in medical journals and by lectures to community nurses and doctors of widely different disciplines.

In similar fashion Dott taught workers in varying medical fields, and reached out to individual patients and their families with instruction and messages of hope and confidence, by joining and accepting high office in various societies. Age and disability simply could not wither his capacity for work nor stale his infinite enthusiasm in difficult areas. Epilepsy, Spina Bifida, Paraplegia, and Cancer. Many relatives of those afflicted confirmed that he had instilled in them understanding and renewed confidence.

> In 1965 we started the Scottish Spina Bifida Association. Professor Dott agreed to be our President. It is difficult to find the right words in speaking of him. He would come to our meetings, would understand our anger that there would be no 'cure' for our children, would speak with his soft voice, would smoke his pipe, would chuckle. It was as if his very presence subdued our anxiety.[4]

If these were activities of his retirement, he had during his surgical career, close and active associations with the Chartered Society of Physiotherapy and the Association of Occupational Therapists, with all the implications of teaching therein. In 1962 he delivered the Founders' Lecture, *The Road to Recovery* to the Annual Congress of the Chartered Society in which he confirmed his admiration for the work of physiotherapists in rehabilitation and saluted them as 'A Profession Complementary (as opposed to Supplementary) to Medicine'. He was, perhaps, even closer to the Association of Occupational Therapists. For many years he was President of the Scottish Association of Occupational Therapists and as one senior therapist, Miss Loggie, confirms, gave a tremendous amount of support to the development of Occupational Therapy in Scotland. He was also one of the first Honorary Fellows of the World Federation of Occupational Therapists and was instrumental in getting permission for the first inter-national congress to be held at his old school. On that occasion he delighted overseas delegates by including in his speech of welcome a description of the original Herioter's uniform—'browne breekis of ane tweed clothe!'—and advising them to assume it in order to survive the Edinburgh climate! Miss Loggie concludes:

> He was a marvellous man to work for, or with, as he would have insisted, firm but kind, sometimes rather frightening because his expectations were so high though always centred on the welfare of patients.[5]

Invaluable as these Associations were, the Society through which Dott exerted the greatest influence on the teaching and practice of Surgical Neurology, on the maintenance and improvement of standards in the speciality, throughout the United Kingdom and further afield, was the Society of British Neurological Surgeons. In latter days, seeing this unassuming, slight figure at meetings of the Society, few would conceive that he had been involved in its foundation in 1926 and had been the President throughout the war years, his term of office being from 1938 to 1945. He was first elected Honorary Assistant Secretary and Librarian in 1927 and finally to the supreme accolade of Honorary Membership in 1962. It was a Society dear to his heart and he realised its importance from inception.

He was a most conscientious attender. Carefully preserved programmes of all meetings, during his lifetime, were found in his papers and he left his surgical trainees and colleagues, after he had put them up for membership, in no doubt that they were expected to attend likewise. The Society of British Neurological Surgeons was and still is a most important forum for instruction and discussion in neurosurgical matters. By 1928 Dott had persuaded the Society to meet in Edinburgh and the programme proclaims that it met on 8 and 9 June 1928, with dinner at the North British Station Hotel at 10s.6d. (or 50p) per head! Dott had a whole range of patients for demonstration and discussion, two spinal tumours, facial paralysis, two cases of 'spasmodic wry neck', spina bifida and a fractured clavicle with nerve damage. At 9 a.m. on Friday 9 June 1928 Mr Dott was to be operating at 19 Great King Street with the opportunity for members, presumably in restricted numbers, to view.

In like manner, the ensuing programmes tell of Dott's particular interests of the time, topics which he felt should be brought forward for instruction and discussion, topics which were to be so characteristically associated with him in the years to come.

In 1929 the Society met at Oxford and Dott offered *Observations on Electrosurgery* and *A Case of Angioma Diagnosed by Moniz's Method*. The first concerned his pioneer work with surgical diathermy, the second was a presentation of his first essays into Cerebral Arteriography. At Dublin in 1931 there is Norman Dott on *Chiasmal Lesions*. This favoured topic of his deals with varying pathologies causing damage and dysfunction to the zone at the base of the brain where the optic nerves unite and their fibres cross. He insists on the most accurate perimetry to define the extent and character of the lesion. In London at the National Hospital for Diseases of the Nervous System, Queen Square, in 1933, he puts forward, *Some Observations on Intracranial Aneurysms*. And so his contributions continue through the years.

A year after the Society of British Neurological Surgeons came into being, Mr (subsequently Sir Heneage) Ogilvy of Guy's Hospital initiated The Surgical Travellers' Club. Dott valued his membership of this greatly with the opportunity, thus given, for travel to other surgical units and the maintenance of his connection with surgery in general and its advances. Numerous other Societies and Associations in the United Kingdom and abroad elected him to membership and requested instructional lectures.

Individual surgeons and departments invited him to visit, to lecture, to discuss, to demonstrate. In the United Kingdom, on the occasion of prestigious invitation lectures, although he might discuss some important surgical topic as in the Victor Horsley Memorial Lecture on *Brain Movement and Time,* he felt freer to discuss important matters of surgical training and organisation as in the Hugh Cairns and Alexander Welsh Memorial Lectures. Abroad it was more appropriate to remain with clinical subjects. If his theme in the former could be summarised, it was to suggest that the artificial division between surgery and medicine was no longer tenable, and medicine, in its wider sense, should be taught and practised upon physiological systems, the central nervous system, the gastrointestinal system etc each encompassing the two therapeutic arms.

He also wanted to see a service peopled with specialists enabling ready cross referrals. *My Utopia is a land so thickly peopled by specialists as to leave no 'No Man's Land' between them* was his message to the combined meeting of the Royal Medico-Chirurgical Society of Glasgow with the Medico-Chirurgical Society of Edinburgh when they discussed Carotid Cavernous Arterio-Venous Fistulae, on 1 March 1939. For the training of the doctor and subsequently the specialist he advocated an earlier start and the earlier achievement of consultant status. He wanted the basic studies of chemistry, physics and biology to be completed at school and, emphasising early consultant appointment, he claimed that the best flow of original ideas came between the ages of twenty-eight and forty. After all, he said, he had been in charge of a teaching department at the age of twenty-seven! Certainly he had been the only surgeon practising neurosurgery in Edinburgh at that age! As Vice-President of the Royal College of Surgeons in Edinburgh, he had his forum for such matters but it was his successor in the chair and later President of the College, Professor F J Gillingham who saw the introduction of a Specialist Fellowship Examination and Diploma in Surgical Neurology. However Dott was to claim that one of his important achievements was the recognition of the importance of Surgical Neurology and the inclusion of neurosurgical subjects in the examination for the Fellowship of the Royal College as then constituted.

The countries Dott visited are legion and the departments, congresses and symposia within them even more numerous. If the host was an ex-Edinburgh trainee, Dott was expected to continue to impart advice and to give instruction on the lines, which had been so beneficial in Edinburgh, if not directly to the trainee, who was now in a senior position, then to his staff. Dott obviously enjoyed these relaxed 'paternal' encounters. In addition operations might be watched and discussed. Rarely he was persuaded to take part. Patients might be brought to see the great man for a second opinion or to discuss and illustrate a mode of treatment. Lectures would be expected and advice sought on planning of neurosurgical services. Among hand written notes by Dott about one of his trips to America, we find these lines and this degree of involvement: 'Dinner at Cave Dwellers Club with Doctor and several psychiatrists . . . forgot to go for the wives after dinner. Had to go back to hospital and re-inject tic keeping ladies from 9.30 p.m. until 11.10 p.m. in car waiting—baby due a feed at 10.30 p.m.!' Mrs Dott herself was very tolerant, but what about the young host and hostess's infant daughter denied her natural rights by neurosurgery? We don't have her comments but many a neurosurgical wife could fill them in.

The zenith of Dott's career as a teacher of surgical neurology was surely the invitation for him to be the Honoured Guest at the Congress of Neurological Surgeons in Toronto in 1968. He was asked to deliver some 'Introductory Remarks' and then to address the Congress with a group of papers on some of his own chosen topics.[6] This he did admirably with the relaxed confidence of the elder statesman. There was no need for him to take up any of the acerbic stance that is sometimes found in the younger less secure. He taught with gentle pleasantry, reinforcing the lessons with homely tales, notwithstanding the erudition of his audience. Disarmingly he revealed his essential 'Scottishness' and loyally did the ghosts of Parlane Macfarlane, Sandy Thomson and a host of Burns-like characters bear him up, as he mounted the distinguished rostrum. 'Carotid Cavernous Arteriovenous Fistula' was delivered on 26 September 1968.

In her secluded cottage by the tall elm trees, the gamekeeper's wife was sitting knitting by her comforting fire, one evening in the spring time. Her children were grown up and had left the parental home. On a sudden she heard a repeated crying sound, which she supposed might emanate from a young crow that had fallen from its nest, for there was a rookery in the trees and the crows were there nesting. She arose and went forth to find it. She failed to do so but she observed, as she searched, that the crying sound seemed to accompany her. So she rightly deduced that the noise came from her own head. When her man came in, he heard it too; and noted that he could just hear it at a distance of four paces from his wife. Next day the district nurse called for her cup of tea, and heard this strange tale. She put her ear to the patient's head and expressed the opinion that it was the crying of seagulls. She told the doctor and he took occasion to come round that way to investigate the mystery. He put on his stethoscope and declared that what he heard was exactly like a nest of suckling rabbits. He had heard of patients being disturbed by bees in their bonnets, others by bats in the belfry, but here was a more serious matter—either seagulls on the slates, gull in the skull or rabbits in the rafters! The doctor went home to think about these things. The gamekeeper's wife took a quiet placid interest in these several suggestions and in the source of them but was quite undisturbed. A few days later it was noted that her left eye was becoming prominent and appeared bloodshot.

An unforgettable description of the developing symptoms of a Carotid Cavernous Arteriovenous Fistula, that dangerous communication between intracranial artery and vein, the management of which he went on to detail. The phrases are finely measured in their descriptive pawky humour. Even as he pronounces them, is he not deliberately contrasting the Old World with the New? Fully able to hold his own in the New World, yet his spirit casts back across the Atlantic to that Trossachs village and the mellow ghost of his Highland ghillie friend for added support, as he lectures this large audience of attentive neurosurgeons.

So the invitations to formal lectures were multiplied and were often accompanied by election to an important neurosurgical or medical society of the country concerned. On occasion a plaque was unveiled or a ward named after him. The Dott ward was one of the new wards in the Liverpool neurosurgical centre taking company with other famous neurosurgical names, Horsley, Jefferson, Cairns.

Yet in spite of the public acclaim, Dott achieved his greatest influence on the practice of surgery not by formal teaching and academic precept but by example; the day-long, night-long beacon of his tremendous discipline, a discipline engendered by his favourite formula: 'What is best for the patient is a touchstone we can and should apply to all these problems and their solution.' And again: 'Just apply that simple test to all you do, in practice, your personal service to individual patients, in teaching others your knowledge and art, in research for improvement of your service to future patients.' Such words did not come frequently or easily but were enunciated publicly on rare occasions in later life. How much more he silently and consistently put them into practice throughout his surgical career. Listen again:

> Stern and puritanical in demeanour he rose betimes and ordered his day with iron self discipline, which he also imposed, without difficulty on all associated with him. He did no formal teaching of his staff. We learned from him by watching his face and hands and by absorbing his casual remarks. We learned so thoroughly that it has amused and impressed the writer in later years to observe some of his disciples displaying unconsciously but most faithfully the Chief's personal attitudes and characteristic utterances in their own routines with religious exactitude.

We have heard that these were the words with which Dott described Cushing.[7] How well they bear repetition as a description of Dott himself. This way he trained many who travelled to all parts and endeavoured to maintain similar standards in the care of patients. Increasingly too he received applications from men of high calibre to come to Edinburgh to complete their training under him. So much so that in 1958 he wrote to the Secretary of the Society of British Neurological Surgeons Mr D W C Northfield with the words, 'The Edinburgh Department of Surgical Neurology is absolutely inundated with requests for relatively senior training in Surgical Neurology for periods from three months to several years, from India, Africa, North and South America, Australia and several European countries especially the more eastern ones Yugoslavia, Poland, Greece.' He goes on to suggest 'the setting up of a central register by the Society of British Neurological Surgeons for distribution in the United Kingdom of such trainees who cannot be accommodated at their centre of choice.'

In addition to the direct training of surgeons and associated staff he received requests for advice on establishing neurosurgical services from places as far apart as Africa, South America and Malaysia and the planning of more than one unit in the United Kingdom closely reflects the ideas he established in Edinburgh.

Did these strict disciplines breed a compliant, unimaginative trainee? Most Dott disciples have already answered that question and shown their enterprise by travelling half the world over to secure the training of their choice before returning to their homelands to establish enviable reputations. Most of them, still, if they correspond or meet, share, with wry humour, reminiscences of the disciplines to which they subjected themselves voluntarily. However senior they may be, they will admit, if caught in a moment of honesty, that still as they complete an operation, whatever its complexity, they find themselves glancing over their shoulder to see if that familiar figure is not there and half expect to hear an equally familiar comment, 'Uh-Huh!' if all is well or 'That won't do doctor!' if something is wanting!

But reminiscences come from all grades of staff and it is unfortunate that all cannot be heard.

> I was theatre sister in Ward 20 at the Royal Infirmary from 1946 to 1948. He worked extremely hard and expected his staff to do likewise. He had a cosmopolitan team but neither creed nor colour bothered the Chief. His concern was the individual's ability to work conscientiously for the benefit of the patient. The bulk of his major surgery was done at that time at Bangour, his day starting at 9 a.m. After that a rather weary looking Professor Dott would return about 6.30 p.m., sometimes later to Ward 20 back in Edinburgh. He would then commence a complete ward round, missing no detail on each patient. The round would finish about 9 p.m. and thereafter the registrar and I would have to tackle lumbar punctures and sundry dressings.

54 Norman Dott joins the distinguished Roll of Honorary Fellows of the Royal Society of Medicine: Sir Hector McLennan, President, presents the scroll, 16 July 1968.

55 'and advice sought on planning neurosurgical services.' Professor Dott and Mr Block examine the theatre table to Dott's design at the opening of the new Dundee Department of Neurosurgery, also called Ward 20.

56 A surgeon of international repute. Professor Dott with Professors Ramamurthi (right) and Kalyanaraman (left) in India (centre).

57 Neurosurgery in India? Dott in deep discussion with Nehru.

58 Professor Dott addresses the late Shah of Persia on behalf of colleagues.

Early in my sojourn on the team, I learned there were no 'on or off' duty times, that one was on call 24 hours. Somehow we accepted this fact very readily. There were rare relaxations however. On one or more occassions he took the staff to the Medical Society Ball, held at that time in the Assembly Rooms. We were also treated to front seats in the Bertram Mills Circus when they visited Edinburgh. For the Chief the purpose of the latter visit was to observe and research some pygmies who took part in the show!

The same sister, Sister Johan Hogg concludes:

At different times we had patients from abroad, brought to Professor Dott for his special skills to operate upon. A few came from South Africa; some came as private patients. The Chief was not concerned with finance, only the betterment of his patient.[8]

How amply is this borne out by Mr Edward Jackson, nearly fifty years after the event, who writes from Cockermouth in Cumbria:

I was a little boy with a headache when my parents took me to Edinburgh to see Professor Dott. The local doctors and hospital didn't know exactly what was wrong with me after they found out that a heap of aspirins didn't seem to make much difference. This was in August 1939. He diagnosed brain trouble and after a period of 'building up' he operated. This I am told was a 12-hour operation, entering my head from the rear, and removing a tumour from the brain. Money was in short supply in those days and my parents were Cumbrian farmers with not too much of it. Professor Dott charged five pounds consultation fee and after the operation, when my parents fearfully asked, 'How much do we owe you doctor?' he replied, 'A packet of cigarettes'! He was truly a most remarkable man with such incredible skill and modesty. To him I owe my life and I shall never forget that. I have been able to lead a normal life and am a television engineer and watchmaker with my own television shop.[9]

Another sister, Sister Kirsty Hose describes Professor Dott:

He was a modest and humble man but he had a great presence. He set the pace and the standards, always the leader of the team. He had a quiet determined manner, charming and dignified, a lovely smile and very sparing with his words. He had a large medical and nursing staff; the doctors came from all over the globe, Americans, South Africans, Europeans, quite a 'League of Nations'; the nursing staff too came from far afield though mostly Royal students. . . Frequently as I opened the door at 7.30 a.m. he would be standing there, 'I'll just do a round, sister', a smile on his face . . . He often paid a visit to his patients at 10 p.m. and met the night nursing staff. There was sometimes an evening telephone call to the ward to enquire after a specific patient. He was extremely nice to his patients and always listened to what they had to say. He always saw the patient's family before an operation.[10]

Similarly his example was not lost on one of his occupational therapists.

> Professor Dott was of course the Patron of our Association and one of the few physicians at that time to take a holistic view of his patients. He cared just as much for the street sweeper as he did for a celebrity. His humility and concern influenced me throughout my professional life. I learnt more from him and his head Occupational Therapist in that short spell at Bangour than I did throughout the rest of my training. It kindled in me a lifelong interest in neurology.[11]

And how did he teach that cosmopolitan, 'League of Nations', group of young surgeons who had come to learn from him? As sister remarked 'he set the pace and the standards'. Even after his hip operation in Manchester, he convalesced in Ward 20, in a specially chosen room near the operating theatre so that with his location, with case records brought to his room, and with discreet enquiries from nursing staff and resident, he could still keep his unvarying watch on standards. Like sister, medical staff found him 'very sparing with words'. Of course he used them when necessary, explained how the patient's position on the operating table could be bettered to avoid cerebral congestion, described a particular technique, answered a well reasoned query. Mostly, though, learning was by listening and watching; listening perhaps as he explained to patient and relatives the reasons for an operation and what he hoped to accomplish; watching continuously. Watching in operating theatre, on ward round, in X-ray room, and above all watching oneself to avoid falling short of the standard set. And was this teaching effective? In 1960, in connection with the opening of the new Department of Surgical Neurology, Professor Dott was encouraged to write his own curriculum vitae. He details the teaching activities of his department and concludes with modest pride, 'It is not without significance that four Professors of Surgery and the premier Professor of Psychology in Britain are trainees of the Department.' On a less exalted plane, recollections of thirty years on from one of Dott's assistants give some indication of enduring value.

> This incident occurred about three weeks after I started working in Ward 20. As you know, during the initial period, in true Cushing tradition, your chief never greeted you or spoke to you; in fact you were invisible as far as he was concerned until such time as he deemed it fitting to acknowledge your presence. Anyway, after I had been there three weeks, he suddenly turned round to me while we were at a patient's bedside and said, 'Tell me Lipschitz, what are this patient's cerebrospinal fluid findings?' I got such a shock that, without thinking, I said, 'Fairly normal, Sir!' He then stared at me without saying a word for his usual half-minute of deadly silence—his customary weapon. Then he turned to Robin Lowe and said, 'Robin tell me, is there something wrong with our laboratory? Don't they tell you there are so many

cells per cubic millimetre and then tell you the types of cells? And then don't they tell you what the protein is in milligrams per cent, and the sugar and a Langhe's colloidal gold test and a Wassermann Reaction and report all this? Or do they just report "fairly normal"?' This again was followed by half a minute of silence and then he looked at Watson and repeated the question, 'Tell me Watson is there something wrong with our laboratory et cetera?' Again there was half a minute of silence. Harris was next. 'Tell me Harris is there something wrong with our laboratory?' So the question went round deliberately from one member of the team to the next. There were about fourteen of us standing there. So the point was made. I can assure you that since that day I have never used the word 'fairly' and do not allow any of my staff to use it!

Another recollection carries a never-to-be-forgotten lesson.

We were removing a meningioma, a benign intracranial tumour, and had been at it for about ten hours, in Ward 20 theatre, which overlooks Heriot's school. In the school grounds there was a cadet parade and the band was playing. Suddenly Professor Dott commands, 'Diathermy.' The other assistant, entrusted with the diathermy needle, had allowed his attention to wander across to the Heriot's parade. Coming to, he grabs the needle and, in proffering it, inadvertently touches Professor Dott's face with it as the Professor activates the system with his foot pedal. He sustains a small burn. The assistant pales, puts the needle down on the sterile instrument trolley and waits. Again there was the usual pause. Then quietly, 'The fact that you don't like me and stick a diathermy needle in my face, when the machine is on, is personal between you and me but,' and he does raise his voice at this juncture, 'next time you put an unsterile instrument down,' (for the face was unsterile) 'on top of my sterile instruments, I will throw you out of the theatre!' He then made sister change all the drapes and instruments for new sterile ones. [12]

She, because of all the trouble entailed, would undoubtedly have underlined Dott's lesson in sterility in the memory of this unfortunate registrar, who had allowed his attention to be distracted during a ten hour operation!

Sister learnt 'early in my sojourn that there were no on or off duty times'. Equally early the same lesson came to one of the trainee registrars.

Shortly after my arrival in the famous Ward 20 unit, I was entrusted with the evacuation of a subdural haematoma. This is a relatively simple procedure in which holes are drilled in the skull to drain a collection of blood from the surface of the brain. Unfortunately there is sometimes a tendency for the fluid to reaccumulate. In this case the operation was completed satisfactorily and the patient made the rather dramatic recovery in consciousness that not infrequently follows in this type of case. All was well and the weekend approached. I studied the duty list carefully. There was no sign of my name for the weekend, so decided to take the opportunity to explore Scotland, to which I had newly arrived. Unfortunately the patient did reaccumulate fluid but was drained uneventfully. Nevertheless my first encounter with Professor Dott on Monday morning was a brief and never-forgotten lesson, 'Your patient had to be operated upon again. It would have been better for him if you had been here!' There was no arguing this softly spoken statement. I realised that duty lists in Dott's Ward 20 merely indicated who was to be first in line for emergencies not who was off duty![13]

One of the distinctive ways in which the Edinburgh School of Surgery maintained its outstanding reputation was the Saturday morning meeting, sometimes irreverently termed 'The Deaders Meeting'. Every Saturday morning during term time, surgeons of Edinburgh and surrounding districts, very often accompanied by distinguished visiting surgeons, would congregate in the main surgical lecture theatre at the Royal Infirmary, or sometimes at one of the other hospitals, to listen to each of the surgical units in rotation. Each had to publish and discuss all deaths which had occurred in the unit in the previous year. Discussion and questioning could be searching and critical. Surgical neurology, by the nature of its work and the number of serious head injuries which were admitted usually had to present a fair quota.

One year, while still a registrar, I was considered fit to present the deaths at the imminent meeting. This entailed a great deal of work, studying all the case records and X-rays, defining the exact cause of death and whether there had been any avoidable complications and preparing oneself to answer any conceivable question. However it was finally accomplished and I felt I had marshalled my facts satisfactorily. So I was not unduly perturbed when Professor Dott approached me a week before the meeting with the characteristic words, 'I'd just like to hear what you have to say. Saturday would do admirably.' So the Saturday before Ward 20's turn for the 'Deaders Meeting' I told my wife, 'I may be a little late for lunch, Professor Dott wants me to run over the cases with him.'

How grievously I was mistaken. 'This one died because half his cerebral hemisphere was shattered,' I might say, attempting to pass on to the next one. But that was not good enough for Dott. How had the accident happened? Was it avoidable? Had there been any delay in transport to hospital, any delay in hospital? Had the patient's position been correct for transport? Then damage to the cerebral hemisphere is not sufficient cause of death for Dott. Has surgical decompression been sufficient? Are there any small haemorrhages in the brain stem? So the questions—and many others—came relentlessly and were repeated for each case. My poor wife; I think there was a brief break for a late lunch and then an afternoon session which went on well into the evening. Indeed Sunday morning and Sunday lunch time had passed before Dott was satisfied that the reputation of the department was secure.

Needless to say the next Saturday I faced the distinguished audience with a confidence that was well founded and I have never forgotten the lessons learnt. Many a time since sometimes during the hours of the night, as I have struggled with a severe head injury or troublesome cranial operation, flagging energy has been stimulated by the thought of the questions I would have to answer to Dott if I let this patient slip through my hands. In the imagination this has continued long after Dott's retirement and death. In turn I have tried to impart these standards to my own assistants.[14]

In conclusion a recollection from the same source.

Unrelenting he was with the high standards, which he demanded, but how kindly and caring with advice, when it was sought. 'If I can be of help, remember that I am just across at Chalmers Crescent,' were the words he left me with as I was about to assume consultant responsibilities because of Dott's own retirement. Needless to say I had no thought to avail myself of this kindly gesture until fate and common sense decreed otherwise. Here is how it fell out.

Hardly had the young captain, in an English County Regiment, and the physiotherapist, recently come from home, been married in war time Hong Kong, before the Japanese had invaded. Cruelly separated in the fighting, the harsh divorce continued as they were made captive and, with no thought for family ties and yearning, men were callously herded from the women and children, whom they had so recently left to defend the island. They were sent to separate camps in Japan. The regimes were harsh, communication impossible, gaolers (except for one notable exception) unrelenting. One shipload of prisoners was torpedoed and sunk on the voyage. It was eighteen months before word filtered through to the despairing wife in the women's camp, that her husband had survived the shipwreck. Callously they had not been spared news of the sinking. Can it be wondered that despite this fleeting injection of hope and as month cruelly followed month, their hopes of ever being reunited steadily declined? With the war's end and repatriation through India hope seemed reckless and thoughts were forced into plans for resuming bleak celibacy in the United Kingdom. The sudden confrontation and unexpected reunion in that humid staging post was nothing short of miraculous.

With such furnacing, the jewel of their bond became more precious, even though the years passed, war time memories faded, and the captain and his bride became the general and his wife. They surely didn't deserve the further catastrophe that fate had in store for them. Bound for a holiday in their beloved Perthshire, she had a cerebral haemorrhage in the overnight sleeper as it neared Edinburgh. She was transferred to hospital and the angiogram confirmed the anticipated aneurysm. It lay however in an unenviable site on the basilar artery, most difficult of access and closely associated with vital brain stem functions. The patient, recovering from her initial haemorrhage, as usually happens, and her husband, awaited an opinion.

How swiftly and finally could the almost inevitable recurrent haemorrhage or a badly planned operation sever the ties which had endured battle, shipwreck and internment. As I turned over these matters in my mind, I remembered Dott's parting offer and reached for the telephone. What I did not then realise was that Dott himself, over thirty years previously, had trodden a similar, though much more formidable path. It was incomparably more formidable because, as he stood alone, casting all care for his reputation aside, he was stepping into the unknown territory of aneurysm surgery.

The familiar unhurried tones came back quietly over the telephone with an immediate response, 'Just come right over and bring the X-rays.' There was no difficulty in those days about parking outside number Three Chalmers Crescent, the quiet backwater so convenient for the Royal Hospital for Sick Children, the Royal Infirmary and the University. The small wicket gate, the fuchsia, were familiar from previous visits. If they had not been, the little brass plate with the single word 'Dott' on it confirmed the householder, if not his eminence.

White-coated Barbara answered the door and ushered me into the study. There he was, his greeting friendly, perhaps a little more relaxed since pressures had eased on retirement. A brief résumé of the case was given and the X-rays handed over for study. The minutes ticked by unhurriedly. Dott's reputation had never depended on snap decisions. It rested mainly on action formulated after careful consideration of every aspect of a problem.

There was time therefore for observation and reflection, as he carefully studied each X-ray from all angles. The same slight figure, in grey tweed suit with watch-chain and key across the waistcoat, sat behind the massive desk. Leaning slightly backwards, his stiff leg was out-thrust for comfort. His face had changed little over the years. That surprisingly small head capped by greying hair, which showed no signs of receding; hair which was so closely waved that, had one not known the person, artifice would have been suspected. The sculpted face had no spare flesh apart from the wrinkles, which etched a determined mouth and pointed to those penetrating eyes, which only occasionally relaxed into the semblance of a twinkle.

This was the same figure of that first encounter those years ago but so well remembered; the encounter that had led, somewhat inconsequentially, to an invaluable training under Dott.

It was at a meeting of the Society of British Neurological Surgeons. Thoroughly overawed, I was standing talking to my current chief, who had just delivered a paper on an ingeniously gentle forceps for temporarily occluding a blood vessel during aneurysm surgery. The slight, unassuming figure limped over and greeted us. I, the young registrar, was introduced and courteously acknowledged. 'I was interested in your paper,' he said. 'We were trying something on similar lines a little while ago.' The tone was entirely encouraging and congratulatory. As the technical discussion continued, no further hint of priority or of competition was introduced. The matter seemed to be concluded by the explanation that the unknown figure was the famous Professor Dott. However, by then I had determined that I must seek my next appointment under the unassuming man who obviously presided over a very benign and unexacting regime!

On appointment to Edinburgh, shortly afterwards, it took only a matter of days to discover that this was an entire misapprehension, and a little while longer to find in a cupboard a series of fine unpublished diagrams from a decade or so previously, which illustrated forceps very similar to those described by my former chief!

My reverie was brought to an end as Dott turned and, with an unhurried but considered emphasis said, 'You have got to operate, otherwise she will die.' The very words, with which he had commanded himself on that unique occasion those many years before.

Balanced by this weight of experience there was now no room for any lingering doubts. A valuable discussion on operative approaches and techniques ensued but the gem of the whole consultation was that first phrase, 'You have got to operate, otherwise she will die.'

Fortunately the operation was successful and many happy years ensued. Yes, mostly he taught by silent example but equally he could offer telling advice, especially if asked.

Thus Dott taught and continues to teach in many parts of the world and his influence weighs much deeper than mere technical surgery of the brain and spinal cord.

CHAPTER TWELVE

A Noble Thing

Ah! Fredome is a nobil thyng!
(Barbour)

Briefly and without undue formality Professor Dott was notified of his ultimate and most valued honour. Auld Reekie was to crown her son, not with baubles but with the warmth and affection of her freedom. The letter of 23 May 1962 from The Lord Provost told Professor Dott:

> I am writing to you formally to let you know that at a meeting of The Town Council last Thursday, it was agreed unanimously to confer on you The Freedom of the City of Edinburgh. The formal resolution is as follows:
> 'In recognition of the honour and distinction he has brought to the city by virtue of his career as a surgeon and as a teacher in the specialised field of surgery, in which he has been a pioneer.'
> If I may add a personal note, may I say how very delighted I am that this was all agreed to unanimously and we now look forward to the occasion of the ceremony on Friday 6th. July.

The letter was signed by Sir John Greig Dunbar Lord Provost.

Preparations went forward immediately. Among the first tasks was to make certain that the Lord Provost's office was fully informed about Professor Dott's career and distinctions. The help of Doctor Raeburn, the Senior Administrative Medical Officer of the South Eastern Regional Hospital Board of Scotland was enlisted. He readily supplied all the details and also an amusing but telling afterthought. 'One of Professor Dott's characteristics is that he usually manages to persuade other people to agree with what he wants!' As the senior, he is surely echoing the experiences of many in administrative posts who found themselves yielding to Dott's persuasion, if not insistence, as he fashioned the neurosurgical services.

The Usher Hall was the chosen venue. Charles McKean[1] describes it as 'an octagonal domed expression of industry's support for the arts . . . set askew on a difficult site.' He gives it a 'grandiose interior.' The average Edinburgh citizen is not so critical: it's the Usher Hall; it's part of

Edinburgh; it's impressive. He may have been to a concert inside or met someone outside. It is just possible that he may have registered his complaint about the extraordinary chiming clock that has been erected in front of it; equally he may have defended this timepiece. Certainly, when the architect, Stockdale Harrison, set to work in the early years of the twentieth century his efforts were largely funded by Sir Andrew Usher, of brewing fame. It was an appropriate setting, then, for honours to a surgeon who had persuaded another industrialist, Sir Andrew Grant Bt of Glenmoriston, the Chairman of McVitie Price the biscuit manufacturers, to endow his imaginative schemes for brain surgery in Ward 20 at the Royal Infirmary.

'Askew on a difficult site'. We must accept the expert view but surely Dott, on the day, as he mounted the platform and faced rank upon rank of his fellow citizens to receive his honour, realised that it was looking benignly down Lothian Road to that spot no distance away where an unknown youth, nearly fifty years and two world wars previously, lay with fractured limb and shattered motorcycle. His impetuousness had flung him injured to that same spot, to sow the first seeds of this whole saga, on a Lothian Road dusty from horse-drawn vehicles and the adjacent railway goods yard.

The 'grandiose interior' with extensive ground floor, upper tier, grand tier and organ gallery, has seating for some 2,760 persons. If there were any initial doubts as to whether this vastness would be adequately filled they were soon dispelled. Numerous cards of invitation in differing colours were printed and eagerly sought. All aspects of city life and tradition were to be represented as well as friendly neighbouring burghs, from whom Dott's skills had not been withheld. The High Constables, of ancient foundation, the Fire Services, skilled with modern appliances, were there. The Services, the men of peace, the Church, the Law, the uniformed and those of sober suit—all attended. Innumerable bodies and organisations had sent chosen members with their goodwill; listing would be invidious. There was, of course, plentiful representation of medicine, both surgical and physicianly, with office bearers of both The Royal Colleges of Surgeons and Physicians. Perhaps dearer to Dott's heart were the nurses and nursing organisations, a pristine semi-circle upon semi-sircle of starched white caps and gloves, and the professions, as Dott would have it, 'complementary not supplementary to medicine', physiotherapists, occupational therapists, speech therapists, social workers, the very backbone of patient care as practised by him. These were women and men to whom, he readily owned, his success and fame owed much. Many hospital authorities wrote requesting tickets for such staff because of their affection for him and their pride in shared work.

Special emphasis was on youth: Scouts, Guides and the schools. Every age and every grade was numbered there, but pride of place went, naturally, to the very regiment of Herioters in their striped ties and smart blue blazers.

59 The freedom of the City of Edinurgh. The youngest Burgess, accompanied by Mrs Dott, receives the casket from the Lord Provost, Sir John Greig Dunbar, who has Lady Dunbar by his side, 6 July 1962. Courtesy of *Edinburgh Evening News.*

And then the patients. In his subsequent speech The Lord Provost was to say how touched he had been by the large number of 'grateful patients' who, on hearing of the proposed ceremony, had called at The City Chambers requesting tickets. Dott too would have been moved, and faced with them individually, would undoubtedly have recalled the details of many of the struggles, which they had endured together, still visible by a slight limp, or minor scar or skull deformity. No journey, however tedious, would have kept them from this occasion. Meticulously he answered congratulatory letters on these lines.

So much for official invitations originating in The City Chambers. What of Professor Dott's invitations? This was a very modest list, offered tentatively; no attempt here to impress the influential; a few relatives, the occasional friend or colleague, Barbara, the faithful housekeeper among retainers. Certainly he did not forget his staff, his secretaries, his junior doctors. Many of the latter came hurrying off the wards for the surprisingly brief ceremony, for was it not an unyielding principle of Dott that patient care ceded to no individual or occasion however glorious? Then who could have imagined that Norman Dott, on the point of retirement could have summoned up his early teachers to give them credit for setting him on the right road? But Miss Fraser Lee from that first private school in Hailes Brae and Mr William Gentle from Heriot's were there as important guests.

All sat intermingled to pay tribute to this exceptional man.

Preparations were meticulous; no hitch would be tolerated. The police were alert; transport was available to take the principal participants to lunch at The City Chambers after the ceremony. The City parks and gardens provided flowers to enhance and humanise that 'grandiose interior'. Mr George McPhee, Dip (Mus Ed) RSAM, FRCO, was engaged on the mighty organ (at a fee of eight pounds and eight shillings!). The Reverend Dr H C Whitley, from St Giles' Cathedral was to offer the opening prayer.

These then were the folk that the benign though mighty Usher Hall was preparing to receive as the hands of its new and upstart neighbour moved towards twelve on that July day. Those with specific duties or forming part of a uniformed cadre arrived early. Others, more relaxed, strolled up, recognised and greeted friends before dispersing to various entrances, dependent upon the colour of their invitation card. Lothian Road carried its normal week day traffic. Pedestrians and passengers in Edinburgh's characteristic maroon coloured buses might have wondered what unbilled concert was taking place at this unusual hour. Others might have read in their *Scotsman* or *Evening News* about the famed brain surgeon, who lived among them and of the proposition to confer upon him the Freedom of the City.

Those that arrived early were impressed to see the platform vividly decorated with summer flowers but, above all, the Grand Tier and Organ Gallery filled and enhanced by row upon row of nurses in those gleaming white caps and gloves to form an appropriate backdrop to the ceremony. In their midst, the organ played and the gathering audience was entertained by its notes and by friendly chatter.

The organ reaches a crescendo now as the platform party mounts the rostrum and moves into position, led by The Lord Provost and his mace bearer. The light catches the chains of office. It is a solemn occasion as befits this great city, but the slight smiling figure of Norman McOmish Dott, as he limps behind to take the place of honour, reassures all that friendliness and humanity will pervade. All have played some small part and no one, least of all himself, will be tempted by their own importance.

The organ voluntary dies down and after the opening prayer. The Lord Provost steps forward and, presenting the ceremonial scroll and silver casket, admits Professor Norman McOmish Dott to the Honorary roll of Burgesses with the following words

Ladies and Gentlemen,

It is many years since a ceremony of this kind took place in this city and I make no apologies from the Town Council that this should be so, for the honour which we are about to confer on a distinguished son of this City is not one which should be lightly conferred. It is for this reason that I am particularly proud to occupy the position I do at this moment, for it gives me the privilege of welcoming on behalf of the citizens of Edinburgh, Professor Norman McOmish Dott to this platform this morning. It is an additional pleasure that we also welcome his wife and daughter and son-in-law, Dr and Mrs Calvin Hider.

Ladies and Gentlemen, I have been told, on excellent authority, of the Professor's persuasive powers and the manner in which he gets his own way. I can tell you that it required no persuasion on my part, or anyone else's, when the proposal to confer on Professor Dott the Freedom of his native City was put to the Town Council.

The proposal was not only accepted unanimously by the members, but with enthusiastic acclamation, for throughout her long history, Edinburgh has delighted in honouring men and women who have served their country faithfully and well, and in serving their country have bestowed undoubted benefits on mankind. When one becomes involved in human frailty and suffering, I can think of no-one who has conferred greater benefits on mankind than Professor Dott. Through his skill and his knowledge in the realm of specialised surgery, he has restored to health many people who have been grievously afflicted.

I will not reveal the intimate details of his age, only say that about the beginning of this century he was born in Colinton, the son of a Fine Art dealer who was interested in social work. After attending school in Colinton and at George Heriot's, he began an apprenticeship in Engineering which was of short duration. Like many youths he was interested in cycles and motor-cycles, and as the result of a cycling accident he landed up in the Royal Infirmary. This must have been the turning point of his career, because during his treatment in the Royal Infirmary his interest in surgery was aroused and on his recovery he began his studies in medicine.

To do justice to his meteoric career in medicine would involve a discourse of many hours, and I must therefore beg you to accept the knowledge of his remarkable career which I am certain is already known to most of you. I would however like to make the point that Professor Dott's fame as a surgeon is by no means a local one and that we in Edinburgh bask in the reflected glory of his achievements in many lands throughout the world. We, in this country, are so accustomed to the fame, and indeed prosperity, of everything pertaining to the United States of America, that it is indeed comforting, to say the least of it, to know of Professor Dott's recognition in that vast Continent. At the same time, I am sure Professor Dott would be the first to acknowledge his debt of gratitude to the Rockefeller Foundation of America in making a most generous appropriation of money to enable him to develop a proper department of Surgical Neurology in Edinburgh.

His long list of publications would at first sight entitle him to rank as a best seller, as I am sure he must be within the specialised field of his contribution to literature.

During the last war he was Consultant to the Army in Scotland and organised the 'Brain Injuries Unit' at Bangour Hospital, and from there directed the treatment of service personnel. It was mainly for this war medical work, which brought to the forces the standards of civilian management, including rehabilitation in Surgical Neurology, that our guest this morning was awarded the CBE.

Professor Dott, I must tell you how very touched I have been since the news of this ceremony was released, at the large number of people, referring to themselves as 'grateful patients', who have called at the City Chambers for invitations to attend the ceremony. All this, together with your world wide reputation, must, I think, give you tremendous satisfaction.

And now, the City of your birth gathers you to herself and in her own simple yet distinctive manner offers you the greatest honour it is in her power to bestow—the 'Freedom of the City'. I think that I must warn you that it confers neither rights nor privileges, but it is a symbol of the high admiration of the people of this City for your genius and powers of healing—in recognition of the honour and distinction you have brought to the City, by virtue of your career as a surgeon and as a teacher, in the specialised field of surgery, in which you have been a pioneer.

Professor Dott I ask you to accept this Casket containing a suitably illuminated Scroll which constitutes you our youngest Burgess.

The Professor accepts the scroll and casket, so fittingly to repose in later years, in the Royal College of Surgeons in Edinburgh. How would this man, no stranger to adulation and honours in other climates, respond to this gesture from his birthplace, a city renowned for cloaking the true warmth of its feelings by a mock play of east wind and west end hauteur? He seemed to speak from his heart and unfold for the first time, his whole ethos.

Let his own words in their charm and modesty speak for themselves.

My Lord Provost, Magistrates and Councillors of the City of Edinburgh— My Lady Provost, My Lords, Ladies and Gentlemen— A gathering such as is assembled here today displays certain noble and inspiring characteristics of our way of life—a loyalty to constituted authority—a respect for our glorious history—a generous recognition of service wherever this has been attempted to be faithfully rendered.

My first impulse is that of profound gratitude for my Burgess and Guild Brother Scroll, for its elegant and precious casket, and for the generous and kindly terms with which you, My Lord Provost, have presented it.

My first claim on my Freedom is freedom of speech—which, by your leave, I shall indulge in briefly.

The Roll of this Signal Honour, dating back to the fifteenth century, is an inventory of those who have contributed notably, personally and by virtue of office, to the weal of our dear City, to the weal of Scotland, of Britain, of the British Commonwealth of Nations and of the World—Churchmen, Statesmen, Sailors, Soldiers and Airmen—ancient and modern, those learned and able in the Law, Musicians, University Administrators and learned Professors, Poets, Authors, Captains of Commerce and Industry; and some Doctors of Medicine.

Your gracious and generous act today in selecting a doctor—a surgeon—a University Professor—represents, as I believe, your desire to place on record Edinburgh's affection and high esteem for her Medical Profession, her University, her Royal Medical Colleges and her Medical School. I love our dear City. I admire the judgements and acts of her City Fathers—and Mothers (in these days). I am a loyal citizen and I bow to your judgement and your act.

That you have selected me, as a representative of these estimable and important bodies, I value much more highly than any other compliment that has been paid or could be paid to me—the Freedom of my own City—of the Capital City of Scotland—of this City golden with sunsets of the past—and rosy with dawns of the future.

When we felicitate or pronounce valediction on our friends, on important occasions—birth, marriage, other ceremonial events, we wish upon them health, prosperity and happiness. Note well! Health first; then the frills—prosperity and happiness. It is perhaps not inappropriate then, that you should choose to honour your *Medical Profession*—the keepers and restorers of your healths.

You have honoured the Medical Profession with the Freedom of the City of Edinburgh in the past, and thanks to Mr Cousland's loving work, I have been able to trace twelve medical Freemen. The first five of these—1617-1668—were eminent medical men—Physicians to the Monarch of the day—honoured usually on the occasion of a Royal visit to Edinburgh, and the compliment was perhaps as much to Royalty as to the Profession or the individual. However, in this category Edinburgh had the good fortune—or was it far-sighted wisdom?—to enrol Dr William Harvey, the great discoverer of the circulation of the blood—and that within five years of the publication of his famous *De Motu Cordis*—long before it received general recognition. That was in 1633 when Charles I came to Edinburgh for his Scottish Coronation and Dr William Harvey accompanied him as Physician to the King. Then in 1766 you turned towards leaders of Medicine in your own City—Professor John Gregory—and later his son, Professor James Gregory—who provided that mildly explosive aromatic powder, upon which, with porridge, many of us elder Edinburgh citizens were reared. Then my Lord Provost, you restricted your choice to medical giants—men who have made momentous contributions to World Medicine—Dr Jenner of Vaccination fame in 1804, Sir James McGrigor, father of the RAMC and of modern Military Medicine, Sir Astley Cooper, notable surgical pioneer, Professor Sir James Young Simpson, who introduced chloroform and was a noted pioneer of modern obstetrics, and the great Lord Lister, who introduced antiseptic surgery.

Now after a 'medical suspense' of sixty-four years your choice lights upon—Norman Dott. I can assure you that over-modesty has not been a conspicuous fault of his; but what embarrassement you place him in! I feel like a pigmy, peeping about among the legs—or should I say toes—of these medical giants. I could not reach to touch the hems of their garments; even if consciousness of my unworthiness did not prevent me. This picture, my Lord Provost, will, I hope convey to you the magnitude of your generous act towards me.

My Lord Provost, you will be proud to recall that of these eight medical giants, whom this day's ceremony summons to mind, no less than five were Edinburgh men, and four were professors in the Town's College or later Edinburgh's University and Medical School. What a record that is—the main contributors to healing in the past 200 years. You do well to honour the Faculty of Medicine of your University, your Royal Medical Colleges—your Edinburgh Medical School. They are the guardians of your future medical profession. They are also a powerful influence for Commonwealth Unity and for World Peace. The Brotherhood of Medicine is the strongest world-wide Fraternity that exists; and Edinburgh has by far the largest proportion of Post-Graduate Medical teaching of our British Medical Schools; here doctors of all Nations assemble to learn and to carry Edinburgh Medical Tradition all over the world.

When medicine is honoured, those professions that are complementary to medicine are included, professions without which doctors, and especially hospital doctors, would be devastated and helpless. I see many nurses present. They have come to honour this occasion; but I consider that they are here to take the homage and to accept the affection that is their due.

The specialised field of surgery in which I have practised and taught is prehistorically ancient and also ultra-modern. After your great Freemen, Lord Lister and Sir J Y Simpson, had opened the gates to modern surgery it was Sir William Macewen—another Scotsman—one who laboured in your Province of Glasgow—who pioneered the modern brain and spinal cord surgery—that was from 1879. In the 1920's the lead in Surgical Neurology was carried forward by Dr Harvey Cushing in Boston, USA. How important are our international bonds, and how magnanimous our American cousins! I learned of Cushing—carried there by the Rockefeller Foundation's generosity and later supported by it through the War years. It is not strange that former Freemen appear in any story of development; we owed our first home—Ward 20 of the Royal Infirmary of Edinburgh—to the munificent gifts of Sir Alexander Grant, Freeman of the City of Edinburgh, and of his son, Sir Robert—of biscuit fame.

It were impossible for me to acknowledge individually in these brief remarks all those who have guided and encouraged towards the development of brain surgery in Edinburgh; but I hope they will accept a global acknowledgement. I must, however, express my indebtedness to my first teacher—Miss Catherine Fraser Lee who was later headmistress of St Trinneans School; to Mr William Gentle, my first science teacher, and later Headmaster of George Heriot's School; likewise to the late Sir Henry Wade, to the late Mr

James Methuen Graham and to the late Sir John Fraser, my preceptors in the art and science of surgery.

Another Freeman of the City of Edinburgh appears—this time from the year 1617—Dr Robert Balcanquell, Dean of Rochester, George Heriot's trusted friend, and maker of the wise rules that governed Heriot's Hospital and Trust. I see a number of fellow Herioters present here. You and I owe much to the learned and perspicuous Dean Balcanquell—how much, I realise as I approach the evening of my life—how much you will discover as you too carve out your careers in these stirring times. It is some thing to be a Herioter. Some other Edinburgh Schools have since followed Heriot's example.

Talking of 'carving', there are, as it were, two sides to surgery—the surgeon and his team on the one hand—the patient on the other. It is proper, seemly and appropriate to laud and honour the great pioneers of medicine—as your Free Burgess Roll so well illustrates; but we pay insufficient homage to the great, courageous, pioneer patients. When I recall those patients who, with implicit faith and unfaltering courage, have adventured with me into the unknown I realise that they should be standing here rather than their surgeon. Their courage implies an apprehension of risk—it is indeed fear under control—their faith is in the properly constituted authority of the doctor.

These are the heroes and the heroines who, in the nature of things, must remain unsung; and in which Scotland is so richly endowed. They shone forth here and there in the publicised adventures of War; but they are with us always; they are our heritage; they are bred here—in Edinburgh.

Scotland—the Laird, the Minister, the Doctor, the Lawyer, the Dominie and the people—it is the happiest and the most rewarding land in which to practise medicine. I mentioned that doctors from all lands assemble here to learn and carry Edinburgh traditions of medicine all over the world. They learn valued science and techniques from the doctors; but they learn faith and courage from Scottish patients—and that patient-doctor relationship is the most precious gift they take with them from Edinburgh, My Lord Provost.

As I mentioned, I approach the period when it is time to lay down the tools of active surgery. I shall do so with no misgivings as to the future of surgical neurology in Edinburgh. Those who have built with me in later years are young and strong, and more are coming forward—medical science progresses with accelerating speed—they will serve you better than I have been able to do.

But my Freedom of the City of Edinburgh, I carry with me from this place—I shall never be too old or too tired to carry it proudly—the greatest gift I could have ever dreamed of.

As his last words were spoken, those who had served him for years, used to him meeting each crisis of operation or administration with cool logic and resolve, noted that uncharacteristically, he was visibly moved by this most cherished honour. The platform party moved away to a celebratory lunch in The City Chambers. The remaining audience broke up, coalesced again in fleeting groups for brief recollections, then finally dispersed. Fittingly, the Department of Surgical Neurology was soon about its routines again. Many patients did not know that anything unusual had occurred.

Strangely, there was no evening ward round by Professor Dott that evening.

CHAPTER THIRTEEN

The Man's the Gowd

The rank is but the guinea's stamp,
The man's the gowd for a' that.
(Burns)

Yes, the man's the gowd, as the world well realised in the case of Norman Dott, who more than once was called upon by troubled countries to advise and care for those injured under sensitive political circumstances: now a Cypriot youth, paralysed by wounds in the back, now a Greek Deputy, grievously injured in the head. Thus Dott was raised shoulder high by a Greek crowd awaiting a miracle from him to save their stricken Deputy.[1] His University of Edinburgh also raised him high, appointing him to a chair and awarding him an exalted honorary degree. His Sovereign created him a Commander of the Most Noble Order of the British Empire for his war time services. His medical peers showered him with honours and golden opinions. His patients have wrapped him in their rarest breath of praise and affection. Above all else—and this in his own estimate—the citizens of his birthplace honoured him with the Freedom of the City of Edinburgh: an exceptional gesture.

Inevitably one searches for the man behind the transition from that small boy in a Colinton garden to the master surgeon of world renown. Equally inevitably it is impossible to discover and present a single composite picture of such a character. As soon expect a piece of Edinburgh crystal to retain all its sparkle without the multiple facets which reflect the various shafts of light.

Before seeking the differing viewpoints, you have to consider whether there was indeed a man other than the entirely absorbed surgeon.

There was.

If you pursue the same analogy, there were facets of Dott which every now and again lit to themes entirely unconnected with medicine and surgery, although what usually flashes forth is a reflection of his overwhelming care for humanity and his pursuit of the highest standards in the practice of medicine.

In 1931 Norman Dott wrote to Geoffrey Jefferson regretting that the latter had had to postpone his visit to Edinburgh. He then detailed some of the neurosurgical facilities that he was achieving and agreed that he would be in a better position to entertain him on a later visit. He concluded:

> There is yet another reason why I am glad you have delayed your visit. I have recently become engaged to be married and when you do come up, I should like you to meet my fiancée.

He also notified Cushing, who replied:

> I can't tell you how pleased I am to have received for Christmas that delightful picture of you and your dog. I don't know which of you looks the more alert and intelligent and I hope you will both take it as a compliment. It is quite evident that your fiancée is going to have her hands full keeping you both down and in teaching you to lie down in the corner when you become individually too great a nuisance. But then that's her business and not mine and it is just as well that she knows beforehand just what kind of canines she is going to take in hand.

Is this entirely light-hearted banter? Cushing's was a sternly serious soul. There may be a vein of studied comment in his reply, which over the years Dott took to heart. Addressing the Glasgow women students in 1946, he confessed to having drawn his inspiration, strength and comfort mainly from females. But if a kaleidoscope of loyal nursing sisters, doctors, physiotherapists and secretaries passed thorough his mind as he said as much, it was to his partner that he paid the great tribute on the day of his Freedom Ceremony, 'I owe my wife that support that has sustained me.'[2]

As his father had hoped, Norman Dott had hit on 'a very fine mate', and a very practical one. A practical man himself, to the very bone, a man whose life orbited inexorably around his work, did others even see something professional about his marriage to Margaret Robertson in 1931? Having served as his secretary for a period before the marriage, and given the years of support and encouragement for his career afterwards, it would be unkindly easy to write off their courtship as a neurosurgical romance and their long life together as one of clinical convenience.

That was how it was sometimes seen, by outsiders who remained outsiders. Her first appearance in Norman Dott's life suggests a rather staid young woman of secretarial efficiency, gradually evolving into the tall, grey-haired bespectacled lady recalled by many of Dott's staff. In truth she was shyly self-sufficient. There was always a suggestion of quizzical or wry amusement about a gentle smile that was never far from her mouth and eyes. Having conversed with the high and mighty of the medical world, yet wedded herself to one of the most eminent in the land, a sterling man quite undisfigured by vanity, she was not much impressed by status and honours superficially imposed upon cracked gold. And so, like her husband, she was not a spendthrift with words; usually a few kindly inquiries in a low voice. Like her husband also, she was always courteous, however junior her contact. She referred to her husband as 'The Professor' and handed out boxes of his slides, carefully selected for the particular lecture to which a doctor was allocated. This was one of her life's many and willing responsibilities, the careful nurturing of the slide collection.

Such was the infinitely patient, devoted and loyal lady who found them the house Dott was to inhabit for the remainder of his days, at No 3 Chalmers Crescent in the Marchmont district of Edinburgh. Found him a house mere steps from his work places, but made him a home whose warmth always drew him back from work or distant lands. She furnished it with her favourite flowers, patient welcome and the chatter of children, so that her sister, who knew, exclaimed unexpectedly, 'They got on famously—he was not at all an austere man!'

A transformed man, perhaps?

Immediately opposite them, at the junction of the crescent with Warrender Park Road and Sciennes Road, the long, needling spire of the Argyle Place church would have directed the thoughts of a less practical-minded man than Dott to questions of God and eternity. He never attended the church. His life's obsession lay in the treatment of bodies rather than souls, and the house was strategically placed between the Royal Infirmary of Edinburgh and the University of Edinburgh in the one quarter and in the other, just along Sciennes Road, the Royal Hospital for Sick Children.

Into that quiet Marchmont house, on 11 September 1933, there came the thin pink crying of the next generation: Jean Margaret Douglas Dott, Professor and Mrs Dott's only child. Peter McOmish Dott, who was living with his son and daughter-in-law at Chalmers Crescent, knew the joy of his grandchild for eleven months. He had begun to experience the condition known as intermittent claudication, with cramp attacking his legs after walking short distances. It worsened, and with blocked circulation of the feet, he developed a gangrene of the toes, which resulted in surgery. David Wilkie carried out the amputation and Sister Dickson, who never left the family until she died, attended faithfully to his dressings. Ultimately he was totally confined to a wheelchair and died of failure of circulation and a terminal bronchitis.

Just at this time Jean started to take her first steps.

Cushing had been informed at once of her birth and had written back immediately expressing his delight. He wrote again early in 1936 when Jean was a toddler of two:

I am delighted to have your New Year's letter giving a full account of yourself
and enclosing an entrancing photograph of Jean—an amazing child with a
Bible in one hand and a hand grenade in the other, sitting like Humpty-
Dumpty on a wall. I am so afraid she is going to fall off, for there's no telling
how high the wall might be.

Is Cushing again blending the whimsical with serious warning? In his
super-subtle way he may well be referring to a child set too high on a wall
of expectation, with an inheritance of Presbyterian rigidity and explosive
potential. It is ironic to consider the number of doctors and surgeons who
had and were still to battle their way to the famous Cushing's attention, and
yet this small girl, still some twenty-two years short of medical qualification, was already receiving his considered assessment.

By 1936 Dott leaves Cushing in little doubt as to how he sees the rôle of
father. 'Here is a portrait of the most important person in our establishment,' he says, referring to a picture of Jean. Over the years Professor Dott's
correspondence tells of taking Jean, while still young, with himself and Mrs
Dott, to a neurosurgical meeting in Algeria: tells of his inviting an eminent
neurosurgeon to join himself, Peggy and Jean in touring the Highlands of
Scotland, where things 'more important than surgery' will be experienced:
tells of her, after tuition from her father, as being accomplished with rod and
line: tells of his pride when she qualified as a doctor. One weary registrar
commented that he knew of only one day in the year when Professor Dott
could be guaranteed not to operate, and that was the day Jean was playing
her violin in the school concert at George Watson's Ladies' College in
George Square. For Norman Dott, undoubtedly, Jean was the apple of the
family tree.

The apple did not keep the doctor at bay. Jean married Dr Calvin Hider,
an anaesthetist at Edinburgh Royal Infirmary and three more fruits of his
eye were to sweeten Professor Dott's age: three grand-daughters, Jaqueline,
Katherine and Susan, born in 1960, 1962 and 1965. They brought him great
joy and pleasure. By this time he was the Grand Old Man of Neurosurgery
and their coming returned him, in many ways, to the Colinton cradle of
innocence, a world of children and animals and innocence and laughter.
Frequently the three girls went straight to Chalmers Crescent from school
and nearly always had Saturday lunch with their grandparents. When they
were sick and off school they often stayed there, where Mr and Mrs Dott
welcomed them and they were looked after by the housekeeper, Barbara.
In spite of the stealing years and increasing disability, he did lots of walking
with them. Through the quiet quarters of Marchmont and the Grange and
Morningside to the Blackford Hill or the Hermitage, following its leaf-
strewn river, then around Arthur's Seat to the shores of Dunsappie Loch,
with the blue coasts of Fife before them and the green contours of the
Pentlands behind, came an old man and his three grandchildren. The old

man wore a long greyish raincoat with an ancient leather belt which did not match. Beneath his knickerbockers clumped a rather heavy pair of boots. He sucked on an old pipe. Had it not been for the three girls laughing and dancing round him as they waited for their cones from the summertime ice-cream seller, he might have been taken for a passing tramp.

The cones were forthcoming. Not that he was prone to spoil his little ones, who quickly learned to respect the admonitory gesture of the walking stick. A spanking might be administered only on occasions of the utmost naughtiness, as for instance when they sat down and ate all of the dog's chocolate drops. But such occasions happened hardly ever, and though he set a high standard of behaviour, they enjoyed pretty much the run of the house, being allowed to play with everything. Everything that is, except for his collection of beautifully cared for and sharpened tools which lined the boiler-house wall and which were not under any circumstances allowed into small hands.

Nor were they kept out in the cold when their granda was talking to eminent visitors in his study. They knocked and were never refused admission, roaming around his desk with its papers piled like leaning towers of Pisa, its scattered scribbling pads covered in jottings, its shining, sharpened pencils and clutter of mementos from trips abroad and foreign visitors: paperweights guarding their own bright little miniature interiors; the tray from Rio de Janeiro, the pot pourri bowl from China, the curios from India, the three little bears from Hungary. And the grotesquely carved head with the dog's bone resting underneath—Beelzebub guarding the bone, as Dott told his awed grandchildren.

Then he took them on his knee and they played with his old-time watch chain and the key which hung from it. Sometimes he would say it was the key to his heart: at other times they would bend their heads, fascinated, when he told them it was the key of wisdom. Ah, but where was the lock? And so they were ever searching for the lock it would open. Medical matters forgotten, he told them about the kelpies and sprites that haunted the Highlands and Brig o' Turk, and about the spunkies that danced on the daisies in Colinton Kirkyard, where their great-grandmother, Rebecca Dott, was sleeping the last sleep.

Perhaps encouraged by the presence of grandchildren, a hedgehog and a tortoise joined the rest of the creatures that were a familiar part of the Dott establishment. Norman Dott the scientist was, as we know, kind and caring towards his laboratory animals, but harking back to the old Hailes Brae days, he was in himself extremely fond of animals and was never without a dog. There was a nondescript bundle of hair with legs sticking out everywhere which he called Spider. Latterly he was devoted to a mongrel called Sally, who enjoyed driving with him and the time came when neither moved anywhere without the other. Most callers at No 3, however, and

facing page

60 Norman and Peggy, man and wife, outside St Giles Cathedral. Two of the bridesmaids (on Norman's right) are Peggy's sisters.

61 A very youthful Dott of thirty-four now engaged to be married. Harvey Cushing could not decide whether Dott or his dog looked the more intelligent and alert.

62 Norman and Peggy on holiday in the Trossachs.

63 Young Jean on the fisherman's knee. He doted on this only child.

64 Father and daughter.

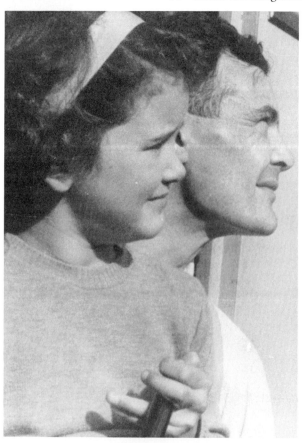

65　'Three Castles' was his preferred brand of cigarette. Dott was sometimes known to charge a packet of cigarettes as his fee.

66　The work went on in Chalmers Crescent often late into the night.

67 The Samoyeds guarding Norman's most prized possession.

68 A touch of Hailes Brae brought to Chalmers Crescent. Kelty at her bell demanding entry. The photograph was taken by Dr Wilder Penfield in July 1959.

69 Norman Dott practised fishing as he practised surgery, with professional intentness, patience, skill—and rewarding results.

70 Under her father's tutelage young Jean grew up to be a skilled fisherwoman.

71 On holiday with Eric and Sally, September 1940.

72   Visiting the Udvarhelyis in October 1969.

73   Back home at Chalmers Crescent.

neighbouring dogwalkers, remember the white Samoyeds and how insistent he was that the dog was not to blame when he tripped over one of them and fractured his recently grafted thigh.

He had not been long discharged from the Royal Infirmary where at his suggestion, if not insistence, Sir Walter Mercer had shortened and reset the bone of the right leg to match his old injured left leg. The Professor was exercising himself with the aid of one of the Samoyeds in the garden when he tripped over the dog and fell. The ugly cracking sound and accompanying pain did not need any diagnostic skill on his own part to confirm that the leg had refractured and Dott had to be embarrassingly re-delivered to the orthopaedic ward so soon after they had completed an excellent job. His one concern was to convince the doctors that the accident had been his own fault and not the dog's.

Towards the end of his life he could be seen garbed in an extraordinarily all-encompassing top coat which covered him protectively from neck to ankle so that dogs could extend their enthusiastic greetings to him with their muddy paws without dirtying his suit. It was the mark of a lifelong, perhaps slightly ambivalent interest in and relationship with dogs. The first successful steps in his career had been dependent upon animal work in Sharpey-Schäfer's physiological laboratory and at the end of his career he returned to the Wilkie laboratory to carry out work on cerebral hypothermia which he hoped to continue to the benefit of mankind.

From time to time some of the pets were reminded of the ambivalent honour that was theirs in being residents of No. 3 Chalmers Crescent. Remembering the system used by Spunkie in Hailes Brae. Dott taught his Marchmont cat to demand his right of entry to the house by ringing a bell. As an added refinement he also learned to wait politely after the first ring, but if on looking through the window he saw no sign of stirring to accede to his request, he rang a second time more imperiously. Already we have referred to Dott's delightful descriptions of animal behaviour in a letter to Lord Adrian. This is the letter in which Dott, leading on from the acuity of a dog's sense of smell and obviously bearing in mind his knowledge of some of the primitive neural pathways of the human brain, refers to the strong emotional appeal of smell, though minimised in humans, and its intellectual associations. Hence the smell of pinewood is intensely evocative of his happy Scottish childhood.

Animals apart, the house at Chalmers Crescent received a constant stream of visitors, often unexpected and usually distinguished. They mingled easily with the hotchpotch of people who always seemed to be about: men and women who came to the door begging and were never turned away without a cup of tea and a sandwich, Barbara the housekeeper, the maid Bridget who had been taken in from one of the hospitals with a deformity of her neck and shoulder and somehow became adopted, Delaney the odd job man who looked after the cars, Sister Dickson, Jean's friends who stayed from time to time, later the grandchildren, and stray flights of foreigners who settled for varying periods. The most notable of these was Doctor Kate Hermann who lived with the Dotts during the war. Professor Dott's loyal neurologist, she had received a note in Hamburg enabling her to escape the Nazis who had marked her out for her outspokenness. She succeeded by the finest of margins in slipping through the net, took a ship to Methil in the manner of Dott's Huguenot forebears, and landed in Fife with tuppence and a stamp in her pocket. And she too was adopted. Patients too called in latter days. Mrs Dott was described by her housekeeper, not surprisingly, as 'a most accommodating person'!

Some of these visitors had to be accommodated not only with bed and board but with special fare appropriate to their culture and religion. Dark-skinned people with a taste for hot food, ladies in saris and sarongs, Jews, vegetarians and connoisseurs of quaint culinary fancies. Rationing was a fact of existence during and after the war, but so also was Professor Dott's preference for plain, simple meals in the Hailes Brae style. Dignitaries who came to the renowned Professor's table expecting to fare sumptuously would have received a salutary lesson in the virtues of good, wholesome Scots kitchen, even although every effort was made to defer to the traditions of their cuisine, and of course if Dott the fisherman had been wilier than the Highland or Border salmon, the table might be graced by the king of fish. Inevitably though, meals were irregular as work dictated, sometimes the household was three quarters of the way through a meal before Professor Dott arrived home, always to a tumultuous welcome from family, children and dogs, and thermos flasks of food and coffee had often to be set aside for his late return. He did enjoy a very short lunch break, followed by a few minutes sitting stiffly with outthrust leg before going back to work.

He worked harder than most men.

There was no designated off-duty time in Professor Dott's world. His secretary would continue working with him until half past four on a Saturday afternoon and he himself would frequently be working on the Sunday: a seven day cycle going on for as long as was necessary. A major flaw in this great man whose iron will and constitution kept him going in spite of his own physical handicap, is that he failed to recognise the sheer inability of some people to cope with the rigours of such a regime. A registrar who did *not* peel off, but who survived to enjoy his own success, lamented that he was not allowed to leave the ward for six weeks. When he asked permission to go out and have a haircut the Professor had the barber come in and see to it in the ward itself. This, though, was in part amused irony, for the registrar and his wife were subsequently rewarded for their endurance by a clutch of well chosen festival concert tickets.

Even the elements could not contain him. An occupational therapy student at Bangour recalls the day when a monumental snowstorm cut off the hospital and the ambulances stopped running. Not one of the usual staff was able to get through for the weekly professorial round. With immense relief she, the sister and the grateful house surgeon, all resident in the hospital, sat down in the grip of the white bewintered world to enjoy a relaxing cup of coffee, all the more welcome for being unusual if not illicit. Stolen waters are sweet—and bread eaten in secret is pleasant. Suddenly Dott appeared out of the blizzard like God out of the whirlwind, dismaying with his all-powerful presence. Without a single word of comment he walked in and started his usual meticulous ward round.

A man of mettle.

The faithful tried hard to emulate him and to please him. Some came close.

As a compensation for such a reign, Dott often appeared bearing tickets to various concerts and shows. He had an almost child-like weakness for the circus and would take his staff personally if one were near at hand. He enjoyed theatre, cinema, the opera, Gilbert and Sullivan and all kinds of classical music.

But Dott himself had little in the way of spare time. When he shut the door of No. 3 behind him in the evening that was not the end of his day's work. It continued well into the wee small hours, where this wee small man with the mighty vision and the huge capacity for his task, worked on in the pale puddle of anglepoise lamplight and the cluttered towers of medical papers on his desk, blue skeins of tobacco smoke drifting in a hazy, lazy fragrance over his head as he toiled on, not sparing himself, unstinting, unremitting, into the dead watches. Opposite his house was a guest house where students were lodged. At that time Marchmont was an academic warren of landladied undergraduates. One of these students, later to become a journalist wrote to *The Scotsman* newspaper about the beacon in the dark that kept him company as he pursued his own studies. That star of enlightened industry was the yellow burning of Professor Dott's anglepoise. Youth's a stuff will not endure, says the poet, but Dott's energy was quite literally a burning and shining light to all the place, and an example to the flagging or late-returning roisterers of academe.

In the morning the door opened and the other Dott appeared: a man with a dog, and a little girl in a Redskin headdress and outfit playing around them; a man pruning his roses or admiring the beautiful fuchsia whose scented galaxies crimsoned and purpled the porched entrance to the house.

Norman Dott animal lover, Norman Dott gardener, Norman Dott doting father.

There was little indoors other than his study to suggest that this was the home of an eminent neurosurgeon. A few skulls with holes drilled in them, sitting on a chest in the hall, one or two pictures on the walls illustrating the dark doings of early surgical operations, some portraits in oils—not the orchards of art that might have been expected to grow out of his background. A great many freshly cut flowers and plants among the cluttered confusion of its rooms—garden things placed there by the gentle, bright hand of Mrs Dott.

Here he was in all senses at home. Whether sitting under the sun on his workbench by the backdoor, his fingers fiddling instinctively with lighter or pipe or whatever lay to hand—or indoors listening to music, rarely reclined on the living room couch while Jean played to him on her violin. 'Let me hear that phrase again,' he might say. And, if she were doing a duet with Joan Hay, her classmate and friend: 'You a bit softer, I think, and perhaps you a bit louder.' Or some such technical correction. Music took the place of art in filling the house: the walls brimmed with Bach's Brandenburg Concertos. He played them for hours after hours.

Warm, friendly hours.

Or he sat in his long-armed brown armchair on the right of the fireplace, his left leg thrust out in front of him as always; Peggy in the companion chair on the left. As always. There were occasional bursts of laughter from him as something funny came up in conversation or reading. Sometimes he would say in his slow voice, with its ironically lazy-sounding overtones, 'I had an idea, Peggy'. And then he would go on to discuss with her some such matter as a forthcoming trip or visit, or maybe a holiday.

They did everything together, even when holidays meant, as they invariably did, fishing, and though bored to tears Peggy rowed him manfully round his favourite lochs for days on end, much preferring this to the formalities of the congresses abroad. In Stornoway they occupied an extremely isolated cottage, a much travelled groceries van providing the frayed end of the lifeline to civilisation and there Dott fished the stars round the sky, enjoying the soothing balm of solitude.

To achieve the full benefits of the contemplative man's recreation it was sometimes necessary to pack both of the Alvis cars with the large amounts of fishing tackle that were a serious part of holiday planning. Fishing was not a mundane relaxation with Dott. From his earliest days in Colinton it was an obsessional sport into which he poured the same concentration and attention to detail that he applied to his surgery. Without such zealously practical devotion he would never have enjoyed the art. High thoughts did not come to him as the moon marbled the lochs at Achray and Katrine during Easter and the water rustled mysteriously to the stirrings of the fish.

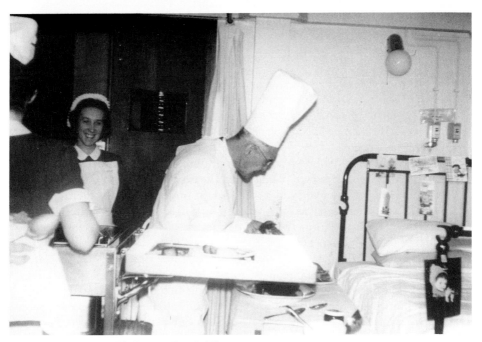

74　Operating on Christmas Day? The famous surgeon carves the Turkey for the patients in Ward 20.

75　And afterwards the plum pudding, brought in by the chef himself. Dott's visit to his patients on Christmas Day was sacrosanct.

Or, if they did, he never said. The closest he came to philosophy was when Sister Ross retired to Brora and he went up on fishing holidays to visit her and sat chatting for hours over the pots of 'Tinkers' Tea', the very same brew with which he liked to refresh himself after an arduous spell in theatre. Under his tutelage Jean was soon a keen and skilled fisherwoman. She could guddle a trout in the burns and carry it home in a basket of rushes she had gathered and made herself. Taught by a master angler. And if the ghost of Parlane Macfarlane ever whispered to him on the nights of the fishes, he would have dismissed it as the splashing skirts of the loch shores, the invisible breath of a sea trout—or the tread of a footstep in some half remembered furrow of the human brain.

Even on Christmas Day—perhaps the one day in the year when most busy men can be guaranteed to fortify themselves in their households against the cares of work, Dott did not remain on holiday. Instead the whole Dott family sallied forth to Ward 20 to visit his patients and make them as merry as they could. This ritual was sacrosanct. And if there were any specially ill patients to be dealt with, or operation which needed his skilled and practised intervention, it went without saying that he was available. Dott was known to leave important social functions, walk into the Royal Infirmary in full evening dress and go straight into his operating clothes, if he were needed in an emergency. In the life of this great family man there was simply nothing that came before his calling. He put his work first, his family next, and finally, if at all, he considered himself.

Perhaps the one great luxury he allowed himself was his cars, and there is no doubt that they were better looked after than the Professor's own person. From the youthful enthusiasm for motor bikes in the long sidecar of one of which he was humorously reported to carry odd bodies for dissection, he graduated to a Morris Cowley and then to a DFP a French built car of an unusual type which appealed to him. Its trick of slipping into reverse gear by accident and shooting unexpectedly backwards in the Edinburgh streets gave him ample opportunity to be under the bonnet and getting things to rights. He tinkered with it constantly until it perished in a fire. 'A glorious end,' he commented to Eric, to whom he had given it.

Then came the famous Alvises. He was extremely fond of these two beautiful Alvis cars with their long raking bonnets, the one named Bira and the other Tortoise. The latter was allocated to Mrs Dott, though she would sometimes find on routine school or social trips that it contained embarrassing pathological specimens left there if the Professor had happened to borrow it. Much heart searching discussion was gone through before the Alvises were exchanged for a Bentley, which offered a more comfortable ride to Dott's injured hip.

76   Bira and Tortoise, the famous Alvis cars.

Mr Peter Walton, a retired consultant surgeon, still has a memory of fifty
years ago when he was a very young resident but desperately keen on cars.
He had seen Dott arrive in his gorgeous Speed 25 HP Alvis. Despite the
rather formidable setting of the Royal Infirmary main corridor with its
statuary and legacy boards, and the fact that Dott was a consultant, the
neurosurgical consultant, and he was a young resident, his enthusiasm
allowed no restraint. 'Mr Dott, Sir!' he said, 'I saw your beautiful Speed 25
Alvis. But is it not a bit heavy on petrol?' Dott replied, 'It was, but I took
the pistons out, put liners in the cylinders and reduced it to a Speed 20, so
now it's more economical to run!' And this from a surgeon. He never forgot
it.[3]

Dr David Tulloch, another enthusiast, called Professor Dott into
consultation at the home of a patient. It was a very distressing painful
syndrome but as Dr Tulloch watched the road from the patient's house for
Dott's approach he began to have second thoughts. The pain was intractable
but the condition was not truly neurosurgical. Was he troubling the great
man unnecessarily? As he pondered, with increasing disquiet, his attention
was focused and disquiet gave way to admiration.

> The small dark shape grew steadily larger and was soon seen to consist of an
> enormous black car with an immensely long bonnet, gleaming radiator and
> very handsome open coachwork. It was an Alvis of the nineteen thirties. From
> it stepped Norman Dott and pleasant greetings were exchanged. 'Is it a Speed
> 25 or a 4.3?' I asked. 'It's a 4.3,' he replied. I was deeply impressed

remembering that this model had registered the fastest acceleration figures of pre-war road tests. I regretted not having appeared in my 4½ litre Bentley of 1930 vintage.[4]

Impressive as this rather aggressive automobile was, it was Dott's strangely contrasting kindness that left a lasting impression on Dr Tulloch.

For the next two hours Norman Dott devoted his whole attention and the full force of his personality to the consideration of the patient, his wife and their problems. There was no treatment in the true sense that he or anyone else could offer but he made practical suggestions in management in order to achieve the maximum in comfort and well-being that was possible, or at least to minimise pain and distress. By sheer force of his compassion and concern Norman Dott inspired the patient and his wife with courage that sustained them for the remainder of their life together.

His love for his Alvises became legendary. Mr Thomas Stewart remembers his grey 4.3 litre Alvis Tourer.

I was an apprentice mechanic and 18 years old at the time. When he brought his car into our garage it was my duty to drive him back to the Royal Infirmary and sometimes I had to collect the car from the Royal Infirmary. When I delivered his car to his home I used to meet his wife and family and they all chatted to me. He had a great knowledge of cars. Professor Dott and I spoke in great detail about the insides of a car. When his own car needed repair, he knew exactly what the problem was and would request repairs exactly as he described. He was also particular as to who carried out the work and sometimes, the choice having fallen on him, Mr Archie Anderson would find Dott beside him helping to take off the cylinder heads![5]

Professor Lipschitz, 'Lippy' he was to all and sundry in those days, confirms how very, very human Dott was in some of his attitudes. One day he was returning to Edinburgh from Bangour Hospital, seated beside Professor Dott in one of the Alvises, with Miss Jacqueline Robertson his secretary and sister-in-law in one of the back seats. 'Lippy, this car is running rather well isn't it?' said the Professor, turning to Lippy at 98 miles per hour. Lippy replied, 'Yes sir, but it doesn't seem to be tuned to perfection.' His foot went down harder and at 105 miles an hour, 'You see, she is running well.' Lippy persisted. 'No sir, she doesn't seem to be running quite so well as she should.' As he put his foot down further, 'Jackie' from the back seat rammed her umbrella into Lippy's back with the words, 'Shut up! Stop winding him up or he'll ride this car until the bloody engine bursts!'[6]

It should be stressed that Norman Dott was a superb driver, that these were different days on clear roads, that the quoted speeds he is reputed to have reached are probably more illustrative than accurate, and that he had too much professional experience of head and spinal injuries resulting from road traffic accidents ever to behave dangerously himself. Nevertheless he was often in a hurry, sometimes to arrive at an emergency case, and one former nurse recalled how the police between Edinburgh and Bangour used to look the other way when they saw him speeding by. The hands that steered the wheel had great work to do elsewhere. 'As for me,' she said, 'I just shut my eyes.'

Doubtless his delight in feeling the power of these fast-driving cars was in some sense a compensation for his disabled frame and the liberation of a caged spirit. Pain and disability were ever present or threatening. He was forced into periods off work for treatment, some short, one in particular relatively long. In January 1948, shortly after being appointed to the Chair of Surgical Neurology, he started leave of absence which eventually had to be extended to twenty months. Dott himself describes how, as a boy of nine, he attended the outpatients of Dr John Thomson at the Royal Hospital for Sick Children with a painful hip. The fear was that it was a tuberculous infection but this was discounted and Dott himself considered it a resolving Perthes disease. There is no evidence that the condition persisted into adolescence, or that it gave him any lasting trouble during schooldays. He did not play ball games but he enjoyed swimming. We have seen how in his motorcycle accident in 1913 he suffered a compound fracture of the tibia and a fracture of the neck of the femur on the left side. Although he was fortunate, for those days, to recover from such injuries, the effects dogged him all his days. The left hip was stiff and painful and the leg foreshortened in comparison to the right. This caused him to limp and throw further abnormal stresses on the hip and spine, compounding the pain and disability.

At different times he persuaded eminent colleagues, both neurosurgical and orthopaedic, to carry out various operations to improve matters. A fusion of the left hip was the province of a famous orthopaedic surgeon, Sir Harry Platt. A cordotomy is an operation to section the nerve fibres carrying pain sensation from the lower limb in their course through the spinal cord. This was performed by an equally famous neurosurgeon, his friend Sir Geoffrey Jefferson. Ingeniously, as we know, he persuaded an Edinburgh orthopaedic colleague, Sir Walter Mercer, to shorten his good right leg to bring his legs into uniformity and diminish his limp. It was when he was not long into convalescence from this last operation that he tripped over the dog and refractured it. It was also at some point in that saga that he had found the pain in his little toe, if not intolerable, at least not to be tolerated and had injected it with local anaesthetic and amputated it himself.

Did this far from robust physique have a bearing on his personality and achievements? Of course it must have, but not in any anticipated manner. He had ample excuse for developing querulous traits or for abandoning effort, with pain as the excuse for lack of success but this was not his manner, and if anything he disparaged such a reaction.

'The stoics are few nowadays, and I think the Welfare State rather favours the neurotic, dependent attitude: "I have a pain, and it is somebody's duty to take it away."' No, Dott's ultimate transcendence of pain lay in his life-long efforts to remove other people's. All that his staff could report in this matter were long operations carried out to the final detail beyond the demands of conscientious surgery; the occasional unobtrusive rubbing of his painful thigh during a lengthy ward round; perhaps an extra cigarette over the cup of 'Tinkers' Tea' at the end of an operation. A keen observer might detect a slight sense of relief and relaxation as he sat down in his chair leaning slightly backwards and stretching out his left leg before discussing a particular patient or topic. Shortly, however, the regular voluntary contractions of his left thigh muscles might be seen disturbing his trouser leg. Once, when he was explaining a proposed operation to a patient not overendowed with either intelligence or grace, he was interrupted by the patient's wanting to know 'What was he doing there?' How many would have swept this impertinence brusquely aside! Not so Dott. He gave a courteous explanation, carefully tailored to the man's intellect, of the benefits of regular quadriceps muscle exercises in painful, stiff limbs, and then resumed his advice to the patient.

Doctor Margaret Munro applied for a job as Dott's resident in 1945. She was wearing a caliper as the result of a previous attack of poliomyelitis, and found Dott with caliper and crutches from one of his operations. She still recalls, with pleasure, the informality of their first meeting, the interview. 'How do you manage these awful things?' he said, pulling up his trouser leg to show her his caliper! This informality, as was the experience of others, did not prepare her for the tremendously hard work entailed in being Dott's house surgeon. He was a patient himself in Ward 20 during part of her appointment. He might, she said, awake at about 6 a.m., decide to shave, then conduct a ward round of his patients from his room!

One day there had been a pit accident with a stream of casualties. After the initial hectic rush, things began to quieten. Then at about midnight the Alvis was seen to enter the front courtyard of the Royal Infirmary, Dott having just decided to have 'another wee look at some of the patients.' They went to the orthopaedic ward to see some of the multiple injuries, who also had head injuries. Dott, with caliper and crutches, and Munro with caliper, attempted to enter. The resident dismissed them sharply. 'No casualties here, you go to Accident and Emergency!' 'Possibly the resident had been too brusque with potential patients for Dott's liking,' comments Dr Munro. 'I can't imagine that it was his own dignity that concerned him; in any case, Dott kept him on a full and protracted neurological ward round until approximately 2 a.m.!'

Like Dr Munro, others found the same indefatigable spirit even when he was confined to bed in a ward. His orthopaedic teams, physiotherapist, house surgeon, registrar, have the best stories of bed and traction beams vibrating to enthusiastic exercises, of orthopaedic side wards converted into neurosurgical offices with telephone and X-ray viewing boxes installed. They tell of interest in and advice offered about their patients, a special injection technique advised—almost insisted upon—for a fellow patient noisy with pain. And yet there was time for a late night informal chat about work and music with the house surgeon on his last round of the day; informal yet informed.

No, Dott's disabilities did not deter him from his driving ambitions for surgical neurology, nor from the enjoyment of his fishing. He was often sighted on his Highland beat in less than favourable conditions long after others, not so intrepid, had left the river. They did not deter him from extensive travelling and lecturing which he increasingly enjoyed during his retirement. There was an occasional reference in his notes to position in a car or plane seat, an extra cushion, but no curtailment in the enthusiasm for world tours. He seemed to regard his body as divorced from his driving spirit. It was as if he had been saddled with the care of another patient, who must not intrude too much but, if it proved necessary, must receive the same meticulous clinical assessment as others. On occasions this led to entries in his own clinical records, the exact nerve roots involved, the degree and location of pain.

> Knee considerably swollen; it too is quite painful and very stiff at first . . . Drove car over to Royal Infirmary today, can't reach hand brake and clutch a bit heavy for left knee and foot . . . On 18/4/49 operated on two trigeminal neuralgias; my back and shoulders rather sore, but good results.

A more mundane upset gives us the supreme example of his spirit and command over his troublesome body. He notes on one of his foreign tours:

> Excellent clam soup that kept me up most of the night. My stomach seemed to keep these back and I would wash out quite effectively by drinking much and vomiting until clear of them—could keep to schedule.

And that was no ordinary schedule of visits, lectures and travel. If his disabilities did not deter him from his course they sharpened his appreciation of other people's suffering and did not lead him to be too critical of others' complaints.

> I do not belive that a neurotic patient's over valuation of pain is a contra-indication to surgical treatment. Rather it is an indication in favour of it for ultimately it is the patient's valuation of his pain that is of real importance.

Throughout his active surgical life, Dott saw to it that his patients were relieved of unnecessary pain and suffering and, as we have seen, made an extensive study and practice of surgical relief of intractable pain.

It was in retirement, that bowel cancer struck Dott; retirement, when most people, after such an active life, would be turning to relaxation and amusement. He had turned instead to deep involvement in the socio-medical aspects of 'those conditions for which I have not been able to do enough during my active surgical career', epilepsy, spina bifida and hydrocephalus, paraplegia, cancer. He had been invited to high office in many of the appropriate voluntary societies. Was cancer going to make him succumb and cry 'Enough' to fate? Far from it. He realised that the unfamiliar colostomy was an intolerable burden to some patients, so he studied and commanded his own. Soon with encouraging slogans such as 'Never missed a meeting either in London or Edinburgh' and the attitude that a colostomy was almost as convenient as the normal system of voiding, he was quite unembarrassed in launching an energetic campaign to help others in a similar situation (he would have damned the word 'plight'). At the age of seventy-three he now develops improvements in apparatus, writes to the medical press, lectures community nurses, general practitioners and surgeons. He instructs and comforts patients, brings them to Chalmers Crescent to show them how to manage their colostomies. He sets up a stoma clinic to this end. All his old energy and attention to detail appear to be preserved as he writes minute instructions for the measurement and placing of shelves for the benefit of these patients. Whatever fate had in store for him Norman Dott determined to turn to the benefit of mankind.

He was in fact, though not everyone on his staff realised it, one of the kindest of men.

His caring and compassion came out especially where children were involved. One nurse recalled a little girl of five, the daughter of a farm labourer in Aberdeenshire, and helpless with a brain tumour. After she had been operated on she became steadily more lively until one day Dott took her home for tea. When she returned to the ward the staff crowded round her like wasps round jam, agog to hear of her experience. They were delighted when she told them in her broad Aberdeenshire that she 'had played wi' wee Jeannie Doatt and had breid wi' banana spreid on' t, an' choccy biscuits for tea.'

He would come from Edinburgh to Bangour to be with a child some nights before an operation was due and asked the nurses to do something special for the youngster's coming round and recovery. 'In the best way you can, make it like a party for him,' he said. And the nurses did his bidding, as best they could in war time.

Often Dott saw to it himself. Many a patient, old now and frail, brightens with the remembrance of the doll or toy given to them by the man who saved their lives and took away their pain. The first doll I ever had; the donkey on wheels I learned to push around to help me walk again, and which Professor Dott let me take home when I was 3½ years old—such stories of his kindness could fill up another biography. Nurses too were struck by these touches. A boy with a brain tumour had a 'Dismal Desmond' dog from Dott. The great brain surgeon himself bandaged the dog's head just like the child's, to make sure that this would take up his attention when coming out of the operation.

It is time to allow just a scattering of these former patients, staff and acquaintances to have their fuller say.

Many times we hear of a kindly, unassuming person who never entered a ward without acknowledging the nurse at the door, however junior. There was no imperial sweep into the ward with retinue dancing frenzied attendance, like some consultants.

A nurse remembers with amusement:

> My friend was in the Nurses' Sick Bay and I was visiting her. She had been asked to try out a new bed which had been designed for the neurosurgical department. While I was visiting, a small, rather insignificant man came in and crawled under the bed to inspect it. We sat having tea at the window, assuming that this was an engineer. Sister then came into the ward and said, 'Have you seen Professor Dott?' We both immediately replied, 'No', when a voice from under the bed said, 'Yes! here I am sister' and out came our engineer: Professor Dott.

Then there is a delightful snippet, from the pathology technician.

> Only three weeks into the job but proudly in a new white coat, I was sent to the corridor to clean the specimen jars and cabinets. I had scarcely moved on to the section dealing with the Central Nervous System when this gentleman arrived and, passing the time of day, asked if I were enjoying the work. When I said I was he started to show a keen interest in the mounted specimens asking what they were. I, not knowing one part of the brain from another and with all the confidence of a beginner, gave a glowing account. The gentleman then departed in the direction of the Professor's office. A short while later the Professor's secretary shot from her den like a bullet and administered a severe reprimand to me for not showing such an important person as Professor Dott directly into her. For the rest of the morning I skulked in the basement for fear of meeting again the man to whom I had been so foolish. A few months later, I was despatched, with a photographer, to Ward 20 to take some photographs that Professor Dott had requested. Not unexpectedly he was there to check that all was done exactly as he wanted. It wasn't long before he recognised me, turned with a smile and enquired how my anatomy was progressing hoping that it had improved somewhat since the last meeting.

This kindly understanding comes out again and again. Professor Ritchie then working in the Physiology Department and meeting students not long embarked on their medical careers gave an example. It is a well known scourge of the young medical student, overburdened with these new studies, to be suddenly afflicted with the symptoms, or so they seem, from his hurried referral to the only text books available to him, the symptoms of the most dire and lethal conditions known. Many have been struck by acute cancer of the rectum, tuberculosis or brain tumour, only to be miraculously cured by careful examination and reassurance. When they confided in Dr Ritchie, as he then was, he said that strangely, as a super specialist might be thought inappropriate, he used to refer them to Professor Norman Dott. With him they would receive such a considered hearing, thorough examination and kindly authoritative reassurance.[7]

So the vast crowd of witnesses flocks to the bar, clamouring for hearing.

He was an extraordinary man, he instilled such confidence in his patients and their relatives and they were never afraid to ask him the simplest of questions. But he was also a very ordinary man. One day a fellow nurse, new to the ward asked him to get her something while she was working with a baby. She thought he was the ward porter! He did as she asked without enlightening her as to who he was.

Nothing was ever any trouble to Mr Dott. To staff and patients alike he was always a perfect gentleman, and one had to marvel at his kindly approach to so many war-wounded lads. Bitter at being maimed for life, with his help they slowly came to accepting their fate . . . His love of humanity and care for everyone made him loved and respected by all who had the privilege of helping him in any way . . . My memories of those days in Ward 20 and Bangour are vivid and clear. Through his attention to detail in observance my training was early enhanced and the building of my character indebted.

He was a tall slim lad with a slight limp in those early days of the 30's in the Sick Children's Hospital—very shy, but always with a smile and a 'good morning'. The children just loved him and we could hear them calling 'Mr Dott' from all over the wards. Especially when they were getting better, they were always shouting his name . . . This is only a little remembrance from an Old Age Pensioner who can still hear the children calling, 'Dr Dott! Dr Dott!'

In addition to operations he always seemed to be in attendance at the bedsides, day and night . . . He usually addressed his patients by their first names or nick-names. He created a wonderful atmosphere in the wards. As well as the service men and civilians with head and spinal injuries, there appeared to be scores of folk arriving at that particular time—folk on crutches, in wheelchairs, some never having walked for years. In a very short time Mr Dott had them marching round the ward singing *Let him go, let him tarry, let him sink or let him swim* . . .

He grasped me tightly by the hand and I was astonished by the strength of such a small man. He refused to let go of my hand until I'd agreed to the operation. All the time I could feel those eyes of his boring into the back of my brain . . . After the operation he rubbed his cheek gently against mine and said he was so happy to see me on my feet again.

And the smaller tributes from letters sent and calls made, they pass through the mind and across the page like bright birds.

I shall never forget that small man with the marked limp, grey wavy hair and rimless spectacles.

The staff always called him 'The Quiet Man' and the title seemed to suit him admirably and to sum up his whole being.

He was totally dedicated to the great work he was called upon to do. When operating on the most seriously ill patients we would sometimes feel like dropping, but we drew strength and inspiration from him who was a true servant of God.

Watching my son grow up over the years, I often give a prayer of thanks for the great skill of Professor Dott.

He exuded a charisma I had never experienced before. From the outset I was intrigued by his pleasant and gentle attitude to me. He was so different from any other doctor or high-ranking surgeon I have ever met.

Often when he made his round he was dressed in an ordinary lounge suit and he reminded me of an ordinary working man wearing his Sunday best. I vividly recall his limp and the fact that he always seemed to be smiling.

It may be difficult to believe that when asked 'What do we owe you, docor?', his reply was 'A packet of cigarettes', but he was the kind of person who would react in this way—a nobleman without peer, yet who was completely ordinary.

He was concerned for the poorest child as he was for the wealthiest one.

He gave new life and hope to thousands of suffering people.

Everyone had faith in him. He inspired everyone who came in contact with him. When you walked into his presence you knew at once he was someone special.

'Dott' was an honoured name in our household.

He operated on a blind man to correct his sleeping pattern and out of the blue the man regained his sight. I can see his face still grinning from ear to ear.

He was a lovely person—more like a gentleman farmer than the brilliant surgeon he really was.

I shall be eternally grateful to that marvellous man.

77, 78 and 79 Studies by Grace Alison, the photographer on whose pituitary Dott had operated.

That kindly gentleman with the quiet voice had tears in his eyes when the wee fellow died. Previously he'd come down the ward holding his hand.

Many a patient who thought they were crippled for life walked out of Bangour.

This great man gave us a wonderful father!

Professor Dott has never left my thoughts since the day he saved my life.

I've thanked God for the gift of healing that was given to that quiet man. I felt a personal sense of loss when I heard of his death.

I have seen him making patients walk and care when they had lost all hope.

This brilliant surgeon was a gentle, caring person, never too busy to listen and comfort.

One of God's most caring and kind gentlemen.

My mother spoke of him in the same tone used for the Queen.

He was a very simple and kindly man and liked working class people.

A sincere, simple person.

One of my dearest friends . . .

It is easy to dig up darkness in people's lives, and there was none in Dott's. It is equally easy to eulogise, and, in doing so, to idolise. But the voices that speak here are those of people who worked with him and were treated by him, not those of the authors.

Can a crowd of witnesses, then, be sometimes wrong?

Sometimes, yes. The patients never saw the martinet, the man whose way of doing things was the only way, in his own single-minded view. They were not aware of the seemingly unreasonable demands made on the time and energy of a dedicated but often drained staff. The humility seen by the sufferers was a personal one only: professionally he was far from self-abnegating. How many great men are, or can afford to be? A golden idol sometimes has its feet of clay. Yet in pointing to Dott's, no-one has said 'clay'. The platform for such a gesture, such a word, was offered publicly. At worst the man himself comes away with streaks of bronze—but still glittering.

There is one angle from which many patients saw their distorted view of Dott and perhaps saw what they wanted to see.

He was not a religious man.

All that he was ready to concede in this respect was the need of the human soul for worship, and his regard for Harvey Cushing fell little short of that. He described how Cushing sent a body of disciples, himself among them, into the world to form a close knit international brotherhood. In the devotion to himself and the ideals which he inspired in them he resembled the great religious founders more than any other medical man so far appearing in the pages of history.

Nevertheless Dott's was not a religious zeal and knowledge of him in his lifetime and perusal of his papers must suggest a guarded agnosticism. This he sometimes cloaks in whimsey perhaps in deference to some in his audiences. He is starting to outline his own philosophies when he quotes on more than one occasion, 'Philosophers tell us that happiness is proportional to our contribution to the weal of our fellow men', and gently, one step further.

> A very happy man this John D Rockefeller, whether you speculate that he is still viewing his achievement from some celestial vantage point; or conclude that, while still upon earth, he could see far enough to realise that millions would bless his memory.

This address to the Rotary Club of Edinburgh continues,

> Theologians give us an interpretation of laying up riches in another place. Be that as it may, I think that the happiness and satisfaction of service comes to the servant here on earth.

Then, there are, from other speeches, light-hearted, sidelong swipes at religion. He tells us that his ancestors found themselves, 'in a land largely overcast by the baleful ecclesiastical discipline of Calvin and John Knox, yet they throve.' And again, 'I have spent some times in the outer Isles. The road to them is sweet. Out there the stricter Puritanical Sects still prevail—and the lunacy rate is unusually high!'

When he addressed the Edinburgh Philosophy of Science Group he might have, given the opportunity, revealed his deepest soul. But not so. He took for his title 'The Human Brain as a Mechanism'.

Did he from his extensive experience of probing the brain in life go on to suggest a site for the soul and its activities? Wisely, no. 'I suspect,' he said, 'that man's understanding of himself is a pursuit without an end.' He went on to quote what T H Huxley wrote in 1870:

> I can find no intelligible ground for refusing to say that the properties of living protoplasm result from the nature and disposition of its molecules . . . and, if so, it must be true in the same sense and to the same extent, that the thoughts to which I am now giving utterance, and your thoughts regarding them, are the expressions of molecular changes in the matter of life which is the source of other vital phenomena.

He ended by posing the question: 'When death comes and the whole brain with the rest of the body suffers dissolution—does the mind survive?' And he offered the reply:

> I once had the occasion to present a portrait to a dear colleague on behalf of a Society of Surgeons. On their behalf it was suggested that the portrait presentation represented the highest compliment the Society could pay—its expressed opinion that the recipient was worthy of immortality. We noted several categories of Immortality—Celestial and Terrestrial, and of Terrestrial—Biological and Personal, Social. We brain surgeons—knowing nothing of Celestial Immortality—chose to associate our gift with the terrestrial division. Our colleague was well provided biologically with promising progeny to two generations. We knew his stock in terrestrial, social and personal immortality stood high—his important contributions to the structure of medical science and his lasting influence for good. We associated our portrait gift with that.

Well-worded agnosticism. On such imponderables he simply refused to be foolishly drawn.

In politics too there is an easy pitfall.

He was one of a small party of Scottish doctors who visited Russia in 1937 and subsequently reported their impressions to the Medico Chirurgical Society of Edinburgh. Dott described his visit to St Isaacs Cathedral then used as a sort of 'anti-religious' museum and expressed his belief that 'it has been relatively easy for the Russian to renounce his former creed, the more especially as Communism and Lenin worship supply an idealism and hero worship which the human soul requires.'

This is a considered observation. At no time is there any suggestion of Dott's leaning towards Communism or extreme left-wing politics. Two of the myths which accompany the evermore tenuous tail of the comet are that Dott refused or was refused a knighthood because of his political convictions. As already stated, he was never even offered the knighthood, though many felt during his lifetime and afterwards that he deserved that honour. As to why he never received it, speculation is futile. All we know is that he tended to decry politics and politicians, believing that his duties lay in the brotherhood and influence for peace of world medicine. Kindness is not Christianity and love of one's fellow men does not fall under the flag of any political Party. Dott's compassion was often mistaken for piety and his altruism for socialism.

What his upbringing ensured above all was his Scottishness. He enjoyed describing himself as an old Edinburgher who had spent sixty-three of his sixty-four years in or about the city, and in the nine years that followed that remark nothing changed his willingness to stay on Scottish soil, firmly rooted in the capital city.

Like many famous Scots he was practical to the fingertips. 'I am a craftsman rather than scientist or philosopher,' he told the Edinburgh Philosophy of Science Group. The ingrained practicality of the man was with him from childhood, as we know, and as he illustrated himself when addressing a Burns Club, with an autobiographical story:

Aged about ten, I had been fishing a burn all day up behind Ben Ledi. Fatigued, I tramped homeward in the gloaming, half asleep on my feet. Thus I was passing through a long field below the farm, where the Cashaig burn joins the main water, and I came to a familiar dip where the path crossed a rivulet. From the hollow the north east sky was bright with the after glow; the two familiar little hazel trees were silhouetted against it. But there was something more! 'I there wi' something did foregather, that pat me in an eerie swither!' Two gigantic men—at least three Scots ells in height towered above me. Their adjacent arms were linked, their free arms set akimbo. They were breathing heavily, as if poised for devastating action. They swayed ominously from side to side, as if about to fall upon me. I was as one petrified and I could feel my hair bristling. Aghast, I strained my eyes at them—and their details are clearly imprinted on my mind now. They wore tricorne hats, frock coats; and I could discern the gold braided frogs and bands that embellished their hats and coats. They wore knee breeches and buckled shoes. As I stared, those giants broke off their threatening swaying, wheeled to the north and disappeared into the gathering gloom. Their heavy footsteps had a cantering rhythm and as they receded one of them uttered a neighing sound—very like a horse. I was shaken and now very wide awake and felt rather foolish. Nevertheless, I mended my pace and kept a very sharp eye on 'hillocks, stanes and busses' for the two miles I had still to go. I remember the relief of seeing the cottage lights; also that, once inside, my 10 year-old appetite and my sleep were not deranged; but I refrained for some months from mentioning my awful experience. In daylight, next day, I did carry out some field researches; and found that a couple of large Clydesdales with blazed faces were put out to graze in that field; and that they often stood together, swaying their heads in unison.

How typical of the ten year old Scots boy that he returned the following day to 'carry out some field researches' and so dispel any supernatural shred from his inquiring mind. The practical Scotsman grew out of that small boy in the ways that have been described. His coal merchant at Chalmers Crescent remembers that although central heating had been installed, the Professor's preference was for the old-fashioned coal fire. However, Dott had rigged up a special system from the central heating inside the house whereby the heat could be channelled out to the dogs' kennels in the back garden, allowing them the full benefits of convenience heating.

The former manager of an Edinburgh shop which stocked fishing tackle recalls how Dott came in and asked for a wading staff to be specially designed for him for a fishing holiday in Norway. The staff was in two pieces and was so designed that weights could be attached to it variously dependent on the flow of the strong Norwegian waters—the greater the strength of the current, the greater the weight attached. The whole object was to prevent wear and tear on his wrists and hands. The staff was both designed and made at the workshop, where Dott came down more than once to satisfy himself that it was going to meet his requirements. It did, and a letter of appreciation duly came. Dott's appreciation was often expressed, when appropriate, with a generous chunk of salmon.

'A surgeon,' he told one patient, 'is no more than a joiner.' Ignoring the ironic overtones of this ridiculously self-disparaging remark, it contained, in the case of Norman Dott, something of a truth. His hands could not be still. Perhaps the best example of this part of his personality is provided by the patient who writes that after he had removed the tumour from her brain—she was only a few years old at the time—he mended her yo-yo! She recalls little of the events before and after the operation; it is the picture of Dott sitting on her bed mending the yo-yo that remains. The craze for this now popular child's plaything was on in 1932. It is easy to picture Dott's hands, perhaps more fascinated by the new toy than they had been in performing what for him might have been a relatively routine operation.

This genuine humility—at times it was virtually anonymity—can be seen in his housekeeper Barbara's memory of him cracking away to the bin men outside his front door; can still be seen in a faded rectangle on the gate of No 3 Chalmers Crescent, where once a name-plate read simply 'Dott'.

If the man's the gowd, as his hero Robert Burns said, then he offers us much of value. A sense of humour, like Burns? Yes, with no false dignity and no mock modesty. He confessed to the ladies of the Clarinda Edinburgh Ladies Burns Club that he himself had experienced alcoholic diplopia at no less a place than 'Auld Ayr':

> Auld Ayr, wham ne'er a toon surpasses
> For honest men and bonnie lasses.

> As a very young consultant, I was urgently summoned to Ayr by Dr Geekie—the then medical patriarch of the region. To do the occasion justice, I fortunately hired a uniformed driver and his ancient Rolls Royce. The good doctor took me forthwith on our business. The patient's condition was alarming enough but fortunately one quite amenable to judicious control by me and to cure by Mother Nature. This we duly set in hand; and then repaired to his home for a sumptuous repast well accompanied from his carefully studied and furnished cellar. He was a good wise doctor and he dealt more lightly with my driver than with his greenhorn consultant and guest. As he guided me to my car, I was astonished at the duplication of the street lamps; and grateful for his arm to 'keep me sicker.' I had no other apparition on that occasion but was brought to with a blast of frosty air, as my driver opened the car door to consult me, having lost his way on the Lanarkshire moors in the 'wee sma' oors.'

He also had a strong sense of history and felt he owed much of what he was and what he had achieved to his ancestors and his parents. He was deeply grown in Scotland and in particular Edinburgh, though he had a great affection for rural and Highland Scotland. He was grateful for his education, both at home and at Heriot's. Politically others might label him left, but he let them get on with it and committed himself to medicine and its possibilities for the welfare of mankind, brotherhood and peace. Others in his work might see him as unrelentingly austere, but he was kind and friendly at heart, though often outwardly reserved. He was abstemious but liked his toddy by his bedside and good Scots kitchen. He enjoyed music and fishing, yet with a seriousness that his work and temperament would lead you to expect. Children and animals played close to his soul. A perfectionist who insisted on doing things his own way; a fast driver and inveterate tinkerer with anything mechanical; a humanitarian who remained agnostic; a restrained speaker and correspondent who burst out laughing at circus clowns. Fisherman, gardener, grandfather, spouse. God to his patients, God-*and*-the-Devil-in-one to his exhausted staff—he was at the same time the most ordinary and the most extraordinary of men. Crusty? Undoubtedly; some never penetrated the crust. Gentle and human? Yes, if in his opinion you merited the discovery.

Who or what is at work in the currents that drift beneath our slow formation? History, topography, tradition, genes, God? Some folk, like Faustus and Job, curse the parents who engendered them, shake their fists at the stars, blaming anything and everybody, even down to the books they read, the apple they ate. Others, like Norman Dott, can only suppose that their mission is to return thanks to whatever gods they think may be, with the hands that earn their daily bread. And, if there be no gods, simply to do as the good book commands.

'Whatsoever thy hand findeth to do,' say the scriptures, 'do it with all thy might.'

And Dott did.

Such was the private man who shadowed the famous brain surgeon whom the world recognised, applauded, honoured and mourned.

CHAPTER FOURTEEN

Golden Lads and Girls

Golden lads and girls all must
As chimney sweepers come to dust.
(Shakespeare)

And so the curtains closed at last on this tight little band of brothers and sisters who had played so happily together—as, one by one, and in their different ways, they took their leave of one another and of life itself.

All except Dr Eric Dott, who by 1929 had started up a small practice in Eltringham Gardens, off Robs's Loan, in the west of Edinburgh, and who, after a long and successful career in medicine, is still sixty years later a bright rememberer of ninety. Without his loving and enthusiastic recollections, made from his quiet home and walled garden in the charming seclusion of Canaan Lane, this story would have lost immeasurably. There he lives still, with two of his three sons, and is a delightful reminder of a vanished Edinburgh and era.

The first death was Jean's. It came tragically early.

Impetuously she gave up her art, in spite of her obvious talent, and after a brief spell of nursing went on to the Labour College in London, where she met and wed Percy Sephton on 18 May 1923. Together they committed their future to an amelioration of the world through Socialism. Three months after their marriage they left for Canada, meaning to spend a belated honeymoon holiday with sister Margaret and her husband on their ranch at Gabriola Island.

Things went badly wrong. They had not long been there when a duck shooting party was organised for the ranch. In the dim light Jean was accidentally shot and was rushed to the nearest hospital at Nanaimo, off Vancouver Island. There she died less than twenty-four hours later. It was 9.20 p.m. on 2 September. She was twenty-seven. Her father was on holiday at the time with Eric in Brig o' Turk when the first telegram arrived, fraught with tragic potential. Peter McOmish Dott was standing with his son in the window of the peaceful old family cottage when the second telegram came with its chilling intimation of mortality. Looking through the glass at the familiar scenes of his daughter's childhood, McOmish Dott said very quietly, as if to himself, 'Well, there's a *very* bright little life gone.'

Miss Catherine Fraser Lee penned a moving tribute which appeared in the St George's Chronicle in February of the following year. She is mistaken in implying that the Sephtons intended to remain in Canada but there is no mistaking what she thought of her former pupil.

IN MEMORIAM

JEAN DOTT

God has given us memories that we may have roses in December, and how beautiful are our memories of Jean!

It is true that her school life at St George's was all too short for many of us to get to know her well, and she was not one whom it was easy to know, but where she did give her love and friendship, what a rich gift it was!

The first picture I see is a tiny, bare-legged childie standing in that beautiful Colinton garden with the Pentland Hills in the background. Around her the birds are clustered, some settling on her head and arms, and feeding out of her hand. Or again I see her with her head resting on dear Mailla, her beloved donkey, while Jackie, the tame crow, perches on her shoulder, and the pussy rubs himself against her legs.

What a wealth of love she gave to animals!

Again I see her looking out at you from beneath her sou'wester (almost the only head covering she ever wore), that picture which she painted of herself, and which we hoped was to be but the first of many wonderful pictures from her brush.

But no, not that way did she feel she could best serve mankind, and to our sorrow she gave up all her art work to train as a hospital nurse. Her childhood's sympathy grew in depth and was given without stint to those in pain and need.

Yet even here she felt she could not give all she longed to give; so forth she goes to get a wider training to equip herself better to help the downcast and the sad.

Her training in London was full of interest and the enthusiasm with which she threw herself into it was delightful to see. She entered the Labour College to prepare herself for the work nearest to her heart—the uplifting of the lives of the wage-earning masses of the people. It was while in London that she met her husband, and the last picture I have of her is with him, once again in that beautiful garden, when I said goodbye to them both before they set out for Canada.

How full of promise the future seemed to be! I had never seen her so perfectly happy before, for Jean had always, even in her most self-sacrificing service, been full of questionings and doubt. As I said goodbye I felt that here at last, in love and service in a new country, far from cities with their sadness, among the creatures she had always loved, she would find the answer to her eager questionings.

But God ordered otherwise, and while still her bright happy letters were coming home, the cable was received, and we knew that she had 'out-soared the shadow of our night' and entered that great city, where we no longer see through a glass darkly, and where sorrow and sighing flee away

December 1923   C FRASER LEE

Norman Dott was stricken for the second time. His mother had died six years previously: his sister Jean was his great favourite.

'She was the best of the five,' he said, in his grieving admiration, 'the very best of all of us!'

A lively spark of a girl.

Three days later she was buried in Nanaimo cemetery.

Margaret joined her in the same cemetery twenty-six years later, almost to the day, in 1949. She had gone to Canada in the first place out of a period of psychological difficulty arising partly from her position as the youngest member of a mercurial clutch of children. Gradually she grew somewhat apart from the others, reticent and shy, eventually announcing that she would like to go abroad.

At first she passed a rather unhappy period with a family known to the Dotts—the Laws, who owned a ranch on Gabriola Island. They treated her unsympathetically, more like a servant than the daughter of family friends, and her misery increased. Then Mrs Law's brother, Arthur Millward, came to stay to help out on the ranch, which was not doing well. He was drawn to Margaret at once, assessed the reasons for her wretchedness, and they grew close. Shortly afterwards the Laws decided to sell the ranch and he decided to take it over and marry Margaret at the same time. McOmish Dott bought the ranch in his daughter's name and set them up there. Millward worked the ranch well: a good life opened up for Margaret at last. She was married on 25 August 1922.

Again unhappily, her life was also shortened.

In 1934 Norman was lecturing in the USA and went to Canada to see his sister. It was on that visit that he detected a heart murmur indicative of a valvular defect. When Margaret became pregnant three years later she was advised to have an abortion to avoid the risk to the heart that would be involved in having the child. This she utterly refused to do and her daughter Barbara was born without mishap in August 1938. Eleven years later Margaret took influenza which did play havoc with her strained heart—and Barbara was left motherless.

Kathleen, after her early disappointment in having to abandon her academic and career prospects, was married exactly one year after the tragic shooting of her sister. On 1 September 1924 she became the wife of Walter Schlapp, son of Otto Schlapp whose family had been made so welcome at Hailes Brae and the Trossachs. So Kathleen too became a mother, then a grandmother; after a long and happy life knew widowhood and grey hairs,

80 His sister Jean in the drawing room of Hailes Brae.

81 A highly talented artist, Jean abandoned her artwork and looked first to nursing then to Socialism as a means of serving humanity. Full of vitality and sparkle, she was the victim of a tragic shooting accident at the age of twenty-seven.

and eventually died in a nursing home in the south. She had failed greatly, becoming wandering and forgetful and confused in her thoughts.

She had outlived Norman by a decade.

In 1970 Norman Dott developed cancer of the lower bowel and he chose as his surgeon Mr Tom McNair, later to be President of the Royal College of Surgeons of Edinburgh, to see to his resection. This left him with a colostomy, which in turn led to his setting up of the stoma clinic at the Astley Ainslie hospital.

By then he had given up smoking his cigarettes—a severe pain in the chest after a fit of coughing in Norway had convinced him to take to the pipe, which his musing hands were forever cleaning. Increasingly Mrs Dott would wake up in the middle of the nights and find him sitting in reverie, smoking quietly all to himself, that familiar plume of tobacco smoke etched uncertainly on the air as the hours dwindled down towards another morning.

He had been retired for just eleven years when he recognised the onset of the symptoms of an aortic aneurysm expanding and on the point of rupture. Again he put himself into the care of his chosen surgeon, Tom McNair, and in assessing his own condition he chose the path of terminal care rather than heroic surgery, confessing that he now felt 'tired enough'. Such was his laconic comment on his case and on his own wishes in respect of it.

What could be more fitting than that one of his nurses from Ward 20, one who had returned to the service after marriage, should be sent down to the surgical ward in the Royal Infirmary, to help with his nursing care? Nurse Margaret Simpson pays Professor Norman McOmish Dott the following moving tribute:

> My memories of that room and of the Professor lying there are still clear. Quiet and undemanding, accepting the routine monitoring without question, he reminisced in a faint voice when I mentioned that I worked in his theatre thirty years before. I recall his dignity and calm above the pain. I had always thought what an honour it was to have worked alongside such a brilliant neurosurgeon all those years ago, but I felt it a privilege to have nursed the great man so near his end.

After reminiscing in that faint voice, he said no more.

If he saw pictures in his mind that language could no longer unlock, they would have been bright splinters of a happy past: of love and companionship and fulfilment; of honours and early struggles and such toil; a life well spent. A silver casket and a scroll, perhaps? Hosts of grateful well-wishers thundering their applause; the long, lit vistas of nurses and ward rounds and white-coated doctors; faces lined with suffering and flooded with relief; a white-haired old ghillie in a boat on the hushed loch; the looming sides of a horse in Lothian Road and a taxi bearing down. And so on, ever backwards, past a genial bearded bear in tweeds, a gentle smiling lady with a squirrel's finesse, sitting at a piano reading poetry and singing old songs . . .

And a garden full of children's laughter, a dell dancing with water and the dappled sunlight. And two small boys standing hand in hand by the Water of Leith, green leaves a-floating, castles of the foam. The world lay all before them, where to choose their place of rest . . .

It was on 10 December 1973 that rest finally came.

A Monument without a Tomb

If there's another world, he lives in bliss:
If there is none, he made the best of this.
(*Burns*)

He had set up his accustomed stance as, in spite of the early hour, the hurrying figures on the Middle Meadow Walk steadily increased in number. A kenspeckled presence, the newsvendor, commanding the busy crown of this pedestrian artery so well conceived by the City Fathers. As he faces the hum and hubbub of Lauriston Place, the grey bulk of the Royal Infirmary lies on one shoulder and on the other the buildings of the medical school. So, although folk are passing in all airts, they are for the most part the stuff of youth, and seem to be making for these two edifices. Particularly at this corner the bitter December winds of Edinburgh nip the sunless faces and impart a tracing of blue even to the well-weathered logbook of the newsman's stoic features.

A steady scattering of darker complexions tells of students drawn from warmer climates by the reputation of Edinburgh medicine and surgery. Clearly this corner of Auld Reekie is a familiar image, carried in many another head that lies beyond the Forth. The students and scholars speak with many accents and tongues, and, over the years, not a few of them have come to hear the homely Scottish voice of Professor Norman McOmish Dott speak of brain and spinal surgery. They hurry on with intent eyes, each wrapped in his own concerns; some anxious about imminent exams; others freer from that worry for the moment, more relaxed. Few have time to spare for the wares of world affairs offered to them from the newstand: wars and rumours of wars, no doubt, and nation rising against nation: a bombing in Belfast, a coup in a little kingdom. The occasional purchaser gets a glad grunt from the custodian of the press. He has never quite supplied the classic picture of his Cockney counterpart—the frenzied shouting, the waving poster, the outstretched paper: Russia mobilises, Yanks reach the moon, Cuban crisis explodes. In the douce heartland of Edinburgh gravitas and

dignitas prevail. But today he has ignored the headlines and crayoned large on his billboard the three stark words: Dott is dead.

Dott is dead

Among the first to read this announcement, as he makes his tired way from the Royal Infirmary to the Royal College of Surgeons, is Mr Tom McNair. Of course he knows that Dott is dead. Had he not been chosen by Dott as his surgeon three years ago and operated upon him successfully? Are not his discussions with Dott still vividly imprinted on his mind? Those discussions so very recently completed in entire agreement and concerned with the appropriate management of this new and fatal condition. For Dott had developed that complication of ageing vessels, an aneurysm on the main aortic artery. This pioneer, who had so courageously carried out life-giving operations on others' aneurysms, also knew full well when, wearying of effort, the time had come to cease from the struggle and pass with peace and dignity into the limbo he professed he knew nothing of: the undiscovered country, from whose bourn no traveller returns.

Mr McNair turned to the newsman and asked him why he had substituted his own headlines, ignoring the splash of intelligence of the front page. 'That,' he replied, pointing to the three words on his billboard, 'is more important to Edinburgh folk than what's in the paper today.' A brief but heartfelt nod of agreement was all the surgeon allowed himself before he and the newsman turned, each to resume his daily round.

In nearby Ward 20 the news gradually spreads. The nurses, early on duty or coming off night duty, hear it first. Doctor speaks to doctor. *Dott is dead. Professor Dott died last night.* There are new faces who barely knew him. Others of longer standing pause to reflect on the familiar figure who has passed; the martinet, the watchful Hydra of neurosurgical standards. Routine telephone calls between the Head and Spinal Injuries Unit at Ward 20 and the Department of Surgical Neurology at the Western General Hospital carry the simple message, as do doctors finishing a spell of duty at the emergency unit and driving to that other wing of Dott's Kingdom. There is only one fitting response: patient care continues uninterrupted but with renewed allegiance to Dott's legendary high standards.

More slowly the news of Dott's death comes to neurosurgical outposts around the globe; to Dott's far-flung trainees. Condolences and tributes pour in; newsprint and medical journals carry obituaries and praise. A moving example is published in South Africa from the pen of Professor Lipschitz—'Lippy' of the 'fairly normal' reprimand those many years ago.

And so Edinburgh paid its last respects at St Giles' Cathedral on 21 December 1973, the winter solstice.

Many came.

Including three grandchildren who had come to say goodbye to Granda.

Yes, Granda who used to sit on a rock by the burn and tell them where to put the stones that fashioned the dams to create their own rivers and harbours, like Robert Louis Stevenson, and like another little boy who had played in the Water of Leith not so long ago. Granda who took them for all those summer walks around Dunsappie Loch, with ice-creams for each, and one for the dog. Barbara the housekeeper was just too grown up. It was to be a very sad and private parting and the girls had promised to choke back the tears which Granda would have frowned upon. But what were all those crowds there for, in that most private of moments, and such imposing looking people, garbed in black—and did that one have a great gold chain around his neck? And there were cameras—cameras were for holidays and weddings, but some of them were crouched like Martians on queer long spider legs. It was all too difficult. Surely no-one would notice, Susan thought, and Granda wouldn't mind, if she wiped her eye on mummy's gloved hand, already comfortingly in hers?

Although eight year old Susan could not, many in that congregation were able to recall the last gathering in triumph at the Usher Hall, which seemed such a short while ago; many were patients, come to utter a last prayer of respect and gratitude.

Thus Auld Reekie praised her son, who had completed his journey from the rural village of Victorian Colinton to the ageless grandeur of the High Kirk, and had scaled such heights on the way: from Sandy Thomson's workshop to the lovingly labelled 'Dott's Workshop', Ward 20 and beyond. Forsaking Dott's Burns, the President of the Royal College of Surgeons raided Shakespeare like a Border reiver of old, ending his valedictory address with the ringing words that Nature might stand up and say to all the world, *This was a man.*

History would want us to conclude: And so they laid him to rest. But this was not Dott's way. Growing weary of teaching of the functions of the brain and its vagaries, he had determined to continue to teach of its structure, even after death: he had bequeathed his body to medical science.

Was that the end?

Not quite.

When preparations for this biography were being advertised, many letters landed on our desk. Fittingly, let one of Dott's former patients have the final word.

Ben Jonson once said of Shakespeare that he was a monument without a tomb. Lacking Jonson's eloquence but expressing greater sincerity, an Edinburgh woman provided Dott—who has no gravestone, no burial place—with his greatest monument: her tears.

She wrote:

When I read in the newspapers of his death, I sat down and wept.

Notes

CHAPTER ONE pp 3 to 9

1   William McTaggart the artist was the father of the co-founder of the Engineering Company. Following an exhibition of his work at Aitken Dott & Son's *c*.1903, McTaggart lent the company the sum of £5,000, which rescued it from financial difficulties. The sum was repaid two years later but the engineering firm was naturally grateful and took on the sons of artistic personalities including Wingate and Colin Mitchell, son of the Principal of Edinburgh College of Art. It was thus no coincidence that the young Norman Dott was apprenticed there.

2   'The Convergence of the Twain', first published in Hardy's *Satires of Circumstance* in 1914, reflects its author's pessimistic view that life's coincidences and ironies do *not* work together towards one good end.

CHAPTER TWO pp 10 to 23

1   From Papers Delivered at Congress of Neurological Surgeons, Toronto, September 1968. Published in *Clinical Neurosurgery*, Vol 16, 1969.

2   The original letter is in the National Library of Scotland.

CHAPTER THREE pp 24 to 37

1   Dr Eric Dott in interview with the authors.

2   Address to Edinburgh Merchant Company Teachers Association, 5 March 1965.

3   Bacon's *Essays* were published in various editions between 1597 and 1625.

4   Tennyson's *In Memoriam* was published anonymously by Moxon in 1851.

5   Letter to Kathleen Dott dated 28 May 1917, National Library of Scotland.

6   From Peter McOmish Dott's Notebook, National Library of Scotland.

7   *Ibid.*

8   *Ibid.*

9   *Ibid.*

10 *Ibid.*

CHAPTER FOUR pp 38 to 57

1   Robert Louis Stevenson's Essay 'The Manse', published in *Memories and Portraits*, 1887.

2   Dr Eric Dott in interview with the authors.

3   *Ibid.*
4   Address to Colinton Burns Club, 21 January 1966.
5   Letter to Sandy Thomson's daughter in 1962.
6   Miss Cathy Morrison in interview with the authors.
7   Address to the Annual Dinner of the Edinburgh University Club of Bristol, 22 January 1962.
8   From Robert Louis Stevenson's *A Child's Garden of Verses*, 1885.
9   Robert Louis Stevenson's 'The Manse', 1887.
10   *A Child's Garden of Verses*, 1885.
11   John Milton's *Paradise Lost*, published in 1667.
12   Robert Louis Stevenson's 'The Manse', 1887.
13   Letter from the Dott family papers, 23 April 1911.
14   Allan Ramsay, 'Imitations of Horace', 1721. Published in the *Tea-Table Miscellany* 1724.
15   No. XXXVI from Robert Louis Stevenson's *Songs of Travel*, 1896. The poem is worth quoting in its entirety:

> The tropics vanish, and meseems that I,
> From Halkerside, from topmost Allermuir,
> Or steep Caerketton, dreaming gaze again.
> Far set in fields and woods, the town I see
> Spring gallant from the shallows of her smoke,
> Cragged, spired, and turreted, her virgin fort
> Beflagged. About, on seaward-drooping hills,
> New folds of city glitter. Last, the Forth
> Wheels ample waters set with sacred isles,
> And populous Fife smokes with a score of towns.
>
> There, on the sunny frontage of a hill,
> Hard by the house of kings, repose the dead,
> My dead, the ready and the strong of word.
> Their works, the salt-encrusted, still survive;
> The sea bombards their founded towers; the night
> Thrills pierced with their strong lamps. The artificers,
> One after one, here in this grated cell,
> Where the rain erases, and the rust consumes,
> Fell upon lasting silence. Continents
> And continental oceans intervene;
> A sea uncharted, on a lampless isle,
> Environs and confines their wandering child
> In vain. The voice of generations dead
> Summons me, sitting distant, to arise,
> My numerous footsteps nimbly to retrace,
> And, all mutation over, stretch me down
> In that denoted city of the dead.

In fact the wish expressed in the poem was not fulfilled. Stevenson died in Samoa and was buried there three years before Norman Dott was born.

16 Robert Louis Stevenson, 'To My Wife', Dedication to *Weir of Hermiston* 1896, the unfinished masterpiece published after his death.

17 Robert Louis Stevenson, 'To S R Crockett from Vailima', from *Songs of Travel*, 1896.

18 Robert Louis Stevenson's essay 'To the Pentland Hills', from *Edinburgh: Picturesque Notes*, 1879.

CHAPTER FIVE pp 58 to 78

1 Address to Colinton Burns Club 21 January 1966.
2 Dr Eric Dott, in interview with the authors.
3 *Ibid.*
4 T J Honeyman, *Three Scottish Colourists*, published by Nelson & Sons Ltd, 1950.
5 Dott's 'Notes' on William McTaggart were published by Constable in 1901.
6 *Ibid.*
7 *Ibid.*
8 *Ibid.*
9 Dr Eric Dott, in interview with the authors.
10 Letter to Eric dated 6 May 1918, National Library of Scotland.
11 *Ibid.*
12 Letter to Eric dated 10 February 1918.
13 Letter to Eric dated 25 February 1918.
14 Letter dated as given in text.
15 Dr Eric Dott, in interview with the authors.
16 *Ibid.*
17 *The Herioter*, Vol 1, as indicated in the text.
18 *Ibid.*

CHAPTER SIX pp 79 to 95

1 Dr Eric Dott, in interview with the authors.
2 Letter to Joe Schorstein (Glasgow neurosurgeon), 21 September 1953.
3 Katie McFarlane, in interview with the authors
4 *Ibid.*
5 *St George's Chronicle*, as indicated in the text.
6 *The Herioter*, as indicated in the text.
7 *Ibid.*
8 *The Herioter*, 1917.
9 *The Herioter Roll of Honour.*

CHAPTER SEVEN pp 99 to 122

1 Patient's letter to the authors.
2 Mr George Smith, in interview with the authors.
3 Dr Alistair McLaren, from an article written for *The Watsonian*, 1987-8.
4 Mr George Smith.
5 Letter to Kathleen dated 25 May 1917. National Library.
6 Letter to Eric dated 18 August 1917, National Library.

7   Copied into one of Peter McOmish Dott's notebooks. The original is in the
    National Library of Scotland.
8   Letter to Eric dated 18 August 1917.
9   Letter to Eric dated 15 February 1918.
10 Letter to Eric dated 1 April 1918.
11 Dott Personal Papers: Address to Royal Medical Society of Edinburgh as
    'Guest of the Evening', Presidents Annual Dinner 1962.
12 Dott Personal Papers: Letter dated 19 October 1965 in response to a request
    from Dr Hovell for information about the place of Edinburgh in the history
    of anaesthesia.
13 Post-script to 12.

CHAPTER EIGHT pp 123 to 137
1   Address to Edinburgh Branch, Institute of Medical Laboratory Technology,
    5 October 1962.
2   See Appendix 'Publications'
3   Dott Personal Papers.
4   'The History of Surgical Neurology in the Twentieth Century', *Proceedings
    of the Royal Society of Medicine* October, 1971, Vol 64, No. 10, pp 1051-5.
    (Section of the History of Medicine, pp 17-21.)
5   Dott Personal Papers.
        Addresses to:
            1   See 1 above.
            2   Presidential Dinner Royal Medical Society Edinburgh 1962.
            3   Borders Clinical Club Scotland 1964.
            4   40th Anniversary Foundation Dinner, Society of British Neuro-
                logical Surgeons, 1966.
6   Dr Eric Dott's Conversations with the authors.
7   See Appendix 'Publications'.
8   Peter Bent Brigham Hospital.
9   'Dr Harvey Cushing MD Memoir for the Centenary Year of his Birth'.
    Scottish Medical Journal, 1969. Vol 14, pp 381-6.
10 See 4 above.
11 See 9 above.
12 Dott Personal Papers, correspondence between Cushing and Dott.
13 See 9 and 11 above.
14 See 12 above.

CHAPTER NINE pp 138 to 175
1   'Centenary Royal Infirmary of Edinburgh—Neurological Surgery', Dott
    1970 and 'The Royal Infirmary of Edinburgh, 1929-1979', E F Catford 1984,
    Scottish Academic Press, Edinburgh.
2   See Appendix 'Publications'.
3   Dott Personal Papers. Letter to Mr A C H Watson.
4   Letter to authors.
5   Sir Thomas Browne, *Religio Medici,* published without this seventeenth
    century doctor's consent, in 1642.

6   Conversations with authors.
7   James A Ross, 'The Edinburgh School of Surgery after Lister', 1978. pp 59-67. Churchill Livingstone, Edinburgh.
8   Dott Personal Papers. 'Statement re Surgical Neurological Work in Edinburgh', Dott 1930.
9   Dr Eric Dott. Conversations with the authors.
10 See 7 above.
11 *Ibid.*
12 Dott Personal Papers. Letter to Professor Wilkie, 3 June 1931.
13 Letters to authors.
14 Dott Personal Papers. Letter to Professor Wilkie, 26 September 1929.
15 Dott Personal Papers. Letter to Professor George Robertson, December 1930.
16 Dott Personal Papers. Correspondence with Dr E A Carmichael.
17 'The Royal Infirmary of Edinburgh 1929-1979', See 1 above.
18 Letter to authors.
19 Letter to authors.

CHAPTER TEN pp 176 to 216

1   Professor Edwin Bramwell, Transactions of Medico Chirurgical Society of Edinburgh, 1932-3, Vol 47, p 238.
2   See Appendix 'Publications'.
3   Botterell is actually in error. The date of the operation was 22 April 1931.
4   Dott Personal Papers. Letter to Mr Joe Pennybacker.
5   Dott Personal Papers.
6   See Appendix 'Publications'.
7   Letter from Mr George Newell to Authors.
8   Dott Personal Papers.
9   *Ibid.*
10 Dott Personal Papers. Undergraduate Lecture 1930, 'Preparation for Operation'.
11 *Ibid.*
12 B Bramwell, 'Spontaneous Meningeal Haemorrhage', *Edinburgh Medical Journal,* 1886. Vol 22, p 101.
13 C P Symonds and H Cushing, Guy's Hospital Reports, 1923, Vol 73, p 139. C P Symonds, 'Spontaneous Subarachnoid Haemorrhage', *Quarterly Journal of Medicine,* 1924. Vol 18, p 93.
14 Dott Personal Papers. 'Specialism and Generalism in the Utopic Medical School', Address to the Women's Medical Society, Edinburgh, 16 February 1932.
15 Transactions of the Medico Chirurgical Society of Edinburgh, 1932-3. Vol 47, pp 223-4.
16 Dr Eric Dott, Conversations with the authors.
17 See 15 above, p 224.
18 See 1 above.
19 Dott Personal Papers. Address 'Medical Travels' to Borders Clinical Club, 5 January 1964, and to Netherlands Society of Neurological Surgeons, Zwolle, 2 May 1964.

CHAPTER ELEVEN pp 217 to 234

1   Dott Personal Papers. 'Statement re Surgical Neurological Work in Edinburgh', by Norman M Dott, 1930.
2   Professor A E Ritchie CBE, Letter to authors.
3   Dr David Bowsher, Letter to authors.
4   Letter to authors.
5   Letter to authors.
6   Clinical Neurosurgery, 1969, Vol 16, Williams & Wilkins Co, Baltimore.
7   'Dr Harvey Cushing, MD Memoir for the Centenary Year of his Birth', *Scottish Medical Journal*, 1969, Vol 14, pp 381-6.
8   Letter to authors.
9   Letter to authors.
10 Letter to authors.
11 Letter to authors.
12 Professor R Lipschitz, letter to authors.
13 Author.
14 Author.

CHAPTER TWELVE pp 235 to 244

1   Charles McKean, 'Edinburgh, An Illustrated Architectural Guide', 1983. The Royal Incorporation of Architects in Scotland and The Scottish Academic Press.

CHAPTER THIRTEEN pp 245 to 279

1   In 1963 Professor Dott flew to Salonika to advise on the care of Gregoris Lambrakis, an Opposition Deputy in the Greek Chamber of Deputies, who was also a surgical gynaecologist and university lecturer. He had sustained a severe head injury during the dispersal of a political rally. Professor Dott was asked to act as spokesman for the group of specialists who had been assembled. He describes how, 'Professor Slykov (from Moscow) and I were seized by the crowd and carried shoulder high to the hospital entrance to shouts of, "God give him life!" Unfortunately it was not possible to save the patient.'
    In the previous decade, Professor Dott had flown to Cyprus to consult about a youth paralysed by a back injury during that island's troubles. He brought him back to Bangour Hospital for prolonged treatment and rehabilitation. He was a familiar figure, well remembered by many of the staff of that time.
2   Response at celebratory luncheon, City Chambers.
3   Mr Peter Walton, letter to authors.
4   Dr David Tulloch, letter to authors.
5   Mr Thomas Stewart, letter to authors.
6   Professor Lipschitz, letter to authors.
7   Professor E Ritchie, letter to authors.

Appendix

Curriculum Vitae and List of Publications as prepared by Professor Norman Dott, the last entries being in 1972, shortly before his death in 1973

SECTION I CURRICULUM VITAE

DOTT, Norman McOmish
Date of birth: 26 August, 1897

DEGREES AND OTHER QUALIFICATIONS

MB ChB Edinburgh University 1919
Fellow of the Royal College of Surgeons. Royal College of Surgeons, Edinburgh, 1923
Honorary MD University of Edinburgh, 1969

ACADEMIC DISTINCTIONS

Syme Surgical Fellowship, 1921
Rockefeller Surgical Fellowship, 1923
Liston Memorial Jubilee Prize for Advances in Neurological Surgery, 1932
Sir Victor Horsley Memorial Award and Lectureship, 1960
President Society of British Neurological Surgeons, 1938-47
(Portrait presented by the Society, 1960)

PREVIOUS POSTS HELD

Resident House Surgeon, Royal Infirmary Edinburgh, 1919-20
Clinical Tutor, Royal Infirmary Edinburgh, 1921-3
Lecturer (part time) Department of Physiology, Edinburgh University, 1921-3.
Assistant Surgeon, Chalmer's Hospital, Edinburgh, 1923
Assistant Surgeon, Deaconess Hospital, Edinburgh 1923
Junior Associate in Surgery, Peter Bent Brigham Hospital, Boston, USA (with late Dr Harvey Cushing) 1923-4
Honorary Surgeon, Royal Hospital for Sick Children, Edinburgh, 1925
Neurological Surgery Conducted in Private Nursing Homes, Edinburgh, 1924-31
Surgeon in Ordinary, Deaconess Hospital, Edinburgh, 1929

Consulting Neurological Surgeon, Jordanburn Nerve Hospital, Edinburgh, 1929
Associate Neurological Surgeon, Royal Infirmary, Edinburgh, 1931
Director, Brain Injuries Unit, Bangour Emergency Medical Service Hospital, 1940

Early activities in general Surgery were combined with a part-time lectureship and experimental work in Physiology. From this, and in recognition of distinguished achievement in it, came the training period with Harvey Cushing in Boston and the start of a career in Surgical Neurology. From 1924 to 1932 it was possible to practise paediatric surgery while developing surgical neurology. From 1932 all energies were required for developing surgical neurology. In 1937 Sir Alexander Grant generously provided for a new Department of Surgical Neurology in the Royal Infirmary, and the Rockefeller Foundation assisted in its equipment.

PRESENT APPOINTMENTS WITH DATES OF APPOINTMENT

Neurological Surgeon, Royal Infirmary, Edinburgh, 1937
Consulting Neurological Surgeon, Royal Hospital for Sick Children, Edinburgh, 1935
Consulting Neurological Surgeon, Deaconess Hospital, Edinburgh, 1931
Honorary Consultant in Neurosurgery to the Army in Scotland, 1941
Surgeon in Charge, Department of Surgical Neurology, Western General Hospital, Edinburgh, 1960. Vice President, Royal College of Surgeons of Edinburgh, 1957
Chairman of Surgical Staff Committe, and of Medical and Dental Staff Committee, Royal Infirmary, Edinburgh, 1960
Medical Officer, Regional Stoma Clinic, Astley Ainslie Hospital, Edinburgh, 1972

Early in the 1939–45 War, the Rockefeller Foundation of America was interested in Britain's welfare and sustaining her medical progress. They made, through Edinburgh University, to Professor Dott an appropriation of some $27,000 over six years for those purposes in respect of Surgical Neurology. This made it possiblel to develop a proper Department of Surgical Neurology, with a properly balanced staff of wide scope. This was integrated with the Emergency Medical Service and later with the National Health Service (1948) and it did much to raise the standards of hospital service provision in staff and in equipment in those important early days of the service.

TEACHING EXPERIENCE

Lecturer in Paediatric Surgery, Edinburgh University, 1925
Lecturer in Neurological Surgery, Edinburgh University, 1932
Professor of Neurological Surgery, Edinburgh University, 1947
Stoma Care, 1972

RESEARCH

Under conditions of 1914–18 War developed anaesthesia in Edinburgh, was first to employ and popularise in Edinburgh the now universally employed endotracheal intubation-devised instruments and apparatus in this connection, 1914–18.

With Sir Edward Sharpey-Schafer, and as a young general surgeon in 1922–3, conducted first researches into histamine induced gastric secretion, using special experimental gastric pouches. The methods then used have been revived for modern research (A P Forrest in Glasgow, 1959.) Experimental ablations of pituitary and thyroid glands were studied, and again the methods then used have been revived for modern research (Harris Guy's Maudsley Medical School, London.) It was for this work that the Medical Research Council awarded a Rockefeller Travelling Fellowship which carried the recipient to Harvey Cushing in Boston, USA. Thus it was through research work that Surgical Neurology was developed as a career, 1922-3.

During the years 1925-35 Paediatric Surgery was practised as well as Surgical Neurology, and requests are still received for reprints of publications of researches into 'Anomalies of Intestinal Rotation' etc. Contributions were made to modern surgery of Congenital Dislocation of Hip, Cleft Palate, Intussusception, Congenital Misplacements of Intestines, etc in the form of new instruments or improved methods.

From 1924 a series of some forty major publications on aspects of Surgical Neurology appear. Most of these represent new and original work on a developing subject, for example demonstration by angiography of an intracranial aneurysm and successful operations for these lesions were first carried out in Edinburgh. It is now an important and world wide activity. In later years, the enhanced possibility of operating under artificial cooling of the brain was studied in 1954, and as recently as December 1960 Professor Dott led a team of six to Oslo to study and bring to Edinburgh latest advances in this field.

Much of this research or experimental work may be summarised as follows:

    1918-20 Endotracheal Anaesthesia
    1920-2 Laboratory on gastric secretion
    1919-22 Laboratory research on Hypophysectomy and Pituitary Stalk section
    1920-1 Anomalies of intestinal rotation
    1925-35 Cleft Palate
    1927-56 Cerebrospinal Fluid Circulation and Pathologies
    1929-60 Cerebral Surgical Diathermy
    1929-62 Cerebral Angiography and Aneurysmal Surgery
    1940-60 Brain Displacement and related Cerebral Ischaemia
    1940-50 Spinal Decompression
    1954-62 Hypothermic Cerebral Surgery

The Department of Surgical Neurology has by far the largest teaching activity of any such department in Britain. It amounts to some forty-seven and a half hours a week. It has developed under-graduate teaching, postgraduate tuition, teaching of the nursing and other supplementary professions, and teaching of specialist trainees by apprenticeship. These latter come from all over the world and only a selection of applicants can be accommodated. The new building at the Western General Hospital is furnished with modern staff conference and student seminar rooms; and furnish an example in teaching hospital design. It is not without significance that four Professors of Surgery and the premier Professor of Psychology in Britain are trainees of the Department.

Has served his profession, his school, and his country with some distinction. Has pioneered Surgical Neurology in Edinburgh and contributed largely to its advancement. Has developed a department of Surgical Neurology, one of the largest and best in the world with a high international prestige. Has done much to reintegrate Surgical Neurology with General Surgery and Medicine. Has developed the largest teaching department of Surgical Neurology in Britain. Has designed and caused to be created and equipped the most advanced Hospital Department for Surgical Neurology in the World (for the present!), and in doing so has advanced hospital standards in Britain. Is at present advancing new experimental and clinical work of major importance.

As Vice President of the Royal College of Surgeons of Edinburgh he chaired the committee charged to prepare evidence for the Royal Commission on Professional Remuneration and was largely responsible for the evidence submitted. Similarly he chaired the College Committee to prepare evidence for the Joint Working Party on Hospital staffing, whose report is now imminent.

WAR SERVICE

Volunteered in 1916 but not accepted owing to hip injury, completed medical studies and took part in holding the 'home front' in civilian medicine during latter part of 1914–18 War.

During the 1939–45 War, as consultant to Army in Scotland, organised 'Brain Injuries Unit' at Bangour Hospital near Edinburgh and directed the treatment of Service Personnel (Navy, Army and Air Force) in Scotland and at this base hospital for neurological cases. It was mainly for this war medical work, which brought to the Forces the highest standards of civilian management, including rehabilitation in surgical neurology, that Professor Dott was awarded the CBE in 1948.

OTHER INFORMATION, AWARDS, HONOURS, MEMBERSHIP OF SOCIETIES, COUNCILS, COMMITTEES

Awarded CBE 1948.
Fellow of the Royal Society of Edinburgh, 1936
Member (Foundation) of the Society of British Neurological Surgeons
Member of British Medical Association
Fellow of the Royal Society of Medicine
Honorary Fellow, College of Physicians, Surgeons and Gynaecologists of South
    Africa
Honorary Fellow of the Royal Medical Society of Edinburgh
Honorary Member of the Society of American Neurological Surgeons
Corresponding Member of the Harvey Cushing Society
Fellow of the Association of Surgeons of Great Britain and Ireland
Member of the Medico Chirurgical Society of Edinburgh
Senior Member of the Scottish Society of Experimental Medicine
Member of the Pathological Club of Edinburgh
Member of the Scottish Ophthalmological Club
Honorary Fellow of the Faculty of Radiologists
Member of the Societe Clovis Vincent, France

Corresponding Member of the Societe de Neurologie de Paris
Honorary Member of the Scandinavian Neurosurgical Society 1946
Honorary Member of the Societe de Neuro-chirurgische Studiekring, 1947
Honorary Member of the Societe de Neuro-chirurgie de Langue Francais
Honorary Member of the Sociedad Luso-Espanola de Neuro-Chirurgia
Honorary Member of the Societa Italiana de Neuro-Chirurgia, 1951
Honorary Member of the Sociedad Neurologica de Buenos Aires, 1953
Honorary Member of the Academia Peruana de Cirugia 1953
Honorary Member of the Sociedad de Neuropsiquiatria y Medicina Legal de Lima, 1953
Honorary Member of the Sociedad de Neurologica y Neurocirugia, Montevideo
Honorary Member of the Sociedad de Neurocirurgia de Chile, 1961
Honorary Member of the Sociedad Chilena de Neurologia, Psiquiatria y Neurocirurgia, 1961
Guest of Honour, Faculty of Medicine, University of Buenos Aires, 1961
Honorary Member of the Glasgow University Medico Chirurgical Society, 1961
Honorary Member of the British Association of Paediatric Surgeons
Member of Honorary Advisory Council of Canadian Association of Occupational Therapy
Honorary Fellow of College of Speech Therapists, London
President, Scottish Association of Occupational Therapists
President, Society for Research into Hydrocephalus, 1961
Corresponding Member, Societe de Chirurgie de Lyon, France
Elected Vice-President, Royal College of Surgeons of Edinburgh, 1957
Chairman, Surgical Staff Committee, Royal Infirmary, Edinburgh, 1960
Chairman, Medical & Dental Staff Committee, Royal Infirmary, Edinburgh, 1961
Honorary Member, International Medical Society of Paraplegia, 1962
Elected Honorary Academic of Academia Mexicana de Cirugia, 1962
Freeman of the City of Edinburgh, 1962
Professor Emeritus, Edinburgh University, 1962
Honorary Member of the Harvey Cushing Society, 1963
Honorary Member of the Section of Sciences of the Polish Society for Arts & Sciences Abroad, 1963
Representative of the Royal College of Surgeons, Edinburgh, to the General Medical Council, 1966
Member of the General Medical Council, 1966
Representative of the University of Edinburgh on the Central Consultants' and Specialists' Committee (Scotland) 1956-62
Representative of the University of Edinburgh on the Central Consultants' and Specialists' Committee (United Kingdom) 1963-6
Member, British Medical Association Central Ethical Committee, 1968-9
Member, representing University of Edinburgh, George Heriot's School Board of Governors, 1955-62
President Heriot Club 1966-8
Member, representing General Medical Council, of the General Dental Council, 1969
Member of the Physiology Society

Member, The Research Defence Society
Member, The British Council for the Welfare of Spastics
School of Speech Therapy, Edinburgh
Scottish Surgical Paediatric Club
Anglers Cooperative Association
Electro-encephalographic Society
Scottish Electro-encephalographic Society
Scottish Society of the History of Medicine
Cockburn Association (Edinburgh Civic Trust)
Ancient Monument's Society
British Society of the History of Medicine
Association of Neurological Sciences
British Empire Campaign for Cancer Research (Edinburgh Committee Chairman)
Scottish Epilepsy Association
Epilepsy Society of Edinburgh
American Neurological Association
Scottish Spina Bifida Association
Society of Neurosurgeons of South Africa
Honorary President, World Federation of Neurosurgical Societies
Honorary President, Scottish Paraplegic Association
Honorary Fellow, American College of Surgeons, 1968
Hughlings Jackson Lecturer, Montreal, 1955
Victor Horsley Memorial Lecturer, British Medical Association, London, 1960
Guest of Honour, Faculties of Medicine, Universities of Rio de Janiero, Buenos Aires, Cordoba, Santiago de Chile, Lima and Quito, 1961
Egas Moniz Memorial Lecturer, University of Lisbon, 1967
Guest of Honour with Mrs Dott, Congress of Neurological Surgeons, Toronto 1968

SECTION II PUBLICATIONS

* Marks those publications, which, in the author's (i.e. Dott) opinion, are important.

'A New Gastro-Enterostomy Clamp', *Ann Surg,* 72, 771-4, 1920
'Cardiac Massage in Resuscitation', *Br Med J,* 1, p 192, 1921
'The Pituitary Body in it's Relation to the Skeleton, with notes on Experimental Surgery', Thesis, Edinburgh University, 1922. (Accepted for Syme Surgical Fellowship)
'The Use of Clamps in Gastro-Enterostomy: A Suggested Improvement in their Design', *Lancet,* 2, pp 661-3, 1922
'Hydrocephalus', *Br J Surg,* 10, pp 165-91, 1922-3 (With John Fraser)
'The Physiological Consequences of Gastro-Enterostomy', *Br Med J,* 1, p 351, 1923
'Hydrocephalus', *Trans Med Chir Soc Edinb,* 37, pp 1-19, 1922-3 (With John Fraser)
*'Observations on the Isolated Pyloric Segment and on it's Secretion', *Q Jl Exp Physiol,* 13, pp 159-76, 1923 (with R K S Lim)

'An Investigation into the Functions of the Pituitary and Thyroid Glands. Part 1: Technique of their Experimental Surgery and Summary of Results', *Q Jl Exp Physiol*, 13, pp 241–82, 1923

'Apparatus for Insufflation Anaesthesia Demonstration', *Q Jl Exp Physiol*, 13, 1923. Supplementary Volume, Proceedings of the 11th International Physiological Congress, pp 104–5

★'The Syndromes of Experimental Pituitary Derangements', *Ibid.*, pp 105–7

'The Influence of Experimental Pituitary and Thyroid Derangements upon the Developmental Growth of Bone', *Ibid.*, pp 107–8 (With John Fraser)

'Experimental Jejunal Ulcer', *Ibid.*, pp 109–10 (With R K S Lim)

'A New Aseptic Method of Intestinal Anastomosis', *Ibid.*, pp 122–4 (with John Fraser)

'The Pyloric Secretion', *Ibid.*, p 170 (With R K S Lim)

★'Anomalies of Intestinal Rotation: Their Embryology and Surgical Aspects: With Report of Five Cases', *Br J Surg*, 11, pp 251–86, 1923–4

'Aseptic Intestinal Anastomosis, With Special Reference to Colectomy', *Br J Surg*, 11, pp 439–54, 1923–4 (With John Fraser)

★'A Consideration of the Hypophyseal Adenomata', *Br J Surg*, 13, pp 314–66, 1925–6 (With Percival Bailey)

'Transfusions and Infusions', *Surgery of Childhood*, John Fraser, Vol 1, pp 43–73, Arnold, London, 1926.

'Pituitary Disorders', *Br Med J*, 2, pp 1040–8, 1926

'Volvulus Neonatorum', *Br Med J* 1, pp 230–1, 1927

'A Simple Method of Intestinal Anastomosis Illustrated by Three Diverse Cases of it's Application to the Large Intestine', *Trans Med Chir Soc Edinb*, 41, pp 55–60, 1926–7

'Diseases of the Pituitary Body', *The Medical Annual*, pp 374–87, 1927

'A Case of Left Unilateral Hydrocephalus in an Infant Operation Cure', *Brain*, 50, pp 548–61, 1927

'The Occurrence of Brain Tissue Within the Nose: The So-Called Nasal Glioma', *J Lar Otol*, 42, pp 733–45, 1927 (With Douglas Guthrie)

'Case Report Arterial Angioma of the Brain', *Ibid.*, pp 24–5, 1932–3

'Operations on the Brain; Operations on the Vertebral Column and Spinal Cord', *Operative Surgery*, ed A Miles and D P D Wilkie, 2nd ed, Oxford University Press and Milford, London, 1936

'Paroxysmal Neuralgia and Other Pains in the Jaws and Face', *Br Dent J*, 58, pp 616–25, 1935

'Traumatic Lesions of the Optic Chiasma', *Brain*, 58, pp 398–411, 1935 (With H M Traquair and W Ritchie Russel)

'Organic Basis of a Psychosis; Report of a Case', *Br Med J*, 1, pp 744–6, 1936 (With W M C Harrowes)

'Pituitary Tumours: Their Classification and Treatment', *Br Med J*, 2, pp 1153–5, 1206–8, 1936 (With J H Biggart)

★'Chronic Progressive Hydrocephalus', *Trans Med Chir Soc Edinb*, 50, pp 113–28, 1935–6 (With E Levin)

'The Early Diagnosis of Intracranial Tumour', *Br Med J*, 2, pp 891–5, 1937

★'Intracranial Aneurysms and Allied Clinical Syndromes: Cerebral Arteriography in their Management', *Lisb Med*, 14, pp 782-814, 1937 (With K Hermann and S Obrador)

'Russian Guides, Medical Schools and Research', *Trans Med Chir Soc Edinb*, 32, pp 44-56, 1937-8

★ *The Hypothalmus*, Oliver and Boyd, Edinburgh and London, 1938 (With W E Le Gros Clark, J Beattie and G Riddoch)

Foreword. An Introduction to Clinical Perimetry by H M Traquair, 3rd ed Kimpton, London, 1938

'Intracranial Tuberculoma', *Edinb. Med J*, 46, pp 36-41, 1939 (With E Levin)

'Post Traumatic Carotid-Cavernous Arteriovenous Fistula', *Trans Med Chir Soc Edinb*, 53, pp 103-12, 1938-9

Brain and Skull; Head Injuries; Meninges and Brain; Cranial Bones (With G L Alexander) *Thomson and Miles Manual of Surgery*, ed A Miles and D P D Wilkie, 9th ed, Oxford University Press and Milford, London, 1939

'Injuries of the Brain and Skull', *Surgery of Modern Warfare*, ed H Bailey, E & S Livingstone, Edinburgh, 1941

'Recent Experiences of Intracranial Surgery', *Trans Med Chir Soc Edinb*, 42, pp 132-212, 1927-8

'Hydrocephalus Simulating Tumour in the Production of Chiasmal and other Parahypophyseal Lesions; *Trans Ophthal, Soc UK*, 51, pp 232-46, 1931 (With A H H Sinclair) 1931

'Clinical Record of a Case of Exomphalos, Illustrating the Embryonic Type and it's Surgical Treatment', *Trans Edinb Obstet Soc*, 52, pp 105-8, 1931-2

'Case Report, Cystic Pituitary Epidermoid Tumour', *Trans Med Chir Soc Edinb*, 47, pp 173-4, 1932-3

'Discussion on Anaesthesia in Intracranial Surgery', *Proc R Soc Med*, 26, pp 953-5, 1933

★★'INTRA CRANIAL ANEURYSMS: CEREBRAL ARTERIO-RADIO-GRAPHY: SURGICAL TREATMENT', *TRANS MED CHIR SOC EDINB*, 47, pp 219-40, 1932-3★★

'Management of Head Injuries', *War and the Doctor* Baltimore pp 89-98, 1942

'Foreword', *Acute Injuries of the Head*, G F Rowbotham, E & S Livingstone, Edinburgh, 1942

Injuries of the Brain and Skull (With G L Alexander and P Ascroft)

Surgery of Modern Warfare, ed H Bailey; 3rd ed, E & S Livingstone, Edinburgh, 1944

'Skeletal Traction and Anterior Decompression in the Management of Pott's Paraplegia', *Edinb Med J*, 54, pp 620-7, 1947

'A Contribution to the Surgery of Hydrocephalus in Childhood', *Proceedings of the Sixth International Congress of Paediatrics*, Zurich, 26 July 1950

'Facial Pain', *Proc R Soc Med*, 44, pp 1034-7, 1951

'Spinal Epidural Abscess', *Br Med J*, 1, pp 64-8, 1954 (With A Hulme)

'Tumours of the Brain and Spinal Cord', *British Practice in Radiotherapy*, ed E R Carling and others, pp 330-49 Butterworth, London, 1955 (with R Mc Whirter)

'Bilateral Lumbar Plexus Lesions Simulating Cauda-Equina Compression', *Lancet*, 1, pp 688-91, 1955 (with A R Taylor)

'Palliation in Cancer', *Proc R Soc Med*, 48, pp 706-8, 1955

Presentation of Sir Geoffrey Jefferson for the Honorary Fellowship of the Royal

College of Surgeons of Edinburgh, 10 July 1957 *Jl R Coll Surg Edinb*, 3, pp 75-7, 1957-8

'Foreword', *Traquair's Clinical Perimetry*; 7th ed G I Scott, Kimpton, London, 1957

'Repair of the Facial Nerve in Traumatic Facial Palsies: Intracranial Nerve Grafting According to the Method of Norman M Dott', by K Kettel, *Archs Otolar*, 67, pp 65-6, 1958

Promoter's Address. Medical and Dental Graduation Ceremony, University of Edinburgh, 16 July 1958. Private Print, Edinburgh University Press.

'Chronic Arachnoiditis and Hydrocephalus in the Surgical Management of Acoustic Tumours—A Plea for Early Operation', *Proc R Soc Med*, 51, pp 897-8, 1958

★Facial Paralysis—Restitution by Extra-Petrous Nerve Graft, *Proc R Soc Med*, 51, pp 900-2, 1958

★'Mechanical Aspects of the Cerbrospinal Fluid Circulation—Physiological, Pathological, Surgical', in *CIBA Foundation Symposium on the Cerebrospinal Fluid*, ed, G E W Wolstenholme and C M O'Connor, pp 246-64, London, 1958 (with F J Gillingham)

'Discussion on the Treatment of Intractable Pain', *Proc R Soc Med*, 52, pp 987-9, 1959

★'Presentation of Wilder Penfield for Honorary Fellowship of the Royal College of Surgeons of Edinburgh', 21 July 1959, *Jl R Coll Surg Edinb.*, 5, pp 80-1, 1959-60

★'Brain Movement and Time: The Sir Victor Horsley Memorial Lecture', *Br Med J*, 2, pp 12-16, 1960

★'Lesiones Expansivas Intracraniales', in *Proceedings of the IX Congresso Latinoamericano de Neurocirurgia*, Mexico, 1961 Ch IV(b), pp 549-54

'An Introductory Review. Presidential Address. The Cerebrospinal Fluid Circulation and Hydrocephalus', *Develop Med and Child Neurol*, 4, pp 259-62, 1962

'The Road to Recovery', (Founder's Lecture) *Physiotherapy*, October 1962, pp 266-9

'Hypophysectomy for Advanced Cancer of the Breast', *Proc R Soc Med*, 56, pp 389-98, 1963 (with H J B Atkins, M A Falconer, C N Bateman)

'The Dentist in Relation to Medical and Surgical Neurology', *Br Dent J*, 115, pp 273-5, 1963

'Facial Nerve Reconstruction by Graft Bypassing the Petrous Bone', *Archs Otolar*, 78, pp 426-8, 1963

'La Circolozione del Liquido Cerebro-Spinale', *Osservazioni Chirurgiche Minerva Neurochir*, 7, pp 100-3, 1963 (with F J Gillingham)

'Neurosurgical Classics XXIV: Intracranial Aneurysms: Cerebral Arterio Radiography: Surgical Treatment: by Norman M Dott', *J. Neurosurg*, 21, pp 892-901, 1964

'Discussion: Carotid Cavernous Arteriovenous Fistula', *J Neurol Neurosurg Psychiat . . .*, 27, pp 579-80, 1964

'Foreword', *Acute Injuries of the Head*, by G F Rowbotham; 3rd ed E & S Livingstone Edinburgh and London, 1964

'Address to Newly Elected Fellows—Ceremony of Presentation of Diplomas, The

Royal College of Surgeons of Edinburgh', 10 February 1966, *Jl R Coll Surg Edinb*, 11, pp 236-7, 1965-6

*'The Arteriovenous Malformations of the Brain: Review of 115 Cases', *Acta Chir. Acad Sci Hung*, 7, pp 111-28, 1966 (with J J Maccabe)

'Spontaneous Spinal Epidural Haemorrhage During Anticoagulant Therapy', *Br Med J*, 1, pp 522-3, 1966 (with I Jacobson, J J Maccabe and P Harris)

'Training the Specialist Surgeon. Cairns Memorial Lecture', *Lancet*, 2, pp 1305-7, 1966

*'The Third Sir Hugh Cairns Memorial Lecture', *Private Print for Society of British Neurological Surgeons*, Oxford University Press

'Reflections on the History of Surgical Neurology (Summary)', *Scottish Society for the History of Medicine, Report of Proceedings*, 1966-7, pp 10-11

'Address to the Scottish Association of Occupational Therapists at it's Annual General Meeting', 18 March 1967, *Scottish Journal Occup therap*, 69, pp 4-6, June 1967

'Postscript in Appreciation of Almeida Lima, following his Fourth Sir Hugh Cairns Memorial Lecture—Beyond the Diagnosis', 19 May 1967, *Private Print for the Society of British Neurological Surgeons*, Oxford University Press

*'The Life and Work of Egas Moniz. Memorial Lecture at International Neurological Reunion in Lisbon', *Private Print for Instituto Alta Cultura and Fundacao CalousteGulbenkian*, Lisbon

'Address to the Scottish Spina Bifida Association at it's First Annual General Meeting', 19 March 1967, *Private Print for Scottish Spina Bifida Association*

*'Presentation of Lord Florey for Honorary Fellowship of the Royal College of Surgeons of Edinburgh', 11 November 1967, *J R Coll Surg Edinb*, 13, pp 112-14, 1968

'Harvey William Cushing. Biographical Note in Munk's Roll', *the Royal College of Physicians of London*, Vol 5, 1969, pp 93-5

Acknowledgement of Honorary Fellowship of the Royal Society of Medicine, 16 July 1968

'Introductory Remarks to the Congress of Neurological Surgeons at Toronto', September 1968, *Clinical Neurosurgery*, 16, pp 23-6, 1969

*'Intracranial Aneurysmal Formations' (Toronto 25 September 1968) *Clinical Neurosurgery*, 16, pp 1-16, 1969

'Surgical Treatment of Epilepsy—Note on Temporal Lobectomy in 1927' (Toronto 26 September 1968) *Clinical Neurosurgery*, 16, pp 312-14, 1969

*'Carotid—Cavernous Fistula' (Toronto 26 September 1968) *Clinical Neurosurgery* 16, pp 17-21, 1969

*'Training and Accreditation of the Specialist Surgeon' (Toronto 27 September 1968) *Clinical Neurosurgery*, 16, pp 22-9, 1969

*'Disintegration in Specialist Medicine—Modern Patterns of Reintegration' (Toronto 28 September 1969) *Clinical Neurosurgery*, 16, pp 30-42, 1969

'Obituary Notice on Paul Martin MD, *Brit Med Journ*, 2, p 704, 1968

'Obituary Editorial on Lieut Col John Cunningham MD, *Scottish Journ of Occup Therapy*, 75, pp 5-6, 1968

'Dr Harvey Cushing MD, *Scot Med Journ*, 14, pp 381-6, 1969

'History of Surgical Neurology in the Twentieth Century', *Proc Roy Soc Med*, 64, pp 1051-5, 1971

'Paraplegia and Spinal Paralysis in Scotland', *Paraplegia*, 9, pp 194–203, 1972

'Colostomy After-Care and the Stoma Clinic' (with Lt Col J Fraser MD) *Health Bull*, 30, pp 162-5, 1972

Index